SAGE ANNUAL REVIEWS OF STUDIES IN DEVIANCE

Volume 1

SAGE ANNUAL REVIEWS OF STUDIES IN DEVIANCE

Series Editors: EDWARD SAGARIN
CHARLES WINICK
The City College of the City University of New York

Deviance is one of the most important, exciting and stimulating areas in sociology. It covers the entire spectrum of activities and people who are disvalued, denigrated, punished, ostracized, and in other ways made to feel undesired and undesirable in society—whether this be for something that was done (as the commission of a crime), or for some peculiar stigmatic status. It extends into criminology, social problems, social pathology, and numerous other areas. Despite many texts, readers, and countless journal articles, there has never been a serial publication devoted exclusively to deviance. It is to fill this gap that this annual series is being launched.

Volumes in this series:

Volume 1. Deviance and Social Change (1977)
EDWARD SAGARIN, Editor

Volume 2. Deviance and Mass Media (forthcoming 1978)
CHARLES WINICK, Editor

DEVIANCE and SOCIAL CHANGE

Edited by
EDWARD SAGARIN

SAGE PUBLICATIONS / *Beverly Hills* / *London*

For information address:

SAGE PUBLICATIONS, INC.
275 South Beverly Drive
Beverly Hills, California 90212

SAGE PUBLICATIONS LTD
28 Banner Street
London EC1Y 8QE

Printed in the United States of America

International Standard Book Number 0-8039-0804-0 (cloth)
International Standard Book Number 0-8039-0805-9 (paper)

Library of Congress Catalog Card No. 77-72937

FIRST PRINTING

CONTENTS

DEVIANCE
Introducing a Series

EDWARD SAGARIN

Even in the midst of the information explosion, only a few areas in the social sciences have seen such a sudden spurt of intellectual interest as has deviance. Within sociology, where it has found a snug position as a subdiscipline, or a field of specialization, it was a word seldom encountered until the 1930s. In the Encyclopedia of the Social Sciences that appeared in the early part of that decade, there was no entry under deviance; in fact, the word did not even appear in the index. At the time, it probably would have been difficult to locate a single book in the behavioral sciences that had "deviance" in its title. Four decades later, a bibliography of such books would probably run to over 100 items, and of articles in a variety of professional journals many times that figure.

It is not only the quantitative expansion, but also the intellectual ferment, that has marked the interest in deviance. It is a field of study that has seen sharp debates, over anomie theory, labeling perspectives, conflict orientations, and many others, and the debates show no signs of subsiding. It is a field that has its roots simultaneously in sociology (with background particularly in what once was discussed under the rubric of social disorganization) and in psychology (with a similar background in abnormal psychology, psychopathology, forensic psychiatry, and the like). Theorists have had to come to grips with deviance. How is deviance accounted for in a theoretical perspective on the nature of society? Or on the nature of man? What are the consequences of deviance for a society, for a social class, or any other social group, for the deviants themselves, and for the nondeviant population that has come to be called, in a sociological appropriation of an essentially psychological word, the normals?

Journals of many sorts are found that have opened their pages to writers on deviance. They are scholarly publications whose titles and orientations show interest not only in sociology and psychology, sometimes in political science and less frequently economics, certainly in psychiatry, but they are more specialized, focusing on social problems, urban life, crime and delinquency, sexual behavior, medical sociology and health, mental retardation, disability and rehabilitation, and so one could continue. To add one more journal to a list so long that few specialists have time to read was a temptation, but it appeared that the need for a specialized serial publication in deviance, while indisputable, could better be served by an annual volume. It is with this in mind that the present series is being launched.

There are advantages to a volume that covers the broad spectrum of the field itself, the field being deviance, and whose editors choose the material solely on grounds of interest and quality: for originality, scholarly contribution, the stimulating nature of the ideas put forward. We have opted for another course, namely, thematic volumes, each annual being on deviance in one of its specific aspects. Our immediate projection for the future, following the present volume which launches the series, is for studies centered around deviance and the mass media, deviance and the ethics of human research, and perhaps, although we have not planned more than two years into the future, deviance in cross-cultural perspective, deviance in historical perspective, deviance and language, and numerous other themes that come to mind.

However, it appeared paramount, natural, almost inevitable, that the first volume in a deviance annual series should be devoted to social change. The debate over the relationship of these two phenomena continues (nor do we expect it to be settled by the papers written for this book). Theories of society have been rejected because they cannot accommodate deviance, or because they see (or some of their critics claim that they implicitly suggest) deviance as an excrescence, an illness, an abnormality that must be removed from society. Marxists have sought to construct a social conflict view of society that would not only account for deviance but would integrate it as part of the conflicting forces in society. Ideologues have hailed deviance, or at least many forms of it, as being the wave of the future. Formal sociologists, deriving largely from Simmel, have seen deviance as bringing about a new view of the old order of things, causing adjustments, accommodations and changes (not always progressive, one sometimes forgets); and functionalists, deriving from Durkheim, have seen deviance as assisting in the cohesion and unity of the vast majority of the society, the upright persons who cast out the wayward and the transgressors.

It was to fill a gap in the serial literature of deviance that this annual series has been launched, and to bring together a variety of thinkers and viewpoints on deviance and social change that this first volume in the series has been published. We know that interest in deviance will not diminish in the years ahead, and we hope that the annual thematic volumes will make a major contribution to the proliferating literature.

DEVIANCE AND THE PROBLEM OF SOCIAL CHANGE
Introducing A Volume

EDWARD SAGARIN

At one time, sociologists and political scientists were wont to think of a society as a very orderly and ongoing system—a set of behavioral patterns, groups of people, rules and laws—that somehow meshed together in what Robert Bierstedt, for example, called, in a book by that title, a "social order." No one, certainly not social scientists, nor even political conservatives, thought of that order as having reached such perfection that improvement and progress (words which imply change) were unnecessary. There were wars, civil and international, malnutrition, and slavery (although the latter was not always recognized as an imperfection by society's rulers, nor even by the contemporary social philosophers), and then there were those outside the pale of the respectable society who flouted the rules and disobeyed the laws. Nonetheless, most societies survived, and there was indeed social order, even if there was a great deal of disorder concomitant with it.

Later, under the influence of Marx and most recently of militant liberationist movements, sociologists readily admitted that society was possible (proven by the very fact of its existence), but it is riddled with conflict, if not pandemic disorder. The conflict is between interest groups, class groups, ethnic and racial collectivities, sometimes directed against one another, and sometimes against the political entity in which power is vested: the government and its legislative, executive, judicial, and particularly military and police arms. Some have questioned whether there is consensus as to what the norms ought to be. Within this order or disorder, or combination of the two, there are those who, individually or collectively, on occasion or regularly, violate the rules in such a manner as to bring down upon them the hostility of others: these are the deviants within the society as a whole, or within some group of it.

The problem of deviance and its relationship to society itself as a self-perpetuating although changing system, and to the survival or downfall of that society, has attracted considerable attention. Deviance in America is probably too wide, penetrates into too many circles of all social classes, manifests itself in flagrant and obvious ways and (one has come to suspect) is probably or possibly as widespread in manners protected by secrecy, for sociologists not to be concerned with many fundamental issues. How is society possible with so much deviance (if indeed there is as much as one suspects)? What is there about the nature of the social structure (the problem that Robert K. Merton faced in his extraordinarily important work on anomie and deviant behavior) that generates, reduces, or confines deviance? What are the limits of tolerance that a society can extend to various forms of deviance without the society ceasing to function with minimal efficiency as an ongoing order? What function does deviance play in uniting or disuniting a society, by placing the transgressor outside of the pale of the group, as Emile Durkheim contended and as Kai Erikson delineated in his studies of the witchcraft trials in Salem?

One can continue with the questions, but one such problem is the central theme of this book: namely, the relationship between deviance and social change. Does social change generate deviance, or even deviant personalities, because it leaves people in a state without firm beliefs in the traditional world into which they were socialized? Does deviance, on the other hand, generate social change, perhaps by dramatically calling attention to the failures of a society, or by making demands for concessions on the groups having a monopoly of power, or—to look in an entirely different direction—by inciting a more severe social hostility, be it repression, backlash, indignation?

That deviance is related to social change is widely accepted in social science, but what the relationship may be, how it functions, brings forth theoretical problems and calls for empirical evidence that is only beginning to become available. That scholars look at these related concepts from various perspectives, with different theoretical approaches and drawing upon diverse examples and substantive areas, will be readily apparent from the contributions in this book. Let us look at these pieces individually as well as in groups, and then see the directions in which they are pointing.

One of the fascinating aspects of the study of deviant behavior is that it encompasses such a diversity of people, social classes, and types of activities. Some sociologists have complained that the emphasis is on lower-class persons, and that this represents a social class bias in the study of this as a subdiscipline of sociology; whether the rich literature on white-collar and upper-world crime provides a balance is debatable. But if deviance is a study of those rejected, punished, reacted to unfavorably by large groups of powerful people in society, it hardly seems to be a bias to study such rejects, although one may well be biased by defending the rejection. In what may be the most dramatic and startling conceptualization of upper-class and lower-class people as pursuing different but socially analogous modes of activity, Talcott Parsons and Dean Gerstein bring together the oval office and the slum, the power-hungry and the heroin-hungry deviants. In the equilibrium model of society for which Parsons and his colleagues have become spokesmen, the forces within a society tend to work toward stability (a word not to be confused with stagnation). Departures from this system tend to become strains upon it, and the system undergoes change, becomes restored to a state of equilibrium, often with adjustments brought about by the existence of the deviants. The new equilibrium can be, in the words of the authors, "complete restoration of the status quo ante," or may involve fundamental changes in the social structure. In the Watergate-heroin duo, the system worked toward containment, which involves one might say change but not fundamental change, almost cosmetic and surface change, but not complete restoration.

The very title of Jack Douglas's article travels to the heart of the subject matter of this book. He is dealing with "creative deviance," a term that goes beyond the one popularized by Merton when, in his famous paradigm, he wrote of "innovative deviance." In a sense, all deviance is creative, although all deviants are not (for they may be slavish followers of others similarly situated, having in common with these others some deprivations, needs, goals, frustrations, or perceived oppression at the hands of more powerful groups). Although the deviance may be coopted by society, ignored, or repressed, the social hostility brings forth, in Douglas's theme, the trio of shame-pride-rage. We have seen the first in sexual deviance, the second in political and racial, the third in political as well, but they overlap, are in flux, work simultaneously, and develop, or tend to develop, their counter-pride and their counter-shame. Under what conditions of suppression, suffering, and submission these reactive forms come into existence, whether they are conscious or acted out without understanding of sources and implications, are delineated by Douglas. But this is the theme of deviance and change (it is personal as much as social change that Douglas is here outlining, except that the personal change is very much social, both in its implications and in its manifestations). Deviance usually involves a type of behavior which contravenes the morals sufficiently strongly that the powerful groups in society, the keepers of the morals, develop within the deviant sufficient shame, as well as resort to the self-protective measures of secrecy and deceit, to contain and control the transgressions. Thus we have a second dimension of deviance and social change: the experience of living in a world in which one is forced into deceit and made to feel a sense of shame can generate a counter-reaction, bringing about change not only in the individual deviant, but galvanizing him and others like him into a collective social movement, sometimes enraged, and directed toward effecting change in the society.

And now we pass to Harriet Zuckerman, in what is a most original and provocative work, on deviant behavior and social control in science. For those who have thought of deviance as residing in the flotsam and jetsam of society, Zuckerman's article offers an unusual challenge. Here is deviance not only in upper social strata (some of us have come to expect this, what with the "robber baron" stories of the great American fortunes, and the political and official deviance cynically believed to be widespread), but in a highly educated profession whose qualified members are generally regarded by the public (or so at least it is thought) as being above the world of lies, deceit, chicanery, plagiarism, falsification, and the like. Not that scientists may not be liars, deceivers, and tax evaders, for certainly there is no reason to believe that they are more pure in morals and law-abidingness than others of similar education, social class, and income (which means that they can aim low and still be on a moral level with their peers), but that their scientific work should itself be subject to deviant acts on their part goes outside the realm of what is generally thought of as deviance within sociology. The quantity of such acts may indeed be few (compared to the proportion of politicians who indulge in political deviance, or teenagers in heroin addiction), and some of them have become matters of public information, *causes célèbres,* such as Piltdown Man. It is not that Zuckerman undertakes to contend that deviance of such type may be more common than suspected, although if she extended her thesis to social science, the rarity might tend to disappear. Rather, she demonstrates what there is about the nature of science, the structure of science as a social institution, that makes such acts tempting and conceivable, how despite rules of reproducibility and other factors, they are committed and not always immediately suspected, denounced and exposed.

The system of social control in science hardly breaks down because of the deviant cases, but it is far from perfect, particularly insofar as society may find even a few cases of deviance in science beyond tolerance levels. Present theories of deviance, Zuckerman contends, are inadequate, or only partially adequate, to explain the phenomenon she is perceiving. Deviance thus becomes its own mechanism for change, but within the framework of deviance and social change, it would appear to me that the deviance that Zuckerman describes is most likely to generate change within the institution of science, its social control systems and its norms, rather than in society in a broader sense. For reasons germane to the uniqueness of science as a social institution and its place in society, deviance is unlikely to bring forth a relaxation of the norms and an acceptance of what was formerly deviant (a problem to which I shall return in discussing Winick's chapter), but more stringent measures, more effective control, what under other conditions can be described as enhanced repression.

From scientist to physician may seem like a small shift, for many would place medicine as a branch of science and physicians as a subgroup of scientists. Aside from important definitions and concepts that, for some, would place the practice of medicine as a pursuit quite unlike the "practice" of science, from the sociological view the norms governing the two areas diverge to such an extent that there is little basis for viewing the two as one. Deviance by physicians and other health care practitioners, not as citizens, fathers and mothers, or autoists, but in their capacity as professionals, has come to be widely accepted and is part of Americans' cynical view of their world. Front page stories in leading newspapers tell us that physicians perform operations in large numbers purely out of greed, unable to justify the surgery in medical terms. It is not unusual to read of physicians who operate health care factories, milking patients and government of hundreds of thousands of dollars. All this aside from the deviance of medical quackery, of endorsements of nostrums from pharmaceutical companies for a high fee, of malpractice (the honest error, that Zuckerman describes) and the coverup of malpractice by perjury and other methods for the obstruction of justice and protection of peers and cronies (see Parsons and Gerstein, if the memory needs refreshing).

It is interesting that medical deviance has generated public indignation unlike that of scientific deviance, and it is not only the frequency of the former that is crucial here, but it is the immediacy of the issue for the public. Widespread deviance of this sort, in an area for which there is such public sensitivity, calls for social control, and while a medical establishment, rich and powerful and prestigious, would like to be its own gatekeeper, the ramifications and the enormity of the deviance make this prospect unlikely, although there will be no lack of input by such establishment physicians in changed and strengthened control mechanisms. While I would not argue with the conclusions that Arnold Birenbaum draws from his own material, coming to the rather pessimistic view that organizational criminal behavior is going to be protected by the governmental elite in a capitalist society, I believe that he himself shows that when deviant behavior in certain areas (and health care is one such, particularly in a society like the American) becomes publicized, abusive, cynical, threatening to large masses, it calls into being changes within itself or from without. That these changes are insufficient, and again particularly in an area like health care, would lead the sociologist to the theoretical problem of noting under what conditions social change is palliative, and under what conditions it goes to the root of a social problem.

When going to the work of Henry Barbera, we are still in the area if not of science then of technology. That invention has brought forth changes in social institutions, norms, the very structure of society, has long been noted; one need only go to the work of Ogburn on cultural lag to become deeply immersed in this issue. What Barbera has shown us is something seldom noted before: that the users of the new technology may be reviled and despised, in short the deviants, for having embraced the innovative when the society was rallied around the traditional. The example that he uses to demonstrate this thesis is no doubt an extreme one: the invention of the gun. No amount of denunciation was going to make the gun and its users lose out against old forms of conflict. Technology introduced change as sweeping as any in history, something to be compared with the printing press, or before it the wheel or the alphabet, and after it the atomic bomb. What is challenging here is the extent, if at all, that the technological innovators, as the deviants who become the midwives for social change, can be applied to a more generalized theory of deviance, at least on a limited level (that is, limited to deviance and technology).

The Zuckerman, Barbera, and Birenbaum articles have some degree of unity, in that they deal with science and technology; the next two, those by Richard Moran, and Albert Ellis and Linda Eckstein, deal with various aspects of political deviance. By political deviants, all of these authors are speaking of those who rose up in individual or collective rebellion, or at the least allied themselves with such rebels, and this rebellion was against the power groups in their societies (unlike the Watergate deviants discussed by Parsons and Gerstein). In so doing, most of the people described in these papers resorted to methods of violence, lawbreaking, or insurrection (although Moran includes in his general study some who could not be so described).

The papers by Moran on the one hand, by Ellis and Eckstein on the other, come to a sort of implicit clash, although they are not beyond some effort at reconciliation. In the world at which Moran is looking, the people are what might be called "normal deviants," but the word "normal" is here being used in the psychological sense, "deviants" in the sociological. They have come to political conclusions which lead many of them to extreme measures, but there is nothing to indicate a psychological, psychopathic, or neurological basis for their behavior. On the contrary, it is inherent in the climate of the times, the war in Vietnam, the youth and student rebellions, and the emergence of liberation movements of various sorts. If political deviance has its aim in social change, then to whom can one look in order to find the deviants? Ellis and Eckstein, while finding in the population at large a wide spectrum of desire for change, of political dissatisfaction with things as they are, believe that those individuals who become most actively committed to carrying out such change by any means whatsoever (variously called extremists or fanatics) have deep-going psychological problems. These writers do not take a sanguine view of change being instituted by "mad geniuses," by people with unbending monomaniacal urges that their way must be adopted, or else all humanity will collapse (or should).

What we are faced with here, and it is a problem that has been looked at before but hardly in the depth that it deserves, is the personality of the most innovative deviant. Often, the normative values of the viewers have made them see their subjects entirely differently, depending on the causes to which they were dedicated. But it is entirely possible, if the Ellis and Eckstein thesis is found tenable, that genocidal murderers and fighters for freedom can have in common certain personality characteristics, and that these are the characteristics brought to the fore by a political climate calling for a political deviant leadership.

It is fitting that we follow this with an example of the deviants who have put across their view, their way, and have been a leading force in transforming some aspect of a society from deviant to normative. This is what Charles Winick has done, in his study of changes in the social acceptability of sexually explicit material. Nor is sexuality the only area where sweeping changes have been seen over the course of a few years. In the lifetime of this writer, there was not a restaurant or hotel in New York outside of Harlem where a black person could eat or sleep; a few years pass and interracial restaurants and hotels are so taken for granted, not only in New York but in the South and in many small towns and hamlets of America, that it is difficult to convince young people that it was ever otherwise.

Winick has given us a very special and important statement of this phenomenon, however, for it is not merely that what was once deviant became normative (although he might well be exaggerating the extent to which the winds have shifted, but that is another question), but the deviants themselves, through flouting laws and norms, were the instruments for bringing about the change.

Many would not look upon women in terms of deviants, although career women were so defined by Fred Davis some years ago. Nor was feminism a deviant social movement or a social movement of deviants. But what Nanette Davis has examined is the relationship between a movement for social change and the destigmatization or the removal of deviant connotations from some of those it champions, and at the same time she suggests how social change can generate deviance as well as diminish it by the institutionalization of formerly disvalued patterns of behavior.

(In this introductory essay, I shall do no more than mention the valuable work of Fred Montanino, whose essay on trends in the literature of deviance was not meant to be confined to deviance and social change, although many of the references and discussions therein will be useful for that purpose.)

The people brought together in this volume have focused on a fundamental sociological (and social) issue. There are areas of agreement and disagreement among them, and some raise questions that they do not answer. In sum, and as a group, they all raise serious questions for sociological study, that go to the heart of two fundamental aspects of society: the nature of deviance and the nature of social change. No scholar looking at these matters, whether in their broader aspects or as applied to a specific substantive area, will be able to ignore those who have done fundamental groundbreaking in these essays. More than that, I am confident that these will be takeoff points for scholars for many years to come.

1

TWO CASES OF SOCIAL DEVIANCE
Addiction to Heroin, Addiction to Power

TALCOTT PARSONS
DEAN R. GERSTEIN

I. INTRODUCTION

In this article we will try to present two examples of socially structured deviant action which are of a special type within a much broader range. They are both cases where pursuit of the deviant pattern has proved to be a "losing game" and where, therefore, any tendency it may have had to spread for a time comes to be checked by the operation of countervailing forces and, from the point of view of its impact on the larger social structure, either to be eliminated or, more likely, to be "contained." These are the cases which, in other respects, are very dissimilar, of heroin addiction on the part of rather small minorities of the population of urban communities, and the action of former President Nixon and a "faction" of persons close to him in the Executive Branch of the Federal Government, which eventuated in the resignation of Nixon from the Presidency in August, 1974.

The two cases have in common that they have not, and we hope to show, could not have spread directly to the point of becoming major foci of far-reaching change in the structure of the society as a whole; indeed this is what we mean by their at least having been "contained." In the earlier stages of such a movement or process, however, it may be difficult to predict its longer-run fate. Like various others its very most conspicuous feature is that it is innovative,[1] in the one case with respect to personal behavior, in the other with respect to the conduct of governmental affairs. Such innovative patterns of action, however, can seldom be accurately diagnosed in an early stage on the question of what the consequences of widespread adoption in the society might turn out to be. Not only is it exceedingly difficult to diagnose the potentials of a tendency to change, it is also equally difficult to appraise the significance of objections and resistances to it. Any major change in a going society will encounter objections and resistances just because it is change; in that sense, all going societies or smaller social systems are "conservative" or have relatively strong "vested interests" operative within them which, in a variety of possible ways and degrees of intensity, are likely to react negatively to any considerable or prospectively considerable disturbance of their status quo.

There is one apparent type of exception. Some kinds of social systems, like the organization of scientific research, are built around the expectation of certain types of change, so that if the state of knowledge in the relevant field has not changed in a suitable time period, this is an index of the failure of the organization to perform its functions properly. But even here, the difference is relative, for the disturbing type of change is deviation from the expected pattern of growth, so that tendencies to maintain the relevant body of knowledge in an unchanged state would be treated as deviant, because it would change the pattern of "normal" operation of the organization.[2]

Thus innovative changes in social systems, involving social structure, the action of participant individuals, or the relevant cultural symbol-complexes, are always in one sense "deviant," i.e., relative to more or less firmly institutionalized expectations. Their introduction, usually first on a small scale (but not always), can then have different kinds of consequences, which will depend *both* on the nature of the innovative processes, which is meant to include not only the "kind" of innovation concerned, but also the vigor, competence, and resources with which it is pressed, *and* the nature of the countervailing "reactions" to the innovative attempts, be they accepting, indeed often encouraging in various respects, or, conversely, resistant and rejecting, including manifestation of violent opposition.

We therefore suggest that, apart from the processes of their stimulation, i.e., their genesis and strength, the fate of innovative social processes is the outcome of a highly complex set of selective processes, which involve complex interaction between (1) the pattern content of the innovation, which may be more or less acceptable in the relevant sectors of the society or may arouse more or less serious opposition, (2) the bearers of the innovation, i.e., the population groups which come to be committed to it in varying degrees, (3) the ways in which they organize to promote it, (4) the kinds of antagonism these efforts arouse in others, the more or less strategic position of both proponents and opponents; and the like. Indeed not to be forgotten is the fact that both promoting groups and oppositional groups, and individuals, are always more or less divided and ambivalent with respect to the issues at stake. It is scarcely too much to say that a theory of social deviance, to be workable, must be an integral part of a more general theory of social conflict, including tools for understanding not only the genesis of such conflicts, but the alternative outcomes which may be cumulative escalation to a catastrophic breaking point, various modes of endemic persistence, possible resolution, and others.

This, however, would be a very large order for a modest venture in the theory of social deviance. As noted above, we will confine our substantive discussion to two cases which, as we shall argue, could not have come to be models for the wider reorganization of the relevant sectors of the society, or personality or cultural patterns. In doing so, however, we wish to keep the reader aware of the openness at the margins, of patterns of deviance in the narrower sense and of those innovative patterns which have come to be insulated against higher levels of spread or dominance.

This leads over to the consideration which involves the possibility that the spread of an innovative pattern might, beyond certain points, prove to be destructive of the social or other action system in which it appears. It is thus almost patent that a society composed of a very large proportion of severe heroin addicts, say of the order of 50%, if a large-scale complete society, would be, to say the least, in severe difficulties, both internally and in its relations to others, e.g., of economic competition. Similarly it is not difficult to imagine that a society in which the pattern of the Nixon "clique" came to be very highly generalized in the affairs of formal organization, governmental and otherwise, would also be in serious difficulties. It thus seems to us that this development was something like an incursion of a Hobbesian struggle for power into a critical part of the social system.

In the perspective which we have just put forward, we think we can speak of a continuous and endemic process of pattern-innovation in social systems. These innovations are complex products of all manner of combinations of the factors which determine human action, comprising clearly some which are integral to the social system itself, others, like psychological or cultural processes, which are more peripheral. Once appearing, however, such innovative tendencies impinge on the network of factors often called the system of "social control." There will be a selective process engendered by this articulation. From the point of view of the fate of these innovative patterns, in and for the structure of the social systems, we may call this the problem of institutionalization. If, that is to say, such a pattern comes to be fully incorporated into the structure of the relevant social system from personality and cultural sources, then we speak of it as having become *institutionalized.* There is a very wide variety of outcomes which can occur as a result of these processes, of which full institutionalization is only one. The complete disappearance of the innovation is the extreme opposite to full institutionalization. In between lie in particular various levels and degrees of partial institutionalization, of limitation and tolerance short of generalization, for example. Thus we do not think it likely that a time will come when the great majority of Americans will spend even several years of their lives as heroin addicts, or that the overwhelming majority of organizations will be controlled by power-seeking factions like the Nixon clique. At the same time we think it unlikely that either type of deviance will be permanently and totally extirpated from American society, especially if one fits heroin addiction into a wider variety of severe personal addictions. Much the more likely outcome is varyingly effective "containment" with persistence of the institutional definition of the pattern as deviant.

In spite of objections from the sociological left, that use of the equilibrium concept is an index of a fatally conservative bias, a cryptic defense of the status quo, we feel that, since it is one of the master concepts of modern science generally and social science in particular, theoretical progress with our problem will be greatly facilitated by its incorporation into our analysis.

We have one cogent reason for this. Much of the discussion of problems of deviance has apparently, and on the whole rightly, stressed the negative aspect of action of that sort toward the institutional complex in question. This of course is a definitional criterion of deviant behavior. It is, however, seldom if ever the whole story. First, the normative complex relevant to a given mode of deviant behavior, as of that of other types, is not a simple matter of violation of a single specific norm, but rather of the violation of one or more specific norms within a much broader complex of normative factors. Such complexes are in the first place seldom nearly perfectly integrated within each, so in violating one norm an actor may well be conforming with another which in some connection is just as important. Second, normative aspects of an action situation by no means stand alone, but are interdependent in complex ways with nonnormative or conditional factors, a distinction which itself is empirically relative. Assessment of these two sets of factors and of their relations to each other requires careful and detailed analysis. The temptation to facile trapping in the "fallacy of misplaced concreteness" is very strong.

It therefore seems to us that use of the concept of a social system in equilibrium as a reference point is a very helpful analytical device in dealing with these problems. The concept of equilibrium need not be static, but may formulate the outline of an orderly process of change, like the growth of an organism. For present purposes, however, it would use the assumption that, with the system in equilibrium, the mode of deviant action in which we are interested would not yet have appeared. We then proceed to try to identify the "disturbances" of the equilibrium state which account for the genesis of the deviant pattern, with some estimate of quantitative magnitude of the "size" of the deviant phenomenon, and of the strength of the "forces," always a combination, never a single "cause," which account for it. An analysis can then proceed to consider the counteracting forces and the balance attained, in the empirical setting chosen for study, between forces making for deviance, and for restoration of equilibrium or containment, which would be a new state of equilibrium.

A very useful model, taken from another discipline, namely economics, is that put forward, many years ago, by Joseph Schumpeter (1934) in his book *The Theory of Economic Development.* Schumpeter's primary interest was in the analysis of certain processes of economic change. The first, rather long and elaborate chapter, however, is entitled "The Circular Flow." This chapter delineates an economic system in a state of relatively stable equilibrium. Then in subsequent chapters the author systematically introduces the factors of disturbance of this state which can account for the kinds of changes in that state which he is interested in explaining. It goes almost without saying that the end-state of the processes he analyzes is not a return to the initial state of equilibrium, but a very substantially altered state. The fact that he used an equilibrated state as a reference point clearly does not imply that he believed its maintenance unchanged was somehow more likely empirically or more desirable than its change. Rather, he used the conception of a circular flow as a reference point for the theoretically orderly analysis of a process of change.

We have stressed above that the genesis of deviant patterns always involves multiple causal factors. These of course have to do with the fact that no system of human action, social system, personality or cultural system is ever perfectly integrated. To take the social system focus, there are, particularly in complex societies, many types of conflicts of varying severity, important areas of anomie in which normative expectations are ill-defined, as well as areas in which pressures to conformity are particularly severe. In all of them, furthermore, individual persons are situated and have to act. We therefore think that the old and often controversial concept of *strain* is essential to a theory of deviance, indeed is just as essential a reference point as is the concept of equilibrium.

For purposes of this discussion we mean by strain, features in the situation of an individual's action, above all social and cultural, but even including the physical environment, which tend to "make it difficult" for an individual actor (or class or type of actors) to fulfill the "normal" expectations of the role or role-set. What we define as deviance is one type of response to situations of strain in this sense.

For purposes of this essay we therefore use the term strain to designate the negative aspect of the interface between the individual as personality and the social system in which he participates. This is the area of interrelations where, from the point of view of the individual participant, there are felt to be discrepancies between individual needs or desires and the expectations, demands, or obligations defined as emanating from social sources "outside" the individual's control. The occurrence of strain, in the sense defined here, we take to be a major empirical indicator that deviance and/or social change, relative to the circular flow of behavioral equilibrium, is taking place. Evidence of strain is recurrent in the case of heroin addicts as well as participants in the Watergate affair.

The case of the Nixon group is not analyzed here primarily in psychological terms. Even in such a case, however, one does not speak relatively concretely about action processes without attempting at some level to characterize "typical" attitudes or motives of individual participants. Thus to varying degrees the evidence suggests that members of the group were sensitive to the fact that their actions would be in a variety of respects disapproved outside; hence, there was a stimulus to secrecy. In the case of heroin addiction, then, the focus on the problem of the participant personality is much more immediate. In both cases we use the concept of strain as one focus in accounting for individuals' participation and on the other hand for characterizing the impact on them as personalities of the conflicts in which they became involved through their participation.

We have worked out the analyses, which will be presented in what follows, in terms of a rather technical theoretical scheme. We felt, however, that, for purposes of exposition, to couch our whole discussion in those terms would place an undue burden on readers who are not schooled in the formal aspects of what we call the "theory of action." Perhaps, however, we have not been fully consistent in adhering to a relatively nontechnical level.

First we can refer the interested reader to sources where he can find an exposition of these technical matters. The most important, because the most recent, is the "Technical Appendix" to Parsons and Platt, *The American University* (1973:423-447), but also other parts of that book. The same book also contains ample references to other parts of the conceptual scheme, such as the generalized symbolic media of interchange, the pattern variables, etc.

There are, however, one or two specific technical matters which, because they will appear later in this exposition, should be briefly commented upon here. These concern two principal concepts. The first is the existence, in many human-symbolic contexts, of what we call, following game theory, a "non-zero-sum" set of possibilities open to actors in a social interaction system. In Section II, it is made clear that the "medicinal" use of morphine and heroin had to be combined with its "recreational" use to generate the essential features of the "heroin addiction culture" which is the primary reference of the analysis.[3] From the point of view of the heroin user, this means that there are benefits to be gained beyond the alleviation of pain or related sorts of distress in the direction of the achievement of positively pleasurable states. It is the combination of these two which is necessary for addiction to take hold.

In the Watergate case the counterpart is the conception that political power can be something more than an instrumentality of implementing the traditional obligations of office, but that it can open up opportunities for political innovation beyond that. The potentialities in both cases can, from the point of view of personalities and social systems of reference, be either predominantly constructive or destructive, but in either case the relatively open opportunity needs to be there.

Such openness of opportunity implies, if it is to be meaningful, that the actors of reference will command sufficient resources to take significant advantage of them. Insofar as resources are generalized and "fluid," or can be made so, there is in such situations incentive to keep or build up sufficient fluid resources to maximize advantages from this point of view. In this kind of context, borrowing terminology from economics, we refer to an interest in the "liquidity" of the resources commanded by an actor or set of actors. Indeed a very important aspect of the relevant systems of action concerns the balance between keeping resources in "circulation" through processes of output and input, and keeping direct control of what, from the point of view of the actor at hand, is an adequate supply of resources, at the expense of circulation. This is one of the most important lines for defining the relations between unit and collective interest in systems, and from both points of view, for defining the relations between short- and long-run interests.

For resources not being currently consumed there are, as economists tell us, two alternative modes of use. One of these is that they should be "invested," which means, in the relevant sense, being put to "productive use," but thereby withdrawn from immediate consumption expenditure. The other alternative to consumption is "hoarding," i.e., maintaining the control of such resources in "liquid" form without the kinds of commitments to refraining from momentary and "whimsical" decision to withdraw them, which investment implies.

We will suggest below that heroin addicts have been pushed in the direction of hoarding resources, in this sense free access to heroin, and that the Nixon group were pushed in the direction of hoarding power. We thus mean to assert that such categories as investment and hoarding should be understood in our discussion as extending beyond their established economic meanings, but without challenging the correctness of such meanings. One important precedent is that of Freud (1961) who defined his concept *cathexis* as the "investment of libido" in a particular object-relationship, which is surely psychological rather than economic in reference.

We now proceed to the analysis of our two disparate but theoretically related cases. We begin with heroin addiction, precisely conceived as a pattern of socially deviant action, because it is closer to what the "common sense" of sociology considers to be deviance. After presenting this, we then present the salient features of the Nixon-centered "power-drive," if we may appropriately call it that. Then, in the final sections of the paper, we will undertake a comparison of the two and the formulation of a few conclusions for the theoretical field of the analysis of the genesis in social systems of deviant patterns, the nature of the balance between these and the counter-active forces, as we have called them, and hence the differential outcomes of different kinds of innovative tendencies in social systems.

II. THE FIRST CASE: HEROIN ADDICTS

We will start our exposition by an outline discussion of the heroin addiction "subculture," referring to the pharmocological problem but not elaborating on it, centering rather on its psychological and sociocultural aspects. Analytically speaking we will thus be concerned with the place of the phenomenon in the whole general system of action, with cognizance taken of its biological aspect. We will also include a brief account of its historical development, since we think that some understanding of its place in changing sociocultural situations, and of its own transformations over time, is essential to understanding the phenomenon from our predominantly sociological point of view. The "Watergate phenomenon," which will be discussed in the next section, on the other hand involved primarily phenomena internal to the social system, centering on the genesis and utilization of political power. Even here, however, broader considerations have either to be made explicit or to be assumed. Two categories stand out. The first is the matter of publicly relevant morality which, as in the heroin case, is not unrelated to legality. Both the addiction community and the "Nixon group" had their problems with the law. The second concerns psychological problems of the motivation of individuals, which are not, as we will point out, entirely differently structured in the two cases.

The case of heroin is thus empirically quite different from that of Watergate. Concern with the criminal social actions of heroin addicts, tied in with the law-and-order theme of the first Nixon administration, certainly propelled the massive wave of governmental activity directed against heroin circa 1970. But it is impossible to understand or explain the heroin phenomenon without central attention to matters at the general action level; to issues of personality, cultural change, and behavioral dynamics. The heroin phenomenon is furthermore no brief spasm of disorder which appeared, worked its way through a life cycle of action and reaction in a few years, and is now past. Rather, this phenomenon, which reached its lowest level during World War II, has expanded in successive waves since 1946, and there is currently no end in sight; while to find a beginning, one must return to the nineteenth century. In this section, we will first trace the history of the heroin situation in the United States, which will not be as familiar to most readers as the headline events of Watergate (see Terry and Pellens, 1928; Burroughs, 1953; Lindesmith, 1965; Fiddle, 1967; O'Donnell, 1969; Brecher, 1972; Musto, 1973, for a variety of perspectives on the historical development of heroin and opiate addiction generally in the United States). We will do so first in concrete historical terms, and then in a more theoretical vein. We will conclude by summarizing the equilibrium characteristics of the situation, with some comparative and predictive remarks.

During the nineteenth century, opium-containing patent medicines and injectable morphine (introduced circa 1860) were the most effective medicines known for nearly all diseases. They could not cure—but they alleviated pain with uniform efficacy. Subsequent to the Civil War, the folk use of opiated nostrums (most often not so labelled) was equivalent to use of all aspirin-type remedies today, while morphia was comparable to modern analgesics, sedatives, and tranquilizers combined. Neither was regulated by law. Recreational opiate use—smoking, drinking, and to a lesser degree injection—was also widespread, although most notoriously among unemployed Chinese railroad laborers, a focus of growing racial fear and persecution.

Unrestricted opiate importation expanded steadily after 1800, levelling off in the 1890s when there were an estimated 300,000 "habitués" and millions of casual users, many (in both groups) unknowing. By this time, coalescing medical opinion that opiates were too indiscriminately used led some states to legislate registration of suppliers. Loopholes for patent medicines, and the ease of interstate transport, rendered these laws ineffective. But in the first decades of the twentieth century, a confluence of additional pressures generated the first federal narcotics statutes: labelling provisions included in the Pure Food and Drug Act of 1906, the Smoking Opium Exclusion Act of 1909, and the landmark Harrison Narcotic Act of 1914, which required licensing of all importers and dispensers. The pressures behind these measures included the professionalization, with attendant protectionist efforts, of medicine and pharmacy; fortuitous moves to gain diplomatic advantages in contending for the fabled "China trade," and a moralistic crusade (with very strong xenophobic components) parallel to that resulting in liquor prohibition. During and after World War I, this xenophobic moralism, exacerbated by police activity and fear of German and Bolshevik "subversion," resulted in transformation of the Harrison Act into a de facto prohibition on the supply and possession of opiates for addiction maintenance, with particular attention being directed to the most recent, most effective opiate, increasingly popular among newer users: diacetylmorphine, first marketed in 1898 by the Bayer cartel under the trade name Heroin.

From 1915 through 1945, the pharmaco-medical initiation, support, and treatment of addiction contracted steadily, as narcotics officers prosecuted thousands of physicians and druggists. Efforts to withdraw addicts using various methods (many quite bizarre by modern medical standards) were largely unsuccessful in producing immediate abstinence in the short term. This lack of encouraging clinical results, harassment by narcotics police, and adverse public attitudes, caused medical practitioners to abandon the field of addiction treatment, until only the two Public Health Service operated narcotics prison-hospitals, at Lexington (opened in 1935) and Fort Worth (1938) continued medical treatment and research on opiate addiction (Eddy, 1973; Walsh, 1973a, 1973b; Musto, 1973). Police action against illicit opiate suppliers, the generalized depression of worldwide trade in the 1930s, and finally the disruption of international smuggling and intense domestic manpower mobilization of World War II caused the number of actively addicted Americans to decline to a small fraction of *fin de siècle* levels, while casual opiate use was reduced to trivial significance. In thirty years, a flood of opium had been reduced to a trickle of terpin hydrate.

The decade subsequent to World War II witnessed a series of "heroin epidemics," as the rapid onset of heroin use in a population has come to be called—although it should be understood that the term refers simply to an increase in experience with heroin use, implying nothing about progression to addictive use, or a "disease" concept (development of the "epidemiological" approach can be traced in the works of Dai, 1937; Chein et al., 1964; Finestone, 1966; Ball and Chambers, 1970; Hughes and Crawford, 1972; Greene and DuPont, 1974; Hunt and Chambers, 1976; and Rittenhouse, 1976). The "epidemics" occurred among young people, mostly males age 15 to 25, in the most impoverished neighborhoods of the largest American cities: New York, Los Angeles, Chicago, Detroit, Houston, Washington, D.C., and others. Little systematic research was conducted on these epidemics as they occurred, but a cluster of social-cultural changes can be related to this onset. First in importance, the massive internal migrations of war workers and their families to these cities, continuing after the war, along with the rapid demobilization of millions of servicemen, created an unprecedented pool of young urban dwellers unemployable in the recessionary postwar economy. Those with middle-class aspirations and high school diplomas were shunted into higher education by the G.I. Bill. Many of the remainder, especially among a few ethnic minorities, were not absorbed by conventional economic, educational, and other institutions, and became the substrate for postwar "street life" and the reorganizing "underworld," which concentrated in this period on three interlocked industries: redistribution (so to speak) of consumer goods, gambling, and drugs. A variety of imported and domestic intoxicants, including heroin, refined from Turkish opium and imported via Mediterranean and Caribbean ports, and Mexican morphine base (slightly refined opium) crossing the borders of the Southwest, found a ready market within this group, oriented toward expressive consumer values and lifestyles independent of the conventional labor market.

It was not necessary aggressively to merchandise heroin, as nineteenth century snake oil salesmen hawked their product; it was popular by virtue of its unconventionality, cheapness, and lack of knowledge about its latent physiological properties. The "epidemics" spread through local neighborhoods as fads, first among older street youths and then among their younger siblings and admirers. In most areas, only after many months or even years of popularity did addictive aftermaths become widely recognized. It remains unknown what proportion of neophytes continued the use of heroin after initial experimentation, or what proportion became organically addicted (suffered physiological withdrawal) at some point in their usage; no numbers are available, except data on how many became identified as drug users through later police action.

It *is* known that in the postwar decade political interest in the heroin traffic, aroused by the Federal Bureau of Narcotics and the McCarthyite revival of xenophobic moralism, led to drastic increases in penalties for narcotic violations, reaching the statutory extreme of the death penalty. The subsequent impact of these attitudes and laws (especially their "conspiracy" provisions) on importer syndicates, and such fortuitous events as the overthrow of the Batista regime in Cuba (which dislocated Havana-based transatlantic smuggling), multiplied the cost of heroin in the early 1960s. Meanwhile, the well-publicized anti-heroin campaign of Synanon, and firsthand exposure to addicted peers among city youth, made its negative potential better known (Feldman, 1968; Preble and Casey, 1969; McCoy, 1972). The concurrent employment boom and low wartime birthrate combined as well to reduce the pool of unemployed youth. In consequence of all this, a lull in the incidence of new addicts, or at least of concern about the "epidemics" as such, occurred in the late Eisenhower and Kennedy years.

Thousands of individuals addicted during earlier periods continued to use opiates and reappear for "the cure" (methadone detoxification by the dose reduction method, and several months of room and board) at Lexington and Fort Worth, and at New York City's Riverside Hospital (opened in 1952). Increasing medical and legal experience with these groups of identified addicts led to a concerted articulation of policy by respectable liberal physicians and attorneys: addiction was deemed a chronic relapsing disease, immune to short-term detoxification and criminal sanctions. Long-term rehabilitation, involving clinical maintenance therapy if indicated, was advocated by many health professionals, particularly in New York, where both elite physicians and heroin addicts were concentrated. It is important to note that, in the face of knowledge derived almost solely from seriously addicted individuals, it was widely believed among researchers, clinicians, and the public (and vigorously confirmed by the addicts themselves) that heroin addiction was an inevitable concomitant of drug use and so intractable an affliction that once acquired, it could not be self-limited without intense, consistent, external support (Joint Committee, 1961; Hoffman, 1973).

In alignment with the social welfare commitments and strategy of the Kennedy-Johnson administrations, and under the impetus of legal and medical professionals, community-based treatment such as "civil commitment" in Synanon-styled therapeutic communities, supervised parole, and publicly supported methadone maintenance began to take hold; the latter expanded dramatically as the billion-dollar-a-year Nixon administration "war on heroin" heated up. Methadone maintenance, in effect substitution of a legal opiate for illegal heroin, was advocated as an inexpensive solution to a growing addiction problem, which came to be associated in the public mind with "street crime" on the one hand, and the "hippie movement" on the other. Invented by German scientists during World War II (trade-named Dolophine in honor of Adolph Hitler), methadone's own opiate properties were downplayed in the light of highly publicized early success in keeping a select group of New York addicts in treatment and not committing crimes to support their prior heroin habits (Chambers and Brill, 1973; Lukoff, 1976).

The heroin epidemics of 1965-1975 were somewhat different in character from their postwar predecessors (DuPont, 1973; Levengood, Lowinger and Schoof, 1972; Hunt and Chambers, 1976). Although centered in the same poor neighborhoods of the urban giants, they developed as well, although at later points in time, in most smaller urban centers, reaching even into the suburbs, and included a higher incidence than ever before (although still a small minority in all) of middle-class youths and of females. These epidemics were associated with three events unique to the era: the Indochina war, the arrival at adolescence of the post-World War II "baby boom," and what we have called the "expressive revolution." American involvement in Southeast Asia triggered a massive rupture of youthful faith in American moral and political integrity, and a massive expansion of transport across the Pacific—a natural trade route for Indochinese heroin, the cheapest, most plentiful in the world. While the customary price of retail heroin sold in the United States did not decline appreciably, it unquestionably became far more widely available. Due to the baby boom, large numbers of young people again flooded the educational and labor markets in this period, straining socialization resources and contributing to a rapidly reviving unemployment pool. These three elements—the breakdown in solidarity fed by protest against the Vietnam War, new supplies of Asian heroin, and the increase in unsupervised leisure time among young people—joined with a catalytic cultural development: the romanticization of intimate experience (of which drug-induced states were paradigmatic) that became a focus of adolescent and young adult expression in the 1960s. While the addictive (and other damaging) potentials of heroin and other drugs were not unknown, the importance of such phenomena was devalued relative to the central impetus to explore private experience; while disengagement from all authoritative or conventional pronouncements and beliefs (especially those regarding drugs), relative to direct experience, further reduced the relevance of such warnings. Recreational use of drugs became a central token in the expression of peer solidarity.

From 1965 and through the early 1970s, the incidence of drug use, including heroin, increased steadily, as public concern mushroomed and was channelled by events. The initial phobic reaction partially exhausted itself in fulminations and legislation against LSD and "speed." Widespread experimentation with marijuana, particularly among middle-class youths who almost universally failed to "graduate" into heroin addiction, helped to further deflate the inflammatory aspects of the drug issue. The heroin problem did not receive renewed public articulation until the early 1970s, when the availability of methadone maintenance as an authoritatively pronounced successful treatment for addiction, and the well publicized concentration of law enforcement energies on "higher ups" in the heroin supply chain, forestalled the punitive moralistic response to addicts themselves which had marked prior outbreaks of attention to the subject in this century.

When the termination of American combat involvement in Indochina broke the Southeast Asian connection, the price of heroin again rose by multiples, partially through a decline in quality; that is, the ratio of opiate to adulterant in retail heroin decreased from the 25% range to the 5% range, until brown Mexican heroin (typically a more potent but less refined mixture) began to fill the supply channels. By this time, despite the backlash against methadone (owing to its widespread appearance on the street market in Eastern cities, and the distress many users experienced when withdrawn from maintenance treatment), this had become a prominent factor in both public perception and policy regarding heroin, and in the character of heroin use itself. The viability of the "chronic disease" model of heroin addiction, and concordant lessening of moral stigmatization attaching to addiction per se, became an established feature of current views, such that calls from legitimate sources for heroin maintenance became increasingly common (National Commission on Marijuana, 1973; Lidz et al., 1975). For users of heroin, the resort to methadone maintenance as a mode of continuing addiction during periods when, previously, withdrawal and abstinence would have been necessary; the possibility of avoiding incarceration much more successfully; and the prospect of using heroin in combination with methadone fairly indefinitely—all have changed long-term career prospects, in ways that are not yet entirely apparent.

Even as the disease concept gains public credibility, a revised view of the nature of heroin use has begun to form in the scientific subcommunity concerned with the problem, which group has expanded in numbers, knowledge, and respectability since the advent of methadone treatment, the expenditure of some quarter of a billion dollars on research, and formation of the National Institute on Drug Abuse. Indications have appeared over the past decade of study that: (1) many more individuals have experimented with heroin than became addicted to it; (2) abstinence over a long term, not enforced by institutionalization behind walls, is quite common among people who have been seriously addicted; and (3) many people presumed to have been heroin addicts were and are "polydrug" users with no demonstrable physiological dependence on heroin. The decades-long search for a "nonaddicting opiate" and a strictly neurochemical explanation of addiction, while not over, appears to have lost much of its salience, and more complex accounts of the phenomenon, incorporating systematic psychological and sociocultural variables, appear to be gaining credence (Young, 1973; Levin, Roberts and Hirsch, 1975).

In the succeeding pages of this section such an account, putting the historical background we have sketched above into more systematic theoretical terms, will be offered. We wish to demonstrate by so doing that such an account, drawn directly from the framework of action theory, is capable of concisely describing the deviant phenomenon, and explaining how it has come to be involved in processes of social change.

Opiate consumption in the nineteenth century occurred under two primary sorts of general action controls. First, cognitive judgments of professional and folk medicine of the time held opiates and opiated compounds in high regard, espousing first opium, then various tinctures, then morphine salts, and then heroin as welcome instruments in the technological control of behavioral deficits induced by bodily dysfunctions. The steady expansion of belief in the technical efficacy of these drugs was the major component in the rise in United States consumption rates during the 1800s. The second matter specifically concerned the recreational use of these drugs, as mutual practices carried out among friends to frame and facilitate occasions of relaxation and sociability. Unquestionably, there was potential for a combinatorial effect between these two sectors of opiate use: they were not simply additive, but each augmented the other beyond the simple sum of their parts; what we have called a "non-zero-sum" or "investment" phenomenon.

This occurred on two levels, psychological and sociocultural. In regard to the first, the combination of use for relief of behavioral deficits, and use for the induction of a relaxed (or other valued) mood, generated the possibility that absence of the relaxed mood associated with the drug might itself come to be seen as a behavioral deficit, for which consumption of the drug is indicated. This type of control sequence, quite familiar in operant learning theory, can be considered paradigmatic for self-directed learning processes in humans. In the current psychobiological conceptualization of "drug dependence," it is only insofar as the latent physiological properties of opiates retard or contribute to the acceleration of this learning pattern that the generic behavioral category "drug dependence of the morphine type" is distinguished from other sorts of drug dependence (Eddy et al., 1965). Conversely, insofar as consumption of the drug for repair of perceived behavioral deficits is learned effectively, the action involved in acquiring and consuming it may become additionally gratifying, as a display of competence. Insofar as this is personally valued, an increment to the overall capacity for personal goal attainment occurs.

In this context, an important theoretical distinction can be drawn between the consumption of opiates (which we may simply refer to as "use") and dependence classifiable as "addiction." Addiction is a type of "value addition" to simple use; the point at which a concrete case might be designated addiction depends on the quantity value-added, and that in turn on a contextual factor. The question revolves critically about the degree to which the behavioral pattern involved in opiate acquisition/consumption becomes incorporated into the personal goal structure of the individual in relation to the allocation of organized personal effort (competence) directed toward other goals. Clearly, one extreme is that the individual pursues no other goal; we would clearly designate this to be addiction. But ordinarily, people are also thought to be addicted when operating at levels considerably below this limit, although there is much imprecision in common usage. We do not wish to dictate here, but would simply suggest that addiction (or the "severity" of such) may best be concretely defined by the degree to which pursuit of the drug effect displaces, prevents, or interferes with the development of generalized competence, selection of alternative personal goals, and effectiveness in allocating competence toward such goals. Unquestionably, the degree to which sociocultural factors heighten the cost—in terms of allocations of competence—of acquisition of the drug contributes largely to determining the level at which a concrete definition of addiction is set.

The second context in which non-zero-sum combinatorial processes occur is sociocultural. The relationship between standards and sentiments of right and wrong, on the one hand, and accepted facts of social structure and institutional solidarity on the other, entail significant potentials for such processes. In one direction, the professional and folk medical approval of opiate consumption, in combination with the sociability characteristic of recreational use, could result in regular, solidary relations between suppliers and consumers (and among each), that would generate new subcultural symbolism giving meaningful significance to opiate consumption, beyond either its technical or recreational foundations. In the other direction, situated perceptions of the value of opiates, in concert with institutional respectability among users, could generate morally justified demands for the inclusion of opiates as an intrinsic constituent of the social order. Both of these investments clearly occurred during the pre-Harrison Act period, but had evidently reached their limit by the turn of the century.

A crucial theoretical point to be noted here is that the non-zero-sum feature applies as well to negative potentials in the overall action pattern; that is, to processes which may be referred to as "disinvestment." Such reductions in the investment sectors may multiply or accelerate an overall decline in the action pattern. This point is central to analysis of the changes in the position of opiates which occurred in the first decades of the twentieth century.

These changes derived largely from a twofold alteration in the cultural evaluation of opiates. The growing clinical awareness of addiction syndromes led to formation of a medical consensus that, on the whole, initiation of opiate treatment was entirely too frequent, and usually poorly managed. This occurred contemporaneously with the cumulation of scientific medical advances associated with such figures as Pasteur, Koch, Osler, Reed, and Cannon, which were rapidly rationalizing medical practice. At the same time as the standards and overall knowledge of medicine were improving, the early registration laws and muckraking attacks on the pharmaceutical industry exposed the unappreciated extent of opiate content in patent medicines. Secondly, the moral crusades characteristic of the time, which led to landmark reforms in civil service appointment, antitrust legislation, industrial hygiene regulation, suffrage extension, and liquor prohibition, extended as well against the use of opiates, which came to be viewed as destructive to national moral character. The movement was directed not so much toward limiting the initiation of opiate use (the focus of medical concern), but against the extant addicts and addiction per se. Fear of the Chinese, associated with opium smoking, and connections in the public mind between opiates and cocaine, a drug phobically portrayed as inciting sin and violence among Negroes, served to inflate the crusaders' moral position in regard to opiates. The rampant anti-German feeling of World War I, and anti-Bolshevism resulting from the Soviet revolution, added the fear of intentional foreign subversion of American moral fiber to these domestic bogies. The recreational use of opiates was denied the status even of a disreputable vice, instead coming to be seen as vicious, sinister, and gravely defective in moral worth.

Under the impetus of these definitions, societal institutions increasingly withdrew support from suppliers and consumers of opiate compounds. That medical efforts to withdraw addicts in the early 1920s were largely unsuccessful, while the science of the day was unable to demonstrate any medical cause for relapse, undermined contrary efforts to retain moral legitimacy for addicts or casual users; the actions of narcotics police, in jailing and thereby stigmatizing as criminals thousands of opiate-connected individuals, destroyed the basis in social respectability which had been a component of nineteenth century addiction.

By the 1930s, then, individuals who used nonpatent opiates, particularly in the large urban centers in which medical practice was most modern and police enforcement least lenient, came to rely almost exclusively on clandestine, illegitimate sources, liable at any time to be lost because of police activity or other reasons. In consequence of this instability, and of their own need to avoid police and the condemnatory views of others, addicts grew increasingly dependent on each other for support, of which they had precious little to provide, at least on the social level. The rapid deflation of sociocultural investment in opiates thus drastically reduced action in the two consumption sectors, such that maintenance of opiate use as a goal remained viable almost exclusively among individuals in whom the psychological investment in opiates was quite extreme.

The large numbers of addicts jailed subsequent to the Harrison Act threw them into contact not only with each other, but also with petty criminals of all sorts. Opening of the federal narcotics hospitals then isolated addicts from other criminals, while throwing together individuals from all across the country who had little else in common besides sharing the pursuit of opiates as a personal goal. Sheltered in these environs, and clustering together in byways as inconspicuous as possible while out of prison, these addicts generated, in these years, a sector of control of action which had not been prominent during the period of opiate consumption prior to the Harrison Act, one particularly concerned with the fit between individual identity and style. In the language of action theory, this sector is concerned with processes that we designate as "savings" or "liquidity" phenomena: they define potentials for action in fully codified, highly transferable fashion. In the case of addicts, what occurred in this period was a crystallization of meaningful stereotypes of mythic dimensions: the "junkie" and his "fix." This nearly self-contained realm of subcultural symbolism, concerned with the special personal needs and wants of the addict, played a highly significant role in seeding the new wave of recruits to heroin in the years following World War II.

The expansion of the consumption market after 1945 depended first of all on development of a greatly expanded pool of "high risk" individuals after the war, for whom the new supply of opiates was available. However, the notion of "high risk" (from epidemiology) must be defined in general action terms, and involves a second area of action liquidity. There are two central aspects to this. First, the fact that conventional opportunities for occupational mobility were, after the war, essentially closed to a large group of individuals, while opening for so many of their cohort, meant that their evaluation of the significance of conformity to mainstream social norms was deflated; such a group can be thought of as withholding their expectations of social reward, and thus in a position to engage in behavior innovative or deviant by normative standards, without much "opportunity cost." Second, the lack of conventional controls over this group by the socializing institutions, in the form of career opportunities and established kinship relations, undercut the grounds for rational evaluation of life chances attendant to their situation; thus they were in a position to experiment with what might be seen as chancy or improbable combinations of social strategies for mobility.

In another and final respect, as well, this group held a position of considerable liquidity in their action position. Heavily overrepresented by black, Puerto Rican, and Italian first and second generation urban immigrants, they shared a cultural milieu accented heavily upon expressive values—deference to virtuosity of style. In the context of the impoverished urban landscape in which they lived, this required making do with a limited and inconstant set of material cultural resources, a fluid willingness to experiment with any new fashion and display both bravado and mastery with whatever minimum of materials were at hand.

In this context, then, the first set of postwar epidemics becomes comprehensible, particularly given that there were few experienced users of heroin in these groups who knew of its addictive potential and could offer clear social example; and given also the cultural mystique of heroin that was available in the argot of the criminal "underworld" due to the earlier association with addicts. These epidemics appear to have derived neither from primary changes in what we have called the consumption sectors of action, nor from positive sociocultural or psychological investment in opiates, although these did develop somewhat as black market syndicates perfected importation routes and new addicts were generated from the ranks of users. In the main, however, these epidemics provided an outlet for an available pool of unspent, otherwise undirected energies in the internal action environment. The vague imagery of heroin as an esoteric potion became more explicit symbolization and identification by young street users. They built the heroin world from its prewar collection of exotic Chinese pipe terms and petty schemes to an alluring, dialectical mythic opposition: the slick-hustling, unruffled pusher cruising his silver Eldorado past the greasy, sniffling dope fiend begging his cotton fixes. As well, they created, with the aid of the police, politicians, and syndicates, a system of behavioral markets in which their life chances became a calculable matter involving clear aggregate probabilities. None of this was evident at the outset, nor was it the result of explicit plans; these action codes were built up through a decade of reciprocal action.

The limitation of these epidemics occurred mainly as a result of saturating the high risk pool as here defined. Further limiting the growth of addictive consumption were the closure, in this period, of other cultural elements to the expressive aspects of heroin symbolization, the restriction of increasingly expensive heroin to clandestine channels, and the increase in antiheroin ideology as negative addiction consequences became better known.

The epidemics of the 1960s and 1970s partially involved a regeneration of the conditions of the early postwar period on a wider scale. The extension of peer controlled leisure time among both middle- and lower-class youth, coupled with widespread adoption of expressive standards and interests in the period, made available a large new population during a fairly short period of time, in a liquidity position corresponding to "high risk." But additional factors specifically affecting both the sociocultural investment and consumption sectors modified developments in this period. Vietnam-related experiences reduced the institutional solidarity between American youth culture and the dominant institutions of the society, and elevated the sense that "oppression" and injustice were widespread in American society (a process begun by the civil rights movement). All sociocultural disincentives to morally stigmatized practices suffered from this development, not least those regarding drug use, which was undergoing an independent renascence of cultural signification. As a result, the structure of control over heroin, which had been stabilized in the late 1950s, shifted toward higher levels of use, including addiction. The involvement of heroin in the "polydrug" orientation of young people made a recreational pattern once again viable, while the advent of methadone maintenance, in line with the chronic disease model of addiction, signified that the medical rationality underlying addiction maintenance, which had disappeared as a factor in heroin control not long after the Harrison Act, was becoming reasserted. The concentration of the "war on heroin," in its enforcement aspects, on the nonusing "big-time operators" in the heroin trade, with the focus of dealing with addicts turned to narcotic treatment, including increasing calls for heroin maintenance from legitimate sources, is the logical extension of this secular trend.

What, then, is the current control situation with respect to heroin? The primary consumption sector remains the social-recreational one: nearly all users are initiated via the fortuitous involvement of heroin in a primary relationship of friendship or intimacy. Insofar as strict controls over the medical administration of opiates to neophytes can be maintained, this promises to remain the case. For most users, this social-recreational context remains the framework of their heroin involvement.

The increased psychological investment by which we define addiction onset has important consequences for the consumption sector, particularly when it cuts sufficiently into allocation toward other psychological investment processes that a general disturbance of developmental equilibrium can be identified. The result of such detection is a rapid reduction in the overall rate of social support for the heroin user, not only for heroin use per se, but for all personal goal-attainment so long as addiction continues. Reciprocally, psychological investment in addiction quite commonly involves a rapid reduction in levels of personal motivational support of conventional social institutions that are not heroin-linked. The exceptions to these dual processes are diffuse solidarities partially incorporating mutual heroin use, provided they are not destroyed or converted into strictly instrumental associations by the disintegrative character of the heroin social system. This disintegrative character, and the withdrawal of support from heroin addicts vis-à-vis the rest of the societal community, is in turn a result of the steep gradient of sociocultural disinvestment in opiates, which leads to the need for clandestine activity, the instability of the clandestine market, and the degradation resulting from exposure of heroin system membership.

How, one must ask, can an individual be drawn into the heroin addiction-investment process, given the prospective withdrawal of social support so entailed? The answer lies largely in terms of the liquidity factors defined above. First, insofar as heroin is a drug of exotic expressive significance, it exercises unmistakable appeal to those interested in exploring the limits of expressive activity, that is, with a well-developed sense of adventure. Such an orientation tends to discount current or incremental social-motivational support in favor of maintaining potentials for psychological investment. An inherent danger of all heavily expressive orientations, however, is that their preference for maintaining openness or liquidity in personal style and identification may result in investments whose payoff in support is not merely low or zero, but negative. It is by no means necessary for this to happen; psychological investments by no means necessarily eschew outcomes favorable to increase in social recognition or attachment. But expressive liquidity requires a degree of indifference to support. Moreover, when negative outcomes result, in order for liquidity to be maintained, a further reduction in overall support in the short term becomes necessary. After enough such short terms, the initially unintended consequence of excessive liquidity preference is a total collapse of motivational support.

The second area in which liquidity problems may occur is that of social rationalization. Where intelligent appraisal of life chances clearly differentiates positive and negative outcomes attached to social contingencies, people ordinarily follow "good risk," traditionally successful career pathways. However, where selection of positive outcomes is made ambiguous—by rarity of example, social contradictions, or randomness of opportunity—then high risk or simply non-rational choice patterns become more probable and attractive. This once again involves a devaluation of consumption increments relative to maintaining investment potentials. In this instance it is not social recognition which is discounted, but cultural recognition in the form of demand for cognitive capacity (e.g., technically trained skills), and the converse, available cultural standards and knowledge. Maintenance of the liquidity preference in the face of repeated disasters in cognitive outcomes eventually results in a total collapse of cognitive support.

In brief, the initiation of heroin use occurs at the highest rates in the "high risk" populations as defined by liquidity preferences which we have specified above, although it can occur in any diffuse relationship which is solidary on other grounds, in which one member is a user. The development of addiction investment, however, is confined largely to the high liquidity groups, for whom the outcome of addiction, while not sought as such, is most compatible with their overall action positions. This is true because and insofar as they are disposed to continue even "bad" psychological investments.

Overall, until the rapid spread of methadone maintenance treatment programs in the early 1970s, the invested heroin addict faced bleak prospects on the long term. While the heroin action pattern held considerable appeal for the segments of the population defined here by excessive liquidity preference positions, the career trend pointed to steady reductions in personal production and consumption capacity. The rates of morbidity, mortality, dereliction and lengthy incarceration combined to produce a considerable annual attrition. The downward trend is well-recognized by symbolic complexes within the subculture; the loss of social recognition as well as the acquisition of personal characteristics symbolic of the "broken-down junkie" or "stomped-down, hope-to-die dope fiend" signify the minimization of potentials for personal goal-gratification characteristically resulting from extended addiction.

With the advent of methadone as a legitimate treatment procedure, several modifications in career path became possible. First, reestablishment of functionally specific solidarity between opiate consumers and suppliers in a socially supported market—that is, between addict "patients" and treatment personnel—became possible again following the long lapse. The support of sufficient numbers of addicts for such programs, and the relative cognitive legitimation of addiction within a "chronic disease" model, has altered the severity of sociocultural disinvestment, although powerful degradation features remain in effect. Enough cognitive credit has been extended to addiction as such to permit some ten thousand addicts to have become employees of treatment programs during the "war on heroin" and to encourage various employers to hire "ex-addicts" despite open knowledge of their status; in previous periods, only by obscuring their addiction histories could heroin addicts maintain legitimate employment careers.

Methadone maintenance has, therefore, provided some alternatives to the long-term career prospects of addicts, reducing incarceration, dereliction and death rates while establishing firmer conventional social controls over career courses. Insofar as mixed heroin/methadone maintenance (the current practice in British narcotics clinics) becomes viable, it will almost certainly reduce the cultural mystique of heroin, thus cutting down its attractiveness to the high-risk groups whose propensity, largely determined by politico-economic and youth-cultural considerations, to a great extent determines the overall incidence of heroin use and addiction. Depending on the further softening of sociocultural disinvestment, the average severity of addiction where present (in the action, not necessarily in the physiological sense) will decline, although the prevalence of addiction among users may increase somewhat as enforced abstinence becomes less necessary. This will depend too on the nature of addiction treatment admission policies.

In summary, we can expect the incidence of new heroin users to decline steadily over the remainder of the century, while the prevalence of addiction will continue to rise for a few more years, stabilizing as the postwar high-risk cohort ages. The trend of sociocultural disinvestment is moving toward the acceptance of higher *rates* of addiction in return for reductions in the *severity*.

III. THE SECOND CASE: THE NIXON POLITICAL CIRCLE

As we noted in our introductory statement, in empirical content, the case of the deviance of the inner political circle of the Nixon administration was very different from that of the nearly contemporaneous peak of the heroin addiction culture. The former, to the discussion of which we now turn, was concerned with problems of their political power position, at the center of the federal government of the United States, whereas the latter was concerned with the highly personal problems of, shall we say, individually not very prominent citizens. We have, however, deliberately chosen these contrasting cases in order to show that, in spite of their conspicuous differences, there are certain features in common which on the one hand are of special interest to theoretical social science and which, in turn, we do not think would have become evident to anybody except through theoretical analysis of the sort we are attempting in this article.

The Nixon clique pursued political power, as any political group aiming to achieve and maintain political control of the central government of a great nation must, and as a matter of course does, usually in ways considered to be more legitimate than not. The peculiarity of the Nixon episode, by virtue of which we venture to call it deviant, consisted, however, of certain strategies which were adopted in the group's operations. On the one hand, as in any presidential campaign, they had to rely heavily on the traditional basis of status in the institutionalized social system, mainly the mobilization of support through the party system—in this instance the Republican Party—and then within the legitimating framework of the constitutional system. The Nixon group utilized these resources of support, but they deviated by resorting to a constricted segment of their "base." This was a highly selective set of components of this supportive complex consisting above all of the President's "staff" appointees, a base which in turn proved to be highly unreliable "in the crunch."

In the background lay the fact that since the Eisenhower era the Republican Party had been in something of a state of disarray. As the heir presumptive of Eisenhower in 1960, Nixon had little difficulty securing the nomination, but he lost the election by a narrow margin to Kennedy. Later he ran for governor of California, but was defeated, whereupon he announced his ostensible retirement from politics. The 1964 Republican Convention saw a bruising battle between the right and moderate wings of the Party, which resulted in Goldwater's nomination, but was followed by his disastrous defeat by Johnson.

In 1968 it was the Democrats' turn to be in disarray, with Johnson's withdrawal from the race, and the tension over the Vietnam War at a high pitch. In this situation Nixon reentered the lists, easily won the Republican nomination and this time won the election by a very narrow margin against Humphrey.[4]

Thus Nixon, who could never be accused of lack of ambition, was seriously insecure in his first term. Probably the overarching aspect of that was the mounting opposition to the Vietnam War, the seriousness of which Johnson had understood. The narrowness of his electoral margin was related to that, as was less so the fact that there was a strong Democratic majority in Congress.

At any rate, it seems to us that Nixon missed a great opportunity. As a newly elected, outspokenly conservative President, he could have emulated de Gaulle in the case of the Algerian War and moved decisively to bring the war to an end, "cutting" American losses. Instead he decided to temporize, putting forth the formula "peace with honor," and letting the war drag on throughout the first term and well into the second; indeed, it was still going when he resigned. To be sure he did combine this temporizing with an imaginative set of moves toward the Communist world in the opening to China and the policy of détente toward the Soviet Union. But holding on in Vietnam as he did made these moves much less convincing as a major reorientation than they might have been, and they left him exposed to mounting opposition, much of which presumably would have been cut off by a settlement. (One wonders whether he ever seriously considered this alternative.)

Almost certainly one major factor in his position was, as was true of Ford after him, his fear of the Republican Right—one might say that the policy toward China and Russia was daring enough from that point of view. However that may be, as luck would have it, the early part of his first term saw the culmination, in 1969 and 1970, of the wave of student disturbances. That these were not, as many have held, in any simple sense "caused" by the Vietnam War, is clear from the fact that after the Cambodia incident of 1971 they subsided without any fundamental change in the Vietnam situation. They did, however, serve to activate not only the opposition, but certain of the sentiments of Nixon and his associates like Mitchell, of hostility toward "radicals" of every sort, but in particular as they were linked to "intellectuals." There developed a generally repressive attitude in this connection, manifested in the Agnew campaign of speeches (which was planned in the White House) and various repressive measures against demonstrations and the like.

In rationalizing such attitudes, a major part was played by the plea of the necessity for strict "national security." Abuse of this plea, which was not invented by the Nixon administration, had one particularly important effect, namely the alienation from the Nixon camp of a certain sector of the intellectual community, on whom the government had been growing increasingly dependent.[5]

One major path to deviance could lead from here. National security has, certainly since World War II, long been a major basis for the justification of secrecy, which in the nature of the case puts government in an adversary relation to journalists and the other mass media. Governmental secrecy of course also impinges on a wide range of private rights in such spheres as the classification of documents and the clandestine gathering of information, as through wire-tapping and the opening of mail. Not least, of course, have been problems raised by the clandestine operations of such agencies as the CIA. It is well known that secret operations of any sort increase the difficulties of control; conversely publicity, or public access to information, facilitates a wide variety of controls, though not all. This is an old battle, especially with reference to government, but also more broadly in modern societies, e.g., with respect to the maintenance of business secrets.

Another important point about secrecy concerns its relation to attitudes of suspicion. There is a reciprocal relation between secrecy and distrust, in that when secret operations are known to take place, or are suspected, for persons inclined to distrust those involved, the very fact of secrecy increases the presumption that something is being hidden for unacceptable reasons. It almost goes without saying that complete openness is impossible in many important human contexts. Privacy, if only for personal reasons, confidentiality, e.g., of discussions prior to arriving at a collective decision, indeed executive privilege within limits, all have their strong justifications. But there is equally no doubt that secrecy and opportunity for abuse are highly correlated. It is exceedingly difficult, in modern democracy, to draw a reasonable balance, or to devise mechanisms for doing so.

A variety of circumstances seems to have exacerbated these tensions for the Nixon administration. First probably was mutual suspicion between its members and the mass media. Second was difficulty of relations with the Congress, not only because of its size and the consequent opportunity to "leak" information, but due to the fact that majorities in both Houses were political opponents of the President. Similar considerations applied to the various administrative agencies. Then it seems to be the case that, even apart from fear of the revelation of specific wrongdoing or other serious "secrets," the Nixon group, including the President himself, were unusually suspicious of others and prone to impute hostile motives to them, even if they were ostensible political allies, e.g., in the same party.

Theoretically it seems to us that the problems of trust and mistrust and their relations should be treated as part of the influence complex, i.e., that part in which influence is most directly interchanged with political power. [6] In the sense in which we use the concept, power depends on trust, but above all on the legitimacy of the authority under which it is used. Power, however, carries the sanctions of bindingness, whereas influence we conceive to be a medium of persuasion. Hence the resistances to use of the two media are likely to be different. In both cases the person or group, the action of which it is intended to affect, is presented with choices, but the choices are differently structured because the sanctions are different.

It seems, however, to be true that by and large things were relatively normal during most of Nixon's first term, the most overtly abnormal element being the campaign against opponents of the Vietnam War and their associations with radicalism, student dissent and the intellectuals. On the positive side was the relative popularity of the moves toward China and Russia. Also, though the inflationary trend began, the economy did not yet present severe problems.

Probably the most serious deviant pattern characteristic of the first term was that of secrecy with respect to the conduct of the Vietnam War. The most famous incident came to be the secret bombing of Cambodia. In this as in other cases there was particular resentment because congressional leaders were not even informed, to say nothing of being consulted, and of course no public announcements were made. It is extremely difficult in the conduct of a war to define and draw the line between secrecy and legitimate claims to information, but in this period the Nixon administration clearly overstepped those limits on a considerable scale. This is one main reason why they wanted to keep the Pentagon papers from being published (see Sheehan et al., 1971).

Probably the most severe tendency to break away from legitimacy came, however, in planning the campaign for reelection in 1972. A major move was taking control of the campaign away from the Republican National Committee and putting it in the hands of a special "Committee to Reelect the President" (CREEP). John Mitchell resigned as attorney general in order to chair that committee. The committee in turn, as has subsequently come to light, engaged in an extensive repertoire of clandestine and semiclandestine operations which would presumably have been much more difficult to manage under the National Committee of the Republican Party.

These more and less clandestine activities seem to have taken place on two main fronts, the distinction between which is central for our analysis. One was in the direction most directly symbolized by the "dirty tricks" which were meant to influence opinion. The most notorious of these was the letter, proven to have been issued over Senator Muskie's forged signature, referring to French Canadians as "Canucks." This was published during the New Hampshire primary campaign and seems to have done Muskie a great deal of harm with the voters. The authorship has definitely been traced to an agent of CREEP. The famous Watergate breakin itself was essentially of this pattern. The raid, again conducted by agents of CREEP, eventually was alleged to have occurred with the President's knowledge. It was designed to get, from the Democratic headquarters, information about prominent Democrats which could be used against them politically. The breakin to the office of Daniel Ellsberg's psychiatrist belonged in the same pattern. It was designed to secure derogatory information about Ellsberg which could be used to discredit him and thereby counteract the "leaking" of the Pentagon papers. All three of these incidents, and many others, clearly involved criminal acts (see White, 1975).

The second direction of operation concerned financial resources. Just at a time when Congress and large sectors of the public were becoming newly concerned about the political influence of large campaign contributors, CREEP launched a particularly aggressive fund-raising campaign, which seems seriously to have overstepped the normal bounds. Certainly the normative standard for such contributions is that they should be voluntary gifts. Such standards can be deviated from in two principal respects. The first is by the use of specific inducements, the most familiar case of which is bribery, namely the offer of specific financially valuable considerations if the contribution is made. This is the most familiar kind of "corruption" which is endemic in the American type of democratic government. That, however, it is by no means confined to the United States is made clear by the Lockheed Corporation's record of dealing with officials of a variety of foreign goverments. [7]

The other aspect of this deviant direction is the utilization of a superior power position to impose terms of exchange relative to command of economic resources. In the operations of CREEP this seems to have taken mainly the form of approaching large potential financial contributors by "demanding" substantial contributions, implicitly and sometimes explicitly, on pain of the threatened imposition of sanctions on the client which were within the capacity of central government to implement, such as antitrust action, investigation of a company's affairs by the IRS, and so forth. Here the voluntariness of the contribution comes into question and the procedure easily shades over into some form of "extortion." There seems to be no doubt that in the campaign to reelect there was considerable resort to such methods of fund-raising. Often carrying out the implicit or explicit threats would involve one or more government agencies in what were, by most standards of procedure, deviant operations.

It has, however, long been the case in the American system, that it is difficult to draw the lines between legitimate and illegitimate fund-raising. The requisite degree of "freedom" or voluntariness of valuable gifts is difficult to define, and the reactions of the recipient which are in some sense contingent on "giving" behavior cannot precisely be stated, without laborious processes of legal development.

There is much evidence of these practices reported in the various discussions of these events, such as the works of Bernstein and Woodward (1974), Woodward and Bernstein (1976), and especially that of Theodore White (1975). The essential point for our consideration is that, in dealing with the problem of mobilizing financial resources for political purposes, the Nixon group tended to deviate rather seriously in two directions, namely that of overstepping the line between voluntary contribution and bribery by specific inducements, and in the other direction, modifying the voluntary character of the contribution by the introduction of explicit, or more frequently, implied threats of negative sanctions, which were realistically possible because they were made in the name of the current controllers of the machinery of government.

It is another important question how far the inner group in the executive branch is in fact in a position to "bend" the legitimate control over executive agencies for the benefit of "political" interests in this special, relatively narrow sense. The evidence suggests, however, that in the short run for a determined inner group, there is usually considerable leeway. This is partly because, in such a complex system, there is necessarily a good deal of ambiguity in the normative structure of administrative regulations, so that they can be "interpreted" in a variety of ways. On top of that, however, like other "interest groups," administrators are vulnerable to "pressures" of various sorts and degrees, so that just such a determined group as we are talking about, backed by presidential power and prestige, would be able to impress a pattern of deviance from the more or less firmly institutionalized norms of administrative procedure. The evidence suggests that this in fact happened on a large scale.

Of course such action involves certain risks. Probably the most important immediate one was that of activating groups which were injured or outraged by these procedures to take recourse to various kinds of political or legal action. Indeed, as we shall see, this was one of the primary paths by which the countervailing forces achieved effective counteraction. It is notable, as Jonathan Schell (1975) has said, how cavalier the members of this group were about the dangers to them of mobilization of forces of legality when so much of their action was in violation of legal norms. Certainly they tended to rely too heavily for their own good on protection behind the curtains of "national security" and "executive privilege."

The view seems to be justified that the two contexts so far reviewed constituted one main basis of the temporary success of the Nixon group in being able to consolidate and extend their immediate power in the federal government by overstepping the bounds of deviance. These were the fields of the mobilization of various kinds of political support, especially from groups having relatively clear-cut and self-conscious interests in the maintenance of a political regime with this kind of orientation. Secondly, it had to do with the mobilization of financial resources, especially for electoral purposes, but when the faction was sufficiently deeply mired in the illegalities of their operations, this extended to what can only be called protection money, particularly vividly illustrated by the offer of substantial sums to the Watergate burglars if they would refrain from revealing what they knew.

The advantages involved, however, were inherently focused in the short run, and even then could be maintained only by certain protections and sacrifices which were equally important. We have stressed the dependence on secrecy under the umbrellas of national security and executive privilege. Closely related to this, however, was the cutting off of wider sources of political support by engaging in operations which could not be communicated to wider publics on whom the administration was increasingly dependent in a longer run. One might say that the decisive step in this connection was taking the management of the reelection campaign out of the hands of the Republican National Committee and creating CREEP specifically for this purpose. Of course, a relatively clandestine and shady program of money-raising, the nature of which we have just sketched, was more than usually accessible to the Nixon people because of their close connection with many private groups who commanded large financial resources and were dependent on government favor. This, however, was apparently not adequately effective from their point of view, without resort to the deviant processes we have just described.

The continuance of this short-run success was, however, dependent on the maintenance of a certain kind of insulation from two particularly sensitive contexts of interdependence of a political group at the center of power with important aspects of the larger society. The more obvious is the context that many sociologists have come to discuss as that of legitimation (see Weber, 1968). Of course, one primary focus of such legitimation has lain in the electoral process, and the desire to be in full control at this level provided one of the major incentives to deviance. In the short run, this of course was brilliantly successful, as proved by the electoral sweep of 1972. There are, however, other components of the legitimation context which, without attempting to analyze them too fully, may be classified as the legal and the moral. It should be made clear, since memories tend to be short-lived, that the Watergate breakin occurred in June of 1972, nearly five months before the election. Since the perpetrators were arrested and sent to court, it was impossible to quash all publicity about the affair. It was, however, possible for a considerable time to keep investigation of the underlying and secret ramifications from going far enough to break into the glare of widespread publicity. Indeed, the Democrats proved to be unable to make a serious issue of Watergate and its implications in their campaign of 1972. It has, however, become known subsequently that strenuous coverup efforts were necessary for this to be accomplished. Later, during the second Nixon administration, the storms began to gather and finally broke in full force. This only then made clear, especially as revealed by the Senate committee of investigation chaired by Senator Ervin of North Carolina, that with connivance and/or direction in or very close to the White House, a complicated series of definitely illegal acts had been carried out.

There is, then, an important connection between legality and morality, and the opposition raised readily passed from the one to the other.

The second field in which this deviant enterprise was vulnerable in the longer run concerned the problem of loyalty, with its close connections to political support. This has a number of different aspects. Any such large-scale political system as the American system of national politics necessarily involves solidarities at a variety of levels. It seems particularly important that Nixon chose to depend on a very narrow group of loyal supporters, notably the group with whom he surrounded himself in the White House, and groups very closely affiliated with this, of which a very notable example was CREEP. This reliance on the solidarity of close in-groups was necessarily accomplished to a significant degree at the expense of broader loyalties which were of great significance in the larger picture. If a single one could be noted, it was the importance of dependence on the Republican Party as a whole. The secrecy and "go it alone" practices of the Nixon group made it very difficult to maintain loyalties, for example, with the senior Republicans in Congress, to say nothing of others outside the governmental machinery. It is of course significant that toward the end of the road, notably under the pressure of the investigative operations of the House Judiciary Committee, even loyal Republican Party supporters began to desert the Nixon group.

It was, however, extremely important that once the pressure became sufficiently intense, even members of the other, we can correctly say, conspiratorial group began to desert. To try to forestall this was the primary objective of the payoff proposals and in part actual payments to the Watergate burglars to keep them silent. However, this went to much bigger people much closer to the White House, the most prominent of whom was John Dean, in the very sensitive position of special counsel to the President himself. Dean's testimony to the Ervin committee certainly was one of the truly decisive breaks in the situation. It can fairly be summed up that, in relying on this small factional group within the party, the Nixon administration brought itself into an inherently precarious position because it could no longer command the loyalties of a sufficiently broad group on which its position, particularly when it came under political stress, would have to depend, and as it eventually worked out, even the members of the small group itself began to desert (White, 1975).

In any social and political system, as complex, diversified and pluralistic as the American, there is bound to be a great deal of both overt and latent conflict. Therefore it is no mystery that any group such as the inner group of the Nixon administration would have to face, even after its striking electoral victory in 1972, a great deal of suspicion and hostility, generating continual attempts to test its vulnerabilities. From this point of view, the Watergate breakin and a certain number of other points presented opportunities. In the background, of course, was the mounting disaffection in spreading quarters about the dragging on of the war in Vietnam, the lack of anything approaching a military closure, and the administration's secrecy and disregard of public and congressional opinion in this affair.

However, it seems to us that the "Achilles' heel," as it were, was to be found in the suspicion that there were secret vulnerabilities of which Watergate was a prime example. It seems in retrospect that the first seriously effective exploitation of this vulnerability lay in the investigative reporting of certain sectors of the press. The lead example was the reporting team of Woodward and Bernstein. There soon, however, developed a major competition between the *Washington Post* and the *New York Times* in ferreting out facts about the Watergate story which had been concealed by the coverup policy. Then the electronic media, notably CBS, joined in the chase.

From the beginning, however, this also became a major object of court procedure, with the appointment of a grand jury under the jurisdiction of the Federal courts of the District of Columbia to investigate the affair. It is, of course, well known that Judge Sirica of the District Federal Court played the major role in the judicial process which brought to light an ever-widening range of information about these matters and eventually led to indictment and conviction of some very prominent political personalities, notably Haldeman and Ehrlichman, and even before their conviction, forced the President to dismiss them from their very crucial positions on the White House staff (see New York Times Staff, 1974).

The press and, back of the press, the broadcasting networks developed a growing crescendo of a combination of revelation of secret matters and of condemnatory opinion about the goings-on in the White House and its related organizations. There is no point on this occasion of attempting to detail these matters. Only one or two items may be mentioned because of their special significance.

First, the investigation of the Ervin committee, which included the revelation that a set of tapes had been made in the White House of conversations with various people, generally without their knowledge, raised sufficient furor so that there was the demand that a special prosecutor should be appointed with extensive powers of investigation. This was referred to the attorney general, then Eliot Richardson, and he was primarily responsible for the appointment of Archibald Cox, and agreed with the Senate in relation to its confirmation of the Cox appointment, that Cox should have access to all the necessary information to carry out his mandate.

In October 1973, it will be remembered, this led to a truly major crisis for the Nixon administration in that the President explicitly forbade Cox to follow certain lines of investigation, notably those which included hearing certain selected White House tapes. When Cox refused to accept this presidential prohibition, the President ordered the dismissal of Cox. As we know, Richardson felt that his agreement with the Senate to guarantee Cox the requisite access to information was a point of honor, and therefore rather than obey the presidential order to dismiss Cox, he resigned as attorney general. This provoked the so-called "firestorm" which, more than any other episode, led to the activation of proposals for impeachment before the Judiciary Committee of the House of Representatives, of which Rep. Peter Rodino of New Jersey was chairman. The House Committee appointed an able legal staff and eventually, that is in the summer of 1974, came to the point of formulating and approving articles of impeachment. It gradually built up to the point where the recommendation of impeachment by the Judiciary Committee became certain, and the probability of a favorable vote by the House became also certain. Formally being faced with an impeachment trial was one of the two factors which precipitated Nixon's decision to resign.

The second major action was that of the Supreme Court. It is of course important that, after the dismissal of Archibald Cox as special prosecutor by then Solicitor-General Bork (after his two superiors, Richardson and Ruckelshaus, resigned in protest) the White House was unable to prevent the appointment of a successor, Leon Jaworski, on essentially the same terms as those given to Cox. When the President reiterated his refusal to make certain tapes available, both Jaworski and the House Committee took the matter to court. The Circuit Court of Appeals supported the petitioners and the White House appealed the decision to the Supreme Court. A very dramatic occasion occurred in early August 1974, when the Court handed down a unanimous decision in favor of the petitioners. [8] After some hesitancy the President, we are told on the insistence of his personal counsel, James St. Clair, decided to comply with the order of the Court, and in fact turned over the tapes. These two episodes together crystallized the situation which decided the President to resign. As he himself said, so much of the political support on which he was dependent for carrying out the duties of his office had disappeared that he was no longer able to function effectively as President. Incidentally, he has never publicly admitted that anything he did was illegitimate. [9]

It seems to us highly significant that the mobilization of counteraction to the Nixon deviant faction came to focus at the level of the legitimation of political action on the part of office holders. This reaction would have been far less likely and, if some of it had occurred, far less effective, if it had not been backed by a genuine movement of public opinion activated by the press and the broadcast networks, which, it will be remembered, the early Nixon administration had treated with a great deal of hostility. One may, however, say that being confronted with the kind of evidence which had emerged and certainly being greatly influenced by political opposition to the Nixon administration, Congress, backed by the courts, took the primary active role in bringing the problem to a head. More than any other agencies, two congressional committees brought the pressure to a point which, for the President, proved to be unbearable.

Partly preceding, later parallel with congressional action, of course, was that of the courts of law and legal machinery of government. Here it should be particularly emphasized that, though it is by no means completely exceptional, the American system of government is certainly distinctive in the degree of independence which it has accorded to the courts of law. It is quite possible that in certain other systems which had perhaps best be unnamed—though an extreme would be the Soviet Union—it would not have been possible for courts of law to undertake procedures with such potentially threatening implications for the group in supreme power in the society, as did happen even in the somewhat lower court, namely that presided over by Judge Sirica. This independence of the Judiciary, however, was given a final capping by the Supreme Court's unanimous decision to reject the Nixon appeal to deny both to the House Judiciary Committee and to the special prosecutor access to certain White House tapes. The President was then faced with the stark alternative of openly defying a unanimous decision of the Supreme Court in a situation which made his conviction in the impeachment trial certain, or complying with the decision, which would reveal information so damaging that it would make his continuing tenure in office impossible. He decided to comply, but forestalled conviction in an impeachment trial by his resignation.

A few words should be said here, prior to the concluding section, about the specific points at which the Watergate events can be compared with the case of heroin.

For the heroin case, what we have called the sociocultural investment exchange is the "upper-level" area in the general action scheme (the "lower-level" area is psychological). Similarly, there is an upper-level investment exchange within the social system itself, devoted specifically to the development of interpersonal and institutional loyalties. The Nixon faction was marked by a well-noted tendency to disengage from broader political loyalties—e.g., to the congressional and national party structure—instead concentrating on intense commitment to Nixon and the White House staff. The attacks on the media by Agnew, repression of "left-wing" demonstrators, and harassment of government employees suspected of "leaking" national security secrets all correspond to this phenomenon. Of more direct interest, of course, is the use of CREEP, rather than the Republican National Committee, to manage the 1972 presidential election efforts. The Nixon group's deep suspicion of "radic-libs," and their only somewhat less jaundiced view of government and party "allies," is not unlike the position of addicts toward the action-level counterparts of these: conventional adversaries in the law-enforcement system ("narcs," "bulls" and other "pigs") and fellow members in the heroin system who may turn out to be "snitches," and therefore are not to be trusted beyond necessary minima.

Such narrow bases of political loyalty as Nixon's group displayed lead to problems in sustaining an adequate level of overall political support. We have noted that heroin addicts' support problems were greatly accelerated by societal disinvestment (although in recent years this trend has begun to ease). In the Nixon case, suspicion and overt and clandestine attacks on the (broadly defined) Left were successful in maintaining electoral support of Nixon in 1972 (with a notable absence of "coattails" despite the presidential landslide), but backfired quite dramatically in the succeeding period. The shakiness of the potential support problem was experienced by Nixon's staff during early 1972 as a severe feeling of insecurity regarding the upcoming election. Their actions in consequence, while reflecting the investment situation, are inexplicable without an appreciation of their liquidity position. These are as crucial to the incidence of the deviant activities of Watergate as their counterparts at the general action level were shown to be for the deviant action pattern involved in heroin.

Again, the matter has two central aspects. On the one hand, considerable flexibility in executive ordering of cabinet and regulatory departments was exerted throughout the Nixon years by the White House. "Bending" of administrative procedures to White House dictates was covered by the codes of "executive privilege" and "national security," which carried a double sense: *confidentiality* of administrative deliberation and practice, on the one hand, and broad *discretion* in implementing decisions on the other. Thus, whereas President Johnson felt the need for Congressional mandate support of military policy in Southeast Asia, Nixon did not, so that such events as the secret bombings, to say nothing of secret peace missions (in contrast to the Paris conference) were matters of course. The coverup actions, requiring extensive privileged intervention in Justice Department activities, would have been impossible without this orientation. On the whole, the Nixon White House exercised unprecedented flexibility in these areas of administrative discretion, which use we have characterized as involving the relations between power and influence, and commitments mandated by law.

The second area of liquidity factors involves the exchange of money and influence. Nixon and his subordinates exercised a preference for considerable liquidity in this area, especially under the code of "campaign contributions." The exaggerated importance of these to the Nixon operation was manifest in the unprecedented quantities of cash collected in discretionary CREEP accounts. These sums of money, in concert with a notion of executive privilege carried by the Nixon people into the CREEP operations, and activated by the electoral insecurities of the Nixon group, led to the "dirty tricks" so prominently revealed during the later Watergate investigations. In order to accumulate these sums, it was of course necessary to deviate considerably from customary and (the spirit of) legal standards governing the relationship between political position and economic resources—government and business. Investment in these deviant practices, bordering and overstepping the borders of bribery and extortion, in service of liquidity in the money-influence interchange, was as damaging to the long-term foundation for political support of the Nixon regime as was the narrowing of solidarities noted previously.

But the turning points in the Watergate affair all hinged critically upon reversal or overriding of in-group loyalties, which led to wider and wider exposure of the skeletons in the White House closet; while increasing emphasis on liquidity at the expense of support insured the dissolution of Nixon's power. It is of central significance that the early journalistic exposés depended upon revelations by administration insiders, such as the celebrated "Deep Throat." Similarly, the critical juncture in Sirica's court was the letter from chief burglar McCord; the impact of the Ervin Committee hearings was built upon the testimony of John Dean; the existence of the tapes was revealed by White House aide Butterfield. The release of the tape transcripts, as well as assurance of impeachment proceedings in the House, followed the refusal of Cox, Richardson, and Ruckelshaus to place obedience to the "Commander-in-Chief" (to recall Haig's stark appeal to military codes of loyalty) above solemn commitments to Congress made during Cox's confirmation hearings. Finally, there was the unanimity of the Supreme Court ruling on Jaworski's tape subpoena, despite the incumbency of four Nixon-appointed justices. This of course resulted in Nixon's remaining counsellors, as well as the senior Republicans in Congress, insisting on his resignation, following their learning of the damaging evidence on the tapes. In each case, the leverage of broader moral commitments over narrower personal and administrative loyalties within the Nixon administration operated to reverse the deviant trend of commitments within the Nixon group. The resultant exposure of information, very much at odds with societal standards for the exercise of moral and political leadership responsibility, proved the incompatibility of Nixon's liquidity preferences with continued political support or retention of office.

The parallel to the heroin case in these respects involves the personal degradation—withdrawal of cultural legitimation and social recognition—that derives from exposure of information regarding clandestine heroin market activities. The cycles of degradation, focusing on liquidity, and ultimate destruction of most opportunities for personal goal-attainment, provide a clear parallel to the aborted political careers of so many of Nixon's men.

There are, however, equally cases of "rehabilitation" in both groups, which can be understood as diversions in career pattern. The writing and lecturing of Watergate figures are not unlike the roles adopted by many "burned-out" addicts as antiaddiction educators, therapists and evangelists. Such roles are, of course, self-limiting. More permanent are cases in which all aspects of former identification are submerged so that a "new life" within conventional patterns may be undertaken, such as that embarked on by Charles Colson.

In contrast to the particular persons involved in either Watergate or heroin, it must not be thought that the types of sociocultural phenomena they represent are on the whole en route to extinction. Aggrandizement of power and severe addiction, while perhaps both headed toward lesser incidence at the current time in consequence of ongoing action investment processes, are hardly liable to extirpation, given the degrees of freedom available in contemporary concrete action systems. So long as there remains a consensual majority view regarding such activities as defective in moral worth, and continued efforts to expose and degrade the positions of individuals engaged in them, neither can be more than a "losing game" for most practitioners, confined to small minorities in the population, and unable to generate accelerating disequilibria in action structures. Refinement of "containment" procedures, such as campaign financing reform and methadone maintenance, comprise the primary consequence of deviant outbreaks, such as the postwar heroin epidemics and the Watergate scandal. Far more fundamental disequilibria than these are necessary to create radical change in the sociocultural milieu.

IV. CONCLUSIONS

In conclusion we will attempt to sum up and extend slightly some of the main considerations of our view of deviance and its relation to social change, considerations which are illustrated by the two apparently disparate cases which have been considered here.

We have started with two major points of reference. One is the concept of a system in equilibrium, which is characterized by the fact that the main constellation of forces operating upon and within it tend to the maintenance of a stable state. Any considerable departure from such a constellation of forces has the potential that it will lead to a change of state of the system. Among the forces with such potential effect which we have included as especially important for our purposes are those we refer to as "strain" operating on units of the system or classes of them.

Whatever the disturbing factors may be, the mere fact of an initial direction of change does not alone determine its fate. All are, however, from the point of view of an equilibrated state, both "innovative" and in some sense "deviant." Depending on balances of favoring and counteractive forces, the consequences of the complex combinations of factors may range all the way from complete restoration of the status quo ante to quite fundamental change in the structure of the system of reference.

The two cases we have chosen clearly do not exemplify the case of complete restoration, but of relative "containment." We say relative because, in both cases, while the wider extension of the deviant pattern seems, for the time being at least, to have been contained, there have been indications in both cases that longer-run consequences are not precluded. This seems to be a particularly interesting type of deviance, on which we would like to make a few comments in conclusion.

For the heroin addiction case this longer-run set of consequences seems to relate to the partial legitimation of addiction, with legally sanctioned methadone support, as akin to a chronic disease, the "victims" of which can be expected to lead relatively normal lives in the community, especially through maintenance of viable occupational roles. For the Nixon group case, on the other hand, the longer-run, viable changes have to do with organizational patterns rather than particular persons, namely the possibilities of consolidating a more extended pattern of "executive authority" in government and in other organizational contexts. In this respect we may concede that the Nixonites "had a point" vis-à-vis the mass media (including the press), the Congress, and some of the older, more restricted views of political power systems.

One major trend of social change seems to have been working in favor of both movements, namely the tendency to give action system units wider ranges of autonomy, but under some kind of not too clearly defined proviso that they use it "responsibly." The ways in which in the two cases attempts were made to seize such areas of autonomy were clearly defined as deviant in the prevailing public opinion.

We would like to suggest that the two cases here treated, and a wider range, may be considered in terms of three interrelated sets of characteristics. The first is one we started with in the consideration of the heroin case, namely that there should be two levels, not merely one, of "opportunity" or of expenditure-investment of resources open to participants. In the heroin case we have called these the medicinal and the recreational uses of heroin. The first had become institutionalized as routinely acceptable, the second was presumptively deviant and in certain respects came to be broadly established as such.

In the power-promotion case, the first level was that of the institutionally established uses of influence to gain power through election and, once elected, uses of power in the established operations of government. The second level consisted in the openness of opportunities to extend the range of power, in this case of the executive branch, through a variety of possible procedures.

In both cases these procedures involved two possible directions of seeking access to resources to accomplish their aims. One was to appeal to sources in the wider social system, essentially of support and legitimation, to sanction and in the long run contribute to the institutionalization of the innovative pattern, but of course accepting limits to its domination of the wider system. The other direction was to seek to attain a maximum of liquidity, as we have put it, of the control of resources by the immediate agents, in the heroin case of the individual addict and/or his particularistic associate, in the political case, of the close, supposedly solidary in-group. Given the relative legitimacy of the first direction, the resort to the second, in both cases, is the principal basis on which we have characterized them as deviant. In both cases, something positive seems to have been salvaged of the potentiality for constructive change. However, the particular game in which the participants engaged, through investing their resources, proved to be a "losing game."

It seems pretty clear from consideration of our two cases that, given the context and combination of other factors and forces in which these patterns of the structuring of action appeared, no other fate than their having been treated as deviant and therefore rather sharply contained, as we have put it, could have been expected. Thus in their different ways both came into sharp conflict with the legal system and, back of this, of norms of responsible action.

As between the two alternative directions of seeking access to and control of resources for innovation which we have suggested, the actors in the cases we have analyzed, in both cases, chose what we think can legitimately be called the "regressive" alternative. Having "jumped" into their positions from "high risk" starting points, which made the prospects via the alternative channel unpromising, they very likely both turned, as it were, security-minded by trying to hoard their assets. This in turn led them into deviant practices—e.g., "hustling" in the heroin case, "dirty tricks" in the Nixon case—which, if known, could not fail to occasion conflict with the wider society.

Indeed the vicious circle of deviant escalation, so prominent in both cases, mainly explains another important common feature. It is made clear in our exposition, and further emphasized by one of us (Gerstein, 1975) that in the extreme cases, heroin addiction leads to the domination of the life of the addict by a single goal, namely to obtain his daily or hourly "fix" and a secure access for the immediate future to the supply of heroin necessary for this. In the case of the Nixonites we may speak of an "addiction to political power." Acting in a situation which they felt—rightly as it turned out—to be precarious, they narrowed their concerns to that of maintaining power at virtually all costs. This may turn out to be a commentary on the varying degrees of commitment to other goals, such as for example the famous "profit motive." We suggest that this is compulsive in varying degrees, depending on the circumstances.

There does, however, seem to be one very general set of circumstances in which the regressive syndrome, as we have called it, may have, from the point of view both of system units and the system itself, constructive rather than destructive consequences. This is the situation in which regression takes place in what may be called a "protected environment." We stressed above the ways in which, in our two cases, the "losing game" feature of the deviant pattern was linked to the involvement with features of the more general action or social system, with which the pattern stood in more or less definite conflict. What, however, if some of these forces which, being in conflict, are potentially interfering with the pattern, can be "neutralized" by declaring that there is a sphere in which the innovations can legitimately have freer play without, or with minimal, interference from "outside"?

There are many cases of such environments which are insulated from outside intervention. Thus in the socialization process the child is not, in early years, exposed to the full competition of the larger adult world. Another case is the "sick role" where the patient is insulated against various pressures which impinge upon healthy persons of his status in other respects. Sociohistorical instances could also be given, such as the role of monastic orders in the history of Christianity. Indeed we would suggest that in some cases revolutionary movements may require protected environments in this sense in order to develop to a point where they can compete in the big political arena—e.g., Lenin's "emergence" from exile in Switzerland in 1917 to lead the Bolshevik Revolution in Russia.

From one point of view the protected environment is a mechanism which can help to separate the "sheep" of the constructive potentialities of an innovative movement from the "goats" of its more destructive potentialities. It may well be that the lack or weakness of such mechanisms is a factor in explaining the tragedy of the losing game in which our "players" got involved.

In another aspect what we are calling a protected environment connotes, for the unit so protected, dependency, which has become a highly negative symbol in our time. This of course is to say dependency on whatever social actors or classes of them are the agents of protection, be they parents, schools, physicians, or countries offering political asylum. This idea of accepting a status of "being protected"—not quite "protection" in the gangland meaning—is a condition of being offered a realistic opportunity to develop innovations toward the point of their institutional viability. But many groups are highly ambivalent about this. Taking advantage of such opportunities, however, requires more than hoarding of resources, even though certain states of liquidity, as we have put it, are prerequisites of making progress. There must be the equivalent of what economists call "investment" and a further winnowing and adapting process beyond that. Eventually the innovative urge must "graduate" from the protected environment and make its way "on its own."

This is what, in current phraseology, is often called "liberation" from the state of dependency. Mere liberation, however, without any conditions having been met, may lead to success, but it may also lead to the "losing game." We have clearly not dealt here with all the complexities of the determinants of such differential outcomes. We have merely attempted to "define the situation" in certain respects for the conditions encountered in what, in our very general sense, we call an innovative movement, and for beginning to understand the selective forces which have an effect on its eventual outcome.

NOTES

1. Perhaps a further explanation of our use of the term "innovative" is in order. First, it should be remembered that, in discussing deviance, we are using a "status quo" or institutionalized patterning of action as a reference point, as we note later in this introduction. Relative to that, then, the action we call deviant is by definition innovative, in that it takes a course which is not positively sanctioned in the institutionalized system. As we have stressed, whether it will come to be approved or not is usually difficult to predict in early stages of its development, and judgments on this point should not be too facilely assumed.

2. Even here, however, there are strong countervailing, "conservative" forces controlling and containing innovative patterns, from the level of "new facts" to that of "paradigm shifts," to use Kuhn's famous term. From the mechanical aspects of journal paper-selection to such processes as the creation of new subdisciplines, science operates to conserve its established methods and theories even while encouraging innovation. Equilibrium is a matter of balance between the old and the new—not of excluding one in favor of the other.

3. The heroin analysis is primarily the work of Dean Gerstein, the analysis of Nixon and Watergate primarily the work of Talcott Parsons. Both authors accept responsibility for the entire essay.

4. That Nixon's election in 1968 did not signify a major general swing to the right is attested not only by the narrow margin, but by the assassination of Robert Kennedy in the spring of that year. Had Kennedy lived, he would very probably have received the Democratic nomination and been elected.

5. Perhaps the major symbol of this case came to be the Ellsberg case, but it by no means stood alone (see White, 1975).

6. The distinction between influence and political power and the main patterns of their interdependence are discussed in Parsons and Platt (1973, especially Figure A3, p. 432).

7. For a general sociological discussion of corruption, see Smelser (1971).

8. Justice Rehnquist abstained on grounds of personal interest; hence the decision was 8 to 0.

9. The most comprehensive summary analysis of these events seems to be that of White (1975).

REFERENCES

BALL, J.C., and CHAMBERS, C.D. (eds. 1970). The epidemiology of opiate addiction in the United States. Springfield, Ill.: Thomas.

BERNSTEIN, C., and WOODWARD, R. (1974). All the President's men. New York: Warner.

BRECHER, E.M. [with editors of Consumer Reports] (1972). Licit and illicit drugs: The Consumers Union report on narcotics, stimulants, depressants, inhalants, hallucinogens, and marijuana, including caffeine, nicotine and alcohol. Boston: Little, Brown.

BURROUGHS, W. (1953). Junkie. New York: Ace.

CHAMBERS, C.D., and BRILL, L. (eds., 1973). Methadone: Experiences and issues. New York: Behavioral Publications.

CHEIN, I., GERARD, D.L., LEE, R.S., and ROSENFELD, E. (1964). The road to H: Narcotics, delinquence, and social policy. New York: Basic.

DAI, B. (1937). Opium addiction in Chicago. Montclair, N.J.: Patterson Smith (reprinted 1970).

DuPONT, R. (1973). "Where does one run when he's already in the promised land?" Pp. 1394-1410 in Proceedings of the Fifth National Conference on Methadone Treatment.

EDDY, N.B. (1973). "The NRC involvement in the opiate problem." National Academy of Sciences, Washington, D.C.

---, HALBACH, H., ISBELL, H., and SEEVERS, M.H. (1965). "Drug dependence, its significance and characteristics." Bulletin of World Health Organization 32:721-733.

FELDMAN, H.W. (1968). "Ideological supports to becoming and remaining a heroin addict." Journal of Health and Social Behavior 9:131-139.

FIDDLE, S. (1967). Portraits from a shooting gallery: Life styles from the drug addict world. New York: Harper & Row.

FINESTONE, H. (1966). "Narcotics and criminality." In J.A. O'Donnell and J.C. Ball (eds.), Narcotic addiction. New York: Harper & Row.

FREUD, S. (1961). The ego and the id. Pp. 12-63 in Vol. 19, The standard edition of the complete psychological works of Sigmund Freud. London: Hogarth and New York: Macmillan. (First published in German in 1923.)

GERSTEIN, D.R. (1975). Heroin in motion. Unpublished doctoral dissertation, Harvard University.

GREENE, M.H., and DuPONT, R. (eds., 1974). "The epidemiology of drug abuse." American Journal of Public Health 64(December): Supplement II.

HOFFMAN, L. (1973). "The rise of concern." Pp. 33–48 in A. Etzioni and R. Remp (eds.), Technological shortcuts to social change. New York: Russell Sage Foundation.

HUGHES, P.H., and CRAWFORD, G. (1972). "A contagious disease model for researching and intervening in heroin epidemics." Archives of General Psychiatry 27:149-155.

HUNT, L.G., and CHAMBERS, C.D. (1976). The heroin epidemics: A study of heroin use in the United States, 1965-75. New York: Spectrum Publications.

Joint Committee of the American Bar Association and the American Medical Association on Narcotic Drugs (1961). Drug addiction: Crime or disease? Bloomington, Ind.

LEVENGOOD, R., LOWINGER, P., and SCHOOF, K. (1973). "Heroin addiction in the suburbs: An epidemiologic study." American Journal of Public Health 63:209-214.

LEVIN, G., ROBERTS, E.B., and HIRSCH, G.B. (1975). The persistent poppy: A computer-aided search for heroin policy. Cambridge, Mass.: Ballinger.

LIDZ, C.W., LEWIS, S.H., CRANE, L.E., and GOULD, L.C. (1975). "Heroin maintenance and heroin control." International Journal of the Addictions 10(1):35-52.

LINDESMITH, A. (1965). The addict and the law. Bloomington, Ind.: Indiana University Press.

LUKOFF, I. (1976). "Consequences of use: Heroin and other narcotics." Pp. 121-140 in J.D. Rittenhouse (ed.), Report of the Task Force, q.v.

McCOY, A.E. (1972). The politics of heroin in Southeast Asia. Boston: Beacon.

MUSTO, D. (1973). The American disease: Origins of narcotic control. New Haven: Yale University Press.

National Commission on Marijuana and Drug Abuse (1973). Druge use in America: Problems in perspective. 2nd report. Washington, D.C.: U.S. Government Printing Office.

NEWMEYER, J.A., and GAY, G. (1972). "The traditional junkie, the acquarian age junkie and the Nixon age junkie." Drug Forum 2:17-32.

New York Times Staff (1974). The end of a presidency. New York: Holt, Rinehart & Winston.

O'DONNELL, J.A. (1969). Narcotics addiction in Kentucky. Washington, D.C.: U.S. Government Printing Office.

PARSONS, T., and PLATT, G.M., with collaboration of N.J. SMELSER (1973). "Technical appendix: Some general theoretical paradigms." Pp. 423-447 in The American university. Cambridge, Mass.: Harvard University Press.

PREBLE, E., and CASEY, J.J. (1969). "Taking care of business: The heroin user's life on the street." International Journal of the Addictions 4(1):1-24.

RITTENHOUSE, J.D. (ed., 1976). Report of the Task Force on the Epidemiology of Heroin and Other Narcotics. Menlo Park, Calif.: Stanford Research Institute.

SCHELL, J. (1975). The time of illusion. New York: Knopf.

SCHUMPETER, J.A. (1934). The theory of economic development. Cambridge, Mass.: Harvard University Press.

SHEEHAN, N., SMITH, H., KENWORTHY, E.W., and BUTTERFIELD, F. (1971). The Pentagon Papers. New York: Bantam.

SMELSER, N.J. (1971). "Stability, instability and the analysis of political corruption." Pp. 7-29 in B. Barber and A.J. Inkeles (eds.), Stability and social change. Boston: Little, Brown.

TERRY, C.E., and PELLENS, M. (1928). The opium problem. New York: Committee on Drug Addiction in collaboration with Bureau of Social Hygiene.

WALSH, J. (1973a). "Lexington narcotics hospital: A special sort of alma mater." Science 182:1004-1008.

--- (1973b). "Addiction Research Center: Pioneers still on the frontier." Science 182:1229-1231.

WEBER, M. (1968). "The basis of legitimacy." Vol. I, part I, chap. 3, sec. i in M. Weber, Economy and society (ed. by G. Roth and C. Wittich). New York: Bedminster Press. (First published in German in 1922.)

WHITE, T.H. (1975). Breach of faith: The fall of Richard Nixon. New York: Atheneum.

WOODWARD, R., and BERNSTEIN, C. (1976). The final days. New York: Avon.

YOUNG, J. (1973). The drugtakers. London: Paladin.

2

SHAME AND DECEIT IN CREATIVE DEVIANCE

JACK D. DOUGLAS

Becoming deviant, either by your own definition or by that of an enemy, is commonly, though not always, an extremely complex process. While this is true even in an individual case, it is far more true of all the individuals who are involved in any particular form of diviance and most obvious in the case of all those people invólved in all forms of deviance, which includes everyone in our pluralistically conflictful society. Such complexities are not surprising to anyone who has studied other, more reliably understood, forms of natural sequences or systemic activity, which in that sense can be expected to serve at least as a general analogue to human social interaction. For example, the evolutionary theories which sociobiologists have evolved to explain the highly patterned behavior of even the simplest social animals are extremely complex, as any reading of Edward Wilson's *Sociobiology* (1975) will reveal. Since deviant processes are not generally highly patterned, but, on the contrary, are quite variable, it is remarkable that sociologists and other social scientists have persisted in treating them as if they were really quite simply explained in terms of one or, at most, a few general variables. This persistent simplification is perhaps best understood in terms of a combination of the absolutist assumptions of most of Western common-sense ideas about morality and social order, one of our less valuable traditions derived from the Judeo-Christian culture complex, and the tendency of the pioneers in any science to start out with grand theories that explain everything beautifully—until the science has accumulated enough meticulous empirical evidence to discover the vast complexity of things. Wilson (1975) has rightly noted, with some apparent astonishment, the persistence of such grand theorizing in sociology and compared it to such early efforts in biology. I believe it is even more comparable to the persistence of alchemy in early chemistry, because there is a strong element of mythical wish fulfillment in both, born largely of the fear of death and the greed for wealth in the case of alchemy and of the fear and loathing of social problems and the hope of utopia in the case of the social sciences. Perhaps the social sciences are even more analogous in this sense to astrology—they give a sense of certainty or predictability in a situation of anxiety born primarily of the failure of religious faith.

SUBCULTURE THEORIES AND THE THEORY OF CREATIVE DEVIANCE

Some of our most reliable knowledge about deviance concerns the subculture processes involved in becoming and being deviant. Traditional common-sense (Judeo-Christian) theory explained deviance largely in individual terms. The "evil individual commits evil actions" theory pictured the individual as facing a situation of temptation in which he consciously chooses to commit what he knows to be an evil act. This picture of individual deviance was still dominant in the thinking of theorists like Durkheim, in spite of his social causation theory, and in that of Merton as late as 1957. All of the major studies of deviance done by the Chicago sociologists from the 1920s onward, however, had revealed that subcultural processes of many forms are generally involved in deviance. (I have reviewed the development of these ideas in Douglas, forthcoming; also see Arnold, 1970; and Cohen, 1955.) At the least, as Sutherland had argued systematically, even what appear to be highly individualistic deviant actions, like suicide or homicide, commonly involve some indirect cultural learning of ideas (motives and situations) and methods. (See Douglas, 1967, Part IV.) And most forms of deviance involve a great deal more subcultural involvement *at least at some point in the deviance.*

Subcultural processes play a major part in most major deviant processes in complex and pluralistic societies. In fact, I have recently argued (Douglas, 1977) that such deviant subcultural processes play a major part in most forms of social change in modern societies. Deviance is the mutation that is generally destructive of society, but it is also the only major source of creative adaptations of rules to new life situations, both for individuals and for groups and whole societies. There are, of course, those forms of deviance which clearly are aimed at injuring society and which, therefore, are never successful in becoming the new rules for a supraculture. Murder within the in-group, as distinct from killing in warfare against outsiders, is the most obvious case. But, while this recognition of clearly antisocial or necessarily selfish forms of deviance is of importance, we should not fall victim to the Durkheimian temptation of thinking that we or anyone else can decide unproblematically what concrete forms of deviance are selfish or antisocial and which are not (later called eufunctional and dysfunctional by functionalists), and thus think we can tell which are creative adaptations and which are not. We cannot even say that something like "theft" is clearly antisocial. To the members of society the meanings of taking what is not clearly defined as your property often has highly problematic meanings and I believe that certain forms within certain problematic limits of creative "thieving" prove to be highly adaptive not only for the thieves, but, more importantly, for the people stolen from.

But, while keeping this in mind, it is vital to see that the subcultural theory is generally a truncated theory that looks complete as long as one takes a static view or looks at society at only one time. While there have always existed deviant subcultures (such as the Bacchic cults and innumerable others in ancient history), each particular deviant subculture must be created by individuals at some point in time before it can be transmitted to anyone. There is no direct link between modern orgies and Bacchic cults, but, if there were, then surely at some point in the remote past someone created the Bacchic cults.

The creative subcultural theory of deviance depends on some assumption of individual creativity. I think we shall find the theory far more powerful (more general) by determining the individual processes that go to make it up, especially those that lead to the creation, maintenance, and destruction of deviant subcultures. There are certain individual processes that are common to both the creation of new deviant subcultures and to the joining of already existing ones, and these are crucial to almost all (perhaps all) creative deviant subcultures. The most important of these are the processes of successfully using deception, both of self-deception and other-deception. Having first analyzed these on the firm basis of facts discovered in our field research studies of individuals and groups in transition to deviance, I intend to then use this analysis to show how deceit facilitates the transition of whole societies (supracultures) and even civilizations to highly deviant states.

SOCIAL CHANGE, TRANSITIONAL CONFLICTS OF RULES, SHAME, AND PROCESSES OF DECEPTION

I have argued (Douglas and Johnson, 1977; and Douglas, 1977) that major social change, especially the all-important rule changes that are necessary for any social change to persist, ultimately depends on changes in feelings and perceived situations. Feelings are the independent variable that drives animals, including the greatest symbol creator and user. Thinking, or symbol use, even of the most creative kind, can only change our actions or even our basic ways of thinking by being fused with feeling in the willing of something—the effective choosing of something. Interestingly enough, the most independent effect of thinking in changing our feelings comes from misthinking or mistakes of thought that lead to unintended situations which we perceive and then respond to with feeling and action (see Douglas, 1977).

Rules are of vital importance to human life because they are the genetic code of culture, that is, they are the programmers of action which tell us to act in ways which proved successful in the past (as defined by members of society in the past). Rules are the memory of what was most socially successful in producing the feelings we seek in life (pleasures of eating, drinking, sex, aesthetic joy, etc.). They are enforced by the very powerful (genetically inborn) feeling of shame (and sometimes of guilt, which is culturally highly introjected self-shaming), which are induced by expressions of contempt and ridicule communicated directly by universal body language and more indirectly by more complex cultural elaborations on these.

While man could not long exist, even in the "brutish" state of nature, without these shame-enforced rules, it is also true that he cannot long continue to exist without changing some of those rules, because the world changes in threatening ways both independent of our actions and by unintended effects of our actions; and it is most especially true that we could not improve on our individual or social condition without changing those rules. But attempts to change the rules, especially important rules, elicit the inevitable shaming response, both from others who share the rules with us and from ourselves to the degree we have introjected them. Both the thought and, far more, the act of violation also elicit the fear of being shamed. If the fear is very great it spreads and becomes transsituational fear, which is anxiety. Since shame is such a powerful feeling, there is little possibility in changing our rules or our actions in the face of it unless we face a grave situation that elicits such powerful feelings that it overcomes shame and we react with the ambivalent suppression of shame. This is seen in extreme situations like wars or plagues or famines or anything that threatens everyone's life. The extreme fear and anxiety of such situations can produce a general state of "demoralization" in which people do all kinds of things forcefully, blindly, which would normally be totally shaming.

Given the power of shame, how do we change rules? The answer is simple enough: we violate them without getting shamed or, at least, we expect we will not experience shame sufficiently to make us go back to the old rule-governed patterns of action. If we succeed in doing this, then we can build new rules for our new form of action, primarily by getting others to join us in a new shame-pool—a deviant subculture with its own shame-inducing rules that moralistically reject the old rules. If our subculture gets big enough we can take over by whatever political means is possible. The crucial question is, how do we start violating the rules without producing so much self-shaming and far more commonly, so much fear of shaming by *traditionalists* ("straights") who discover our deviance that we stop our new forms of action before we can get any further?

Obviously, in almost all cases we do not. As Becker (1963) and many other researchers of deviance have long contended, most deviant acts are highly episodic. That is, people commit them and find they are deeply shamed, more by themselves and their immediate reference group (whom they may only imagine is shaming them because they are projecting their own fears) than by getting caught by the traditionalists and subjected to social shame-inducing processes (degradation procedures). So they quit. Having been shamed once for wickedness, or having come fearfully close to it, they are less apt to do it again, unless the taste of the forbidden fruit proved delicious indeed. We can obviously go even further and say that most wickedness, almost all of it, is only thinking, never action, because the thinking elicits too much fear of shame or actual shame. A high percentage of people who firmly commit themselves to do something wicked find they cannot do it when the time comes, simply because their "commitments" were mere thinking, while real action involves facing other people in the situation (potential shamers) and the reality of the risks in the concrete situation, which induces more fear of shaming than thinking normally can.

How, then, do people ever start? The primary answer sociologists have proposed is a variant on the Freudian one: they rationalize shame (and guilt) away. This is the answer given by Sykes and Matza (1957) in their well-known work on "neutralization processes," all of which are really what Freud was talking about under the more general rubric of rationalization. There is no doubt at all that people rationalize their wicked actions. However, rationalization of the "ideation" type Sykes and Matza refer to rarely works to suppress or vent shame and certainly not fears of being shamed or guilt feelings. Since everyone can rationalize profusely, eloquently, and sophisticatedly from the time they begin to talk (or earlier with body language), it seems obvious that rules would never have any significant effect if people could simply talk themselves out of shame feelings. Feelings change talk; talk does not change feelings though it can trigger feelings; reason can sometimes inhibit feelings or even indirectly change them by changing concrete situations which change perceptual inputs to the feelings. It is especially wrong to think that one could possibly neutralize guilt feelings by mere talk. Anyone who thinks that has obviously never felt guilt and has simply not paid attention to the masses who go through life suffering from guilt that they can rarely escape, no matter how many professionals they pay to talk them out of it. Rationalization is mainly intended to provide a social bridge (a social fiction) for other people to avoid the breakdown of social relations that can come from shame. It is a tenuous bridge that works only when people have important reasons to share a fiction with you. It is important in that respect, but not in explaining how people avoid shame (and guilt) feelings or manage them to be able to get merrily or, more commonly, warily on with their wicked behavior.

People evade or manage shame feelings mainly by avoiding concrete situations, perceptions, and symbolizations that produce or trigger shaming or fears of shaming by others or by themselves. They build walls of secrecy (privacy, concretely isolated situations) by evasions, by lying, by self-deception (lying to the self), and by using front-work which has the sharp feel of reality. All of these are really various forms of the general phenomena of deceit and all have the general property of being means to evade shame inducing behavior and feelings, or fears of these, as well as evading related forms of punishment (imprisonment, parental disownership, etc.).

Wherever an individual, a group, a nation, or a whole civilization is undergoing an important transition in rule-governed action, there we shall find the traditional rules in conflict with the evolving patterns of new (deviant) actions, and we shall find these processes of self-deception and other-deception at work and those of managing unevaded shame feelings. The more feelings of shame and pride (the opposite of shame) committed or invested in the rules, the more we find them at work; and, conversely, the less important the rules, the less they come into play. At one extreme we find total individual and social repression of any possible mention of what is really happening—it is unthinkable, hence total deception is necessary for it to happen at all. At the other extreme we find that minor procedural rules for a club meeting are consciously changed with only joking reference to the "revolution," because they never involved significant shame and pride feelings—they were as close to totally instrumental rules as effective social rules ever get.

Children are so much more open to shaming than adults that we often think of shame as a distinctly childish response. In one of the finest phenomenological-existential analyses of shame experience, Lewis (1971) has argued that adults even at times feel guilty of feeling shame, and this creates complex problems of therapy when shame is felt by the patient. It is apparent that adults do not have anywhere near as much conscious shame experience as children. There seem to be two reasons for this.

First, shame is basically a reaction of submission. Its physical manifestations, as described by Laing (1960) as an implosion (shrinking, hiding) of the body, is genetically inherited and is the exact opposite of the explosion or puffing-up of the physical self seen in confident dominance—pride. As adults mature and become more dominant and more confident in that dominance, they feel more pride and less shame. There are a few situations in which confident dominance is suddenly destroyed. One of the most destructive is the betrayal by one's sexual mate. Especially if this is experienced in the full horror of concrete perception *(in flagrante),* the sense of shame is apparently profound (but see aggressive moralism, below). The other situation is that of glaring defeat in battle, business, or whatever the competition is.

Second, like most other things in life, self-deceptions are learned. Children have not yet learned how to effectively defend against the terrors of shame experience. The more experience they have, the more they subconsciously experience reinforcements of those forms of deceptions which best defend them against these terrors. Different individuals, of course, will learn different defenses, depending on both personality dynamics and situational dynamics.

Individuals also learn different ways of managing shame that is not effectively evaded.

The easiest way to see these forms of deception and their efforts is to look at them being done by an individual to evade shaming by others. The more he is doing this evasion work for himself, the harder it is to see or infer them, and the more we must know about the individual's whole life situation to be able even to infer tentatively what he is doing. The best way to say anything about them at all may be to look at how they work in specific kinds of transition situations, from the individual to the civilization levels.

BECOMING A PROUD WHORE

Very experienced whores are generally proud of being whores, at least secretly. Very inexperienced whores are generally not whores at all, at least not to themselves, because it is so shameful to them. And totally inexperienced non-whores generally think of whoring as totally shameful and whores as shameless or incapable of feeling shame, hence totally shameful. This is actually a common finding with people who are not deviants, are just becoming deviant, and have been deviant for a long time; they start out feeling paralyzed by the fear of being shamed or mortified by shame at the thought of it, so they don't do it; they progress to doing it with situationally intermittent feelings of fear of shame and sometimes actual self-shame; and shame becomes pride and confidence if they continue and get away with it—go unshamed.

We have seen this happen in a number of young women whom we knew over several years before they became masseuses (doing sex for money), during their time as masseuses and in some cases after. In addition, Rasmussen and Kuhn (1976) have gotten similar evidence from in-depth, independently cross-checked interviews with many other masseuses. Girls who wind up taking money for sexual acts generally seem to follow a complex path of small *step-wise (quantum-leap) build-ups* to that point. (In those rare instances in which they grew up in the subculture, especially when the mother is a prostitute, they may start with feelings of pride and avoid all this deception.) They go by small quantum leaps over considerable time periods, generally years, from being virgins to being involved in various forms of quite casual sex, finally to group sex and orgies, the latter with admitted pride. This means that they are already well along in the process of de-shaming sex behavior and confidently avoiding shaming by others, but they are still some distance from not fearing or feeling shame about becoming a whore.

Various women who have gotten to this stage of highly casual sex have reported that they felt "shocked" when someone suggested that they do sex for money, even when this is in the form of a disguise, as the proposition is generally done in our society today. That is, generally someone will tell such a girl of some friends who want some beautiful girls to go on a trip with them in an isolated (secret) place (as a boat, a resort in Fiji, or a caravan trip through the West); they want the girls to be willing (not having to submit) to do sex (commonly only strongly hinted); and they are willing to pay very well for such hostesses (a thousand dollars for a week or so is not uncommon). Unless the girl has thought about doing such things and probably talked with friends who are like her or have done it, she generally feels some shock. Though I know of several young women who say they have rejected this offer, it is a situation that is constructed in such a way that it is clearly tempting–it offers quick money (so appeals to greed) and does so in a manner that would involve little direct confrontation with the direct shame-inducing situation of doing sex entirely for money.

The secrecy means no one significant to the girl will know. As the old Chicago hands used to put it, social anonymity is basic to deviance. It is social unresponsibility, or in this case secrecy, hence unobservability, hence non-accountability, that in general facilitates transition to deviance because it evades or minimizes the risk of shaming by others. The fact that she is flattered as a beautiful girl means she should feel pride, not shame; and calling her a friend or hostess or whatnot means that there is no "misunderstanding" about her being a whore or some such shameful thing. Of course, this is merely a social fiction. It has some value in bridging those difficult shame situations, but the chasm of shame still yawns below the bridge, so it does not have that much effect, unless the girl is very "dumb" (i.e., slow at imputing common patterns of social meaning). The use of *indirection,* or the *manipulation of uncertainty,* in giving the money, especially giving it explicitly for something other than the sex, is vital. The more that can be maintained as plausible, the less the shame risk involved.

What we have seen actually happen in great detail is very similar in its shame possibilities. This is the matter of becoming a masseuse. The girls we have watched make this difficult transition in great detail have been college graduates with middle-class (even more upper-middle class) backgrounds. They learned the usual feelings of contempt (shamefulness) for prostitution and all believe their parents feel that way. They do not just fall into this by situational chance. They think about it and generally talk about it with similar friends–testing out the idea and its fateful shame implications. They are all intellectually convinced that sexual freedom and so on are good ideas, but their bodies at this stage are still saying something different–almost a *dread of being shamefully ostracized from society, that is, stigmatized.* When they talk to their friends they seem at first to use indirection–"Wow, I wonder what it feels like . . ." "How do you think people can do that sort of thing?" Then they get more direct, depending on the feedback they get. Their friends were also intellectually favorable and were not really worrying about it because they were not thinking of doing it or in a few cases they already were doing it and were very favorable. This *connection with the insider* is often crucial. The person who is already inside has already overcome most of the fear of shame and may feel pride by now. They provide evidence that shame can be overcome or avoided, or, almost certainly, they *act as if* there is no such thing–shame never comes up, is never mentioned as a possibility. The *matter of fact manner* is the best evasion: *no talk* means there is no abstract *symbolic trigger* of the shame feelings. (Out of sight, out of mind.) Above all, no shameful labels are used. And most certainly girls like these, with their childhood feelings, encouraged to become a "whore" are most unlikely to do so. It is precisely because the word "whore" is the most shame-loaded word used to designate prostitutes that I used it to summon up in the readers the feelings of shame associated with sex-for-money behavior. Instead of using such a shame-loaded word, the opposite is done; one uses a shameless word, indeed a word designating the girl as a pride-worthy giver of health–masseuse.

Even with all of this, however, the girl is most apt to feel the shame risks. She manages the way we manage all emotionally difficult situations, especially those involving shame–she goes up in stages. She almost always makes firm, solemn commitments to do only the least (minimally) shameful form of sex, probably "hand-jobs." She may even sincerely think she can avoid sex for money in the job. The boss who interviews her generally supports this by only hinting at sex on the job. Sometimes he denounces it. (The most daring ask for a sample, but there is no pay for this. It's a "freebie.") Then, of course, she makes an "exception to her rule" and, as one girl said, "I guess my exception has sort of become my rule." But it does so in stages and she stops for any given period of time at that point where she is feeling unacceptable actual or risked (potential) shame. If she continues at it, she is very apt to either find and adopt or else to create a *subculture ethos* which gives her a sense of pride in the work or, at least, rejects the ostracisers, the stigmatizing shamers. With masseuses today the main ethos or ideology which does this is the ethos of sex therapy–helping people with sexual problems, just like a proud doctor, only better. By this time, the girls are able privately to come out from under the evasions, especially all of the self-deceptions about what they are really doing. They will even begin to show their lack of concern with shame and even show a spark of pride by saying, "Well, I guess I have to admit it now, I'm a hooker." She's still not a full-fledged "whore," but that too may come in time as she comes to proudly display her deviation in the face of the traditionalists.

The ambivalences, or conflicting emotions, are apparent in the shifts back and forth that go on, varying with the inputs of contingent concrete situations and personal mood shifts. One day she feels one way and the next the opposite. What the particular feeling is in the early stages of development, when emotions are so great and in conflict, seems to be very situational. She tries subconsciously to manage her life situations to avoid those in which shame feelings will be triggered. If she cannot, she is apt to quit. One girl became very concerned that her parents would discover what she was doing because she could not plausibly explain where she got all the money. I also suspected that this girl continued to feel shame herself, precisely because she was not very good at self-deception or other-deception. She was very open with us about what she did and very articulate in talking about it. This seemed to carry over to her own thinking about herself. She said that whenever she told guys she was a masseuse she could see their "real feelings" (or the shamefulness of it) in their eyes. If she had been more secret with others and more deceptive with herself, allowing her body to move along one path and her symbolic life another, she might not have felt the fear of her parents' shame reactions. As it is, I suspect she may well show the common pattern of withdrawal (backsliding) and return to deviance. Like all others, she is into the new form of behavior because of powerful motives or feelings (greed, often combined with sexual interests that may even remain a secret, or even a self-deceived feeling, within the subculture). These continue and may increase as she has less money. That will tempt her to take the risks again. If she can find ways to decrease the situational risk (like getting away from her parents), then the chances are good she will return and move up the steps of deshaming, perhaps eventually arriving at the stage of the proud flaunter, the professional accolade of a deviant subculture.

GENERAL SEDUCTION PROCESSES

As should be apparent from my description, becoming a masseuse is more a matter of *self-seduction* than of being seduced. That is, the self finds ways, largely subconsciously, but partly consciously ("I must avoid that situation or I'll feel embarrassed," "I mustn't think of that") to allow the body to get around the fears and symbolically or perceptually triggered feelings of shame. There is some element of attempted seduction by others, as seen in the sly attempts of would-be customers to present themselves as casual but appreciative "lovers," not "customers." But that is not very successful or important. This is probably true of the paths followed into most forms of deviance. There are, however, important seduction processes, especially more symmetric or mutual forms of seductions into deviance.

Seduction processes in general are the *purposeful use or manipulation of uncertainty to hide one's real feelings or goals, while at the same time manipulating persons and situations to increase their temptations (desires for deviant things).* The simplest seduction process involves a simple hiding of one's intentions or feelings, normally by presenting oneself in one way and then turning out to be the other way. In this case the uncertainty manipulation, if successful, keeps uncertainty total—one is certain that you are x, when in fact you are not x. That simple process is, however, not normally really possible, though the seducee may conspire to maintain the fiction of belief in the presentation. Normally, all the seducer can do is maintain some level of uncertainty, hopefully enough to make the *felt risk of shame less than the temptation.* In the early stages of seduction, the risk of shame, if kept low enough, can actually be used to titillate the temptation (or amplify it) because danger has its own exciting effect, which can spread to feelings like sex very easily.

The *dilemma of seduction processes is that, in order to increase the temptation far enough, and certainly in order to consummate the whole plan, the actual intent must become more certain, thereby greatly increasing the risk to the seducee, thereby decreasing the probability of success.* (If the rational evaluations can be deranged, this can be avoided. That is the purpose of such things as "liquoring up," getting them "loaded" or "strung out." Since this is understood by experienced seducees, they may even pretend to be deranged in this way in order to appear unshameful to the seducer and/or herself.) The solution to the dilemma consists in increasing the temptation faster than the certainty of one's intentions or feelings, so that by the time the real intent is certain, or would be under normal thinking, the feeling of temptation is so great that one cannot stop in spite of risks of shame or else feeling sweeps away (drowns out) such risk cognition. The most successful seduction processes, in situations in which the seducee feels real risks of shame, seem to consist in slowly building up the temptations by smooth ("natural") small steps which do not precipitate rethinking of the situation (preferably no need to make choices of changed paths of action), providing as traditionally legitimate definitions of each new step and its eventual goal as possible (thereby minimizing plausible shame triggers). These definitions seem to be most successful when they are done only by implication, since talk easily triggers feelings of the risk or actual shame. In other words, the successful seducer seems to use the same methods of deception we have been investigating in the case of masseuses, the only difference being that he is purposefully trying to manipulate both feelings and cognitions of risks to deceive the other person. (I owe much of this analysis to years of discussions about sexual hunting with Paul Rasmussen and others. Some of the ideas are common in the analysis of political and military strategy because the phenomena are similar to those of the war of the sexes, except that sexual war is far more complicated because it can be both zero-sum *and* cooperative—and both at once! See Liddell-Hart, 1954; Schelling, 1960; and Paret, 1976.)

It is common to find in concrete instances that some of both types of processes are at work. That is, individuals are often subconsciously deceiving themselves and others at the same time they are consciously seducing others and, sometimes, even themselves. (People can purposefully put themselves in situations they know they will not be able to rationally control—they will be swept away by feelings in the situation, especially if they cooperate by drinking or using drugs.) It seems especially common for individuals in the grip of temptations (desires for what is deviant) to give the benefit of doubt (that is trust or have faith in) to those who promote the goal without the deviance, especially those who praise the goal and insist it is being given in the name of the traditional rule. The more uncertain the situation (such as due to complexity or ignorance of the person) and the greater the temptation (feeling for deviance), the more plausible the belief in the claim, so the less faith, and deceit, needed. The "Yes, we just met but this is real love" ploy involves the implication that it will lead to the traditional goal of marriage or at least a prolonged relation. It invites a willing suspension of disbelief–faith–in the absurd at the moment of greatest temptation. This is the very meaning of *demagogue, the political seducer of an absurdly faithful people in the grip of a great temptation.*

What we have most commonly observed is a much more complicated and shifting process of mutual seduction in reasonably clearly defined situations of deviance. (Where things are more uncertain about the rules and implications of actions for rules, as in the national economic-political situations we shall shortly be considering, there is more political seduction involved and less mutual seduction. Albert Cohen, 1955:59-65, analyzed some of these properties in terms of "mutual conversions.") These are situations like the nude beach. Anyone there is very apt to know in some way it is a casual sex scene, so anyone knows that sexual pickups are intended for some kind of sexual purpose. There is the serious question of what purpose (since there are many, ranging from the titillating talk in the nude to very serious ones), but the first question is whether any purpose can be served by the encounter. The certainty of the sexual intent makes the manipulation of uncertainty extremely difficult: everyone knows the opening gambit is a gambit. The question then is whether socially plausible *fictions* can be presented that allow evasion of shame. This problem seems greatest for women, since they have the continual realization that, if they are shameful types, then the man will want only the most casual sexual relation, whereas they rarely want that, even when they *think* they should because of their abstract commitment to some faddish ideology. Even if they have no other real desires than the most casual relation, they still have the problem of other-respect, since they cannot be sure "where the guy is coming from." To be "used" is to feel self-shame and other-contempt–"He's laughing at me!" (Because the sex act always involves submission for the female, and submission always involves potential shame, she always faces greater risks of shame.) After prolonged study of the nude beach, we (Douglas, Rasmussen with Flanagan, 1977) concluded that this difficulty of maintaining uncertainty–in the face of the so great certainty of what it was all about–made the beach an extremely difficult sexual hunting scene. Talk seemed to be easy enough, but even the most skillful hunters (or pick-up artists) from years of ferocious campaigning, and there were many of those, found it very difficult to "score." That was a challenge to many, but led most to give up in traumatic despair after prolonged and shaming failure. (Bruised or shamed "egos" were epidemic, and I well remember one of the ultimate devotees of hunting circling warily around one very difficult–unshamed–woman, muttering, "I don't think my ego can take another rejection from her.") This is why it was such a good scene in which to study the deceptions needed in seduction processes. It became clear that any pick-up that became successful had to involve a maximum of coolness or naturalness (it just happened, no planning–which meant it had to be either a real accident or, more commonly, very well planned); a maximum of mutual seductions, so that each helped the other, or both helped the woman, to avoid any more than minimal shame risk; and a maximum of temptation (lust). (The vast importance of "coolness" in our vastly conflictful society has been analyzed by Lyman and Scott, 1970.) These conditions were best met in communal groups of hunters in which the girls introduced the girls to the men and all of them denounced the lone predator creeps (voyeurs, body-displayers, hunters) who made the girls feel shame. A woman striking up a conversation with a woman involved little sex meaning; an introduction was neighborly, not sexual; and they were commonly denouncing the shameful things, hence doing self-respectable ones. These groups also in fact offered the likelihood of something longer-run than the merely casual. It was the most successful way by which the ferocious seducers of both sexes cooperatively seduced themselves into a creative deviant subculture.

POLITICAL LABELING GAMES

I have used deviant transitions like entry to sex scenes to get at the fundamental processes of such transitions from one set of rules to another largely because these processes are starker and better known to most people. Some of the really big changes or reordering of whole societies come from those levels of action and build up by spontaneous natural ordering processes to the national or civilizational level. Even most of those, however, eventually reach the level of political action, first in the form of social movements. It is from political action that the most general changes of society are completed and are institutionalized in legal rules, though the transitions begin at lower levels in most things, especially in democratic societies and decentralized ones. We must, then, analyze political transitions from traditional sets of rules to new ones.

We find that most of the time political changes go through the same kind of transition processes we have seen in other patterns of deviance. People are normally committed to one set of political rules by shame feelings and pride feelings. People in a democracy (monarchy, etc.) normally feel pride in being a "free" people. To be transformed into a tyranny involves most feelings of shame, just as being transformed overnight from the "free French people" into "vassals of German tyrants" involves a veritable shame-shock (depression, withdrawal, downcast eyes). But, before looking at the higher level of such political reordering processes, let us look at the transition individuals make from one political set of rules to another, such as from one ideological party commitment to another.

Whenever people are in transition from one set of political rules to another, we find the inevitable political labeling games by which people deceive others and themselves about the real feeling-meanings of what they are doing. Just as with masseuses, one does not normally go from being a socialist to being a capitalist or vice versa, nor does one go from being an advocate of democracy to being an advocate of tyranny. One's body feelings and actions move off in new directions, while his political labels lag behind him. People move by small political steps in new directions and prevent their feelings of possible shame from the self or, more importantly, from the others being deserted and potentially trying to stigmatize you, by the various means of deception. In fact, people commonly enter a period of drifting, or noninvolvement in any new political label, in which they may stay permanently. This drop-out phase is comparable to the casual sex drift of those who became masseuses. All those who become masseuses go through it, but not all those, or even very many, who go through that make the transition to being masseuses. The same is true of political activities. People who find a political ethos and/or label increasingly unsatisfying are much more likely to simply drop out of political commitments than to move into something deviant from that old position. (That is why "Independents" are now a majority in our era of social transformation.) The more they and their friends (reference groups) invested shame in quitting that old ethos or label, the more apt one is to continue thinking of himself in those terms or to "pass" under the old label while his feelings and actions go off in some new direction. The more shameful the rejection of a given alternative position, the less likely one is to drift by deceptive stages into it; but if he does drift into it, the more likely he is to deceive himself and, even more, deceive others about this commitment. (*Conversion experiences* occur in politics as in anything else. However, just as with scientific creativity or sexual creativity, anyone who suddenly discovers that his political "god has failed" almost always has been deceiving himself for a long time, moving away from the old god and not letting himself notice that. He has been subconsciously "diverted" and suddenly faces a situation in which a choice seems necessary, something he has been avoiding. He now lunges—or takes a quantum-leap—out of the traditional. Diversion precedes conversion; self-deception and other-deception allows the new feelings and actions to build up more or less unnoticed—at least, their symbolic meanings are unnoticed.)

Just as in sexual matters, so in political matters the traditionalists of one's group are waiting and watching for political deviance. The slightest sign of transition out of the true faith will lead to degradation (shaming) labeling. Just as in sex, if the threat of betrayal of the iron-rule seems very threatening, then we get the *contrast of small differences effect* so well known since de Tocqueville: that is, the very threatening deviant is quickly labeled with a very stigmatizing brand. A radical politico who sees the new nonpolitical orientation of a colleague immediately brands him a "conservative." (Of course, just as in sex, all kinds of processes can enter. One may hope it is not real or hope to entice him back, so avoid stigmatizing procedures. And if one hates the other for any reason, especially with the power of envy, the stigmatization comes more readily—very readily.) A conservative politico quickly brands a wandering colleague a "radical." Where there exists a sense of great threat, one is either very good or very bad, not something in-between. In a Puritan society, sex is *very* threatening, so there are only madonnas and whores.

There are also, of course, more conscious seduction labeling processes. One may purposefully mislead other people about his political orientations in order to avoid the stigmatic labeling. One who is a socialist (capitalist) may use all of the seduction strategies to avoid being called one in an antisocialist (anticapitalist) society.

DEVIANT TRANSITIONS OF WHOLE SOCIETIES

Societies normally change very slowly. The slow change allows people to gradually shift by small steps from one set of rules to a revised one. This means they have only minimal need for our complex deception processes. But societies also sometimes change very rapidly. If these changes involve new feelings and new patterns of action, as they are very apt to do if they are great social changes, then the situation will call for a maximum of self and other deceptions and the need for these deceptions will almost certainly lead people to faithfully follow some kind of demagogues who lead them rapidly into the promised land (deviance) under a blazing panoply of traditional labels.

In an age when a society is moving rapidly, but not precipitously, into a new era, in which the society is being steadily but not catastrophically transformed into a different (deviant) kind of society, the people often refuse to see the meaning of the changes. It is as if a whole nation were "sleepwalking" resolutely in an obvious direction, but almost no one, other than a quickly stigmatized Cassandra or two, dares to talk about it. By not talking about it, one evades the shame that he would otherwise feel. By the time anyone dares to talk about it, it is almost the new society, with new rules of thought and feeling, so people can begin to hail the new society as if it were always like that. They may rewrite history or reinterpret it to conclude that, indeed, there never was any deviance; they merely had misunderstood what the society was like, now they understand the really real.

There are, first, the well-known *revolutionary creative deviants* who proclaim the absolute necessity of adopting this or that new brand of rules. Some of these are *revolutionary traditionalists,* people who have drifted into an already long-established deviant subculture which has persistently failed to meet whatever new needs the general populace feels, but satisfy the feelings of some isolated deviants so they persist down through history. Marxism is the best known form of revolutionary traditionalism today. It is very absolutist and does not change to meet new situations, which is precisely what a society in rapid transition needs. But a society in rapid transition is also at times a very threatened society, one that feels it is losing all certainty in life—rules seem to many people to have become impossible because life seems so disordered—perceived chaos (unruled life) elicits profound anxieties. These societies are said by historians to be "in crisis" and in their panic for certainty (ruled order) they almost always turn to an absolutist (compulsive) set of rules which is presented not as new, but the very embodiment of absolute truth of all time and places—that is, religion.

There are, however, some really new forms of creative deviance in most such periods. These are the well-known utopia subcultures that spring up during periods of rapid transition. Most are merely ideas, but some involve people actually committing their lives to new rule-governed ways of behavior in utopian communities. In the 19th century, during the great transition of traditional Western society into industrial society, hundreds of these sprang up, mainly in the United States where they could isolate themselves from traditional rules and enforce their new ones. The same is happening now in a more serious period of disorder, possibly a great cultural crisis, once again in the United States more than elsewhere. California today is honeycombed with thousands of such mini-utopias testing out vast numbers of patterns of creative deviance. Millions of people are drifting step-wise in and out of them continually, facilitated by our vast repertoire of deceptive processes.

Secondly, in a period of general social transition there is a much larger group of people, probably a majority in any period other than crises, who are progressively moving with the transition and adapting their bodies, but protecting their selves, by keeping firm hold on the traditional rules and symbols. These are the *sleepwalking cultural drifters.* They are, of course, reconstructing the meanings of the traditional rules for their everyday life concrete situations, but they refuse to add up the abstract meanings of these many reconstructions, so they are able to spread their abstract rules ever thinner over social life, drifting ever further away. They are by their concrete feelings, choices, and actions creating a new concrete social reality, but evading shame in doing this by continually, more insistently than ever confirming the traditional abstract rules and way of life.

Third, and very closely related to this large group of sleepwalking cultural drifters, we have the *traditionalist symbolic displayers.* These are the "happy warriors" who are often working furiously to destroy the old social rules in their concrete situations of everyday life or politics, but who because of this very fact feel a *cultural malaise,* an uneasiness that gnaws at their consciousness, but which they suppress by frantically reasserting the traditional rules and way of life. They deceive themselves into thinking they are exuberant builders of the traditional society and they compulsively reject any suggestion that they are actually pushing the transition of the old into something totally new. They are especially likely to create a *cultural pageantry* that celebrates the traditional way of life they are unknowingly destroying.

This seems to be what is responsible for one of the remarkable phenomena of human history, the frequently noted tendency of a dying way of life to flare up in an effulgent last-burst of vitality, which is largely a symbolic vitality, but sometimes spills over into a last-gasp reassertion of the traditional practices. Payne (1975) has argued that such a dying burst of symbolic display is most obvious and universal in art forms.

I doubt that there are such uniformities in transitional behavior of a whole cultural group. (Sorokin has shown conclusively that periodicities in whole cultural movements are extremely complex. See Sorokin, 1937, especially the discussion of periodicities in Vol. IV. He concludes that there are general waves of change, but that there are vast complexities to concrete movements.) Rather than finding such things as bursts of symbolic displaying throughout a whole culture in a time of transition, I think we do find universally that many individuals and some groups, which are sometimes dominant groups as in the case of feudalism, respond to their growing malaise (produced by the transition) in this way, while others respond in other ways. Many of the sudden bursts of traditional forms of behavior are simply rational attempts to prevent their death; they are struggles to the death for the old way of life, not self-deceptive behavior. Constantine temporarily revitalized the economy of the Roman empire by recognizing some of the terrible effects of government policies on economic life, which were by then so obvious, so there was a final burst of economic vitality which had excellent effects throughout society. It was not symbolic display activity, but rational action. These last-gasp efforts are almost always doomed to failure because they come after the basic damage is done, so the crisis widens and the situation elicits more symbolic display and other deceptive reactions.

Fourth, in periods of transition, especially of transitional crises, there are almost always politicians who consciously recognize the deep need for self-deception felt by the people still highly committed to the old rules and ways of life. They also recognize how much easier it is to deceive one's self when there are others telling you your deceptions are true. And they recognize how people will support, even adore, someone who meets this need, especially when the need is so great during a crisis when everything seems to be falling apart. Some of these become the flattering demagogues so well known in times of critical transition. Demagogues are, of course, the *political seducers* who use the techniques of deceiving to seduce a whole society into a deviant mode of life, a new set of effective rules. Some of them are merely opportunists who flatter the people's deceptions to get the rewards. Others flatter the deception in order to use them to move the people to a new set of rules, sometimes in a benign way, more often in a direction which they would reject if they saw where they were being led. It is these users of deceptions to facilitate transitions that interest me.

The benign flatterers of deceptions have been well recognized since Plato wrote *The Laws* because he explicitly argued that the religious deceptions of people should be flattered by the wise lawgiver in order to lead them into stable ordered patterns of life. (Dostoevsky's Grand Inquisitor is the modern classic statement of the position.) There have, of course, been these benevolent demagogues, if not terribly many. The classic instance in American history was Alexander Hamilton. The American colonies, having just become states, were undergoing the very anxious and conflictful transition to a national government. Hamilton understood well the dread so many Americans had of a powerful central government. (A large part of the population, especially the southern frontier population, were almost anarchists—and still are.) He thus flattered the beliefs of people that a federal government divided into three functioning and supposedly equal branches would allow them to continue with their locally autonomous form of life, with minimal direction from the federal government. This is the crucial rhetoric of *The Federalist* papers. Hamilton knew very well that such an argument was almost certainly a deception, because he knew that all the history of the Western world from the time of most ancient Greece and Rome showed that there is a principle of immanent growth in government power at work. As Baechler (1975) would put it, government power tends to grow until something more powerful stops it. And, of course, once there is nothing else which in combination or singly is more powerful, then nothing stops it and it becomes the classic imperial bureaucratic state so well known to all the Americans of Hamilton's age in the form of the Roman Empire. Hamilton knew that, if he and others like him could just deceive Americans into a federal government, the central government's power would grow and grow until we had a kind of monarchic central power, perhaps an Imperial Presidency. In any event, such deceptions worked, though Hamilton had only a small part in it; and his expectations have all come true, as we can see the Imperial American Bureaucratic State growing more powerful every year.

Most demagogues, however, have not been very benign. The more normal purpose is to flatter the deceptions of the people in order to seize power, especially tyrannical power. These Machiavellian flatterers of deception often would prefer to be kings or legitimate wielders of power in some other way, but the wiser ones recognize, as Machiavelli and most Renaissance tyrants did, that the very transitional crisis that gives them the opportunity to deceive their way into power, and the very process of deception itself, prevent the existence of any shared rules of concrete government which has legitimacy in the short run (which is generally many decades or even centuries). In a situation of critical transition only tyranny is possible for the demagogue—and probably for any other central power; and his use of flattery of deceits makes this even more so, because the flattery of deceit encourages the widening gap between concrete realities and the beliefs of people, which encourages the forces producing the crises.

While it is not true that all populists are demagogues, it is obvious that all successful demagogues are populists. They must flatter the people to achieve power. Above all, they must flatter the deceptions which people hold passionately and which are conducive to the demagogues achieving power. That is, they *pride the people's deceptions,* thereby amplifying them. (The slogan goes something like this: All power to the people; the people are always right; I am the voice of the people.) The demagogue only leads the people by following their passionate, shame, and anxiety-bred deceptions. The difference is that he knows they are deceptions, so he is not deceived in the situation. He tells the people what they want to hear—what they demand passionately to hear—and then uses the power they give him for this reason to lead their bodies elsewhere, that is, to transform the society into what he wants it to be, generally a tyrannical state in which he is tyrant, because that is the only viable state when most of the people share important deceptions about their world. As one of the most brilliant and successful political seducers in history, Napoleon summed up his experience, "Vanity made the revolution; liberty was only a pretext."

The most common pattern of the rise of tyranny from a democratic state seems to be that of priding the belief of the people that they are moving back toward more democracy. The rising tyrant exudes democracy and extolls it to the heavens. (All power to the people!) The more tyrannical he becomes in fact, the more he must extol democracy, thus the more he prides the deception that the people are getting more free and democratic all the time. All of the symbols of democratic freedoms must be amplified, while all of the realities are being destroyed.

The fifth, and final, reaction to social transitions is that of the *reactionary stigmatizers.* These are the people who recognize that the traditional rules and ways of life are in transition, or dying, and who feel profoundly threatened by this. It is the feeling of dread, of being basically threatened (threatened in your being) by other people, that produces stigmatization, whether it be a physical threat (as in the case of leprosy and, probably, venereal disease originally) or a moral (taboo) one. (Great physical social threats, like sexual competition, probably always get quickly transformed into moral questions.) The reactionary stigmatizer is trying to destroy or exorcise the "evil" people who they believe are providing the threat of social transition. These people are not wrong in believing that there is a transition going on. They are not initially paranoid about the existence of a threat, though their anxiety tends very much to amplify their perceptions of change to the point of paranoia. (They may think they are already living in a tyrannical communist nation when it is only a halfway point, that of socialist big government powers such as we have today in Western societies.) Their general form of self-deception is that of thinking they know who is producing it—the witches. Great social transitions, especially critical transitions, are almost never the work of a single man (though a few, like Hitler, may get very great powers as a result of the crisis) or even of small groups, so the imputation of all the evils to a few is a clue that self-deceptions may be at work. (Hofstadter, 1969, has argued that *political paranoia* is most easily seen in the leap from obvious facts to absurd causes, but absurd only to listeners not feeling the same threat.) The American Puritans in the 17th and early 18th centuries were right to recognize that their world was changing rapidly (see Erikson, 1966). Their hard work was making them rich, new arrivals were making the societies more complex, cities were growing, and other basic changes were happening. The simple life of the Puritans was threatened, especially by the evils of luxurious living. The self and other deceit was in thinking their threat, their anxieties, were caused by the evil thoughts of a few people, witches. Again, the McCarthyites were obviously right in thinking there was an international threat and that their way of life, their rules of Americanism, were rapidly changing—dying—at home. America was caught in the Cold War and the early stages of the Welfare State Revolution that has now transformed our traditional society into a totally different form of society, a society controlled more and more by an Imperial Bureaucratic State. Their self-deception was in thinking all of this was the doings of a few hundred "commies" or "pinkos." In fact, any economic-political analysis today shows that their own behavior, that of voting for government officials who "gave" them farm subsidies and business subsidies of various kinds, was vastly more important in producing the growth of big government that threatened their way of life. That seems obvious, even common-sensical, to anyone who is not governed by the powerful deceits born of greed, shame, and anxiety. But their potential shame at using their votes to get political payoffs of "welfare" from the government was evaded by calling the welfare payoffs "subsidies" and so on and by blaming Big Government or the "commies" instead of themselves. This same kind of "relabeling" deceit has been of profound importance in the Welfare State Revolution in the United States. Americans have been the most intensely individualistic nation in the Western world, perhaps in the whole world; we have been puritanically opposed to big government and made that opposition the basic principle of our Constitution.

We have also had profound feelings of shame at taking welfare "handouts" because this is a symbol of submission, extreme shame. (Many of us who came from poor families literally lived in dread of having ever to take "welfare.") In order for people to gratify their greedy desire for more and more government payoffs, and to avoid their anxieties over economic depressions and other things, they have used their votes to elect politicians who have provided them with payoffs and bureaucratic regulations at a phenomenal rate. America is now more socialized than nations like Germany, which started the welfare state under Bismarck in the 19th century, but it was done here remarkably fast in just two decades. (Of course, some of it started in the 1930s, but there was a long lull after World War II.) Americans know that Germany is a socialist nation, but they never think of their country as a socialist nation. Above all, they do not talk of the American welfare state; they call retirement welfare social security insurance (though it is in no way an insurance program); they call unemployment welfare an insurance program (though it too is no such thing); they call their socialist party by the 19th century name of the individualist freedom party, liberals (though most of these liberals are in favor of more socialist measures than the socialist leader of Germany); and so on almost endlessly. By all of the methods of self-deception and political seduction, demagoguery, we have been transformed into a de facto socialist nation which, because of our shame, must be extolled to the heavens as the "last bastion of free enterprise in the world." Our talk of free enterprise is like jousting pageantry during the waning of the Middle Ages. But, of course, the very crux of the situation is that one dare not say so because that immediately arouses shame and anxiety—if one's defenses of deception fail. Of course, they almost never fail in this particular situation: the fact that America is now a socialist welfare state is one of the most closely guarded secrets in our society, especially among the intellectuals who know all the facts. It is quite taboo to say so in public settings and anyone who violates the taboo is labeled a "McCarthyite" by almost everyone except real McCarthyites (i.e., traditionalist stigmatizers of the changes going on), which encourages everyone to believe the simple statement of fact is stigmatic work. These taboos against talking about embarrassing things, things that would shame those present, are of basic importance in a (privately) conflictful society like America (see Douglas, 1971) in avoiding open conflict. They are grouped under our rules of "niceness" (traditionally called the rules of respectability, decency, or civilization). "Nice" people do not refer to a masseuse as a whore (or even as a masseuse), because it degrades or shames her in traditional public settings (parties, etc.). When someone introduces a girl as a masseuse the person may be "shocked out of her mind," but must not "blanch," and should let it pass with something like, "How nice." To call America a socialist state does not shock many people. It is partly because most people do not know much about European socialist states, even though the comparative facts are sometimes presented in the news media (without ever referring to America as a socialist or welfare state—"God forbid!"); but the primary reason even for this ignorance is the automatic shared deceptive (screening) labeling.

A fragmented society in a time of crisis inspires a veritable *stigmatic war* of all major groups against all other major groups. The people are more and more anxious, more and more actually or potentially shameful about what is happening to their society, and the different groups deceive themselves into seeing various other groups or individuals as the causes of all their own particular troubles. In general, it is their enemies, the perceived threateners of oneself, who get stigmatized—as heretics, witches, traitors, or whatnot. This helps to make enemies more firmly enemies, so stigmatizing all around is encouraged, if not assured.

MANAGING SHAME FEELINGS

The second basic way in which individuals get on warily, and later merrily, with their wicked ways is by managing the shame feelings they cannot evade through secrecy or deception. Just as individuals differ greatly in their ability to inhibit flight in the face of danger, that is, in their degree of courage, so do they also differ greatly in the degree to which they can bear shame without deception, withdrawing, submitting, hiding—going back to traditional ways, conforming. There are probably actual differences in the ability to "put up with" shame, just as there are in the ability to put up with hunger (as in dieting) and physical pain. Some people have more physical fortitude than others, some have more moral fortitude, ability to resist the moral demands and dominance demands of others through shaming and ridicule. Some people even talk of "moral courage" and this seems very appropriate. These people inhibit the deceptions and submissive body reactions in the face of shame. But shame is a powerful feeling. Few people seem able to do much of that simple putting up with it without submitting and returning to traditional ways. So even those with moral courage seem to indulge considerably in some of the other means of managing shame feelings.

Probably the most common and most effective means of doing this is by *venting* the shame feelings, of sublimating them. (Just as one can repress and then sublimate the id, so one can repress and sublimate the superego feelings.) The basic way in which this is done is by displays and angry expressions of *aggressive counter-moralism* (shame-fury). People who are extremly good shame managers respond to the slightest feeling of shame, or just the situation which they subconsciously recognize will arouse that dreaded feeling, with an almost instantaneous burst of aggressive counter-moralism or counter-shaming.

Lewis (1971) observed aggressive counter-moralism or counter-shaming very frequently in her patients. Most of the time, however, we can barely see it in our everyday lives, just as we can barely see the pervasive shaming displays that go on. A barely visible smirk or a fleeting curled lip *hinting* laughing ridicule is all we do in shame displays or counter-shame displays most of the time because of the danger of disrupting social relations, even getting in murderous fights, for doing such things. Most of the time we are not even sure shame-displaying has been done, but our suspicion leads to an immediate venting by laughing inwardly at that "dumb ass," "that stupid son-of-a-bitch," and so on endlessly in creative profusion. When we do express our counter-shaming openly in such dangerous situations we show vast creativity in the subtle manipulations of uncertainty, even more subtle than Mark Anthony's deceitful nonpraise of Caesar's shameful behavior. As long as we are only slightly shamed by our suspicions, we can afford to be subtle because the venting is done by talking to ourselves; but when the feeling of shame threatens to be greater, then we must do counter-shame displays for others to more thoroughly vent our subconscious feelings of shame.

Probably the second most important way in which we vent shame feelings is by doing counter-pride displays, deceitfully taking pride and displaying pride in the very thing which has aroused shame feelings. Counter-pride displays are so commonly mixed with simple counter-aggressive behavior to achieve revenge for the aggressive intent in the shaming display that they can be very hard to observe. We all know the feelings involved though. Consider, for example, the effects on someone denounced (shame-display) as a "warmongering American." If one feels quite confident in his innocence, he may not even respond because he does not want any trouble. On the other hand, he is apt to feel aggressive just because someone is aggressing against him. But it is only when he is "defensive" about this Americanism, that is, when he in fact feels some subconscious shame about suspected warmongering behavior, that he responds with that sharp "overreaction" of preening himself, puffing himself up (stiffened back, stern look, haughty contempt for the inferior, chest out—all very military forceful), and doing pride displays that we call counter-pride (or pseudo-pride).

One of the most important patterns of human aggression involves both aggressive counter-shame and counter-pride. When the shame is profound, especially when individuals fear to attack directly the shamer, so they must suppress the direct attacks on the shamer, there are various possible reactions. At the extreme we can get complete repression of counter-attack and a sublimation of feelings resulting from that. This can produce the extreme *identification with the victorious aggressor,* as seen in British colonies in the native bureaucrats and analyzed in Bettelheim (1943) in the concentration camps. This frequently involves the *ressentiment* syndrome analyzed by Scheler (1961). I suspect that is reasonably uncommon, but over long periods of severe repression it seems to happen. More commonly, people in such a situation become demoralized, shameless, as they simply give up their old rule feelings in the face of the overwhelming situational forces, but do not adopt the new, making massive use of perpetual deceits. This is seen in the withdrawal actions (especially alcoholism) of long suppressed people with no realistic chance of rising again—which appears to be the common American Indian situation (though I realize this will be furiously denied by their romantic partisans). Of course, most such people do not become totally demoralized, any more than those with ressentiment have it totally. What one sees is that most of the time in most situations they react that way and are shameless, but there are times when the old rule-feelings reassert themselves, presumably because some situation in conjunction with thinking triggers them, and at that point we can get spasmodic counter-shaming and counter-pride, even episodic (moody) violence in episodes of shame-rage.

When the suppressed shame is extreme we can easily get the very important syndrome of *shame-pride-rage,* which consists in extreme, often violent, counter-shaming and counter-pride, if the situational threat is not too great. This may all be done symbolically as long as the situational suppression continues, but it may be unleashed in a furious attack, even a murderous-suicidal one if the pain of shame becomes too great to be vented by this vast profusion of display work. When the situation is extreme, especially when any counter-shaming or counter-priding openly can produce instant death, the counter-shaming and counter-priding is done all internally, without a hint of external display work that can be understood by the threatener. A remarkable instance of the overwhelming importance of such counter-displays in protecting oneself from the terrors of shame at submitting to the enemy is seen in the pervasive secret counter-shaming and counter-priding of prisoners of war. Ralph Gaither has described (in personal communication) how he did such counter-venting during his eight-year imprisonment in the "Hanoi Hilton." The men had secretly developed a tap code by which they could communicate with each other in immense detail through the walls and pipes. They used this to maintain personal contact and discipline, which was of basic importance in preventing demoralization and identifying with the oppressor (selling out to the new iron-rules under the most extreme pressure of the fear of death). The feeling of shame from the submission to their demands was profound, but could be partially overcome, vented, by even small but extremely emotional acts of secret counter-shaming and counter-priding. The tap code was vital in doing this, but often the individual could only do self-displays in his mind, less effective, but vital. In one instance Gaither was forced to chop wood but prevented from communicating with any Americans by a guard standing over him with a gun. Gaither not only did the internal "name calling" so well known to everyone in these situations, but also chopped the wood in taps to communicate with the other Americans in camp, thereby outsmarting the "dumb Gook"–shaming him, priding himself–gaining the vital "tiny revenge" of those forced by overwhelming pressure to submit in shame.

There has probably never been a more bloodcurdling account of this shame-pride-rage syndrome than that given by Franz Fanon in *The Wretched of the Earth,* which in essence says in bloodcurdling detail that only blood-revenge can rebuild the pride of once-proud people repressed by wicked colonialist shamers who deserve the worst possible. We have witnessed again and again the common pattern: as soon as the suppression is let up, so that the evil is no longer being perpetrated, the pent-up feelings of shame are vented in explosive assertions of counter-pride and counter-shaming, frequently in trying to kill the erstwhile shamers. Those who do not feel shame, but feel only real pride, and those who are highly suppressed, do not explode in open venting displays; those who suffer the terrible agonies of ambivalent conflicts between continued but suppressed pride and shame from the suppression (submission) are the ones who explode as the "lid is let off." This is the basic *dilemma of repressive power:* even if one wants to get off the tiger's back, it is very dangerous to try.

This same pattern of shame-pride-rage under medium pressure of suppression seems to exist among some of the poor in the United States. The American poor, unlike the poor of more caste-repressed societies, do very often, but certainly not always, have feelings of shame about being poor (Douglas and Johnson, 1977). If they were really suppressed minorities, as some of their romantic deceivers claim, then they would not have much feeling of shame–who feels shame about obvious necessities? But, precisely because it is a relatively open society in which far higher percentages of the poor move upward in money and status (and almost all the poor have friends who have done so) and in which self-reliance and initiative in working one's way up are still the conscious rules accepted by most people, the poor tend to feel shame. The feeling of shame is greatest when they have the greatest chance, which is the case today because of widespread welfare and education programs; and it is greatest when they must deal with outsiders whom they suspect are shaming them for being poor (even when the outsiders are not thinking of them), or pitying them, which is an indirect form of shaming. This feeling of shame is partially evaded by deceits, such as "*they* repress all of us," but the residue in some is vented by shame-pride-rage, which often involves violent displays of warrior pride–puffing up, etc. The "nonutilitarian" delinquent activity analyzed by Cohen (1955) is, of course, very utilitarian in venting the feelings of shame one feels, in getting even at least symbolically for one's dominant shamers, rebalancing at least in part, however inadequately, the account book of pride. Gang boys also often develop elaborate rituals of counter-pride.

Though to vastly varying degrees, all deviant subcultures use counter-shaming and counter-pride deceits and when put under great pressure are likely to go into shame-pride-rage displays. As a rough rule of thumb, we can say that counter-shaming and counter-pride displays will increase with the degree of prior learning of traditional rules (which means ambivalence is most likely to remain high) and with the degree of violation of those rules involved in the deviance (the amount of actual or potential shaming displays by traditionalists); and that they will decrease with the degree of secrecy and social distance successfully maintained from the traditionalists. The counter-shaming and counter-pride displays are most obvious in the ridicule heaped on the traditionalists and the puffing-up of the deviant identity and world—we are so-so superior to those dumb-dumbs. Homosexuality is a beautiful instance of this. Homosexuality is one of the most shamed forms of behavior in our society and it is one of the forms in which the subculture, the "gay world" or "gay community," does very systematic counter-shaming and counter-priding displays.

Finally, there are more conscious ways of managing feelings of shame and guilt. Some people are very adept at consciously cutting off any consideration of subjects that can produce shame feelings and even more of avoiding situations in which they will arise, thereby evading shame feelings to a considerable extent. Some people will curtly demand that "You must not even say such things," or "think such things"—block it out of your mind. If a poor person feels shamed by having to "ask for" a job (and the feeling they have is often that associated with "begging"), then the whole thing can be evaded by not looking for a job, even though this involves a lesser degree of continual shame by remaining poor. The short-run pain of begging can be so intense that the prospect of prolonged low levels or episodes of low levels can far more easily be put up with, just as one might put up with the little toothache rather than undergo the sharp pain of the drill that will end it. Besides, one knows of people who have "made a killing" in the numbers racket, or some other gamble or hustle, so it is easy to dream away the prolonged poverty (symbolically vent it by picturing oneself becoming rich, which elicits feelings of joy).

One frequently used conscious means of blotting out the shame feelings or any other negative feelings is the manipulation of the feelings by using psycho-active drugs. The most popular depressants of these drugs not only make one feel high, but blot out feelings of shame and other painful feelings. Alcohol is the most frequently used method. Just as old Sandpiper feels more proud in his world of fantasied friends when he is drinking, so do most people feel more proud, more confident when drinking. That, in fact, is one of the most frequently given reasons for drinking—it makes you feel more confident by realizing your fantasies, steadies your nerves by repressing fears or derealizing them. It works for many people though it can also become more shaming than anything else if one becomes a "drunk," thereby demanding more of the same cure. Most of the other popular depressants, from tranquilizers and barbiturates to heroin, do similar things. In addition, there are all kinds of addictions that people use consciously to rivet their attention away from some painful situation, such as the fear of an exam or the shame of one's life. Movies and television are very popular addictive diversions of (compulsive) attention from the painful situation, thus from the feelings of psychic pain. Many people, especially those suffering from profound psychic pains like the dread of death and shame, are literally addicts to television, so that they will watch anything to blot out consciousness that triggers the feelings; and they do it knowingly until the "fix" takes hold and blots out the consciousness of why they are blotting out consciousness.

CONCLUSION

All human individuals and all human societies suffer from a great deal of conflict. These are a necessary part of our lives because of the vast amount of conflict built into us by our genetic inheritance. They are highly adaptive for individuals and societies (see Wilson, 1975; and Douglas, forthcoming), but they are very painful. Our vastly complex symbolic abilities and our cunning subconscious processes have adapted to our conflicts and our desire to avoid their pains by developing means, mostly through subconscious natural selection (they work so they are reinforced-learned), but also through very complex forms that are to varying degrees conscious, at least fleetingly, to evade the pains. All of these means, even the conscious ones, involve some degree of deceit, either deceit of the self or of others. These deceits allow us to move forward in life, shifting to adapt to new situations that do not fit our old patterns of ruled-life. They can, of course, become totally unadaptive, as any part of our genetic or cultural adaptation apparatus can in new situations. I would assume that in general we would be more adaptive, and wind up in the long run happier, if we could rely on a high degree of centrally integrated (rational) inhibition of our flights from pains (i.e., use willpower or courage), rather than having to use deceits that may hide some important realities from us. But few people have much of that. The American Indians trained themselves arduously to have the courage or willpower to put up with intense physical pain; and they could definitely take a vast amount. Some people train themselves, or, far more likely, are trained by others and by their situations in life, to put up with pain in this way and even to put up with the pains caused by the truth of one's situation. But this does not seem to be very true for very many people, especially in our kind of society in which absolutist (Puritanical) rules inflict such severe shame for deviance.

Our social world is vastly more conflictful and painful in these ways than simpler societies like those of the American Indians. This seems to be necessarily the case in a complex nation state for the simple reason that our genetic inheritance and our historical cultural development have given us each membership in multiple groups from the family to the nation state, and even in some degree to the world, which involve severely conflicting sets of rules. Our commitment to any kind of government beyond the simple bondings of family and band seems to be possible in good part only because we are able to share commitments to deceptions, which make the state *feel* to us like these smaller groups to which we have genetic bonds. (I would roughly agree with Cassirer's symbolic analysis of *The Myth of the State* (1955) but add these feeling dimensions as basic.) But all of our problems are vastly amplified in a highly complex, pluralistic, conflictful state of international dimensions. Everyone lives in a little vortex of conflicting forces, surrounded by enemies ready to pounce with shame and ridicule displays. The more one reaches out in the society, building ever wider and more conflictful ties with the bigger society, and especially the more successful one becomes, thus the more subject to envy-sniping by shaming-displays, the more this is true. I suspect the most morally courageous of us would soon wither under all of this emotional attack, if we did not have our vastly cunning armory of defending deceits to help us move about our world, especially to allow those vital adaptive transitions in our lives as individuals and as whole societies. (Political analysts have considered some of these deceits in the form of "ideologies," but they have not seen how vastly complex deceits are.) The crucial problem we face seems to be that of maintaining some vital, shifting balance between our need for truth about our situations and selves, so that we can choose adaptively, wisely, and our need for protection by deceit and managing feelings elicited by truth. Many people today are sorely tempted, and some give way to the temptation, to agree with the man in the play "The Goodbye People" who proclaimed, "The truth! When you see the truth coming, lock the doors and paint the mirrors black because the s.o.b. will kill you every time!" It will, indeed, kill at times because the pain is so great. But to go to the other extreme, that of the blissful deceit of madness or solipsism, is eventually more painful by far than is the pain involved in that endless, groping struggle to be wise in living, that perilous struggle to maintain a balance between truth and the need to evade the terrible pains of anxiety and shame it can cause in a world of conflict and uncertainty in which we all face the necessity of sin and death.

REFERENCES

ARNOLD, D.O. (ed., 1970). The sociology of subcultures. Berkeley, Calif.: Glendessary Press.

BAECHLER, J. (1975). The origins of capitalism. Oxford: Basil Blackwell. (Originally published in Paris in 1971.)

BECKER, H.S. (1963). Outsiders: Studies in the sociology of deviance. New York: Free Press.
BETTELHEIM, B. (1943). "Individual and mass behavior in extreme situations." Journal of Abnormal and Social Psychology, 38:417-452.
CASSIRER, E. (1955). The myth of the state. New York: Doubleday Anchor.
COHEN, A.K. (1955). Delinquent boys: The culture of the gang. New York: Free Press.
DOUGLAS, J.D. (1967). The social meanings of suicide. Princeton, N.J.: Princeton University Press.
——— (1971). American social order. New York: Free Press.
——— (1977). Subcultures of deviance. Boston: Little, Brown.
——— (forthcoming). Creative deviance and social change.
DOUGLAS, J.D., and JOHNSON, J.M. (eds., 1977). Existential sociology. New York: Cambridge University Press.
DOUGLAS, J.D., RASMUSSEN, P.K. with FLANAGAN, C.A. (1977). The nude beach. Beverly Hills, Calif.: Sage.
ERIKSON, K.T. (1966). Wayward Puritans: A study in the sociology of deviance. New York: John Wiley.
HOFSTADTER, R. (1969). The paranoid style in American politics. New York: Vintage.
LAING, R.D. (1960). The divided self. Chicago: Quadrangle.
LEWIS, H.B. (1971). Shame and guilt in neurosis. New York: International Universities Press.
LIDDELL-HART, B.H. (1954). Strategy. New York: Praeger.
LYMAN, S.M., and SCOTT, M.B. (1970). The sociology of the absurd. New York: Appleton-Century-Crofts.
PARET, P. (1976). Clausewitz and the state. Oxford: Clarendon Press.
PAYNE, R. (1975). The corrupt society: From ancient Greece to present-day America. New York: Praeger.
RASMUSSEN, P.K., and KUHN, L.L. (1976). "The new masseuse: Play for pay." Urban Life, 5:271–292.
SCHELER, M. (1961). Ressentiment. New York: Free Press.
SCHELLING, T.C. (1960). The strategy of conflict. Cambridge, Mass.: Harvard University Press.
SOROKIN, P.A. (1937). Social and cultural dynamics (4 vols). New York: Bedminster Press.
SYKES, G., and MATZA, D. (1957). "Techniques of neutralization." American Sociological Review, 22:664-670.
WILSON, E.O. (1975). Sociobiology. Cambridge, Mass.: Harvard University Press.

3

DEVIANT BEHAVIOR AND SOCIAL CONTROL IN SCIENCE

HARRIET ZUCKERMAN

AUTHOR'S NOTE: *Research for this study was supported by a grant from the National Science Foundation SOC72-05326 to the Columbia Program in the Sociology of Science. Robert Merton gave the manuscript his usual thorough review and Joshua Lederberg, Marvin Wolfgang, and William Kruskal were kind enough to direct me to apposite materials.*

Deviant behavior in science, as in other departments of social life, involves departures from norms assigned to social roles and statuses. It refers to those deviant acts people commit in their capacity as scientists, not the acts which some commit in the other statuses they happen to occupy: such as child abuse by scientist-parents, tax evasion by scientist-citizens, or religious heresy by scientist-church members.

NORMATIVE STRUCTURE OF SCIENCE

The normative structure in science can be thought of as comprised of two classes of norms, intertwined in practice but analytically separable: the cognitive (technical) norms and methodological canons which specify what should be studied and how, and the moral norms, expressed as prescriptions, proscriptions, preferences, and permissions concerning the attitudes and behavior of scientists in relation to one another and their research. Cognitive[1] and moral norms both implement the goal of scientific activity—the extension of certified knowledge about the natural world—and both "are binding, not only because they are procedurally efficient, but because they are believed right and good" (Merton, 1973:270: Mulkay, 1976).

Deviant behavior in science thus involves departures from sets of cognitive (technical) and moral norms. Cognitive norms refer to the framework of generic methodological conventions, such as the requirements of logical consistency and empirical confirmability (Merton, 1973:290; Scheffler, 1967) or, in terms of Karl Popper's alternative criterion, falsifiability (Popper, 1959). These conventions are generic in the sense that, though differing in detail, at any given time they are much alike in the actual research practices of scientists. Scientists have long tried to cope with the problem of what qualifies as scientific work; what Popper has identified as the problem of "demarcation between science and non-science" (Popper, 1959, Chap. 6; 1962, Papers 1 and 11). In practice, they distinguish between two radically different kinds of nonconformity: between those cognitive challenges to the thoroughly established orthodoxies which are set forth *within* the framework of the cognitive norms of science and those challenges to established knowledge which move *outside* that normative framework. The first kind is not generally defined as deviant behavior while the second is decidedly deviant in the sense of being beyond the pale of science.

Thus, the seeming paradox that norms of science call for both conformity and nonconformity is of course no paradox at all. The *approved form of conformity* is to the cognitive standards of what is defined as constituting scientific work while the *approved form of nonconformity* involves original contributions that advance upon previous claims to knowledge by denying their validity, as in the case of Lee and Yang who theoretically disproved the law of the conservation of parity in weak physical interactions. Correlatively, the *disapproved form of nonconformity* involves rule-breaking of a very different kind, one in which the cognitive standards of scientific work are themselves violated, as with contemporary adventures in astrology, while the *disapproved (or at least not greatly rewarded) form of conformity* occurs in work that peers regard as pedestrian.

The obvious and important point, which I shall consider throughout this paper, is that deviant behavior in science relates to greatly differing kinds of cognitive norms with distinctive patterns of peer response to such deviance. Even pathmaking or "revolutionary" changes in science take place within a framework of broadly defined cognitive norms while substantial deviations from those norms are defined by members of the scientific community as nonscience or pseudoscience (with the most extreme specimens being described as "crackpot").

Along with the cognitive norms of science summarized by Merton with excessive brevity was a specimen list of moral norms:

universalism: the norm requiring that truth claims be judged in terms of cognitive criteria, not in terms of personal attributes of their authors;

disinterestedness: "a distinctive pattern of institutional control of a wide range of motives" such that it becomes "to the interest of scientists to conform" by engaging in disinterested activity directed toward the extension of scientific knowledge;

organized skepticism: the norm requiring that truth claims should be subjected to "detached scrutiny of beliefs in terms of empirical and logical criteria"; and

communism (or, as Barber (1952) suggested as a preferable term, *communality*): the "findings of science [as] a product of social collaboration are assigned to the community"; intellectual property is limited to peer recognition (i.e., open acknowledgement) of one's contributions, with "the pressure for diffusion of results [being] reinforced by . . . the incentive of recognition which is, of course, contingent upon publication." [Merton, 1973: Papers 12-14]

To this list which, as we shall see, has been both widely adopted and subjected to organized skepticism, Barber has added individualism, rationality, and emotional neutrality (1952: Chapter 4; see also Cournand and Zuckerman, 1970; Cournand and Meyer, 1976, for further discussion of institutional and individual codes of science).

Violations of these moral norms of science include ad hominem attacks (anti-universalism), the contriving of forged or otherwise fraudulent evidence (anti-disinterestedness); plagiarism and secrecy (anti-communism or communality); dogmatism and shoddy work (anti-organized skepticism), and a range of other actions variously proscribed by these norms.

As in other spheres of social life, the violations of certain norms, both cognitive and moral, are just about universally condemned—even those social scientists who doubt the operation of norms in science reject the practice of plagiarism—while violations of other norms are defined as less serious or consequential.

A SET OF QUESTIONS

When cases of seriously deviant behavior by scientists—fraud or plagiarism, for example—gain public notice, they evoke responses which seem to be out of proportion to their immediately pragmatic rather than symbolic consequences. They even reach the front pages of major newspapers as the culprits are angrily attacked by fellow scientists.[2] The cases surfacing in recent years have involved a wide range of scientists: senior ones and junior ones; Americans, Europeans, and Indians; scientists working in established fields of research and others on the periphery.[3]

Such episodes and the responses to them hold an obvious intrinsic interest for sociologists of science but it is less obvious that they also provide occasions for highlighting certain aspects of deviant behavior generally. In examining the following set of questions, we shall therefore consider their possible relevance to the several theories of deviant behavior as well as the extent to which such study contributes to our understanding of the workings of science as a cognitive and social system.

(1) How is the system of social control in science connected to its institutional structure on the one hand and the differing cognitive textures of the various sciences, on the other? What social and cognitive processes serve to detect and to negatively sanction deviant behavior? Which mechanisms of social control reduce the frequency of deviant acts in science below what it would otherwise be in the absence of these mechanisms? (For a general observation on this last kind of counterfactual formulation, see Coser, 1975:259-260.)

(2) How does the incidence of deviant behavior in science compare with that in other institutional spheres? As we shall see, there are grounds for thinking that extremely deviant actions in science are comparatively infrequent although we note that statistical data on such actions are sparse even when compared with the notoriously inadequate statistics available for other kinds of deviance. Nevertheless, the strong impression remains since we deal here with greatly differing orders of magnitude.

(3) This observation immediately raises the jointly structural and methodological question of what it is about the institution of science that results in the extreme paucity of data on deviant behavior. Why is there no provision for systematic record keeping on such matters?

(4) We have noted that deviant behavior in science involves departures from a composite of cognitive and moral norms. What is the spectrum of such actions ranging from fraud, forgery, and plagiarism at the one extreme, shading off into error—where we shall make a necessary distinction between reputable and disreputable error—to the other extreme involving breaches of what amounts to the etiquette of science?

(5) Reverting to the problem of social control, we address the specific question: How does the distinctive system of intertwined cognitive and moral norms specifically link up with the reward system of science to limit the frequency of deviant behavior and to reinforce patterns of preferred behavior? And finally,

(6) How far does the special case of deviant behavior in science illuminate the various theoretical perspectives on deviant behavior—conflict theory, differential association theory, labelling theory, and anomie-and-opportunity-structure theory?

SOCIAL CONTROL IN SCIENCE

Social control in science depends partly on scientists' internalizing moral and cognitive norms in the course of their professional socialization and partly on social mechanisms for the detection of deviant behavior and the exercise of sanctions when it is detected.

Fledgling scientists soon learn, if they did not know it before, that the faking of evidence in science is its capital crime. Occasional episodes of such fraudulent evidence become and long remain object lessons. For example, in his review of the Koestler (1972) book on Paul Kammerer, the Austrian biologist accused of such fraud a half century ago, Lester Aronson reports: "Although [the] notorious [Kammerer] scandal had reached its climax 12 years before with the suicide of the then illustrious Professor . . . I was familiar with this amazing story, for it was regularly told to biology students as an object lesson. In essence, [we were taught that] falsifying evidence is just about the worst sin that a scientist can commit since such actions threaten to destroy the very heart of the scientific system" (Aronson, 1975:115). We shall return to the reasons for forgery being defined in science, in contrast to forgery in other domains, as the worst of crimes. Here, we note only that the strong sentiments violated by such actions constitute an important component of the system of social control in science.

Once internalized, the norm of organized skepticism—the requirement that truth claims be critically scrutinized by at least some members of the pertinent scientific community—contributes distinctively to the control of deviant behavior. And the norm of skepticism is organized in a double sense. First, it provides moral justification for the conspicuously pragmatic practice of having some peers assigned the task of critically assessing the adequacy of scientific claims. And second, the norm is reinforced by the reward system of science which confers peer recognition on the scientists who identify flaws in the work of others along with the recognition that comes with contributions of their own.

The norm of organized skepticism works in part through anticipatory behavior. Scientists learn rather early that they had better anticipate and take into account the criticisms that others will probably make of their work before, not after, publishing that work. Whether they *feel* skeptical about the validity and adequacy of their own work or not, they learn, if they are serious scientific investigators, that they would do well to act in accord with the norm of organized skepticism or run the risk of having their work dismissed as substandard. As Merton noted some time ago about such anticipatory adaptations:

> Science is public and not private knowledge; and although the idea of "other persons" is not employed explicitly in science, it is always tacitly involved. In order to prove a generalization, which for the individual scientist, on the basis of his own private experience, may have attained the status of a valid law which requires no further confirmation, the investigator is compelled to set up critical experiments which will satisfy the other scientists engaged in the same cooperative activity. This pressure for so working out a problem that the solution will satisfy not only the scientist's own criteria of validity and adequacy, but also the criteria of the group with whom he is actually or symbolically in contact, constitutes a powerful social impetus for cogent, rigorous investigation. The work of the scientist is at every point influenced by the intrinsic requirements of the phenomena with which he is dealing and perhaps just as directly by his reactions to the inferred critical attitudes or actual criticism of other

> scientists and by an adjustment of his behavior in accordance with these attitudes.
>
> Thus, J.J. Fahie quotes Galileo as having written that "ignorance had been the best teacher he ever had, since in order to be able to demonstrate to his opponents [organized skepticism] the truth of his conclusions, he had been forced to prove them by a variety of experiments, though to satisfy his own mind alone he had never felt it necessary to make any." [Merton, 1970:219]

The patterned exercise of skepticism, before and after the event of publication, presumably serves not only to improve the level of scientific craftsmanship but to reduce the extent of fraud that might otherwise be perpetrated.

Also serving as mechanisms of social control are various methodological procedures such as double-blind designs, randomization of subjects, and replicate observers. These procedures operate to curb the tendency toward the unwitting bias and self-deception that awaits the best of scientists. Their use protects scientists against themselves and thus limits their deception of others. It should not be surprising that neglect of simple procedures of this kind evokes indignation or contempt from members of the research community who resent the waste of time and resources. As we shall see when we examine "disreputable" errors in science, investigators who ignore the methodological cautions defined as essential by their particular field do so at peril.

Systems of social control cannot, of course, depend on the internalization of norms alone to ensure reasonable levels of conformity. They must also provide for the detection of deviant behavior and for the exercise of sanctions when it occurs. In science, the institutionalized requirement that new contributions be reproducible is the cornerstone of the system of social control. It has two functions: deterrence and detection.

When socialization fails, as it every so often does, the fact that scientific contributions must be reproducible deters potential deviants who fear the consequences of being caught in the act of faking evidence. The requirement of reproducibility also provides a mechanism for detection of deviant acts both at the time they occur and in the future through efforts at independent replication of research findings. Scientists know that they will be held accountable for their work[4]—there is no statute of limitations on scientific fraud, forgery, and plagiarism—and that such deviant behavior not immediately detected will probably be revealed later when scientific interest in the subject is renewed or when new techniques are developed which make it possible to detect certain kinds of forged evidence. Thus, as we shall see in some detail, the Piltdown Man specimens were not decisively revealed as forgeries for some 40 years until a new form of X-ray analysis showed them to be much more recent than they were purported to be (J. Weiner, 1955; Oakley and Weiner, 1956; Millar, 1972).

Scientists also know in principle that the others working in their own and related lines of inquiry are all potential detectives: "Scientific inquiry is in effect subject to rigorous policing, to a degree perhaps unparalleled in any other field of human activity" (Merton, 1973:3i1). In the process of research, even long accepted contributions periodically come under renewed scrutiny, not by design but as a by-product of using them for further work. Error and deception can thus be uncovered even without intent. (For a case of such apparently inadvertent detection in microbiology, see Rosenkranz and Ellner, 1969.) The requirement of reproducibility therefore serves not only to deter departures from cognitive and moral norms but also makes for the detection of error and deviance.

All scientific contributions are not of course equally reproducible. The potential for true replication varies greatly among the sciences according to their cognitive texture. It is plainly not as feasible to replicate certain findings in observational or largely nonexperimental sciences—such as astronomy, zoology, anthropology, and sociology—as it is in the experimental sciences of physics, chemistry, and genetics. Moreover there are reasons why duplicate findings in the nonexperimental sciences would not be expected; the intervening effects of maturation, social change, and testing effects, if the same subjects are used, all contribute to producing results differing from those first observed. Thus, the opportunity to engage in undetected deviant behavior (particularly in the manipulation of data to confirm one's hypothesis) in sciences of low reproducibility is greater than in the exact experimental sciences and mathematics.[5] (This is consistent with Hagstrom's impression that "fraud is more credible in 'field sciences' such as ethnography and geology" (1965:85).

In part, these differences among the sciences depend on the character of the phenomena dealt with and in part they depend on the level of precision of measurement attained in these fields. It is at least plausible to suppose that it is more difficult to forge or "trim"[6] data (as Babbage, 1975:178, put it) convincingly in fields where precise measurement is commonplace than in fields less given to precision. However, the parameters of expected findings are better established and it may often be relatively easy to predict what data should look like in the precise sciences, and this provides some help to the potential artful forger, but the requirement of reproducibility of results remains a constraint.

Just as the level of precision attained in the sciences affects the chances of uncovering deception, so it also affects the probability of detecting error. Nothing in the social and behavioral sciences remotely approaches the level of precision that often holds in the "exact sciences." By way of illustration, there is the famous case of a fruitful error based on precise measurement. As long ago as the late 1920s, chemists had determined the chemical and mass spectrographic atomic weights of the elements to the fifth decimal place. The physical chemist Harold Urey took the difference between the atomic weights of hydrogen seriously enough to draw the theoretical conclusion that something like heavy hydrogen had to exist in order to account for that difference. Urey's reasoning was sound: he searched for and found heavy hydrogen or deuterium in 1931. But it turned out that the original mass spectrographic atomic weight, as determined by F.W. Aston, was incorrect. Three years after Urey's discovery,

Aston discovered that the original mass spectrographic weight of 1.00778 had to be reduced to 1.00756. Since the conventionally accepted chemical atomic weight of hydrogen was 1.00777, Urey would never have looked for heavy hydrogen, had he known the "correct" weight of hydrogen (see Nobelstiftelsen, 1962:379).

The great differences in precision among fields of science means that the fields also differ in the scale of that gray area that divides acceptable from unacceptably sloppy scientific work. Research in the exact sciences that would be defined as excessively crude might through suitable transformations be defined as faultless, even elegant, in the social and behavioral sciences.

Scientific fields differ not only in the potentials but also in the actual extent of replication. This strong impression is not based on much systematic study of the extent of replication in the various sciences. But Sterling (1959) does report that not one paper published in three major psychology journals in 1955 and in another in 1956 replicated previous work. This extreme result is in contrast to the case for sciences such as physics, biochemistry, and genetics, where replication appears to be far more frequent, especially when the original findings presented are theoretically anomalous or important or both.[7] Critics of the social organization of science contend that in all fields insufficient incentives are provided for replication. And, of course, as long as reproducibility of scientific results remains an ideal not often realized in practice, it cannot serve as a deterrent to the "cooking" of data.

Other cognitive and social contexts may affect the frequency of replication in the various disciplines. It has been said that careful review and reproduction of proofs is rare in modern mathematics because, as one mathematician put it, "contemporary mathematics has become so abstract and fragmented that few people bother to look carefully for errors" (Zahler, 1976:98). Hagstrom has pointed out (1965:229ff) that mathematics is now so specialized that very few mathematicians are in a position to understand, much less to work through for themselves, a good deal of what goes on in the discipline. This, Hagstrom suggests, has created a form of anomie in that field which undermines both the system of social control and the system of evaluation and rewards. But within specialized fields, mathematicians do sometimes closely examine one another's work as illustrated by the recent strong criticisms levelled against "catastrophe theory." The models used in catastrophe theory have received great publicity and extraordinary claims have been made for their applicability to practical problems. As a result, mathematicians who ordinarily confine attention to their own esoterica have been motivated to review the models and to conclude along with their colleague Mark Kac that the claims made for the theory "represent the height of scientific irresponsibility . . . [and] the applications to the social sciences [are] exaggerated and not wholly honest" (Kolata, 1977:350). Perhaps cases involving both the credibility of the field and public policy make for the extended and intensified exercise of organized skepticism.

The incentives for replication implied in the case of catastrophe theory may be more general. Scientific contributions with direct implications for public policy tend to be scrutinized with more than usual care as conflicting values and interests reinforce the search for error or distortion in the work of contending groups. Conspicuous recent cases include studies of heredity and intelligence in genetics and the behavioral sciences and the establishing of acceptable levels of nuclear radiation in the physical and biological sciences. Some claim that the value preferences are especially apt to affect the actual conduct of such researches and that they consequently get more careful scrutiny than usual. The psychologist Leon Kamen disagrees and goes so far as to say that "it's relatively easy to fake it and get away with it, particularly if it matches everybody's preconceptions" (quoted in *New York Times,* January 23, 1977:44). There is no good evidence for or against this assertion. But it should be possible to compare the frequency of replication in research on problems which are variously consequential for public policy.

Perhaps the most important determinant of the probability of replication in the sciences is the assessed significance of contributions. Unsystematic observation of the behavior of scientists suggests that the speed and frequency of replication are directly related to the perceived importance of the reported finding or idea, and this is so, though perhaps not equally so, both when the original contributor is well known and trusted and when he is an unknown neophyte. The experiments by C.S. Wu and her collaborators which showed that parity was not conserved in weak interactions were repeated in numerous laboratories in the United States and elsewhere within days after news of the experiments was released (Bernstein, 1962). Since physicists had long taken the conservation of parity to be universal, until the theoretical contribution of Lee and Yang, these were experiments of immense significance. Similarly the experimental demonstration of what has come to be known as the Mössbauer Effect (a method of producing gamma rays with a precise and predictable wave length) set off a rush among physicists to replicate Rudolf Mössbauer's procedures. That Mössbauer was a youthful unknown may have contributed to the sense of some physicists that they had to judge the reliability of his findings independently. But it was also true that many had tried before to obtain radiation, had gotten poor results, and Mössbauer's procedure, both simple and precise, created "a sensation" in the field (Nobelstiftelsen, 1972:473).

All this suggests that the more consequential the scientific result, the more immediately efforts are mounted to reproduce it and thus the greater the probability that error or deception can be detected. From the standpoint of the system of social control, this is an efficient pattern for deploying scarce resources. Since almost by definition important contributions form the basis for further research, it is efficient to have them become the focus for attempted replication. Other less innovative contributions may in fact escape replication and remain in the literature unchallenged. With limited resources for replication, this would seem to be about as good a criterion as any for deciding whether to replicate.

So far, we have assumed that replication of scientific work will generally detect error or deceptive practice if they are present. This need be so only to a limited extent. The fact that a set of experiments cannot be reproduced, as Medawar (1976:6) has pointed out, need not be "irremediably damaging" to the originating scientist. When this happens, the contributors must explain why the results could not be reproduced. When further attempts to replicate fail, it still will not be evident whether willful deception has occurred or whether the replicators have erred in some unknown fashion. There is no "litmus paper" test that differentiates error from fraud, as one scientist has put it. The main outcome of such attempts is that the original findings are put in question, which from the standpoint of the extension of certified knowledge, is mainly what is required.

When efforts to replicate continually fail, scientists still remain reluctant to assume that a fraud has been perpetrated. The imputation of fraud is often little more than a residual interpretation of the inability to reproduce the original findings. That is, after having been unable to identify the error(s) that may have led to the reported findings, the critical observer might be led to conclude that deliberate deception may be involved. But without direct evidence of fraud or data manipulation, such serious charges, though sometimes privately expressed, will not be made publicly.

Peter Medawar's confession of his own reluctance to call William Summerlin's work into question is revealing in just this regard.

> I found myself lacking in moral courage. Summerlin once demonstrated to our assembled board [Medawar was a member of the board of visitors of the Sloan Kettering where Summerlin worked] a rabbit which he said had received from a human being . . . a corneal graft. . . . Through a perfectly transparent eye this rabbit looked at the board with a candid and unwavering gaze of which only a rabbit with an absolutely clear conscience is capable. I could not believe that this rabbit had received a graft of any kind . . . because the pattern of blood vessels in the ring around the cornea was in no way disturbed. Nevertheless I simply lacked the moral courage to say at the time that I thought we were the victims of a hoax or confidence trick. [Medawar, 1976:6]

Medawar goes on to locate his reluctance to announce fraud within a social context of noblesse oblige and a cognitive context of ambiguity: "Very senior scientists do not like trampling on their juniors in public. Besides it was still possible that for some reason, 'trivial' or otherwise, the story was true."

Although the system for detecting these forms of deviant behavior is reasonably effective in science, it is sometimes not clear, as we note from Medawar's remark, whether error or forgery of evidence has occurred and if it has, who was responsible for it. In view of their membership in a moral community, scientists understandably prefer to assume that error rather than fraud accounts for the unreproducible results.

There is no institutionalized role in the social system of control which is charged with the responsibility for discriminating fraud from error; this responsibility is distributed throughout the system. On occasion, individual scientists will act to the full in accord with the norm of organized skepticism and take it upon themselves to go back to the original records of procedures and data when efforts to replicate fail. Under the norm of universalism, which implies that scientific results should not be linked with the idiosyncratic personal attributes of this or that scientist, and under the norm of organized skepticism which requires that scientific results should be open to exacting criticism, the original discoverers of the unreproduced results can only permit the proposed reexamination. To deny access to the materials would also violate the norm of communality which requires such access, particularly after the publication of findings (Ben-David, 1977:265). It would, moreover, amount to prima facie evidence of guilt. Such a close examination of original data by G.K. Noble of the American Museum of Natural History proved to be the undoing of Paul Kammerer. Noble found that Kammerer's specimen toad had been colored with an india ink-like substance to make it appear that the toad had inherited an acquired characteristic—the so-called nuptial pad usually found only in another species, the midwife toad. (See Goldschmidt, 1959; Zirkle, 1954; Koestler, 1972; Gould, 1972, for diverse accounts of Kammerer's possible involvement in the forgery.)[8]

As we noted earlier, systems of social control must also provide for the exercise of sanctions when deviant behavior is discovered. That part of the system in science is far less organized and less formal than in the far from exacting institutional arrangements found in other professions. There are no institutionalized parallels to the malpractice review panels of bar associations or county and state medical societies and no formal system for meting out penalties for malpractice in science. The system is, as the sociologist of law Donald Black observes, "informal and decentralized, rarely involving litigation or formal action of any kind" (1976:80). In part, this may be related to the circumstance that, outside the domain of applied science, scientists have no clients whose rights require immediate protection. It may also reflect the circumstance that only plagiarism, among the deviant acts in science, is in clear-cut violation of the law. In practice, this means that one set of sanctions for deviant behavior in science consists largely of expressions of resentment, contempt, antipathy, and indignation, with attendant consequences for the deviant. While these sanctions may at first seem weak compared to those occasionally, even rarely, imposed on other deviant professionals (such as fines and imprisonment), research scientists, whose reference groups are largely limited to others like themselves, have little left if they lose their reputation for being trustworthy. Such informal sanctions also gain force by the fact that researchers in the same specialties are apt to know one another. Rejection by respected colleagues who are themselves widely known and respected carries far more sanctioning weight than that issuing from anonymous aggregates.

In cases socially defined as extreme departures from the norms–forgery, plagiarism, and data manipulation–scientists can and do exercise the ultimate sanction of expulsion from the community. Science is no longer an occupation of amateurs and it is rarely possible to practice on one's own without affiliation with a university or laboratory and without financial support for research. Being barred from a position in a research organization or being cut off from the means of scientific production essentially spell the end of an investigator's career. It is unlikely, given the comparatively fast pace of scientific work, that an offending scientist could, as it were, "serve his time," restore his credibility, and be readmitted into the scientific community.

The system of social control in science is a composite of mechanisms for detecting error and deviant behavior (through the exercise of organized skepticism and the requirement for reproducibility) and mechanisms which provide for the sanctioning of communally defined deviance. It is a system which depends both on the socialization of individual scientists and on the "public and testable character of science" (See Merton, 1973:311). How well, then, does the control system operate? How often do scientists flout the norms and engage in behavior socially defined as deviant?

THE INCIDENCE OF DEVIANT BEHAVIOR IN SCIENCE

Almost all those who have bothered to look conclude that seriously deviant behavior in science is rare. Scientists themselves repeatedly note this as fact. The outspoken molecular biologist, James D. Watson remarks, "One's mind never considers fraud as a possibility" (*New York Times,* December 16, 1975:56). His mentor, Salvador Luria, has much the same impression, "Cheating in science is admittedly . . . rare, or at least . . . rarely discovered" (1975:16). Sociologists of science concur. Some years ago Merton referred to "the virtual absence of fraud in the annals of science" (1973:276, 311) and Hagstrom has stated that "serious forms of fraud . . . are rare in science" (1965:85).

Yet these impressions are just that–impressions. The fact is that no comprehensive quantitative data have been collected on the extent of deviant behavior in science or on its distribution. Comparisons of its frequency with deviant behavior in other domains must therefore be made only on the obviously inadequate basis of the cases which have come to public notice. Taking the various forms of seriously deviant behavior together,[9] that is, forgery, data manipulation, data suppression, and plagiarism–willful acts of deceit–the known cases number perhaps several hundred in a cumulative population of research scientists which, over the generations, number something on the order of more than a million, each at work over a span of years.

Were the data available, useful comparisons would deal not with deviant behavior of all kinds but with rates of occupationally-specific deviant behavior. Such data as exist are insufficiently disaggregated to compare, for example, the rates of embezzlement among bank officials, serious malpractice among physicians, and the contriving of fake evidence among scientists.

In the absence of statistics on deviant behavior in science, one can only speculate about its actual extent and distribution. We do not know for example what the relationship is between the few recorded cases and the "true" or underlying distribution from which they are drawn. There are reasons to suppose that the known cases are indeed a fraction of the number of actual cases. For one thing, many scientists can report cases they know of which were not publicized. Luria, for example, reports that he knows of two cases "in which highly respected scientists had to retract findings reported from their laboratories because they discovered that these findings had been manufactured by one of their collaborators" (1975:16).

There are other reasons for assuming that deviant behavior in science is an iceberg phenomenon. As I noted earlier, the detection system of science is directed toward identifying error as well as deception. Since the record shows that a number of (honest) errors have persisted for some time in scientific literature, it is likely that some number of deceptions have also remained undiscovered in the literature and that some subset of these may surface in the future. By way of example of persisting error, geneticists believed for some time that there were 48 human chromosomes (24 pairs); it was not until 1956 that Tjio and Levan looked once again at the tangle of strands which are chromosomes and found to their own and others' surprise not 48 but 46 (23 pairs) (Nobelstiftelsen, 1962:253). The survival of error is in itself a subject for further investigation; here the point is that such survival leads to the inference that deceptions may also remain intact and in equally unknown numbers.

Although condemned to the qualitative analysis of particular cases, we can turn to the general subject of deviant behavior in an effort to lay the groundwork for developing quantitative data on deviant behavior in science. Quantitative studies of deviant behavior generally rely on three kinds of data: official statistics, statistics based on self-reports, and victimization statistics. We need not review the well-known ample evidence that official crime statistics are notoriously inadequate and biased (President's Commission on Law Enforcement, 1967). Such data are, as I have noted, altogether absent in science. Self-reports of deviant behavior have shortcomings. They are, for example, not altogether reliable, with individuals not being consistent in reporting their own deviant acts. But self-reports generally do show higher rates of deviant behavior than the official statistics (see Reiss, 1973). In science self-reported data promise to produce far more systematic information than has been previously available, especially on questions dealing with the less extreme kinds of aberrant behavior.[10] Victimization statistics, as we shall see, should also prove useful in estimating the frequency of theft of scientific ideas although these too have their distinctive shortcomings. Individual scientists do not always know of cases in which their ideas or work have been "pinched," as J.D. Watson is wont to say, and scientists sometimes mistake authentic multiple and independent discoveries for cases of plagiarism (see Merton, 1973).

Informants' estimates are a fourth source of data about the rates of deviant behavior that might be collected. Efforts have recently been made to obtain data of this kind (Mahoney and Kimper, 1976; St. James-Roberts, 1976a, 1976b)[11] but the samples are so small and unreliable as to preclude serious analysis. Since there are theoretical reasons for supposing that the perceived rate of deviance affects individual proclivities to deviate, estimates by informants are not without interest.

In the absence of the kinds of comprehensive statistical information that would allow for systematic review, we can nevertheless raise some questions about the distribution of various forms of deviant behavior in science.

Cases of fraud in science–the outright fabrication of data–do indeed seem to be rare. Among the best documented is the Piltdown Man forgery by Charles Dawson, an amateur archeologist and geologist, which came into view in 1912 when Dawson took some specimens to Smith Woodward, keeper of geology of the Natural History Museum in London. They came, he said, from Barkham Manor, Piltdown, in Sussex and were found when workmen were digging to make some pathways (see J. Weiner, 1955; Oakley and Weiner, 1955; Millar, 1972). From the beginning doubts were expressed about the find, particularly with regard to the question whether the bones were wholly those of a fossil man or whether some also came from a fossil ape. A.R. Wallace, the independent codiscoverer with Charles Darwin of natural selection as the principal mechanism of evolution, dismissed the find out of hand, remarking that "The Piltdown skull does not prove much if anything" (*Nature* 97, June 22, 1916:337). But most scientists in the field came to believe that the find was authentic since "there was nothing to contradict it in the few other human fossils known at the time. Piltdown Man fitted in rather well as a more primitive human being than either Java Man or Heidelberg Man" (Oakley and Weiner, 1956:574). As archeological evidence from other parts of the world accumulated, Piltdown Man seemed increasingly anomalous. As I noted, the development of new X-ray techniques decisively demonstrated that the "fossil" teeth had been artificially ground down. This demonstration finally made sense of the puzzling results of efforts in 1953 to date the skull. At that time, scientists were confused by the apparent fact that parts of the skull were ancient and others were not.

For our purposes, two aspects of the case deserve further notice. First, Dawson himself was not a professional scientist. He obviously knew enough science to produce a convincing forgery but had not been socialized into the scientific tradition and did not count himself, nor was he counted by others, as a member of the scientific community. That this peripheral status may have contributed to his fraudulent behavior is at least plausible, but of course this provides no secure basis for generalization. Similar kinds of fraud have also involved neophytes or peripheral members of the scientific community. For example, the suspect findings reported by the Harvard immunologist, David Dressler, have been attributed to his student assistant (see Note 2 for bibliography). It has also been suggested that an assistant was responsible for the Kammerer fraud of inking the toad specimen (though this interpretation can scarcely account for Kammerer's reluctance to have his specimen closely examined) (Goldschmidt, 1949; Koestler, 1972). But the Summerlin and Gullis cases of admitted fraud (see Note 2) demonstrate that assistants or "outsiders" are by no means always the culpable ones. The case studies can serve only to raise questions about the kinds of research scientists who engage in such extreme deviant behavior.

The Piltdown forgery exhibits another feature deserving emphasis. Like other cases of subsequently demonstrated fraud, it was subject to considerable skepticism from the beginning. This is not altogether surprising since the more theoretically unexpected a reported scientific finding, the more likely it is to be questioned, the more intensively the evidence will be examined and, consequently, the more likely that error or deception will be uncovered. But the absence of any cases of subsequently detected fraud which did not meet with considerable skepticism from the outset suggests that the detection system of science may work reasonably well.

The theft of scientific ideas or plagiarism is often reported as far more frequent than fraud, while insinuations of plagiarism are of course quite common. Merton has detailed a number of cases involving theft and accusations of theft in science as well as other kinds of deviant behavior deriving from efforts to assure one's property rights in science (1973:321ff). Newton, for example, packed the committee established by the Royal Society to adjudicate rival claims between himself and Leibniz for priority in the calculus and proceeded to write the anonymous preface to the committee's report as we know from its having been drafted in his own handwriting. There is every indication that both Leibniz and Newton independently developed the calculus, despite the factional charges of plagiarism. But Newton's intense concern to establish his unique claim to what he knew to be a major mathematical contribution evidently led him to adopt such deviant measures of deception.

The theft of published work is presumably less frequent than the theft of ideas whose ownership has not been decisively established in print. It is, after all, easier to steal unpublished than published ideas and material (Hagstrom, 1965:86). It is not surprising then that recent cases of alleged plagiarism of published scientific work involve the theft of photographs and figures, which one could argue were original, rather than text. (See Editorial Board, *Science* 134(September 29, 1961):946-47.)

Some rough estimates are available of the extent of "victimization" of scientists through the inadequate recognition of their rights to scientific property. Hagstrom (1974:9) reports that a quarter of the 1,309 academic mathematicians, statisticians, physicists, chemists, and biologists in his sample reported that "another scientist [had] published results [I] published earlier without referring to [my] work" even though he probably knew of it. The likelihood of honest but self-serving misperceptions in such cases does not go unnoticed.

Opportunities to plagiarize published work are equally distributed (insofar as the publications themselves are generally available) but there are distinct differences among scientists in their opportunities to pilfer unpublished work. Scientists who serve as referees for journals, peer reviewers for granting agencies, and other kinds of gatekeepers have greater opportunity to deviate in this way. This is all the more the case since the identity of scientists in gatekeeping roles is often kept confidential. But, as we have noted in other connections, opportunity need not be converted into action. If unsocialized Hobbesian men and women were involved, we would expect higher rates of plagiarism among scientists occupying gatekeeping positions than among those not in these structural positions. But we note the countervailing fact that gatekeepers have tended to be established scientists who have demonstrated their ability to identify, develop, and carry through research on their own,[12] thus having less incentive than neophytes to engage in such behavior.

Although plagiarism is plainly proscribed in science, as we shall see here and later on, the norms of scientific property are far less clear when it comes to the ownership of unpublished ideas, problems, and findings. Watson's (1968) account of the discovery of the helical structure of DNA illustrates the presence of gray areas in the norms and etiquette of science. Watson maintains that British and American researchers differ in their willingness to cede ownership to those who have established some proprietary rights to scientific *problems;* Watson's impression is that the British are less predatory than the Americans. He also reports that Max Perutz informed him of Rosalind Franklin's progress in the X-ray diffraction of DNA which Perutz had learned of from a progress report on the work at King's College. But Watson's own account lacks the kind of systematic documentation required to establish the diagnostically essential details. Perutz (1969) has since written that the report to which Watson referred was not confidential and contained no information Watson had not already obtained from Franklin herself. The specific case illuminates the general point: even for so seemingly self-evident a kind of deviant behavior as plagiarism from unpublished work, the ambiguity of norms and the frequent obscuring of basic details of behavior combine to make it difficult to determine whether deviance has actually occurred. It is therefore all the more hazardous to estimate rates of plagiarism in science from the skimpy evidence that is available.

There is somewhat better evidence on the extent to which scientists are secretive about their work. Sustained secrecy violates the norm of communism which, as I have noted, requires that scientists make their work freely available to peers and in effect (if not with deliberate purpose) to exchange such communication for the basic reward of recognition by those peers and by the larger scientific community (Merton, 1973; Hagstrom, 1965; Storer, 1966). The workings of the norm of communism as supported by the reward system of science have been summarized as follows:

(1) The institutionalized pressure for public diffusion of one's scientific work is "reinforced by the institutional goal of advancing the boundaries of knowledge and by the incentive of recognition which is, of course, contingent upon publication" (Merton, 1973:274);

(2) There is the correlative obligation, within the institutional structure of science, for the user of that freely published knowledge to make open reference to the sources to which he is indebted; not to do so is to incur the sanctions visited upon those judged guilty of stealing another's intellectual property (i.e., plagiary); and

(3) The institutionalized reciprocity of incentives for conformity and sanctions for nonconformity were required to work as "part of the public domain . . . [through] the imperative for communication of findings" (Merton 1976:48).

It should be emphasized, moreover, that the norm does not apply equally to all phases of scientific research. Scientists are not obliged to make all the details of their research available until they judge that it is sufficiently advanced to be ready for competent evaluation by peers. What Ben-David has noted about the norms of universalism, disinterestedness, and organized skepticism holds also for the norm of communism: "[the] norms apply only to the evaluation of results to be made public, while hunches are private and are not intended, and usually are not even allowed to be published" (Ben-David 1977:265). This basic distinction between the private and public phases of scientific work requires some emphasis since some observers have concluded that the unwillingness of some scientists to "tell all" before they have finished a piece of research testifies that the norm of communism is thoroughly ignored in practice. (On these stages of research, see Gaston, 1973:122.)

Some evidence indicates that the norm of sharing information serves to pattern much of what takes place even before scientists "are ready to publish." Hagstrom (1974:9, calculated from Table 6) and Sullivan (1975:238) both found that more than four-fifths of their substantial samples of American scientists reported "they would feel quite safe in discussing [their] current research with [all or most] persons doing similar work in other institutions." And these responses refer to the private phase of research before the scientists "are ready to publish." In his study of English high energy physicists, Gaston (1973:117-118) introduced much more relaxed criteria of secrecy, asking whether there was "*anyone* with whom you would not discuss your work [at] certain stages of [your] research." Even so, by the criterion of reluctance to discuss one's work with even a single other scientist (who might presumably appropriate or otherwise misapply the information), 41% of the English physicists report that they would not engage in such "secretive behavior."

If the theft of unpublished research were common, it would seem unlikely that such large proportions of scientists would be willing to discuss their work openly. However, as Hagstrom has observed (1965:88), "secrecy itself must usually be kept secret" since it contravenes one of the principal norms of science and therefore responses of the kind reported here are not easy to interpret.

Blisset provides another data set, comprised of the reports by 789 academic mathematicians, physicists, astronomers, chemists, biologists, and geologists on the perceived behavior of other scientists. He reports certain differences between these fields in the extent of perceived departures from the norm of organized skepticism. He finds, for example, that a high of about 52% of the chemists rejected the statement that "scientists are skeptical even about their own findings until other scientists have evaluated them" as compared with a low of 35% of the physicists who did so (Blisset, 1972:219). He also reports field differences in the extent to which scientists believe that their colleagues violate the norm of universalism. About 65% of astronomers, chemists, geologists, and biologists rejected the extremely worded statement that the "acceptance or nonacceptance of scientific evidence does not *in any way* depend upon the social position of the one who submits it (that is, his institutional affiliation [university or laboratory], his *degree of recognition,* those under whom he has studied or worked" as against 42% of the mathematicians (1972:215, italics added). It is not altogether surprising that this extreme formulation of the norm of universalism—"in any way" rather than "significantly depends"—should elicit responses indicating numerical minorities adhering to it in their behavior. The data suggest that, *as stated* in extreme form, the norm of universalism may serve as an ideal rather than a working norm of science.[13]

Finally, I know of no quantitative data sets on the incidence of departures from the cognitive norms of science, either the generic ones prescribing empirical confirmability, refutability, and logical consistency, or the norms specific to research specialties which express for a given time, appropriate problems, theoretical orientations, methodological procedures, and modes of analysis. It should be possible to assemble such data by expert analysis of the contents of scientific journals and symposia, especially those which are unrefereed and so have not already been vetted for departures from cognitive norms.

So far I have had little to say about which scientists are more apt to deviate but have emphasized instead the incidence of various kinds of deviant behavior. Are rank-and-file scientists more or less apt than eminent scientists to deviate from the norms? D. Black (1976:81-2) and Mulkay (1971:208) suggest that insofar as eminent scientists enjoy a certain immunity from sanctions, they may be freer to depart from the norms. At best, the evidence is sketchy. But whether the Black-Mulkay hunch is correct or not, larger proportions of actual instances of deviant behavior should be publicly identified for outstanding scientists than for rank-and-file scientists, since their lives and works attract far more intense and enduring attention. This holds not only during their lifetimes but, for the greatest among them, long afterwards.

The sustained historical interest in the giants of science, fueled by iconoclastic tendencies aiming to topple the high and mighty, should lead to frequent claims that they were given to breaking rules of various kinds, both cognitive and moral. Thus, it has been claimed that:

- Ptolemy did not in fact make the observations on the equinox which he reported but "slavishly copied Hipparchus to the point of forging observations to obtain agreement with Hipparchus' results" (Toomer, 1975:189). It is also claimed that his star catalogue in the *Almagest* copied Hipparchus. The French astronomer Jean Baptiste Delambre made these charges in the early 19th century and they have been insistently repeated by the American physicist, R.R. Newton (see Gingerich, 1976).
- Galileo did not do certain experiments he claimed to have done for he could not have obtained the reported results. The doubt was first expressed by Père Marin Mersenne in the 17th century (Cohen 1957:14). This was repeated in the 20th century by the historian of science Alexander Koyré (1953).
- Isaac Newton is accused of having violated various cognitive and moral norms, of having "adjusted" his calculations on the velocity of sound and on the precession of the equinoxes, and of having altered the correlation of the value of g with the distance from the moon to make it agree precisely with theory (Westfall, 1973a).
- Mendel, according to the statistician R.A. Fisher (1936), is likely not to have achieved the results he reports since the agreement with theoretical expectation is far too close.
- And, finally, Sigmund Freud is said to have "lied" about or perhaps massively repressed the facts of the discovery of the Oedipus Complex (Cioffi, 1974, 1976).

This truncated inventory of accusations of deviant behavior levelled against the giants of science is arresting but, as one might suspect, the charges turn out to be excessively simplified. Let us review the cases in turn.

- The historian of ancient astronomy, and editor of Ptolemy's works, Otto Neugebauer (1970:191-206; 1975) dismisses the claim that Ptolemy had taken over Hipparchus's much smaller star catalogue. And another historian of astronomy, Owen Gingerich (1976:477), maintains that the accusations are anachronistic, only going to show that the critic R.R. Newton fails to understand that error theory was unknown in Ptolemy's time.
- Evidence indicates that Galileo could have done the reported experiments. They were in fact repeated by T.B. Settle who found that "it definitely was technically feasible" for Galileo to have done them and gotten the reported results (1961:19). Of more general significance, I.B.

Cohen (1957) directs our attention to the standards of reporting scientific work that obtained in Galileo's time which of course differ from standards of a much later time. Experiments were secondary to mathematics and where experimental data differed somewhat from the expected results, the differences were considered "not worth mentioning." Thus even if this was a case of reporting modified data, it did not constitute fraud but rather a kind of selective reporting, quite in keeping with the cognitive standards of the time; in short, the charge itself is anachronistic.

- Newton, it has been suggested, offered the corrections to the velocity of sound as hypotheses to account for the discrepancy between theory and experimental results (McHugh, 1973). But Westfall (1973) questions the evidence for this and maintains that Newton presented his calculations as quantitatively exact. Case still pending.
- Leslie Dunn (1965) and Sewall Wright (1966), two biologists of stature, reject the hypothesis that Mendel presented fraudulent data, indicating (just as we have seen in the cases of Ptolemy and Galileo) that Mendel's procedures must be understood in the context of what was known *at the time* about probability statistics. Dunn and Wright observe that the tallies Mendel made were doubtlessly biased but that this did not at all involve fraud. R.A. Fisher failed to allow for the cumulative effects of Mendel's unwitting tendency to favor expected results in the tallies which may have led him to re-tally only the data which did not fit in with his expectations. After all, the double-blind design had yet to be invented. Wright also notes that the tallies were and are difficult to do. Both also remark on the fact that were Mendel bent on making a case through fraud, he would "hardly" have reported the extreme cases he did (Wright, 1966:174; Dunn, 1965:194).
- As for Freud's repression of the sources of Oedipal theory, it is only Cioffi's claim that most patients did not tell Freud stories of imaginary seductions and that those who did, did not name their parents. No independent examination of the required evidence has been made to confirm or refute Cioffi's (1974, 1976) claim.

What then can we conclude from these episodes about forms of deviant behavior by these giants among scientists? And what do these cases tell us about processes of evaluation of behavior in science? First, since deviant behavior is socially defined, the question of its occurrence must be judged in the context of its time. Acts which appear to be deviant today may not have been so by earlier standards of procedure and proof. Judging historical figures and events of another day by modern standards is a dangerous error well known to historians (they call it "presentism") but this error still turns up in the history of science. Second, the facts of these cases are sufficiently debatable and the documentation too slender to make the evidence of seriously deviant behavior persuasive. Third, the possible "guilt or innocence" of these scientists is of less theoretical interest to us than the apparent fact, expressed by these limiting cases, that everyone in science, including its heroes, is fair game for critical appraisal in the mode of organized skepticism. The pattern of trying to make one's mark in science by toppling contemporary authorities from their pedestals is well known: the David-and-Goliath pattern. It appears that the heroes of science are less often protected from searching criticism than heroes in other domains by being elevated to the plane of the Durkheimian sacred. Fourth, and most in point, these alleged behaviors by the giants of science could be condemned as startling and offensive misbehavior only if they were being judged in terms of shared moral and cognitive norms.

We do not know the responses of contemporary scientists to such historical episodes: how many of these are known to them; whether and how these episodes affect their own definition of norms and acceptable behavior; or whether these episodes matter at all to them. Many scientists are ahistorical in the sense that the history of their fields holds little interest for them. They tend to be future-oriented in their roles as scientists, concerned primarily with the moving frontiers of research. What they need to know about the past in order to get on with their work has been largely incorporated into current formulations. As a result, the history of science remains peripheral. (See Zuckerman and Merton in Merton 1973:506ff.) Since episodes of the kind reported here seem to have little relevance for ongoing work in contemporary science, they may hold no more than antiquarian interest for scientists.

Having noted the virtual absence of systematic data on the incidence and distribution of deviant behavior in science, we briefly consider possible reasons for this being so.

ON THE ABSENCE OF SOCIAL BOOKKEEPING DATA ON DEVIANCE IN SCIENCE

There is no formal rationale for the absence of systematic records of deviant behavior in science, which contrasts even with the limited recording of such data in the practicing professions of law, medicine, and the ministry. Still, the fact is that such records have not been kept.

This may be so in part because scientists are themselves the primary consumers of one another's products and services. Outside the special world of science-based technology (and even there the difference may not be decisive in view of the role of scientist-managers in high-technology firms), scientists, unlike practicing professionals, typically have "clients" who are qualified to appraise the products and services they receive, namely, their fellow scientists. This may account for the absence of institutionalized arrangements in science for protecting clients from unscrupulous practitioners.

Along with this comparative infrequency of lay clients, the institutionalized reward system has scientists receiving their prime rewards (all other rewards deriving from it) from recognition for their work from peers competent to judge it (see Merton, 1973; Hagstrom, 1965; Storer, 1966; and Mulkay, 1972a, on the exchange of scientific contributions for "competent response," as Storer puts it). As we shall see in a little more detail, seeking prime recognition for one's scientific work from a laity unqualified to judge it is defined as violating the norm of disinterestedness in science. [14] The lay society becomes an appropriate audience only when scientists are pleading the cause of social support of science or when they are accounting for the directions that scientific research is taking.

These structural circumstances may also help explain the absence in science, again in contrast to the practicing professions, of a formal code of professional ethics and a body of pertinent law (see Ravetz, 1971: Chapter 11). Without such sets of formal rules administered by some institutionalized groups charged with adjudicating cases of alleged deviant behavior and meting out sanctions for such behavior, there is no basis for a systematic record of indictments and dispositions. As Ben-David has pointedly observed, the role of official scientific academies, such as the Royal Society of London and the Académie des Sciences in Paris, gradually evolved into their becoming "in practice organizations for the public and official recognition of the contributions of individual scientists" (1977:250). Even so, the scientific academies have not adopted the related function of serving as agencies of social control (except with respect to the special case of occasionally dealing with conflicting claims to priority of discovery).

Contributing further to the absence of social bookkeeping data on deviance in science is the circumstance that among the array of departures from the norms of science only one qualifies unambiguously as a violation of the law. That one, of course, is plagiarism. But the few cases of plagiarism in science brought to the courts can provide no adequate basis for estimating the general frequency even of this one kind of deviance. And even these few cases are apt to be unrepresentative, largely involving scientific contributions which happen to be financially consequential.

Taken together, these institutional characteristics may help explain why it is that science, which in its principal activity of research is given to the careful formulation and preservation of detailed records, has not introduced systematic procedures for keeping records of deviant behavior.

FORMS OF DEVIANT BEHAVIOR IN SCIENCE

We have seen that deviant behavior in science involves departures from the composite of cognitive and moral norms that form a spectrum differing in seriousness.

In accord with Durkheimian tradition, acts which violate certain norms evoke deep moral indignation and outrage. Thus when the immunologist Peter Medawar (1976:6) writes that fellow scientists considered it "heinous" for William Summerlin to have painted the skin of a mouse to show that he had effected a successful skin graft between genetically different animals and when the molecular biologist Salvador Luria (1975:15) writes that "falsified scientific findings . . . [are] scandals in science . . . and have a quality of desecration about them," it would appear that the moral consensus has been seriously breached. Such strongly hostile reactions may in turn contribute in unknown degree to the process of social control by reaffirming the moral validity of the norms.

Deviations from Cognitive Norms

It is useful to think of the cognitive norms of science as being of two kinds: generic methodological canons and specific cognitive criteria. The generic canons refer to shared criteria of what is to be taken as satisfactory empirical evidence and to the criterion of logical consistency. The general criteria are tacitly or explicitly utilized in the sciences and transcend even strong differences of scientific judgment on specific cognitive issues. As Scheffler (1967) has observed, the most general cognitive norms have long remained in force to serve as standards for evaluating scientific work even when there appears to be incommensurability of scientific orientations.

The second class of cognitive norms is more or less specific to fields of scientific inquiry. These norms express the shared preferences of scientists, in the given time, place, and discipline, for particular problems, theoretical orientations, methods, and types of interpretation. Norms of this kind are caught up in Kuhn's (1970:181-191) conception of cognitive commitments that are shared by those adhering to the same disciplinary matrix (specialty group). He observes that such commitments include shared exemplars, symbolic generalizations, heuristic models and values, and that they provide criteria for assessing contributions to the scientific field.

Even "revolutionary" changes in science turn out to involve the rejection of comparatively specific cognitive frameworks and their replacement by others rather than the rejection of the more general methodological canons of empirical evidence and logical consistency. When one examines cognitive developments that have been described as revolutionizing a field of inquiry, one finds profound differences obtaining within common general frameworks. The radical changes can be limited to setting forth an unorthodox basic idea or finding or may set out entirely new lines of investigation, with ramifying implications. By way of example, the theoretical contributions by Lee and Yang have been defined as revolutionary since they showed that the law of parity conservation is not universal in physics as had long been thought. Nevertheless, this basic change represented no fundamental break with logico-experimental criteria. The same holds true for the pathbreaking demonstration by the geneticist Joshua Lederberg and the biochemist Edward Tatum that, contrary to the long-held "dogma" set forth in the "founding papers of modern bacteriology" that bacteria merely divided (they were labeled "fission fungi"), bacteria reproduced sexually. This changed biologists' ideas about an entire class of organisms, about the scope of evolutionary adaptation, and formed the basis of the new specialty of bacterial genetics.

The radically new conceptions of nonconservation of parity and of sexual recombination in bacteria, then, with all their major cognitive consequences, were developed within the general methodological framework of empirical evidence and logical consistency. Such positively valued innovations in science contrast with efforts at innovation which involve the rejection of these general methodological standards as well as of particular doctrines or ideas. Scientists distinguish between kinds of cognitive innovation, defining some as deserving serious attention (even if they should turn out to be mistaken) and others as the work of fools or charlatans. That distinction has to do with the kinds of challenges to generic and specific cognitive criteria.

It appears that science is neither as resistant to new ideas, as Mulkay (1969, 1976) sometimes seems to imply, nor as open to innovation as many scientists would like to believe. Plainly, resistance to fundamentally new ideas is not absent (see, for example, Barber, 1961). But as indicated in Cole's (1970) citation analysis of the frequency of resistance, defined as "delayed recognition," it may not be as pervasive as is sometimes assumed.

Reputable and Disreputable Errors in Science

Scientists implicitly discriminate "reputable" from "disreputable" errors.[15] By reputable errors we mean those that occur in spite of investigators having lived up to the prevailing methodological rules of the game and of having taken the normatively accepted procedural precautions against error. When such errors are eventually detected, they do not become occasions for condemning the investigators responsible for them. They are regarded as reflecting unavoidable hazards of research. In contrast, disreputable errors are those resulting from the neglect or violation of methodological canons and procedural precautions. Once spotted, they damage the standing and reputation of the scientist who has fallen into error. The peer response ranges from irritation to downright contempt for the scientist who has wasted time and resources of others in the scientific community who found it necessary to track down and understand errors that "should not have been committed in the first place."

Disreputable error in science is the counterpart to legal negligence: "the omission to do something which a reasonable man, guided by . . . ordinary considerations . . . would do or the doing of something which a reasonable and prudent man would not do" (H.C. Black, 1933:1229). But while the law goes on to consider "willful negligence," that is, "reckless disregard" or "determination not to perform a known duty" (*ibid:* 1234), as more serious than ordinary or inadvertent negligence, scientists adopt the more severe position of not distinguishing between the two. Sloppy craftsmanship is just that, whether the investigator intended it or not. Ignorance of cognitive (technical) norms or accepted scientific practice is considered no excuse for disreputable error.

Disreputable error includes spurious cognitive claims made on the basis of contaminated samples and experimental artifacts, including the wide range of what are called experimenter effects (see T. Barber, 1973). Extreme examples of this class of error have been labeled "pathological science" by the physicist Irving Langmuir (1953). They are characterized, he observes, not only by neglect of proper procedure but also by self-deception on the part of investigators too eager to make original contributions.

Examples of disreputable error are numerous and many scientists have their own list of favorites. The discovery of "polywater" is perhaps a classic (though comparatively recent) case of contamination of data and artifactual results. In 1970, a Russian chemist, Boris Deryagin, claimed to have observed a new form of water which was gelatinous and highly resistant to boiling or freezing. Since water is by far the most abundant compound and has long been closely studied, it is understandable that the announced discovery of a new form of this ubiquitous substance created a sensation among chemists (while evoking extreme skepticism on the part of some of them). Polywater was a truly radical discovery for it was "so improbable, so contrary to nature's laws that only highly unorthodox theories [could] explain it" (Sullivan, 1970).

Within months of the announcement of Deryagin's findings, both American and British chemists (most of them established academic researchers) developed and published theoretical structures to account for the anomalous properties of polywater (Donohue, 1969; Allen and Kollman, 1970a, 1970b; Linnett, 1970). Experimentalists attempted to reproduce Deryagin's findings, most especially to produce enough polywater to subject it to chemical analysis. (Lippincott et al., 1969; Rousseau and Porto, 1970; Kurtin et al., 1970). Efforts to replicate the original findings had mixed success; some reported that they had managed to do so but others concluded that "a variety of chemical analyses show high concentrations of impurities which may account for many of the anomalous properties" (Rousseau and Porto, 1970:1715) and "it is likely that polywater is a hydrosol, consisting of finely divided particulate matter suspended in ordinary water" (Kurtin et al., 1970:1722). The negative findings only reinforced the skepticism that some chemists had about the existence of polywater. For Joel Hildebrand (1970), the Berkeley chemist, polywater was "hard to swallow."

It was not until Deryagin's own samples were subjected to independent analysis by a fellow Russian, V.L. Tal'rose, that the true nature of polywater was discovered. His official report stated that the sample he examined "contained organic substances, including lipids . . . and compounds of fats with phosphoric acid . . . [which] occur in animal tissues and, in particular, are released by humans along with perspiration." (See Davis, 1970, for Russian references.) To put it directly, polywater was no more and no less than human sweat. If contamination and artifact are the essence of disreputable error in science, Deryagin's polywater would seem to be the quintessential case.

R.E. Davis, one of those who had tried to replicate the experiments and to identify the material, described his response to the entire matter ironically but, for our purposes, diagnostically: "American scientists have been *wasting their time* studying this subject unless, of course, it can be identified as a topic of water pollution or waste disposal" (1970:79, italics added). The Tal'rose experiments thoroughly dissolved Deryagin's claims along with the claims of those who had built upon his work.

It is as if the polywater episode were designed to exhibit all the features of pathological science Langmuir inventoried several years before (1953:7). Based on a detailed review of altogether different cases,[16] Langmuir described the symptomatology thus:

(1) "The maximum effect is produced by a causative agent of barely detectable intensity, and the magnitude of the effect is . . . independent of the intensity of the cause."

(2) "The effect is of a magnitude that remains close to the limit of detectability."

(3) Nevertheless, "claims of great accuracy" are made.

(4) "Fantastic" theories contrary to experience are used to explain the phenomena.

(5) "Criticisms are met by *ad hoc* excuses. . . . They always had an answer—always."

(6) "The ratio of supporters to critics rises up to somewhere near 50% and then falls gradually to oblivion."

What is distinctive about cases of disreputable error is not that the investigators proved to have been mistaken. Quite the contrary; many good scientists have been mistaken at one time or another. That is in the risky nature of significant scientific inquiry. Nor is it a matter of those engaged in pathological science having stubbornly retained their ideas in the face of much severe criticism by peers; that is the case with many radically new and later confirmed conceptions in science (which are "resisted" precisely because they depart significantly from certain orthodoxies in their disciplines). Rather, it is that disreputable error derives from failure to live up to the cognitive norms prescribing technical procedures designed to rule out even the most favored hypotheses if they are in fact unsound.

Disreputable error represents a conspicuous violation of the norm of organized skepticism with regard to one's own work. The mixed derision and irritation expressed in the Hildebrand and Davis comments on polywater and in Langmuir's general remarks reflect the sentiment of the scientific community that collective time, effort, and resources should not be wasted on research which would not have come to anyone's attention had the abundantly obvious technical controls been utilized. These responses also reflect the basic tacit assumption in the community of research scientists that mutual trust is essential to its effective workings and that such trust is grounded in most scientists most of the time trying to meet the current standards of craftsmanship.

From all this, it appears that cognitive norms have their strong moral as well as pragmatic aspects.

Deviations from Moral Norms

The same kinds of value contexts appear in instances of deliberate rather than inadvertent violations of the moral norms of science. This becomes immediately evident with regard to the most serious crime in science: the kind of fraud represented by the falsification of empirical evidence. Peter Medawar puts it this way:

> Scientists try to make sense of the world by devising hypotheses. . . . In the ordinary course of events scientists very often guess wrong, take a wrong view, or devise hypotheses that later turn out to be untenable. . . . Nor does [this] necessarily impede the growth of science because where they guess wrong, others may yet guess right. But they won't guess right if the factual evidence that led to formulating the hypothesis and testing its correspondence with reality is not literally true. For this reason any kind of falsification or fiddling with professedly factual results is rightly regarded as an unforgivable professional crime. [Medawar, 1976:6]

As we have noted, the institution of science involves an implicit social contract between scientists that each can depend on the trustworthiness of the rest. Perhaps the first commandment of science dictates that "thou shalt not mislead thy colleagues." Were it otherwise, scientific investigation would slow almost to a halt as each scientist would have to verify for himself all the details of every contribution on which his own work rests. In this sense, the entire cognitive system of science is rooted in the moral integrity of aggregates of individual scientists. Yet as we have seen, along with kinds of inadvertent error, various kinds of falsification of scientific evidence do turn up in the annals of science.

Forms of Fraud

Fraud, the generic term for deliberate deception in science, occurs in three principal forms: the fabrication, fudging, and suppression of data. These correspond roughly to "forging," "trimming," and "cooking," the chief items in that inventory of scientific misbehavior taken 150 years ago by Charles Babbage in the classic volume, *Reflections on the Decline of Science in England,* to which I have made occasional reference (1975:177-182).[17] Forging refers to the recording of observations that were never made and in Babbage's view, the forger does what he does because "he wish[es] to acquire a reputation for science."

So it was with the paradigmatic case of William Summerlin which, after repeated brief mention, now calls for detailed examination. In 1974, the scientific public and the educated public alike were startled by the revelation that a young immunologist at the world-esteemed Sloan-Kettering Institute in New York had confessed to falsifying evidence of having successfully effected skin grafts between genetically different organisms. It was not the alleged corneal graft from a human being to the rabbit with "the candid and unwavering gaze" (described by Medawar) which led to the discovery of faked evidence but the crudest kind of fabrication more than a little reminiscent of the Kammerer fabrication which took place half a century earlier. Summerlin had inked the skin of a white mouse to make it appear that a skin graft from a dark-haired mouse had "taken." Had this been an authentic result, it would have had enormous significance for medicine.

Sometime before the precipitating episode, there had already been doubts expressed about Summerlin's work by members of Sloan-Kettering itself. In England, Peter Medawar and his group, as well as others elsewhere, had tried, without success of course, to replicate Summerlin's results. Since Medawar had not only received a Nobel prize for his pathbreaking work in immunology but was, it will be remembered, a member of the Sloan-Kettering Board of Visitors, this caused no little consternation at the institute. So much so that Robert Good, the director of the institute, arranged for still another investigator, John Ninneman, to try to repeat Summerlin's research. When Ninneman failed to do so, and just before the forgery was detected, Good, Ninneman, and Summerlin were preparing a joint paper to report their failure to reproduce the results of the earlier studies. Meanwhile, technical personnel in Summerlin's laboratory were becoming increasingly uneasy about what they took to be indefensibly sloppy work and excessive claims.[18] As it turned out, a technician spotted the blackened patch upon returning the mouse to its cage and conscientiously swabbed it with alcohol only to discover the inked forgery. He informed Good and the story was out. (For detailed accounts of this incident, see Culliton, 1974a, 1974b; McBride, 1974; Goodfield, 1975; Hixon, 1976. Goodfield, a historian of science visiting Sloan-Kettering at the time, actually interviewed Summerlin on the day of the disclosure just before the news became public.)

The institute promptly terminated its relationship with Summerlin and established a peer review committee to report on the entire affair. After talking with a number of witnesses and examining Summerlin's research records, the committee concluded that a great deal was wrong with his work, all apart from the final inking forgery: [19]

> Dr. Summerlin did indeed grossly mislead his colleagues in respect to this experimental work. . . . This conclusion was reached only after thorough consideration of alternative explanations. . . . The committee feels that Dr. Good shares some of the responsibility for what many see as undue publicity surrounding Dr. Summerlin's claims, unsupported as they were

> by adequate authenticated data. Dr. Good was slow to respond to a suggestion of dishonesty against Dr. Summerlin in a time when several investigators were experiencing great difficulty in repeating Dr. Summerlin's experiments. However, the usual presumptions of veracity and trustworthiness on the part of co-workers would have made it quite difficult for anyone in Dr. Good's position to entertain such a notion. [*Skin and Allergy News,* 5(July 1974):31-32]

On his part, Summerlin maintains that his chief, Good, pressured him to achieve increasingly sensational results in order to bring ever larger sums of research money into the institute and that Good had "turned against" him because his experiments were going badly (Culliton, 1974b:1155). He was also, he said, suffering from acute "mental exhaustion" generated by an "unbearable clinical and experimental load" (*Skin and Allergy News,* 5(July 1974):12). What is most in point for us is the intimation in Summerlin's testimony that some measure of self-deception was also involved, for he seems to have believed that he had truly developed a way of circumventing the rejection of skin grafts (Medawar, 1976:6-7). We shall return to this significant aspect of scientific forgeries later.

The Summerlin case is thus a prime instance of fraud in science. The law differentiates "actual fraud," the "intentional perversion of truth . . . or false representation of a matter of fact" from "constructive fraud" which "although not originating in any evil design or contrivance to perpetrate a positive fraud . . . [has] the tendency to deceive or mislead . . . [and] is deemed equally reprehensible with actual fraud" (H.C. Black 1968:789). In other words, fraud is fraud whether intended or not. The same is true in science.

The Kammerer case of fraud, to which I have referred in several connections, brings out the distinctive role of principal investigators in science. Theirs is the prime responsibility for whatever is made known about the work of their groups to the community of their peers. Kammerer, it will be remembered, claimed to have evidence countering Mendelian doctrine and supporting the Lamarckiam notion of the inheritance of acquired characteristics. He reported having experimentally achieved the inheritance of nuptial pads on the thumbs of a species of toad not originally possessing this characteristic. (See Koestler, 1972, and the creative review of Koestler's book by Gould, 1972.) Upon Noble's exposure of the black thumb pad having been inked, Kammerer maintained his total innocence and declared his ignorance of the forger's identity (Zirkle, 1954:189).

There is still doubt about whether an obliging (or hostile) assistant was responsible for the forgery, but Kammerer's scientific credibility was nevertheless irremediably damaged. He committed suicide not long after Noble's visit and public revelation of the fraud. Not only are scientists expected to oversee the work of their assistants, but also to repeat experiments before publication to avoid the possibility of publishing erroneous work. In the event that this is not done or if error is identified after the fact of publication, immediate retraction is required so as not to mislead colleagues further. Kammerer ignored all these normative requirements. He neither called the body of his findings into question nor volunteered to do the experiments again. He made no effort, however belated, to set the record straight. All this made the Kammerer case a prime example of this form of fraud in science.

Data manipulation, as a second form of fraud, differs from forgery in that the evidence is not made up out of whole cloth but has been altered to make it consistent with theory or hypothesis. Babbage confines such "trimming" of evidence to doctored calculations; as he picturesquely puts it, to "clipping off little bits here and there from those observations which differ most in excess from the mean and in sticking them on to those which are too small" (1975:178). If Newton indeed fudged his calculations, as Westfall claims, this would constitute an historic case of such deviance.

Such manipulation also includes tampering with experimental equipment or procedures to have the data show what the experimenter wants them to show. This form of manipulation with respect to the production rather than the analysis of data is exemplified in the case of Jay Levy, protégé of the senior investigator in the field of extrasensory perception, J.B. Rhine. Levy was discovered interfering with equipment recording the movements of experimental rats so that it appeared that the rats had modified the operation of a random number generator, as the experimental hypothesis predicted they could (see Rhine, 1974; *New York Times,* August 20, 1974).

A third, related form of fraud involves the suppression of data, selective reporting, and comparable operations all serving to make public only that part of the evidence which supports the investigator's theses. Unlike the fabrication and the manipulation of data, the evidence that sees print is genuine enough but the whole pertinent story is not told. This, as we have seen, is the gist of what R.A. Fisher (1936) was attributing to Mendel who, Fisher inferred on statistical grounds, was reporting only the data consistent with the theoretically expected ratios. (Babbage's characteristic term for this brand of misbehavior is "cooking" the evidence, 1975:178-182.)

Although the cooking of evidence may seem a somewhat less extreme form of deviance than fabrication or manipulation, its cognitive consequences for the given field of science are just as dysfunctional. As a result, scientists such as the biologist Salvador Luria feel that "leaving out data that inexplicably conflict with the rest of one's data or with the proposed interpretation is anathema" (Luria, 1975:15). In principle, where ambiguities do not obtain, this judgment is evident to scientists. But in practice, where ambiguities are common, what amounts to the suppression of data cannot always be clearly differentiated from the decisions scientists routinely and conscientiously make not to report certain data judged to be faulty in one or another respect. In this sphere, the acid test for distinguishing deviant from normatively acceptable behavior resides in whether the results are trustworthy and replicable.

Other Violations of Moral Norms

All three forms of fraud—the fabrication, manipulation, and suppression of data—clearly represent violations of the norms of disinterestedness and organized skepticism. The norm of disinterestedness, as we have noted, enjoins scientists from self-aggrandizement in ways that conflict with the institutional, if not necessarily personal, objective of extending scientific knowledge (Merton, 1973:275-277; see Wunderlich, 1974, for a useful clarification).

Plagiarism violates the norm of communism or communality in science. It need not be, like plagiarism in other fields, a matter of misappropriating the immediate cash value of others' work. As we have seen, the norm of communism involves the seeming paradox that, in science, authors must give their scientific contributions away—i.e., publish to the scientific community even without direct remuneration for the publications—if these contributions are to become their own. The apparent paradox is resolved by noting, first, that in science rights of intellectual property are limited largely to recognition by the scientific community of the sources of contributions made to it and, second, that members of that community are obliged to give due credit for those contributions (Merton, 1973:273-275; 1977:48). But plainly, plagiarists claim credit where credit is not due.

Nor is plagiarism in science always a clearly identifiable violation of the norms. Although outright literal pilfering of published texts is comparatively easy to detect, scientific ideas and results have a kind of impersonality that makes them vulnerable to such theft. As Ben-David suggests, "scientific results, because they are specific and are independent of writing style, are easy to steal. Moreover, because of the frequency of genuinely independent simultaneous discovery, it is difficult to detect plagiarism or, in the case of genuine multiple discovery, to assign property rights" (Ben-David, 1977:250). This aspect of the cognitive texture of science, which makes for the appearance of multiple independent formulations of essentially the same ideas and findings far more than in the humanities, introduces its own kind of ambiguity into the application of moral norms that are themselves not put in question. And that the norms have a moral force cannot be doubted: scientists do not respond to plagiarism casually. But if the abstract norm is a matter of consensus, its application to specific cases often is not.

In many cases of priority disputes, for example, only the participants can know whether they each independently made the scientific contribution or whether plagiarism had in fact occurred. There is certainty about oneself and sometimes uncertainty about the other. As Merton has observed, participants in these conflicts are often persuaded that plagiarism has taken place because they *know* that they themselves had arrived at the particular discovery but find it hard to believe that another had precisely the same experience (Merton, 1973:312-316). Outside observers generally do not have even this insufficient access to the facts of the case, yet sometimes hint that plagiarism or theft might have occurred. Thus, Gunther Stent writes that "Bacterial viruses were discovered in 1915 by the English microbiologist F.W. Twort, and two years later—perhaps independently, perhaps not—by the Canadian F. d'Herelle." (Quoted in Duckworth [1976:793] who reviews the Twort-d'Herelle priority dispute and concludes that d'Herelle has been maligned by the suggestion that he might have been a plagiarist.)

The problem of larceny in science is further complicated by ambiguities in the norms themselves with regard to certain forms of scientific property. In some fields, a newly identified problem, and not only its solution, is defined as a special kind of property assigned, at least for a time, to the one who had identified it. This is well brought out in the story that Norbert Wiener tells about himself. Early in his career, Wiener learned from the Harvard mathematician Oliver Kellogg that several mathematicians had identified the problem of "potential distribution" as interesting and were hard at work on it. Wiener, a prodigy who became one of the more agile minds in 20th century mathematics, turned to the problem and soon made rapid progress on it. Upon hearing of this from Wiener, the older Kellogg became acutely disturbed, saying that Wiener's work would interfere with the acceptance of the doctoral dissertations of the two young mathematicians who were also at work on the problem. Wiener remembers:

> I had been aware through Dr. Kellogg's leak, and only through Dr. Kellogg's leak, that other people were working on the problem, but I had no information as to their methods or tools, and my result was genuinely original. Furthermore, I did not accept with alacrity Kellogg's suggestion that I was now an established mathematician, who did not need these papers and who ought to give them up as a charity to youth and inexperience. Both of the candidates were older than myself. [Wiener, 1956:84]

Wiener asserted his property rights to the results he had obtained and told Kellogg that he planned on rapid publication. "This started a storm of antagonism against me, and both Kellogg and Birkhoff [the Harvard doyen of mathematicians] thundered at me from an exalted moral elevation" (Wiener, 1956:85; Hagstrom, 1965:95, also reports on the Wiener episode). There was obviously no consensus on the intricacies of proprietary rights in new problems.

This remains an ill-defined normative region in many fields, with the result that acute conflicts over trespassing on another scientist's problem periodically erupt into the open without lending themselves to a sense of equitable resolution.

As with moral norms generally, so with the norm of communism in science, with its distinctive definition of property as confined to peer recognition of one's scientific contributions. Even when the norm is reasonably clear as tacitly understood or explicitly formulated, ambiguities about its detailed applications often result in conflicting definitions of the situation among scientists about particular instances of seeming plagiarism or of other kinds of intellectual larceny. Since negative sanctions for deviant behavior in the scientific community are applied in the form of diffuse peer responses rather than by specialized courts of inquiry and official decision, these ambiguities serve to moderate the application of specific severe sanctions.

Collective deviations from the norms of organized skepticism and universalism take the form of suppressing radically new truth claims.[20] Ben-David (1977:258ff) has usefully distinguished two major kinds of such suppression: "disciplinary dogmatism" and "disciplinary monopoly." Disciplinary dogmatism, which operates on the cognitive plane, involves such strict conformity to the current cognitive framework of a discipline as to exclude serious consideration of new discoveries which do not fit into that framework. Such was the case, Ben-David reminds us, with the suppression of Semmelweiss' work in the 19th century on the causes and prevention of puerperal fever. Disciplinary monopoly, which operates on the plane of the social organization of the disciplines, obstructs the incorporation of new lines of research that do not fit neatly within the existing boundaries of university departments and laboratories. Ben-David concludes that disciplinary monopoly does more to restrict the development of science than disciplinary dogmatism which, he says, "does not seem to have diminished dissent and independence of thought. In fact, it may have produced more originality and independence. But disciplinary monopolies were detrimental to the development and diffusion of innovations [and] undoubtedly retarded the granting of autonomy and adequate resources to new fields" (Ben-David, 1977:260; see also, Cole and Zuckerman, 1975:141-142).

In the absence of systematic data sets on the suppression of innovative ideas in science, Ben-David reviews discoveries that were at first dismissed out of hand in the 19th century only to be rediscovered and found significant. He observes of those cases (and one might suggest the same for 20th century science) that "what is surprising . . . is not the prevalence of local attempts at suppression but the fact that they so rarely succeeded and that at no point was there any doubt among those with different prejudices that the contest of views could be resolved by accepted scientific procedures" (Ben-David, 1977:259).

Although private resistance to radically new ideas may be widespread among aggregates of individual scientists, public collective efforts to keep those ideas from circulation are exceedingly rare, which perhaps accounts for the regularity with which "the Velikovsky case" is cited as evidence of this kind of suppression. (See Mulkay, 1969; Dolby, 1975.)

Deviations from the Etiquette of Science

As we have noted, the spectrum of deviant behavior in science ranges from serious violations of moral and cognitive norms of the kinds we have reviewed to breaches of what might be described as the etiquette of science. What distinguishes these various kinds of rules of conduct in science is principally the intensity of peer response when they are violated and the associated beliefs about their respective dysfunctional consequences for the workings of science.

Nothing like an inventory of scientific etiquette has been compiled but one begins to identify kinds of behavior that tend to be regarded as bad scientific manners.

Eponymizing oneself. Eponymy—the naming of laws, effects, procedures, and the like after the scientists who have discovered them—has long been a prime form of peer recognition of important contributions. The assigning of eponymies is exercised by the scientific community, not by individual contributors. Eponymizing oneself, except in satirical fun, usurps that collective right and seldom becomes adopted as standard nomenclature. To assert oneself in that fashion is a minor breach of the norm of disinterestedness.

The under-acknowledgement of collaborators' contributions to joint research. As I have pointed out elsewhere (Zuckerman, 1968), scientists signal the relative extent of individual contributions to joint work in various ways, not least through the patterned device of the ordering of authors' names on publications.[21] Although the range of variability is considerable, it has been found for samples of American scientists that thoroughly established scientists, and in particular Nobel laureates, often exercise noblesse oblige by ceding prime authorship to juniors whose careers are less secure. This form of generosity is itself a breach of the tacit understanding in most sciences that the contributions of collaborators to the research should be properly reflected in the publication but, since it errs on the side of generosity rather than of self-interest, this elicits little unfavorable response.

But failure to assign what peer-observers regard as sufficient credit to collaborators, not least junior ones, is taken to breach the norm of communism calling for scientists to give due recognition to one another's contributions. Here again, ambiguity obtains about what would constitute adequate allocations of credit and much variability of practice occurs. A recent case of this sort involved award of a Nobel prize to the radio astronomer, Anthony Hewish, unshared by his young associate, Jocelyn Bell-Burnell, who happened to be the first actually to observe pulsars. Although her name was on the paper announcing the discovery and although she maintains that she has received adequate recognition, others, including the influential astronomer, Fred Hoyle, have criticized Hewish for publicly understating her contribution (*New York Times,* (March 22, 1975):22; *Science,* 195(January 21, 1977):277.)

Ad hominem attacks in scientific discourse. This familiar kind of deviant behavior illustrates the complex dynamics of behavior that can result from norms and institutionally reinforced motives in science. The norm of disinterestedness calls for passionate commitment to the cause of advancing scientific knowledge. In the words of Max Weber, science is a calling, a vocation,

> And whoever lacks the capacity to put on blinders, so to speak, and to come up to the idea that the fate of his soul depends upon whether or not he makes the correct conjecture at this passage of this manuscript may as well stay away from science. He will never have what one may call the 'personal experience' of science. Without this strange intoxication, ridiculed by every outsider; without this passion . . . you have *no* calling for science and you should do something else. For nothing is worthy of man as man unless he can pursue it with passionate devotion. Yet it is a fact that no amount of such enthusiasm, however sincere and profound it may be, can compel a problem to yield scientific results. [Weber, 1946:135]

This passionate disinterested pursuit of knowledge means that one cares deeply about claims to scientific truth, one's own, of course, but also the claims put forward by peers. Caring deeply does not usually lead to affective neutrality. Furthermore, the norm of organized skepticism requires that at least some in the community of scientists subject those claims, so far as possible, to critical examination: when they are put forward in seminars and conferences; when they are submitted for publication and scrutinized by referees; when they are published and are opened up to criticism by larger numbers of peers.

The combination of deep commitment to the pursuit of knowledge, enjoined by disinterestedness, and of socially organized skepticism makes it difficult to meet certain aspects of the norm of universalism. That norm calls for focusing on the quality of scientific work in its own right, not on the personal characteristics, real or imagined, of the scientists responsible for that work. Affective commitment to standards of scientific inquiry makes it difficult to remain impersonal and detached when it seems that those standards have not been lived up to. And if that work happens to be at odds with one's own work, or that of one's "school of thought," we have all the social and social-psychological ingredients needed for the kind of ad hominem controversies that often turn up in the public forum of science.

But the frequency of such behavior does not make it acceptable. Editors of journals will often reject papers marked by ad hominem attacks, and peers will express their sense that such controversies violate the mores of science. As an example, here is a neurologist stating such a response even to the reporting of ad hominem controversies:

> Maugh does a disservice in bringing out the personality conflicts between some individuals in basic protein research. His unfortunate remarks pointing out the antagonisms and controversies in the field do nothing to illuminate the problem and even detract from the scientific value of the article. [Smith, 1977]

The stated irrelevance of "personality conflicts" and the concluding allusion to the quality of the article both reflect a tacit adherence to the norm of universalism (in which personal attributes are irrelevant for assessing the quality of scientific work). It is ironic that the norms of disinterestedness (calling for a prime commitment to the quest for scientific knowledge) and of organized skepticism (calling for critically gauging the merits and demerits of scientific work in terms of current standards) should together provide a normative context making for violations of universalism. Instead of the disjunction between culturally prescribed aspirations and access to socially structured avenues for moving toward those aspirations, which is at the basis of anomie-and-opportunity-structure theory (Merton, 1968:184-248), this type of deviation involves a disjunction (not conflict) between norms, making for behavioral violations of normative expectations.

"Publicity seeking." This is the term commonly applied to scientists who try to make their work "excessively" available to lay publics. In its most extreme form, "publicity seeking" involves making one's scientific claims to discovery available to the general public through the mass media before members of the relevant scientific community have been able to assess them. Going to the lay public for primary legitimation and recognition violates the norm of organized skepticism since it by-passes the primacy of qualified peer appraisal. That is why scientific journals will generally prohibit the release of news of scientific discoveries in the press before they have been published. Even after publication, there are restraints on the extent to which scientists can make their case to lay audiences. There is a good deal of ambivalence in the scientific community about those who seek public attention. True, they may successfully communicate scientific ideas to lay publics, increase the public's understanding of science, and further the possibility of enlarging public support for science. But many scientists remain uneasy about laymen being even implicitly regarded as though they were qualified to pass judgment on the substance (as distinct from the possible social consequences) of scientific work. (We shall know more about these matters with the completion of the proposed Wernick study.)

This short list of infractions of the etiquette of science is perhaps enough to indicate how specific rules of behavior relate to the more general norms. It also suggests that both specific and general rules are subject to redefinition as science becomes increasingly interdigitated with its social contexts (Cournand and Zuckerman, 1970; Nelkin, 1976).

Social Consequences and Normative Change

Social pressures for changes in the norms of science derive in part from the social consequences of large-scale behavior in accord with the norms. The norm of disinterestedness, for example, made the unrestrained pursuit of scientific knowledge an end in itself, irrespective of its social consequences (which were usually assumed to be inevitably beneficial). But as the social consequences of the military and industrial technologies based on science of the purest kind become widely disapproved, science finds itself taking the blame just as it once took the credit. In this way, as Merton observed long ago, "the tenet of pure science and disinterestedness has helped to prepare its own epitaph" (1973:262).

The possible consequences of scientific inquiry may also be defined as undermining other moral values. By way of illustration, when Ladd and Lipset queried some 3,500 faculty members of American colleges and universities in 1975 on their beliefs about restrictions on research dealing with heredity and intelligence, more than half maintained that such research should be restricted. Social scientists were more chary about advocating restrictions than other scientists, but 49% of them favored some restrictions as did 55% of biological scientists and as many as 63% of physical scientists (Ladd and Lipset, 1976:2). Similar willingness to impose some restrictions on research is evident now among scientists and others concerned about the hazards of research on recombinant DNA. The meeting of biologists and biochemists at Asilomar in 1974 resulted in a temporary moratorium on research until guidelines to control investigations could be institutionalized, thereby providing testimony to the growing conviction among many scientists that the values of science are some times incompatible with other significant moral values.

The Phasing of Scientific Research and Conformity to Norms

It has been often suggested that far from abiding by the norms of science, scientists consistently violate them in their day-by-day activities. (See, for example, Barnes and Dolby, 1970; Mulkay, 1969, 1972a, 1972b, 1976; Mitroff, 1974a, 1974b, 1976.) This raises a basic theoretical question of what is meant by behavioral orientation to norms generally, and specifically in the case of science.

Mitroff reports, for example, on the basis of his studies of 42 scientists working on the Apollo Moon Project, that contrary to the proposed technical (cognitive) and moral norms (which I have been examining here), those scientists were not only biased, subjective, dogmatic, and secretive in their actual behavior but, and this is of course the decisive theoretical issue, they maintained that there was nothing illegitimate about their being so. I do not address the complex question of the relationships between norms and behavior which goes far beyond my immediate concern. I note only that norms are of course not behavior, that they are standards taken into account in behavior and standards by which actual behavior is judged.

In more direct point is the nature of Mitroff's claim that scientists defined bias, subjectivity, dogmatism, and secrecy as legitimate, not merely expressing them in behavior. Here we must return to the question we have briefly examined earlier with regard to the phasing of scientific work. In which phases of their work did these scientists regard these "counter-norms" as operative and even legitimate? For, of course, the norms of science refer to public science, not to the private phases which scientific investigators work through to arrive at results they are prepared to submit to their peers as justified claims to a scientific contribution. (See Holton, 1975, on the public and private aspects of science.)

It is not in the selection, formulation, or early work on research problems that scientists are expected by their peers to act in terms of such norms as disinterestedness or organized skepticism. At that phase, deep commitment and involvement with the scientific problems in hand are required for one to continue working on what remain recalcitrant but, it is believed, significant problems. (Remember Max Weber's observation on "passionate devotion" and correlative observations by other sociologists of science who have described the wide range of motives for doing scientific work.) But, as Ben-David noted in the paper to which I have often referred,[22]

> Even the best hunch, as long as it is unsupported by evidence, cannot be judged by preestablished impersonal criteria. One can also not expect *at this stage* either "disinterestedness" or "skepticism" on the part of the investigator. To the contrary, he is expected to be committed and involved with his ideas; otherwise he would be unwilling to risk his time, effort and occasionally also his money on the exploration of a mere hunch. This involvement and lack of objectivity are not contrary to the norms of scientific evaluation; for those norms apply only to the evaluation of results to be made public. [Ben-David, 1977:265, italics added]

The principal theoretical point is that the norms are defined as relevant in the community of scientists for the public, not the intensely private phase of scientific inquiry. This is the phase where judgments are made about the cognitive status of the work—whether it is logically consistent, involves reproducible results, and meets the standards of scientific communication.

The public phase of communication introduces its distinctive problems which the Nobel laureate Peter Medawar (1963; 1967) has raised in the provocative question: "Is the scientific paper a fraud?"

In raising this question, Medawar is not of course referring to the presentation of fraudulent data with the "willful intent to deceive." Instead, he calls attention to the established practice of having scientific papers provide only the information essential for possible reproducibility of results—the barebones of what was found, how it was found, and what has been concluded from what was found. It is in this sense that Medawar can go on to say that if one wants to find out what scientists actually do, with all the episodes of fumblings, errors, and faulty reasoning that often occur before the work is written up for publication, "it is no use looking to scientific 'papers', for they not merely conceal but actively misrepresent the reasoning that goes into the work they describe" (Medawar, 1967:151).

This discrepancy between what scientists have actually done and the published record of what they have done has been noted again and again, even before the scientific paper evolved into its present restricted format. Bacon wrote that there was "never any knowledge [that] was delivered in the same order it was invented" and Leibniz that "I wish that authors would give us the history of their discoveries and the steps by which they arrived at them." (For these and other observations to the same effect, see Merton, 1968:4-6; 1973:351.)

The point is that the institutionalized format of the scientific paper rules out of bounds accounts of the idiosyncratic intellectual biography of the research. This has the paradoxical result that by conforming to established practice, scientists in a sense mislead their readers about what "actually went on." However, since those readers are typically knowledgeable peers, who know from their own experience the sorts of things left out of the paper, there is little risk that they will assume that things went as smoothly as the published account seems to suggest. That risk is reduced further by other materials that do give biographical accounts of ideas or research programs in full-length memoirs or in the short autobiographies of research which are standard fare for Nobel prize addresses and other such occasions. But the question remains whether the cumulative effect of the institutionalized format of the scientific paper can mislead neophytes into believing that research is an immaculate process leading inexorably to new knowledge. This may be what Ernst Mach meant when he observed that scientists misinform in presenting the results of their inquiries by "concealing their methods of investigation, to the great detriment of science" (Mach, 1906:113, quoted by Merton, 1968:5).

LINKAGES BETWEEN NORMS AND THE REWARD SYSTEM OF SCIENCE

Until now, in discussing the comparative infrequency of seriously deviant behavior as gauged by the moral norms of science, we have focused on the combined consequences of socialization and the mechanisms for detecting and sanctioning deviant behavior. But we have only alluded to institutionalized incentives for conforming to the norms.

Sociologists of science have expressed seemingly opposed views about the nature of the linkages between the cognitive (technical) and moral norms of science and its reward system. The issues have been clearly crystallized in an important recent paper by Mulkay in which he concludes that the moral norms are little more than ideologies since they "are not institutionalized in such a way that general conformity is maintained" (Mulkay, 1976:654). He takes the position that strong incentives exist for conforming to the cognitive (technical) norms of science, for producing and communicating "technically satisfactory" information and cites as supporting evidence the Coles' studies (Cole and Cole, 1973) as basis for "the central conclusion of the corpus of sociological research on scientific rewards . . . that rewards are allocated overwhelmingly in response to the perceived quality of the scientific findings presented." But, he goes on to suggest, this is not the case for the moral norms as "there are no compelling reasons for regarding [these norms] as 'operating rules of science' [and] . . . conformity to most of the supposed norms and counter-norms of science is largely irrelevant to the institutional processes whereby professional rewards are distributed" (Mulkay, 1976:641-642).

Although the focus here is on the special substantive case of science, these observations raise general theoretical issues concerning norms, conformity, and deviant behavior. Both the critic and the criticized agree on the premise that institutionalized norms, as distinct from ideologies, must be supported by a reward system. Mulkay cites an early formulation by Storer (1966: Chapter 5) for this general observation just as I quote Storer's specification of the same theoretical premise:

> Neither the abstract statement of the norms of science nor the conception of professional recognition as the institutionally central reward for scientific achievement could separately point to the sources of various forms of deviant behavior in science. But in combination, as here [in "Priorities in Scientific Discovery"], they add dimension and organization to what had previously been little more than a congeries of unconnected incidents involving the "unfortunate" misbehavior of particular scientists. *The basic idea of interaction between the normative structure and the reward structure of science provides a solid foundation for the understanding of science as a social institution.* [Storer in Merton, 1973:283, italics added]

Positive and Negative Linkages to the Reward System

In adopting this premise, Mulkay introduced the double restriction that "Social norms are to be regarded as institutionalized when they are *positively* linked to the distribution of *rewards*" (Mulkay, 1976:641, italics added). The restriction to "positive" linkages and to "rewards" not only departs from the various meanings of institutionalization in the sociological literature (Eisenstadt, 1968) but tends to warp the subsequent theoretical analysis. "Reward system," a sociological shorthand term for a major part of social control systems, refers, after all, to both positive and negative sanctions. Institutionalization involves the linkage of norms to that system of rewards and punishments, not merely "positive" linkages to "rewards" alone. Were it otherwise, one would have to conclude that the prohibition of murder is not institutionalized since society provides no positive rewards for avoiding murder. Only by that same logic could one conclude that the moral as well as the cognitive (technical) norms we have been examining are not institutionalized since the community of scientists provides no positive rewards for avoiding the use of others' ideas without due acknowledgement or misrepresentation through the "trimming" or "cooking" of data. Yet even if we consider primarily "positive" linkages, there has long been reason to think that the allocation of scientific rewards is conditional on conformity to both moral and cognitive (technical) norms.

Scientists who do not conform to the norm of communism cannot expect recognition from their peers since such recognition is contingent on making their work known through publication (Merton, 1973:274). The gradual institutionalization of the scientific journal led scientists to accept the fairly "new norm of free communication through a motivating exchange: open disclosure in exchange for institutionally guaranteed honorific property rights to the new knowledge [being] given to others" (Zuckerman and Merton, 1971:70; see also pp. 68-75 on the process of institutionalization). The institutionalized incentive of peer recognition for open diffusion of one's scientific work is central to the developing exchange theories of science by Hagstrom (1965), Storer (1966), and Mulkay himself (1972a, 1976), who, in spite of his doubts about the norm of communism being institutionally supported, strongly emphasizes the exchange of scientific communications for recognition). It would appear that conformity to the norm of communism not only leads to positive rewards, it is a condition for the operation of the reward system itself.

Scientists are obliged to take part in the social arrangements through which organized skepticism is exercised and they are rewarded for doing so. The institutionalized roles of editors, referees, reviewers, and peer-review panelists are only the more specialized gatekeeping positions for the evaluation process in science. Authority and influence, generally regarded as rewards, go along with fulfilling these functions.

Apart from these specialized roles, scientists routinely engage in public criticism and evaluation of others' work and are rewarded for doing so, since this is in the interest of maintaining standards. Putting into practice severely critical attitudes toward one's own work is also rewarded by peer response. When scientists characterize a piece of research as "rigorous" or even more as "elegant," they are saying that the investigator has anticipated the criticisms that his research might otherwise have elicited.

As I have repeatedly noted, disinterestedness enters into the social and cognitive system of science by contributing to the mutual trust that is central to that system. Rewards are given to those whose research has been found to be trustworthy, not systematically biased for ideological or self-interested reasons. The norm of disinterestedness is institutionalized in the strict sense that scientists are rewarded for adhering to it in the public phase of their work—the contributions they give to their peers—whatever their private motives may be for doing science.

Finally, as Mulkay himself emphasizes, the basic reward of peer recognition is far more often allocated on universalistic than particularistic grounds (Zuckerman, 1970; Cole and Cole, 1973). There are indications also that those who are themselves most highly rewarded in the social system of science are given to judging the contributions of others by universalistic standards (S. Cole, 1970).

All this indicates that the social institution of science provides a composite of incentives and punishments directed toward having scientists adhere to both the moral and the cognitive norms. Yet some sociologists of science have argued that scientists are not significantly oriented toward the moral norms which, in any case, are not institutionalized through the system of social control. One cannot help but notice that the very statement of that view is interestingly self-disconfirming. It represents conformity to the norms prescribing organized skepticism (critical response), communism (public communication), universalism (with the criticism being centered on impersonal theoretical issues rather than being ad hominem) and, it appears evident, disinterestedness.

THEORIES OF DEVIANT BEHAVIOR

Finally we turn briefly to theories of deviant behavior to find out whether anything can be learned about the uses and limits of these theories by examining deviant behavior in science. I consider the four currently principal perspectives on deviance—labeling, differential association, conflict theory, and anomie-and-opportunity structures.

Labeling theory, associated with the work of Lemert, Becker, Cicourel, Erikson, and Kitsuse, is designed primarily to explain the persistence rather than the origins or rates of deviant behavior. It identifies the ways in which social responses to deviant behavior contribute to the development of secondary deviance and thus to the formation of deviant careers. Although labels for forms of seriously deviant behavior in science, such as fraud and plagiarism, are drawn from the law, there is not much overlap between the formal legal system and the informal system of control in science. Scientists themselves have long had nearly exclusive responsibility for dealing with departures from institutional norms. Since the system of social control in science diffuses responsibility for dealing with deviants throughout the community of scientists, the emphasis in labeling theory on official responses to deviance and the ways in which these responses reinforce subsequent deviance does not directly apply to this institutional domain.

The focus in labeling theory on the persistence of deviant behavior and its development into a deviant career is also not quite germane in science. The system of social control in science provides no place for such careers. In the rare instance of a scientist being defined as having committed fraud or plagiarism, he is expelled from the community. If brought back in, it is not in the role of a moral deviant. Secondary deviance of the kind dealt with in labeling theory therefore appears to be a function of the opportunities for remaining at least at the periphery of the institutional domain being examined.

Labeling theory does however help us to understand how a scientist suspected of deviant behavior might be pressured into further deviant acts. Consider, once again, the case of William Summerlin. His early research may have convinced him that he had in fact found a procedure for arresting the disastrous effects of rejection of skin grafts. (Medawar, 1976, believes that this was the case.) Having become convinced, it may have seemed to Summerlin that it was no great departure from the norms to "improve" the evidence which did not clearly show the effect he was sure actually existed. But as others began to express their doubts of the validity of his work, this may have built up pressure for him to "prove" that his earlier investigations were in fact correct. This may have led him into more serious deviance which he believed would not be identified because he was persuaded that he could reproduce his original findings. This speculative account of the process of escalating deviance in response to tentative labeling by peers at least has face validity. Study of the question whether this process actually occurred in Summerlin's case and in other cases of fraud in science would require us to compare the consequences of tentative as distinct from crystallized labels for the formation of cumulating deviant behavior.

Differential association theory, as first put forth by Sutherland, emphasizes the process by which deviant behavior is transmitted. In this perspective, individuals learn deviant behavior by association with those who are knowing about the ways of deviance. But, as we have noted, seriously deviant behavior appears to be rare in science and differential association does not seem to explain the transmission of such deviance. But if we focus on the transmission of standards and values in science, which are not consonant with those generally adopted by the research community, and deal with the notion of subcultures in science, then the idea of differential association directs our attention to the relevance of socialization into the scientific role. It is at least plausible that scientists who were never apprenticed to working researchers or who worked under inexperienced ones are less likely to acquire standards of careful research or a sense of how to deal with problems falling into the vaguely defined normative gray areas we have identified.

More specifically, differential association may account for differing subcultures in science; for example, the greater emphasis industrial and government scientists put on the application of knowledge than on its advancement. Studies of industrial scientists conducted in the early 1960s (e.g., Kornhauser with Hagstrom, 1962) focused on conflicts between the values of scientific research and those of the industrial organization. The newer studies (Box and Cotgrove, 1970; Krohn, 1971) find that industrial scientists place less value than academic scientists on extending scientific knowledge and on peer recognition for such contributions. Glaser (1965) suggests that differential association may help account for these differences in values and kinds of professional commitment. But differential association need not be the only, or even the major, explanation for value differences between industrial and academic scientists. Other social processes, principally those of self-selection, selective recruitment, and selective retention of personnel, account for some of the observed differences. If scientists who are not strongly oriented to the values of "pure science" more often choose to work in industrial laboratories, if they also are more often chosen for these jobs and also more apt to keep them than others, then differential association will account only for value changes in the life history of industrial scientists rather than for gross differences in the values of industrial and academic scientists. Further inquiry is needed to determine whether these selective processes and differential association interact so as to produce greater rates of value-change among the predisposed.

In contrast to labeling and differential association, the conflict perspective on deviant behavior, represented in the work of Quinney and Turk, draws attention to how the rules are made and by whom so that certain actions come to be defined as deviant. It emphasizes the role of those in power in making and imposing rules. These ideas bear a family resemblance to the ongoing discussion in the history, philosophy, and sociology of science about the role of authority in science in relation to scientific advance (Polanyi, 1963). But perhaps a more interesting overlap of current work in the social studies of science with the conflict perspective appears in the role assigned conflict and competition in falsifying scientific hypotheses and ideas. For Karl Popper and others, something like the processes of competition and natural selection operate such that some would-be contributions to science survive attempts at falsification while others fall by the wayside. But there is a basic difference between the perspective of falsificationism and that of the conflict theorists. The falsificationists hold that the fate of scientific contributions has everything to do with how well they withstand cognitive refutation and nothing to do with the interests of those who put them forth. Thus cognitive innovations will be rejected even if they are contributed by members of what conflict theorists might describe as the power elite of science (as in the case of Pauling's work on vitamin C). Given the theoretical differences between the concepts of "authority" and "power," especially in an institutional domain such as science, it is not evident how the study of deviant behavior among scientists can contribute to the conflict perspective or to identifying possible theoretical shortcomings in it.

The anomie-and-opportunity-structures perspective focuses on the sources and rates of deviance rather than on its transmission, persistence, or social definition. Given Robert Merton's long-term interest in this perspective, it is not surprising that his beginning studies of deviant behavior in science (1973: Chapters 13-18) should focus on the consequences of its normative structure. These studies underscore the thesis that anomie theory does not limit the success goal to money success:

> The theory holds that *any* extreme emphasis upon achievement—whether this be scientific productivity, accumulation of personal wealth or, by a small stretch of the imagination, the conquests of a Don Juan—will attenuate conformity to the institutional norms governing behavior designed to achieve the particular form of 'success,' especially among those who are socially disadvantaged in the competitive race. It is the conflict between cultural goals and the availability of using institutional means—

> whatever the character of the goals—which produces a strain toward anomie. [Merton 1968:220]

In science, the institutionalized emphasis upon originality in the form of being there first with significant contributions and upon corresponding peer recognition generates "incentives for eclipsing rivals by illicit means" (Merton, 1973:276). However, our review of the evidence does not find the hypothesized differences in deviant behavior among scientists having differential access to *opportunity* for scientific achievement. Neither Kammerer, Summerlin, nor the other scientists we have noted engaging in deviance were shut off from such access as distinct from their own possible limitations for doing pathbreaking work. This suggests that a marked emphasis on a collectively defined goal may be enough to "attenuate conformity to the institutional norms" even among those who would seem to have privileged access to "opportunity."

In any case, the limitations of the anomie perspective, along with the limitations of the labeling, differential association, and conflict perspectives suggest that a new program of systematic research on deviant behavior in an institutional sphere such as science may contribute to our understanding of deviant behavior more generally.

A FINAL NOTE

Our analysis of deviant behavior and social control in science has turned up an interesting hypothesis that may be relevant for other institutional domains. This is the hypothesis that the greater the socially induced pressure for deviant behavior, the greater the likelihood that it will be detected. For the intense competition built into the institution of science would seem to make for both deviance and for activities enlarging the probability that it will be discovered. The intense competition for making original scientific contributions—the "race for priority"—and the peer recognition that comes with it created pressures for deviant behavior ("undue" secrecy, "cutting corners," even, as we have seen, manufacturing fake evidence). But that same intense competition as a system-property also focuses the attention of scientists on particular problems, intensifies their critical review of others' work in the field, and encourages efforts to check important new truth claims through replication. This should increase the chances that any deviant behavior which does occur will be identified.

It is not evident whether science is special or even unique among social institutions in having the same normative and social conditions pressing for deviant behavior and for its disclosure. The hypothesis loosely resembles Durkheim's famous hypothesis on crime and punishment (Durkheim, 1899-1900, 1964). Durkheim developed the seeming paradox that we should expect to find that societies with low rates of crime should have the most severe punishment; not so much because severe punishment acted as deterrent but because the same strongly held common sentiments ("conscience collective") which led to few acts of serious deviance would lead to even minor infractions being defined as serious. In a formally similar way, I am suggesting that the same normative condition making for intense competition for scientific achievement and recognition helps generate various kinds of deviant behavior in science and the kinds of cognitive activities that should lead to detection of such deviant behavior.

The analysis of deviant behavior in science, then, as in other institutions, can clarify its system of social control. To an unknown extent, that system provides for the recognition and reward of scientific work meeting the collectively esteemed standards and for the detection and punishment of departures from moral and cognitive norms. From this review, it appears that the conceptual framework for understanding deviant behavior and social control in science, though still very incomplete, is further along than the systematic empirical investigation of the subject.

NOTES

1. Mulkay's use of the term "cognitive norms," for example in his 1969 paper and since, strikes me as more appropriate than Merton's term "technical norms," and will therefore be used for prescribed theoretical orientations and technical requirements.

2. See, for example, *New York Times* (January 23, 1977):1; Luria (1975); Borek (1975).

3. Publicized responses to recent episodes include: On William Summerlin, who admitted he had inked the back of a mouse to make it appear that he had demonstrated the possibility of successfully grafting skin between genetically different animals, see *New York Times* (May 25, 1974); Culliton (1974a; 1974b); McBride (1974); Goodfield (1975); Hixon (1976). On M.S. Swaminathan, accused, experts believe unjustly, of contriving to publish evidence on the nutritive properties of a wheat strain, after other scientists had shown it to be false, see *New Scientist,* 64(November 7, 1974):346; *New Scientist,* 65(January 9, 1975):96. The Rosenfeld-Dressler case, involving an allegation of fraud against a student assistant of the Harvard immunologist, David Dressler, see *New York Times* (December 16, 1976):1ff.; Dressler and Potter, (1975). On the case of accusations of fraud against Cyril Burt, one of the major figures in British intelligence testing, see *The Sunday Times* (October 24, 1976):1-2; *New York Times* (January 23, 1977):1ff.; Jensen (1976); Rimland and Munsinger (1977). On Robert Gullis, a biochemist who admitted to having made up experimental data, see *Nature,* 265(February 24, 1977):764; *Washington Post* (February 25, 1977). On fraud and other shady practices in the testing of drugs reviewed by the FDA, see *Science,* 180(June 8, 1973); *Journal of Pharmaceutical Sciences,* 66(February 1977):1. On the case of Jay Levy, protégé of J.B. Rhine and Director of the Institute for Parapsychology, who admittedly tampered with experimental equipment to produce evidence to support the existence of extrasensory perception, see *New York Times* (August 20, 1974); Rhine (1974).

4. Reproducibility is also a mechanism for vindicating those erroneously accused of tampering with the evidence. As we shall see, investigators have replicated Galileo's experiments (Settle, 1961) and Mendel's calculations (Wright, 1966) and concluded that charges of fraud were unfounded.

5. The literatures of the various sciences differ in the amount of methodological detail provided in publications and so differ also in the extent to which investigations can be

reproduced without consulting the original contributor. New developments in scientific publication known as abstracts or "quickies," designed to convey information quickly and briefly, have the unanticipated consequence of reducing opportunities for replication since they provide scanty details of experiments. (See Hagstrom, 1965:96 for further discussion of the implications of this form of publication for establishing rights to scientific priority.)

6. Babbage's inventory and colorful nomenclature for various forms of manipulation of scientific data will be discussed in the section dealing with the varieties of deviant behavior in science.

7. Comparative studies of the extent of replication in various sciences are now underway in the Columbia Program in the Sociology of Science.

8. A similar visit to René Blondlot by the American physicist, R.W. Wood, was the occasion for Wood's demonstrating that Blondlot's methods of observing "N rays" were, to say the least, wholly inadequate. See Rostand (1960) and Langmuir (1953) for accounts.

9. As we shall see, departures from the generic methodological canons of science, those that require logical consistency and empirical confirmation, are also serious breaches (they are often labelled "crackpot" science) but they differ from willful deceptions in that they are public, usually made in the name of science, and challenge the very legitimacy of the cognitive norms themselves. We shall have more to say on this form of deviant behavior.

10. In collaboration with a survey of the professoriate by S.M. Lipset and E.C. Ladd, we are now collecting data on self-reported adherence to the norms of science and frequency of departures from those norms, estimates of the frequency of deviant behavior by others and victimization (inadequate citation of published contributions).

11. Mahoney and Kimper (1976) asked respondents to estimate the percentage of scientists who "suppressed" data, "faked" data, plagiarized others' ideas and writings, and "misrepresented" their methods. Since the return rate was 21%, not much can be said about the reported findings. St. James-Roberts (1976a, 1976b) asked questions along similar lines in a questionnaire published in the *New Scientist.* The self-selected sample of readers returning the questionnaire obviously cannot provide a basis for valid quantitative analysis.

12. Growing efforts to make the occupants of gatekeeping positions more representative of the scientific community may result in gatekeepers decreasingly being established scientists. On the distribution of ranks among referees of *Physical Review,* the acknowledged premier journal of world physics, see Zuckerman and Merton, 1971:83-87.

13. Mitroff (1974a, 1974b, 1976) reports that the 42 moon scientists active in the Apollo mission do not conform strictly to the moral norms but exhibit what Merton (1976) has called "normative ambivalence."

14. This general problem is about to be investigated by Dr. Sarah Wernick of Washington University, St. Louis, Missouri, along the lines indicated in her draft proposal, "The Effects of Public Recognition on the Quality of Scientific Work: A Scientist's Dilemma," April 28, 1977.

15. This distinction is further developed in Lederberg and Zuckerman (1977) which focuses in some detail on "contamination" as a special form of disreputable error.

16. Langmuir describes and analyzes the "pathological" cases of N rays (see also) Rostand, 1960; Price, 1961); the Davis-Barnes Effect; Mitogenic Rays, and the Allison Effect.

17. To forging, trimming, and cooking, Babbage (1975:177ff) adds hoaxing as a fourth form of deception. Hoaxes are intended to last only for a time and then to be revealed for what they are, to the amusement of the hoaxers and the embarrassment of those taken in by them. Babbage's kind interpretation is that hoaxes are a kind of scientific practical joke and not considered seriously deviant behavior unless they are repeated.

18. This provides an instance of the hypothesis that collaborative or team research provides enlarged opportunities for close surveillance and that fraud would be all the more likely discovered in such forms of organized research.

19. The review committee observed that Summerlin did not test the experimental mice to determine whether they were pure strains or hybrids. Had hybrids accepted skin grafts, this would have held no medical interest. His claims to have achieved corneal transplants could not be checked, owing to the absence of properly organized and analyzable records of data, *Skin and Allergy News,* 5(July 1974). Goodfield adds that the optimistic Summerlin misled patients into thinking that research was in progress which would give them help. She observes that he presented a picture not of "Machiavellian deception" but of one unable to deal with the complex situation in which he found himself.

20. Mulkay (1976:643) holds that the norm of universalism has "no content until we formulate it in terms of specific bodies of scientific knowledge, practice and technique. But once we do this, we no longer need the concept of 'universalism.' " But whether one uses the term "universalism" or not, the social and cognitive realities remain. Universalistic technical (cognitive) standards are used to appraise the quality of scientific work, as Mulkay himself indicates in citing the Coles and other research on the subject (see also Chase, 1970).

21. We need not consider here institutionalized patterns of assigning major credit to the directors of laboratories or the heads of university departments which have evolved in various times and places. These conventions are well understood by members of the given scientific community and authorship is interpreted correspondingly.

22. Ben-David's important paper appeared as my own was completed in first draft. Our basic similarity of interpretation of these theoretical issues is reflected in the extensive use I have been able to make of his observations.

REFERENCES

ALLEN, L., and KOLLMAN, P. (1970a). "A theory of anomalous water." Science, 167(March 13):1443-1454.

--- (1970b). "Cyclic systems containing divalent hydrogen symmetrically placed between sp2 hybridized electron rich atoms. A new form of chemical bond?" Journal of the American Chemical Society, 92(13):4108-4110.

ARONSON, L. (1975). "The case of The Case of the Midwife Toad." Behavior Genetics, 5(2):115-125.

BABBAGE, C. (1976). Reflections on the decline of science in England and or some of its causes. New York: Scholarly. First published 1830.

BARBER, B. (1952). Science and the social order. New York: Free Press.

--- (1961). "Resistance by scientists to scientific discovery." Science, 134:596-602.

BARBER, T. (1973). "Pitfalls in research: Nine investigator and experimenter effects." Pp. 382-404 in R. Travers (ed.), Second handbook of research on teaching. Chicago: Rand-McNally.

BARNES, S., and DOLBY, R. (1970). "The scientific ethos: A deviant viewpoint." Archives European Journal of Sociology 11(1):3-25.

BEN-DAVID, J. (1977). "Organization, social control and cognitive change in science." Pp. 244-265 in J. Ben-David and T. Clark (eds.), Culture and its creators: Essays in honor of Edward Shils. Chicago: University of Chicago Press.

BERNSTEIN, J. (1962). "Profiles: A question of parity." New Yorker, 38 (May 12):49ff.

BLACK, D. (1976). The behavior of law. New York: Academic Press.

BLACK, H.C. (1933). Black's law dictionary (3rd ed.). St. Paul, Minn.: West Publishing Co.

--- (1968). Black's law dictionary (4th ed.). St. Paul, Minn.: West Publishing Co.

BOREK, E. (1975). "Cheating in science." New York Times, (January 22):39.

BLISSET, M. (1972). Politics in science. Boston: Little, Brown.

BOX, S., and COTGROVE, S. (1970). Science, industry and society: Studies in the sociology of science. London: George Allen, Unwin.

CHASE, J. (1970). "Normative criteria for scientific publication." American Sociologist, 5(August):262-265.

CIOFFI, F. (1974). "Was Freud a liar?" The Listener (February 7):172-174.

––– (1976). "Was Freud a liar?" Journal of Orthomolecular Psychiatry, 5:275-280.

COHEN, I.B. (1957). "Galileo," Pp. 3-20 in Editors of Scientific American (ed.), Lives in Science. New York: Simon & Schuster.

COLE, J. (1976). "Patterns of intellectual influence in scientific research." Sociology of Education, 40(1967):24-37.

COLE, J., and COLE, S. (1973). Social stratification in science. Chicago: University of Chicago Press.

COLE, J., and ZUCKERMAN, H. (1975). "The emergence of a scientific specialty: The self-exemplifying case of the sociology of a science." Pp. 139-174 in L. Coser (ed.), The idea of social structure: Papers in honor of Robert K. Merton. New York: Harcourt Brace Jovanovich.

COLE, S. (1970). "Professional standing and the reception of scientific discoveries." American Journal of Sociology, 76(September):286-306.

COSER, R. (1975). "The complexity of roles as a seedbed of individual autonomy." Pp. 221-263 in L. Coser (ed.), The idea of social structure: Papers in honor of Robert K. Merton. New York: Harcourt Brace Jovanovich.

COURNAND, A., and MEYER, M. (1976). "The scientist's code." Minerva, 14(spring):79-96.

COURNAND, A., and ZUCKERMAN, H. (1970). "The code of science." Studium Generale, 23(October):941-962. Reprinted in 1975, pp. 126-147 in P. Weiss (ed.), Knowledge in search of understanding. Mt. Kisco, N.Y.: Future Publishing.

CULLITON, B. (1974a). "The Sloan-Kettering affair: A story without a hero." Science, 184(May 10):644-650.

––– (1974b). "The Sloan-Kettering affair (II): An uneasy resolution." Science, 184(June 14):1154-1157.

DAVIS, R. (1970). "Polywater in history." Chemical and Engineering News, 48(September 28):78-79.

DOLBY, R. (1975). "What can we usefully learn from the Velikovsky affair?" Social Studies of Science, 5(May):165-175.

DONOHUE, J. (1969). "Structure of 'Polywater'." Science, 166(November 21):1000-1001.

DRESSLER, D., and POTTER, H. (1975). "Authors' statement." Proceedings of the National Academy of Sciences U.S.A., 72:409.

DUCKWORTH, D. (1976). "Who discovered bacteriophage?" Bacteriological Reviews, 40:792-802.

DUNN, L. (1965). "Mendel, his work and his place in history." Proceedings of the American Philosophical Society, 109(August):189-198.

DURKHEIM, E. (1899-1900). "Deux lois de l'évolution pénale." Année Sociologique, 4:65-95.

–––(1964). The rules of sociological method (S. Solovay and J. Mueller, trans.). New York: Free Press.

EISENSTADT, S. (1968). "Social institutions." Pp. 409-421 in International encyclopedia of the social sciences (vol. 14). New York: Macmillan.

FISHER, R.A. (1936). "Has Mendel's work been rediscovered?" Annals of Science, 1(April 15):116-137.

GASTON, J. (1971). "Secretiveness and competition for priority of discovery in physics." Minerva, 9(October):472-492.

––– (1973). Originality and competition in science (chapters 5, 6). Chicago: University of Chicago Press.

GINGERICH, O. (1976). "On Ptolemy as the greatest astronomer of antiquity: Review of A History of Ancient Mathematical Astronomy." Science, 193(August 6):476-477.

GLASER, B. (1965). "Differential association and the institutional motivation of scientists." Administrative Science Quarterly, 10(June):82-97.
GOLDSCHMIDT, R. (1959). "Research and politics." Science, 109(March 4):219-227.
GOODFIELD, J. (1975). The siege of cancer. New York: Random House.
GOULD, S. (1972). "Zealous advocates; Review of The Case of the Midwife Toad." Science, 176(May 12):623-625.
HAGSTROM, W. (1965). The scientific community. New York: Basic Books.
--- (1974). "Competition in science." American Sociological Review, 39(February):1-18.
HILDEBRAND, J. (1970). " 'Polywater is hard to swallow'." Science, 168(June 19):1397.
HIXON, J. (1976). The patchwork mouse. Garden City, N.Y.: Doubleday.
HOLTON, G. (1975). "On the role of themata in scientific thought." Science, 188(April 25):328-334.
JENSEN, A. (1976). "On the trumped-up indictment of Sir Cyril Burt." London Times (December 9).
KING, M. (1971). "Reason, tradition and the progressiveness of science." History and Theory: Studies in the Philosophy of History, 10(1):3-32.
KOESTLER, A. (1972). The case of the midwife toad. New York: Random House.
KOLATA, G. (1977). "Catastrophe theory: The emperor has no clothes." Science, 196(April 15):287ff, 350-351.
KORNHAUSER, W., with HAGSTROM, W. (1962). Scientists in industry: Conflict and accommodation. Berkeley: University of California Press.
KOYRE, A. (1953). "An experiment in measurement." Proceedings of the American Philosophical Society, 97:224.
KROHN, R. (1971). The social shaping of science. Westport, Conn.: Greenwood.
KUHN, T.S. (1970). The structure of scientific revolutions (enlarged ed). First published 1962. Chicago: University of Chicago Press.
KURTIN, S., MEAD, C., MUELLER, W., KURTIN, B., and WOLF, E. (1970). " 'Polywater': A hydrosol?" Science, 167(March 27):1720-1722.
LADD, E., and LIPSET, S.M. (1976). "Should any research topics be off limits?" Chronicle of Higher Education, (March 15):1-2.
LANGMUIR, I. (1953). "Pathological science." Colloquium given at the Knolls Research Laboratory, December 18. Transcribed and edited by R. Hall (1968). General Electric Research and Development Center Report, 68-C-035 (April).
LEDERBERG, J., and ZUCKERMAN, H. (1977). "From schizomycetes to bacterial sexuality: A case study of discontinuity in science." Unpublished manuscript.
LINNETT, J. (1970). "Structure of polywater." Science, 167(March 27):1719-1720.
LIPPINCOTT, E., STROMBERG, K., GRANT, W., and CESSAC, G. (1969). "Polywater." Science, 164(June 27):1482.
LURIA, S. (1975). "What makes a scientist cheat?" Prism (May):15-18, 44.
MACH, E. (1906). Space and geometry (T. McCormack, trans.). Chicago: Open Court.
MAHONEY, M., and KIMPER, T. (1976). "From ethics to logic: A survey of scientists." In M. Mahoney, Scientist as subject: The psychological imperative. Cambridge, Mass.: Ballinger.
McBRIDE, G. (1974). "The Sloan-Kettering affair: Could it have happened anywhere?" Journal of the American Medical Association, 229 (September 9):1391-1410.
McHUGH, G. (1973). "The fudge factor." Science, 180(June 15):1118-1119.
MEDAWAR, P. (1963). "Is the scientific paper a fraud?" The Listener (September 12).
--- (1967). The art of the soluble. London: Methuen.
--- (1976). "The strange case of the spotted mice." New York Review of Books, 23(April 15):6-11.
MERTON, R. (1968). Social theory and social structure (enlarged ed.). New York: Free Press.

---(1970). Science, technology and society in seventeenth century England. New York: Howard Fertig. First published in 1938.
--- (1973). The sociology of science: Theoretical and empirical investigations (N. Storer, ed.). Chicago: University of Chicago Press.
--- (1976). "The ambivalence of scientists." Pp. 32-55 in R. Merton, Sociological ambivalence. New York: Free Press.
MILLAR, R. (1972). The Piltdown men. London: Victor Gollancz.
MITROFF, I. (1974a). The subjective side of science. New York: American Elsevier.
--- (1974b). "Norms and counter-norms in a select group of the Apollo moon scientists: A case study in the ambivalence of scientists." American Sociological Review, 39(August):579-595.
--- (1976). "Passionate scientists." Society, 13(September/October):51-57.
MULKAY, M. (1969). "Some aspects of cultural growth in the natural sciences." Social Research, 36:22-53.
--- (1971). "Some suggestions for sociological research." Science Studies, 1(April):207-213.
--- (1972a). The social process of innovation. London: Macmillan.
--- (1972b). "Conformity and innovation in science." Pp. 5-24 in P. Halmos (ed.), The Sociological Review Monograph, 18, The Sociology of Science (September).
--- (1976). "Norms and ideology in science." Social Science Information, 15(4-5):637-656.
NELKIN, D. (1976). "Changing images of science: New pressures on old stereotypes." Newsletter: Program on Public Conceptions of Science, 14, Harvard University (January):21-31.
NEUGEBAUER, O. (1975). Studies in the history of mathematics and physical sciences. Vol. 1 in A history of ancient mathematical astronomy (3 vols.). New York: Springer Verlag.
Nobelstiftelsen (ed., 1962). Alfred Nobel: The man and his prizes. New York: Elsevier.
---(ed., 1972). Nobel: The man and his prizes (3rd ed.). New York American Elsevier.
OAKLEY, K., and WEINER, J.
PERUTZ, M. (1969). "Letter." Scientific American, 221(July 22).
POLANYI, M. (1963). "The potential theory of adsorption." Science, 141(September):1010-1013.
POPPER, K. (1959). The logic of scientific discovery (first published 1934-1935). New York: Harper and Row.
---(1962). Conjectures and refutations, The growth of scientific knowledge. New York: Basic Books. London: Routledge and Kegan Paul.
President's Commission on Law Enforcement and Administration of Justice (1967). Task Force report: Crime and its impact: An assessment. Washington, D.C.: U.S. Government Printing Office.
PRICE, D. (1961). Science since Babylon. New Haven: Yale University Press.
RAVETZ, J. (1971). Scientific knowledge and its social problems. New York: Oxford University Press.
REISS, A. (1973). Surveys of self-reported delicts. Unpublished paper prepared for the Symposium on Studies of Public Experience, Knowledge, and Opinion of Crime and Justice, Washington, D.C. (March 17-18). (Revised July.)
RHINE, J. (1974). "A new case of experimenter unreliability." Journal of Parapsychology, 38(June):215-225.
RIMLAND, B., and MUNSINGER, H. (1977). "Burt's heritability data." Science, 195(January):248.

ROSENKRANZ, H., and ELLNER, P. (1969). "Mutant of bacterium paracoli 5099 with an altered DNA: Identification as a flavobacterium." Science, 160:893-894.

ROSTAND, J. (1960). Error and deception in science (A. Pomerans, trans.). New York: Basic Books.

ROTHMAN, R. (1972). "A dissenting view on the scientific ethos." British Journal of Sociology, 23:102-108.

ROUSSEAU, D., and PORTO, S. (1970). "Polywater: Polymer or artifact?" Science, 167(March 27):1715-1719.

SCHEFFLER, I. (1967). Science and subjectivity. Cambridge: Harvard University Press.

SETTLE, R. (1961). "An experiment in the history of science." Science, 133(January 6):19-23.

SMITH, M. (1977). "Antagonisms and controversies." Science, 196(April 15):258.

STORER, N. (1966). The social system of science. New York: Holt, Rinehart and Winston.

STERLING, T. (1959). "Publication decisions and their possible effects on inferences drawn from tests of significance or vice versa." Journal of the American Statistical Association, 54:30-34.

ST. JAMES-ROBERTS, I. (1976a). "Are researchers trustworthy?" New Scientist, 71(September 2):481-483.

--- (1976b). "Cheating in science." New Scientist, 72(November 25):466-469.

SULLIVAN, D. (1975). "Competition in bio-medical science: Extent,structure and consequences. Sociology of Education, 48(spring):223-241.

SULLIVAN, W. (1970). "Startling prospect of a new form of water." New York Times, 28(June):73.

TOOMER, G. (1975). "Ptolemy." Pp. 186-206 in Dictionary of scientific biography (vol. 11). New York: Scribner's.

WATSON, J. (1968). The double helix. New York: Atheneum.

WEBER, M. (1946). "Science as a vocation." Pp. 129-156 in H. Gerth and C. Mills (trans. and eds.), From Max Weber: Essays in sociology (first published in 1919). New York: Oxford University Press.

WEINER, J.S. (1955). The Piltdown forgery. London: Geoffrey Cumberlege, Oxford University Press.

WEST, S. (1960). "The ideology of academic scientists." IRE Transactions on Engineering Management, EM-7:54-62.

WESTFALL, R. (1973a). "Newton and the fudge factor." Science, 179(February 23):751-758.

--- (1973b). "Reply." Science, 180(June 15):1121.

WIENER, N. (1956). I am a mathematician. New York: Doubleday.

WRIGHT, S. (1966). "Mendel's ratios." Pp. 173-175 in C. Stern and E. Sherwood (eds.), The origin of genetics: A Mendel source book. San Francisco: W.H. Freeman.

WUNDERLICH, R. (1974). "The scientific ethos." British Journal of Sociology, 25:373-377.

ZAHLER, R. (1976). "Errors in mathematical proofs." Science, 193(July 9):98.

ZIRKLE, C. (1954). "The citation of fraudulent data." Science, 120(July):189-190.

ZUCKERMAN, H. (1968). "Patterns of name-ordering among authors of scientific papers: A study of social symbolism and its ambiguity." American Journal of Sociology, 74:276-291.

--- (1970). "Stratification in American science." Sociological Inquiry, 40(spring): 235-257.

ZUCKERMAN, H., and MERTON, R. (1971). "Patterns of evaluation in science: Institutionalization, structure and functions of the referee system." Minerva, 9(January):66-100. Reprinted (1973) pp. 460-496 in R. Merton, The sociology of science. Chicago: University of Chicago Press.

4

MEDICINE, SOCIAL CHANGE, AND DEVIANT BEHAVIOR

ARNOLD BIRENBAUM

AUTHOR'S NOTE: *I wish to thank Lewis Antine for his thoughtful comments on an earlier version of this paper.*

The rapid growth of the field of health care has produced new patterns of utilization, new advances in knowledge and new forms of deviant behavior by physicians and other health care providers. Some discussions in the sociological literature have focused on practices which sought to deceive patients, such as spurious nostrums, devices and treatment (Roebuck and Hunter, 1974:302-306). Marginal practitioners, both in and outside of organized medicine, were viewed as making unsubstantiated claims to cure. Unethical practices within the profession of medicine have been accounted for as incomplete professional socialization or the acquisition of inappropriate knowledge, ability, or motivation (Dansereau, 1974:88-89).

Students of the professions have not concerned themselves with deviant behavior which occurs in the medical routine. These instances of fraud, abuse, inappropriate personal conduct and incompetence can no longer be overlooked while the medical profession is publicly criticized for its failure to subject wayward practitioners to stricter discipline.

Medicine has shifted in its organization and structure from solo practice to corporate forms of health care delivery. Medical practice no longer follows the entrepreneurial model, and deviant practitioners cannot simply be seen as quacks. Rather, with the establishment of the health care delivery system as a major industry comparable only to the defense industry, new forms of deviance have evolved which fit these new institutional arrangements. The focus of this report will be on two kinds of deviant behavior related to these changes in health care: (1) the overutilization of services encouraged by certain kinds of medical practices and (2) medical neglect or negligence which produces iatrogenic disorders. Then I will try to examine the procedures and resources available to the medical profession and state regulatory agencies to prevent and punish deviant behavior. Finally, some current and future developments in the area of social control in medicine will be discussed.

The failure of the profession of medicine to regulate itself with regard to these two forms of deviance is evident in the public reports of rule-violating behavior. Abuse of the federally funded Medicaid program of health services for the poor has received extensive documentation and publicity in the Senate Subcommittee report on practitioners participating in the program (Staff Report, 1976). As early as 1973 evidence of the same unethical and criminal practices was uncovered by the *New York Daily News* in a Pulitzer Prize winning series of articles.

In a case of a chiropractor convicted of Medicaid fraud in 1976 (Lubasch, 1976:30), a Federal District Court Judge, Charles L. Brieant, Jr., ruefully suggested that while the defendant was a fine practitioner the evidence showed him to be guilty of theft. Explaining further, the judge presented the basic sociological problem:

> Those greater minds than ours who contrived this Medicaid legislation created a very easy and obvious means to steal public funds. Why did they do this? I think the answer is two-fold.
>
> First, legislators thought that physicians were above that sort of thing because of the education they have, because of the respect they receive from the community and because of the standing they have, that they would not do any such thing.
>
> I think also that the Government believed they did not want bureaucrats intervening between the physician and his patients solely to prevent fraud. Their expectations were not fulfilled, and you are not alone among those who engaged in fraud and there is no excuse for it.

Mounting evidence from medical and nonmedical sources indicates that the profession of medicine has not been effective in maintaining high standards of performance. The technical competency of physicians has been questioned in a study of their knowledge of appropriate uses of medications and in an examination of hospital medical procedures. These data suggest that some physicians inappropriately perform surgery where diagnoses do not indicate its necessity (Brody, 1976a) and that there is widespread ignorance of the correct prescription of medications (Rensberger, 1976b). Estimates have also been made about the prevalence of incompetent or unfit physicians, using epidemiological assumptions.

Finally, educated consumers (and some less educated consumers as well) have taken notice of the fitness of some individuals to practice and the unwillingness of the profession to punish or control those physicians whose behaviors are dangerous to patients. Significantly, a few physicians have begun to educate consumers about how to act in choosing a doctor, what to look for in an examination and what kind of questions to ask (Brody, 1976b). These reactions to deviant behavior in health care services delivery are going to be accompanied by new regulations on accountability where public monies are spent, as in the case of Medicaid and Medicare: In 1975, 27.7% of all health care costs were borne by the federal government and this proportion is expected to increase during the next five years (Department of Health, Education and Welfare, 1976:21). Finally, rising costs for health care services for more affluent consumers have made them ever more conscious of the heavy burden (i.e., Blue Cross) they bear in the form of insurance coverage.

THE STRUCTURE OF ECONOMIC, SOCIAL AND TECHNOLOGICAL DEVELOPMENT

The interpersonal and collective reactions to professionally deviant behavior engaged in by physicians have become more intense as the field of health care has grown into a major part of the American economy. All of the available economic indicators reflect this growth while the population has increased at a much slower rate.

> During the decade from 1965 to 1975, annual national health expenditures increased more than 300 percent, reaching a total of $118.5 billion. Per capita expenditures rose from $198 to $547, an average annual increase of 10.7 percent. Health care outlays as a proportion of the GNP rose significantly from 5.9 percent, reaching 8.3 percent after a three-year period in which the GNP had leveled off. [Department of Health, Education and Welfare, 1976:1]

The financing of health care is now organized around a combination of private and public insurance programs which reduce the likelihood of financial disaster for the person requiring expensive care while making it more certain than in the past that physicians will collect their fees and hospitals receive payment. In New York state, for example, "Medicare and Medicaid provide 41% of the income of hospitals, Blue Cross provides another 22%, and other direct public funds or private insurance funds account for an additional 27% so that 90% of hospital income is derived from third party payers" (New York State, 1976:15). Third party payers will probably assume an even greater proportion of the health care bill in the future under proposed compulsory national health insurance programs.

The unprecedented economic growth in health care has attracted large numbers of women and men who wish to become physicians or paramedical personnel. The field has also attracted considerable amounts of capital, with investments made in service organizations, such as nursing homes, and in the pharmaceutical industry. Capital is attracted to the health care field by profits that are unavailable in more traditional investment channels.

The input of risk capital into the field of health care helps to develop the technological capacities of the industry. Quality improvements in health care techniques have been produced by the introduction of sophisticated diagnostic devices and modes of treatment. Along with improvements in locating and measuring disease states, a broader range of chemotherapies and radiological treatments are available than in the past. This increase in technology represents a second technological revolution in medicine, the first being connected with the invention of ether, the standardization of surgical practices, advances in pathological examinations, asepsis and the germ theory of disease (Freidson, 1970:16).

Maxmen (1971), a physician, has pointed out that there are now available computerized machines which can perform 27 physiological measurements simultaneously. These tasks can be performed by paramedical personnel who are trained to administer and report on these tests. It should be noted that the introduction of technology in health care may improve performance but it does not reduce labor costs, as it usually does in other industries. There has been no decrease in the number of physicians in the United States, but a rather substantial increase during the past 25 years. Moreover, there are now 200 distinctly different health care occupations. Technicians, aides and physician extenders of all kinds are employed to aid the highly trained and specialized physician (Department of Health, Education and Welfare, 1976:21).

Technological advances primarily geared to increasing medical knowledge also produce extra costs to the consumer. Some of the most sophisticated devices are purchased by medical schools or medical centers in order to maintain their attractiveness as research centers to those physicians mainly interested in advancing knowledge or developing new techniques. Whether paid for directly by the consumer or by a third party payer, the costs of these machines (e.g., $600,000 for a body scanning X-ray machine) are often amortized on a per bed basis and are not exceptionally productive in providing revenue for a hospital. They do not increase income by providing frequently used, extensively reimbursable services.

The new technology and the consequent division of labor have created new requirements for their effective utilization. First, the cost of introducing these technological innovations is so great that few physicians in private solo practice can afford them. Moreover, many of these procedures can only be performed on patients who enter a hospital on an inpatient basis, making this organization an even more important source of health care than in the past (Perrow, 1965:948). The result is that increased hospital expenses and extended care facilities account for the greatest part of the spiraling costs of the past ten years in health care (Department of Health, Education and Welfare, 1976:24).

The social organization of health care may be defined as the general standards and specific rules which govern the relationship between physicians and other health care deliverers; these expectations govern the relationship between provider and patients as well. Rules define the network of existing positions and the rights and duties of their occupants. Titles identify positions such as doctor, nurse, blood technician and medical secretary. Some positions are identified internally within a particular organization according to rank and authority, making some surgeons chiefs of surgery and some nurses nursing supervisors.

Variability in social structure is built into the professionally organized field of health care, reflected in conditions and opportunities which influence conduct. Attributes of organizations such as size, extent of contact between various occupational specialists in the division of labor, prestige of an occupation, observability of performance, and contact with colleagues may affect various performers of roles in this field. Each performer of a role is then subject to different structured opportunities to uphold or deviate from the general standards and specific rules which constitute the social organization of a given establishment, such as a hospital or of a professional association.

While most professionals will, at some time or another in their careers, be subject to pressures to violate the ethical code which they have sworn to uphold, it is also possible that these constraints are patterned in such a way that the frequency and the rate of violation will vary from one sector of the profession to another. Similarly, it may be that incompetency in a profession may result from the rationalized organization of the practical activity that constitutes service, creating some opportunities for deviance and few opportunities for formal and/or informal mechanisms of social control to operate. Recent disclosures of abuse and fraud in shared medical practices specializing in Medicaid patients, as well as reactions to incompetency in the form of malpractice suits, provide useful cases for examining how social change in health care has encouraged deviant behavior and the reaction to it.

MEDICAID MEDICINE

Not long ago the physician who served the poor exclusively was a hero to his patients and admired by all. *The Last Angry Man,* a potboiling novel of the early 1960s later made into a motion picture starring Paul Muni, suggested that the profession of medicine encouraged sacrifice and devotion. Many physicians would reduce their fees for the poor and donated some of their time and services to charity patients in free clinics.

If medicine was never a profession made up of mendicants who serviced those in need, it has often been regarded as organized to serve society. Abraham Flexner, a social reformer of the progressive era, advocated the licensing of physicians because it inculcated a communal orientation and made them aware of the need to care for the new immigrant working classes. Writing in 1910, Flexner compared medicine to other practices which supported the newly emerging urban and industrial society.

> Medicine, curative and preventive, has indeed no analogy with business. Like the army, the police, or the social worker, the medical profession is supported for a benign, not a selfish, for a protective not an exploiting purpose [as quoted in Kunitz, 1974:24].

Government intervention, in the form of medical assistance financed under Title XIX of the Social Security Act, made poor people eligible for medical care in a plan which reimbursed physicians for services rendered. Lyndon B. Johnson hailed the plan as the best way to "assure the availability of and accessibility to the best health care for all Americans regardless of age, geography, or economic status" (Staff Report, 1976:1). Instead, Medicaid has led to the formation of a two-class medical care system, segregating the poor even more than in the past. Moreover, it has permitted the proliferation of health care practices which generate substantial incomes and abusive and fraudulent practices. Instead of being organized to serve society, Medicaid practices serve the practitioner. As one dentist told investigators of these practices,

> . . . the way the system is structured the trick is to see as many patients as possible as quickly as possible. Visits must be brief. Accordingly, it is uneconomical to give good care. [Staff Report, 1976:18]

The deviance produced by "Medicaid mills" has its own common culture, relative to these settings and represented by a unique nomenclature. These organized practices in health care provide students of deviant behavior with a glimpse into corporate white-collar crime, usually off limits to observers from the academic world (Wheeler, 1976:531).

It might also be suggested that the nomenclature blurs the distinctly illegal character of the activities, making it possible for people who might otherwise live differently to mentally separate deeds which run counter to professional ethics.

> "Ping-ponging" is the expression given to the most common mill abuse, the referral of patients from one practitioner to another within the facility, even though medically there is no need.
>
> "Ganging" refers to the practice of billing for multiple service to members of the same family on the same day.
>
> "Upgrading" is the practice of billing for a service more extensive than that actually provided.
>
> "Steering" is the direction of a patient to a particular pharmacy by a physician or anyone else in the medical center. [Staff Report, 1976:18-19]

Investigators for the Senate Subcommittee on long-term care brought 200 instances of minor complaints to Medicaid practices in New York City and were overtreated in 70% of the cases. While these procedures were being performed on healthy people, conventional practices, such as taking the temperature and blood pressure of a patient complaining of a cold, were not undertaken. Examinations of ears or eyes were performed in a most unusual manner: a throat was examined by shining a flashlight from a distance of five feet from the patient and without using a tongue depressor (Staff Report, 1976:44).

The growth of these abuses and fraudulent practices was encouraged by the application of the fee-for-service model at a somewhat lower than customary rate of reimbursement. It has also been possible under Medicaid reimbursement to employ various paramedical personnel whose services are billed separately. The more services performed by optometrists, podiatrists, chiropractors and others, the greater the volume of profit to the owner of the Medicaid practice which employs them.

The American Medical Association was very reluctant to abandon the fee-for-service system in the federally funded Medicare and Medicaid programs for fear of establishing a precedent for prepaid health service on a national (or nationalized) basis for the entire population. While there was bitter opposition to Medicare, led by the American Medical Association, before it was made into law, there has been a favorable response after passage and implementation and no organized boycott of patients (Colombotos, 1969:1).

Since the rate of reimbursement from Medicaid for services rendered is lower than rates set in private insurance plans or even Medicare (which sets rates according to customary fees), some physicians have refused to take these indigent patients and other have become specialists in their care. Medicine for the poor not only has its own shared culture but is concentrated in the hands of a few high volume billers, where "7 percent of the doctors practicing in New York City's Medicaid program earned 50 percent of the total paid to all doctors" (Staff Report, 1976:14).

The volume of billing found in a practice seems to be related to financial arrangements. In states where reimbursement procedures can take up to six months (as in New York), financial corporations or factoring firms have acted as collection agents for the practitioners. In exchange for immediate payment, practitioners charge anywhere from 12% to 24% of the face value of the invoices. It has also been pointed out by physicians who participate that the actual interest rate is closer to 48% per year since the factoring firm may receive reimbursement in half the time expected. The use of financial corporations encouraged practitioners to increase their volume to make up for the difference in lost income. Medicaid mills which used factoring firms tended to have practices which had twice the income of other practices. Small practices do not produce enough of a volume of claims, nor a great volume of expenses, to make employment of factoring profitable for owners or investors in Medicaid mills.

Medical practices which specialize in Medicaid patients also engage in business arrangements which, if not clearly illegal, are regarded as unethical. Owners of Medicaid practices are found to lease office space in exchange for a percentage of gross income, and to share fees between two or more physicians for reimbursement for the services rendered by one physician alone. The American Medical Association regards "rebates on prescription and appliances, the ownership of clinics or laboratories by joint stock companies composed in part or in whole by physicians, and the percentage lease renting of pharmacy space for a pharmacy owned by a physician or physicians as clearly unethical" (Staff Report, 1976:67). Enforcements of these rulings of the judicial council of the AMA are up to the local or state medical societies. During the period between 1966-1976 the Medical Society of the County of New York did not expel a single physician for abuse of Medicare or Medicaid and referred 14 complaints to the professional conduct offices of the State Departments of Health and Education (Staff Report, 1976:197).

While these business arrangements encourage overbilling in order to maintain high volume in reimbursement, physicians who engaged in unethical practices are not subject to formal sanctions from the Association devoted to maintaining them. Due to the lack of budget for hiring field auditors and investigators, enforcement by appropriate state and city agencies is very weak and irregular. Medicaid practice owners are well aware of the limited sanctions available to these regulatory agencies. Fines which are imposed are charged against future billing and encourage further abuses and fraud in order to recoup lost earnings (Staff Report, 1976:145). Physicians are also aware that certain illegal procedures such as billing for nonexistent patient visits (or nonexistent patients) involve greater risks than simply overbilling for an actual visit by a patient. These tactics depend on knowledge of the limits of enforcement and risks involved, producing a Dickensian parody of professional behavior.

> You never put through for a patient you didn't see. The patient might have been on vacation or in the hospital. That's the only way that they can hang you. I'm not that stupid. It is stupid to write bills on patients you didn't see on dates you weren't in your office. Other things [kinds of fraud] are all right. But if you put down anything strange, you'd better set a date or a note explaining it. Those are the things to look for. [Staff Report, 1976:59]

The way in which welfare medicine is organized makes it almost impossible for informal peer pressure to effectively enforce the standards of practice. First, the work of physicians in Medicaid practices is insulated from peer review by the nature of their in-house referral system which involves few of the standard medical specialists, except those required in order to receive reimbursement. Many medical practitioners do not have affiliations with medical schools or voluntary hospitals and may deal exclusively with proprietary hospitals which do not set high standards for attending physicians. Therefore, the work of Medicaid physicians cannot be observed, nor can they learn from more highly qualified practitioners. Secondly, many physicians in these practices are either from foreign medical schools or are just finished with residency requirements and are subject to financial pressures which encourage them to seek immediate income opportunities, resulting in further exclusion from peer review.

Patients provide little effective pressure on Medicaid practitioners, and physicians are aware of their weakness. Being unfamiliar with medical terminology, the poor can often be manipulated into a series of unnecessary tests, X-rays and procedures and can be encouraged to return for more of the same.[1] Patients are also not regarded by Medicaid practitioners as effective witnesses against them if their billing is subject to auditing. Since consumers in these cases do not pay for services and cannot exhaust their benefits, there are few incentives for them to become knowledgeable consumers of health care, asking questions about procedures and costs and retaining information about what was performed.

The extension of health services to the poor under Medicaid legislation can be regarded as simply the wasteful practices of welfare state legislation or it can be seen as the result of economic practices which have increased the marketing capacities of providers of services and purveyors of drugs and equipment. As in other industries which have reached this level of development, they seek to avoid declining profits. To meet these needs, more stable markets are sought for products and services, ones which are of great magnitude and constancy (Braverman, 1974:265). Since the medical marketplace, like other marketplaces, is uncertain, providers often seek to *induce* or manufacture a stable demand which can support their needs.

It is also the case that higher rates of profits are sought out by providers of risk capital in those sectors of health care which have not developed fully institutionalized relationships with patients and third party payers. As in other new forms of industry, new forms of production are built upon the employment of marginal operatives, unprotected and unrestrained by more traditional practices and protective associations such as unions. Higher status physicians linked to voluntary hospitals or medical schools would be loath to risk their reputations and participate in the marginal operations disparagingly regarded as Medicaid mills.

While more reputable physicians do not participate in these practices, they tolerate their existence. County and state medical societies are composed of physicians from regions where Medicaid mills flourish; state professional licensing boards are made up of these same physicians. It is important to examine whether physicians can regulate deviant behavior among peers when it takes the form of abuse and fraud, and the conditions under which colleagues will punish deviant behavior.

INAPPROPRIATE BEHAVIOR, INCOMPETENCY AND MALPRACTICE

Professions often depend on a lengthy period of training in which new practitioners must acquire knowledge, ability and motivation as the central means of regulating the behavior of their members. Codes of ethics are also created by professions to remind practitioners of what they can and cannot do. While these formal means of social control do exist, they are more effective in preserving the independence of the professional practitioner than in removing those who behave inappropriately or are technically incompetent. In fact, the increase in the number of malpractice suits in the United States in the last decade and the rapid rise in the cost of malpractice insurance may be partially a result of the failure of formal and informal means of sanction to regulate effectively the medical profession.

State regulatory boards have been very reluctant to revoke the licenses of physicians and thereby remove their means of livelihood. In 1975, Dr. Robert G. Derbyshire of the New Mexico Board of Medical Examiners and Dr. Roger O. Egeberg of the Department of Health, Education and Welfare estimated that 16,000 physicians were incompetent or unfit out of a total of 320,000 licensed physicians in the United States (Rensberger, 1976a:20). While 5% of all physicians are deemed incompetent or unfit, an average of only 66 licenses are revoked every year in the United States. During the period between 1969-1973, 20 states took no disciplinary action at all. Moreover, many of the regulatory boards, such as the New York Board for Professional Medical Conduct, are understaffed and cannot pursue many investigations.

Many state regulatory boards have been limited largely to dealing with cases of misconduct which involve criminal convictions. The New York State legislature, in response to the malpractice crisis, introduced new grounds for defining professional misconduct, including "practicing the profession fraudulently, beyond its authorized scope, with gross incompetence, with gross negligence or incompetence on more than one occasion" (New York, 1976:150).

In addition to introducing new grounds for discipline, the new laws create intermediate penalties, such as temporary suspension of licenses, censure, suspension and retraining, and fines (New York, 1976:149). While this new range of sanctions seems more fitting to the new criteria for investigation and discipline, there is no evidence that more vigorous pursuits of inappropriately behaving or incompetently performing physicians are occurring than in the past. Even formal study of mortality in hospitals where malpractice is discovered does not lead to disciplinary action by county medical societies or state licensing boards (*New York Times,* 1976).

How can this lack of enforcement be accounted for? Some clues may be found in the organizational routine of the profession. The everyday practice of medicine is based on a form of informal social organization which encourages the development of networks of colleagues who exchange services and very often confer on cases. Those practitioners whose work is regarded as substandard may not be utilized by the colleague network and are subject to what Freidson (1970:191) refers to as a "personal boycott." As a result of these informal sanctions, practitioners snubbed in one sector of the field will often move beyond the observability of those who invoked these sanctions. Instead of maintaining contact and seeking to upgrade the performance of the delinquent physician, the upright performers of these roles seek to protect their own reputations and their right to practice independently. As Freidson (1970:199) indicates, there may be several mutually exclusive circles existing in the same region:

> The consequence is that a "single" inclusive profession can contain within it and even encourage markedly different ethical and technical practices, limited in a very superficial way by the common core of training required for licensing and by writings of the leaders of the profession. Insofar as the local practitioner population is large enough, the segregated networks are at least partly ordered by prestige, and only the higher levels are linked in with (and contribute to) the national and international associations representing various formal aspects of the profession.

Rather than conceptualizing the medical profession as a company of equals, Freidson's analysis suggests that various castes may exist, unified only in the fact that they provide medical services and have the same title. Do physicians who begin their careers serving the poor in Medicaid mills, without admitting rights to voluntary hospitals or medical school faculty appointments, remain in that position throughout their careers, no matter how well they do financially? Do physicians cast out of the elite medical care institutions because others judge their work as not up to standards join those who service the lower orders?

More interesting for the study of deviant behavior, such processes of discrediting a member of the profession represent a great deal of structured ambiguity since physicians try not to publicly castigate a fellow physician. Are relations rarely severed in a formal way because one never knows when fellow professionals may meet again or whether the same accusations will be made to the accuser or because there is no group support for these sanctions? While internal exile is utilized in the profession of medicine to avoid embarrassment and possible conflict with the person regarded as deviant, there is also no formal system for upgrading competency. Rarely are efforts made to improve the skills of the physician being sanctioned by taking action which would lead to more supervised practice. The potential for retraining and improvement of performance is there since the upright physician can suggest these avenues. Moreover, both upright and delinquent physicians could separate the deviant acts from the actor himself, providing an opportunity to ceremonialize the occasion and restore belief in the professional who is being questioned to his right to improve. Rather than crystallizing the deviance into an organized career, professionals have the opportunity to restore their belief in the competency or fitness of the physician whose standards need to be upgraded.

The problem of dealing with the organized abuse and fraud of Medicaid practices requires both professional and state intervention. In these instances the kind of interpersonal forms of control suggested in the previous discussion would not be fitting since the deviance under discussion has become a "patterned evasion" of professional, technical and ethical standards. This form of deviant behavior may require the implementation and enforcement of social norms which limit the practice of medicine in such a way that dedication to public service prevails over the physician's right to set the terms of medical practice (Freidson, 1975:127). Such steps would be difficult to undertake unless supported by a substantial minority of physicians wishing to end the two-class system of medical care that we have in the United States. It would mean that purchasing power, either through private or public sources, would no longer be a relevant consideration in determining which patients to treat or how much effort should be expended in each case.

CONCLUSION

If the structure and organization of medicine generates its own deviance and differing rates of deviant behavior, then it is also possible to conceive of the health care delivery system as generating its own reaction to deviance and differing rates of response. The demands for reform in the organization and delivery of health care may well result from structured discrepancies between "culturally induced personal aspirations and patterned differentials in access to the opportunity structure for moving toward these aspirations by institutionalized means" (Merton, 1976:125). Social movements, as Dubin (1959) has noted, may constitute a form of deviance as people seek to develop new institutionalized means to achieve culturally approved goals.

Reform efforts to improve the level of competency of the profession of medicine and reduce the patterned fraud and abuse in Medicaid practices may result from the social changes which have encouraged these forms of deviant behavior. The high volume of demand for health services, increased utilization of technology, and the more refined division of labor can be used to justify the institutionalization of new regulatory practices because older forms of regulation are not adequate. Second, computer technology can be utilized to determine the rates of deviance and identify its differential location in the health care delivery system. Finally, the growth of the health care delivery system has called into being sufficient numbers of physicians who are in contact with each other as promoters of more effective deployment of health care personnel to become concerned with issues related to quality of care as well as distribution. Such "corporate rationalizers," as identified by Alford (1972:143), form a network of medical planners who have already recognized the need for the reallocation of resources. The structured constraints toward social control, to extend the Merton paradigm, are as evident in these conditions produced by social change as the deviant behavior it has produced. The two processes, as always, are connected through the social structure.

While this essay suggests a cyclical character to the relationship between social change and deviant behavior, with efforts to reform medicine following upon these organized forms of nonconformity, there are other predictions which can be made from this analysis. These predictions have more to do with the overall developments in the field of medicine engendered by the reaction to these deviant practices. It can be anticipated that efforts to promote greater social control in medicine will help to bring about greater bureaucratization of that field, making physicians become salaried officials in health delivery organizations of various types.

Medicine, as the preeminent profession, is expected to regulate itself, and while it is clear that many of the unethical and incompetent behaviors discussed here are not standard practices, the current mechanisms of social control are ineffective. While peer regulation through collegial contact may be effective to prevent certain kinds of deviant behavior, other kinds of deviant behavior are not within or fall outside the scope of the group norms of medicine. In other words, rules may simply not exist for which these practices are violations. These unethical practices, as found in Medicaid facilities, may not be regarded by the elites in the field as their responsibility to end because they are not within the effective control of the norms of the group.

That the leaders of any institutionalized sphere are aware of the extent to which actual role performers live up to normative expectations should come as no surprise, given their location in the group (Merton, 1957:342). However, it should also be pointed out that the degree of supervision which can be engaged in by leaders is "itself limited by the norms of the group" (Merton, 1957:343). Close supervision would be a violation in itself of the spirit of collegiality in the social organization of professional work.

Yet even when the norms do not restrict supervision, enforcement is limited by the increased segmentation of the field. Informal means of social control are most effective when there is a great deal of face-to-face contact. The elites in medicine are not always linked to the deviants through an organization which permits the former to exercise control over the latter by virtue of some official capacity. Effective enforcement cannot be promoted immediately unless this kind of reorganization takes place.

What kinds of inducements are there within the field of health care to encourage members of the profession of medicine to seek out more effective enforcement? The greatest inducement would be to maintain control over the means of health care, a right that physicians in many other countries do not have where national health services exist. It is ironic that the original resistance to state regulation of Medicare and Medicaid by the American Medical Association has permitted the growth of routine deviation in the field and has set the groundwork for even more control than was originally anticipated. This constraint toward more social control may reform much of the current structure of organized health care in the United States.

Bureaucratization, however, can be a transforming process that can go far beyond the original purposes of those who seek to reform medicine. The dynamics of coping with deviance in medicine could produce the generalized recognition that the profession is a controllable force in society. The efforts to deal with deviance based on an unregulated fee-for-service system may react back upon the entire field of medicine itself, with consumers and some physicians beginning to realize the incompatibility between the professional norms of service-giving and profit making. Once the reform activities begin, there is no way to stop only with Medicaid fraud and individual incompetency. Structural reform would mean bringing the entire profession into line with the needs of the population and the demands of other health care personnel.

In a volume devoted to the subject of social change and deviant behavior, it is most appropriate to extend this line of reasoning to the subject of public policy and criminal behavior in organizations. There is so little known about the subject because it is so closely supervised by the powerful and the rich. Unlike medicine, there are no technical standards for performance that separate the incompetent from the competent. Ethical standards are of little consequence. Those who are in supervisory and policy-making positions have done little to uncover or correct these forms of deviant behavior. Specifically, why has there been so much reluctance to close off tax loopholes, to develop a realistic corporate tax structure, to impose limits to irresponsible practices of those who have great wealth or use it, to tax income from whatever source derived? Similarly, could not the resources of the federal, state, and local governments in these United States eliminate organized crime, even with some corrupt officials? Why are no major campaigns mounted against organized crime, even just for public display?

The answers lie in examining the role of government in a capitalist society, wherein little is done to restrain corporate achievement, even if it is clearly ill-gotten gain. Such restraint also means that honestly arrived at profits will also be questioned. Capitalism as a class society reproduces itself culturally as well as in social structural dimensions. Organizational deviance may be an enduring part of a social system which often appears to be managed in order for the system to reproduce itself so that there are those motivated to labor and those who are motivated to live off the labor of others. Yet medicine and public health policy as well will probably have to change in order to continue to receive the loyal support of those who produce the goods, services, and knowledge which make this system function.

NOTE

1. The poor seem to be getting form without substance in health care. It comes as no surprise, then, that since the inception of the Medicaid laws in 1964, the patterns of utilization for the poor and the better off have been reversed so that the former were using physicians' services at a somewhat higher rate than the rest of the population. However, better off people were still more likely to take preventive steps, such as Pap tests, eye tests and glaucoma examinations (Department of Health, Education and Welfare, 1976:18).

REFERENCES

ALFORD, R. (1972). "The political economy of health care: Dynamics without change." Politics and Society, Winter:1-38.

BRAVERMAN, H. (1974). Labor and monopoly capital: The degradation of work in the twentieth century. New York: Monthly Review Press.

BRODY, J.E. (1976a). "Incompetent surgery is found not isolated." New York Times. January 27, pp. 1, 24.

--- (1976b). "How educated patients get proper health care." New York Times. January 30, pp. 1, 10.

COLOMBOTOS, J. (1969). "Physicians and Medicare: A before-after study of the effects of legislation on attitudes." American Sociological Review, 34:1-17.

DANSEREAU, H.K. (1974). "Unethical behavior: Professional deviance." Pp. 75-89 in C.D. Bryant (ed.), Deviant behavior: Occupational and organizational bases. Chicago: Rand McNally.

Department of Health, Education and Welfare (1976). Forward plan for health: FY 1978-82. Washington, D.C.: Author.

DUBIN, R. (1959). "Deviant behavior and social structure: Continuities in social theory." American Sociological Review, 24:147-164.

FREIDSON, E. (1970). The profession of medicine: A study of the sociology of applied knowledge. New York: Dodd, Mead.

--- (1975). "The social control of the professions: Toward ethical reform in a 'delinquent community.' " Program of General and Continuing Education in the Humanities Seminar Reports, 3:121-127.

KUNITZ, S.J. (1974). "Professionalism and social control in the progressive era: The case of the Flexner report." Social Problems, 22:16-27.

LUBASCH, A.H. (1976). "Chiropractor given 4-year prison term." New York Times. September 9, p. 30.

MAXMEN, J. (1971). "Goodbye, Dr. Welby." Social Policy, 3:97-106.

MERTON, R.K. (1957). "Continuities in the theory of reference groups and social structure." Pp. 281-386 in Social theory and social structure. Rev. and enlarged ed. New York: Free Press.

--- (1976). "Structural analysis in sociology." Pp. 109-144 in Sociological ambivalence and other essays. New York: Free Press.

New York State (1976). "Report of the special advisory panel on medical malpractice." Albany, N.Y.: Author.

New York Times (1976). "A study of malpractice deaths reported ended without action." October 5, p. 20.

PERROW, C. (1965). "Hospitals: Technology, structure and goals." Pp. 910-971 in J.G. March (ed.), Handbook of organizations. Chicago: Rand McNally.

RENSBERGER, B. (1976a). "Unfit doctors create worry in profession." New York Times. January 26, pp. 1, 20.

--- (1976b). "Thousands a year killed by faulty prescriptions." New York Times. January 28, pp. 1, 20.

ROEBUCK, J.B., and HUNTER, R.B. (1974). "Medical quackery as deviant behavior." Pp. 300-311 in C.D. Bryant (ed.), Deviant behavior: Occupational and organizational bases. Chicago: Rand McNally.

Staff Report, Subcommittee on Long-Term Care of the Special Committee on Aging, United States Senate (1976). "Fraud and abuse among practitioners participating in the Medicaid program." Washington, D.C.: U.S. Government Printing Office.

WHEELER, S. (1976). "Trends and problems in the sociological study of crime." Social Problems, 23:525-534.

5

THE GUN
Trigger for Social Change

HENRY BARBERA

Throughout the Middle Ages the people of Europe were in a period of contraction. From the eighth century through the fifteenth one group of warriors after another carved out huge pieces of European territory. These outsiders came from all directions: the Vikings came from the North, the Moslems from the South, and the Mongols, against whom no European army ever won a battle, came from the East, though they decided on their own to return. The Mongols were followed by the Turks who decided to stay.

On the 28th of May, 1453, the Turks entered Constantinople. Their advance continued, powerful and seemingly irresistible. Northern Serbia was invaded in 1459. Bosnia-Herzegovina in 1463-1466. The Negroponte was taken from the Venetians in 1470. Albania was invaded after 1468. There can be no doubt that "the Turkish menace" was what most deeply concerned fifteenth- and sixteenth-century Europeans. Among the books printed in France between 1480 and 1609, the title relating to the Turks and the Turkish Empire were twice as numerous as those relating to the Americas (Atkinson, 1935).

The reasons for the chronic weakness of medieval Europe are clear enough. To begin with, Europe was not heavily populated (never more than 100 million people). More important, Europeans were divided and constantly busy in "waging wars against each other, staining their hands with the blood of their own people, defiling their arms with the blood of Christian" (Cippola, 1965:17). When composite armies were put together, as during the Crusades, the main result was general confusion. Finally, the military organization of the European potentates was far from being efficient. Europe and more especially Eastern Europe relied on heavily armored cavalry which was colorful but unwieldy. The highly individualistic Western knight was a poor opponent to the strictly disciplined and highly obedient Eastern horsemen.

But in time the situation began to change. Slowly at first and then with increasing rapidity, the Europeans embarked upon a state of expansion, one which has yet to abate. The symbolic turning point must include the capture of Ceuta (1415) in North Africa by the Portuguese, the discovery of America (1492), and the arrival of Vasco da Gama in Calicut (1498). These achievements in external contact and conquest meant that the Turks and all other enemies could be circumvented. Europeans had dreamed for centuries of bypassing their enemies, but lacked the means to do so. Now, with the invention of the gun, that great equalizer, motive and means were conjoined.

The widespread use of the gun did not come easily or quickly. It was met with considerable ambivalence and even resistance by those who would benefit most, but when it came, its greatest impact lay in the wider context of war and society rather than in the practice and art of warfare. Of course, the gun evoked immediate changes in fortifications: to counter the new artillery, the tall, thin walls of the castle had to be replaced or girdled by low and thick ones; it contributed to the development of heavier armor; it slowed down armies in the field and added to the administrative problems; it opened certain tactical possibilities; it inflicted unexpected casualties and introduced a new atmosphere of uncertainty and fear into warfare. But the larger changes brought about through the use of the gun are the structural ones, those crucial changes that make the difference between types of men and warriors, between an estate and class society, between a feudal and a modern state, and therein lies the importance of our subject. It is the story of the great transition between two ages caused in large part by the introduction of a new technic perceived as deviant by a significant number of people and especially by the elites.

THAT HORRYBLE INSTRUMENT OF GONNES

The peculiar violence with which balls and bullets sped through the air led some people to suppose that the speed obtained by a missile fired from a handgun or a cannon was supernatural in origin. Consequently it seemed logical in an age of strong Christian belief to conclude that the invention of the gun was the work of the devil. A modern, who no longer believes in the devil, ejaculates "the son of a gun" without realizing the meaning of his curse.

On the title page of the 1489 Basle edition of Augustine's *De Civitate Dei,* we see devils shooting with guns at the inhabitants of the city of God. In 1499 Polydore Virgil remarked "of all other weapons that were devised to the destruction of man, the gones be most devilische." Virgil attributed their invention to "a certaine Almaine" and continued: "For this invencion, he received this benefit that his name was never knowen lest he might for thys abhomynable devise, have been cursed and evil spoken of whilest the worlde standeth" (Virgil, 1868 ed.:bk. ii, ch. vii). But a culprit was found in a monk named Schwartz. In popular woodcuts and engraving Schwartz is shown inventing gunpowder with the aid of horned and hoofed laboratory assistants.

Around 1500 an anonymous author had this to say about Schwartz (quoted by Straker, 1931:143, from the book, *Of the First Invention of That Horryble Instrument of Gonnes):*

> In the year of our Lord God 1380 . . . one Bertholdus Swartz, an Almayne, did first invent the makying of Gonnes by the putting of the powder of brimstone in a mortar for a medicine, who covered the mortar by a stone, and striking fyer it so fortuned that a sparke fell into the said powder, whereby there arose a very sudden flame . . . and herwith lifted upp the stone . . . a great hight, which thing the said Bertholdus perceiving did this devise by the Suggestion (as it was thought) of the Devyll himself, a Pipe of iron, and loaded it with the powder, and so finished this deadlye and horryble Engine, and then taught it to the Venecians when they had warres against the [Genoese], which was in anno domini 1380.

The deadly and horrible engine was dwelt on not only by noncombatant intellectuals but by men who had seen guns in action; the French surgeon, Ambroise Paré, commenting on the wounds he had been treating, battlefield after battlefield, in the renewed Italian wars of the 1540s, wrote (Paré, 1634:407, and see also Packard, 1921):

> . . . verily when I consider with myself all the sorts of warlike engines which the Ancients use . . . they seem to me certain childish sports and games . . . for these modern inventions are such as easily exceed all the best appointed and cruel engines which can be mentioned or thought upon in the shape, cruelty, and appearance of the operations.

War was in hard fact becoming more impersonal, brutal and squalid. There was less hand-to-hand combat; in spite of considerable advances in their treatment, gunwounds remained more dangerous than those made by steel; the long sieges which characterized so much warfare in the sixteenth century involved lengthy exposure in trenches, and death from exposure and malnutrition became more common than death in action (Howard, 1976).

It was at this point that feudal warriors began to sense the threat that the gun posed to their power and privilege in society. The technology of the knight was the sword, dagger, lance, armor, shield, and horse. All of these took time to learn about, and they were all learned through selected apprentice-master relationships in a closed guild setting. The adoption of heavy cavalry by the Franks from the mid-eighth century and the consequent demand for mounted retainers, expensively equipped and elaborately trained to fight on horseback, formed the military basis of European society. A war horse and possibly a remount, two palfreys for esquires to carry the armor to the battlefield and to equip the knight, and the mail armor itself—all of these were expensive. A suit of mail cost the price of a small farm at the time of the Third Crusade. Later, as plate armor was introduced and the steed had to be the dextrarius, a heavier animal altogether, the cost soared still more. Thus, only the sons of the rich and well-connected could afford to be knights. Alternatively, if a prince wanted a particular man or set of men to act as his mounted cavalry, he had to give them the wherewithal. In those nonmonetized days this meant giving a conditional gift of land with enough peasants to farm it for him.

Throughout the Middle Ages, feudal warriors were preoccupied with the etiquette of personal combat, a steady appetite for battle descriptions in poem and chronicle, and a careful establishment of legal rights and wrongs of specific acts of aggression, although war itself was taken for granted, and arguments for and against it hardly heard. For one reason or another, a knight's main hope of survival continued to be placed in large measure in the hands of God. Knighthood, its duties and also its privileges, along with the moral values of the church, incarnated the chivalric ideal (Painter, 1940).

Since the invention of the gun, the man on horseback could no longer dominate the scene. The chivalric ideal had to wither and the military virtues of courage, endurance, and valor questioned and reinterpreted. The gun was unquestionably a grievance for the horseman who had invested his fortune on his equipment, and for the individual fighting for personal glory rather than for a state or a cause. The idea that war is a trial of moral values, by battle in which the church referees for God, was replaced by a new certainty: that war is a means toward a political end in which the deciding factor is power.

The gun makes all men alike tall, it democratizes war. It is precisely this recognition that prompts the feudal warrior to inveigh against the new means of destruction. So some of the most threatened knights, those who would more quickly slip in rank, began to attack not only the gun as a "devilische instrument" but also the new type of man who would wield it as a base coward. What they attempted to do was join religious and class sentiments against the new technology and the rising townsmen.

To them there was something unfair and fundamentally brutal about killing an armored knight with the new projectiles. In his *Commentaries,* Blaise de Monluc in about 1550 refers to "poltroons that had not dared look those men in the face at hand, which at distance they had laid dead with their confounded bullets," paralleled by Fronsperger's remark that "many a time and oft it happens that a brave and manly hero is killed by a shot from a craven who would not dare look him in the face" (both citations from Hale, 1962:29). The response of Gian Paolo Vitelli to a widespread use of firearms by his enemies shows how the new weapons contributed to a new ferocity. After witnessing in battle the death of many of his companions by gunfire, he began to pluck out the eyes and cut off the hands of all gunmen whom he could capture, deeming it disgraceful that noble men-at-arms should be shot from a distance by low-born infantrymen. When in 1498 he took Buti, a small town near Pisa, he had the hands of all the gunners of the garrison cut off (Taylor, 1921:56). And Bayard–*chevalier sans peur et sans reproche*–supposedly the last great representative of medieval chivalry, shot them when captured. Ironically enough he was himself killed in the battle of Sesia by a ball fired from a handgun (Fuller, 1946:91).

The comments and actions of such actual warriors underlay the protest of the great artists. Ariosto in his famous epic *Orlando Furioso* (1516, libro I, canto 9), narrates how Orlando, his hero and the embodiment of knightly virtues, was forced to face an enemy with a firearm:

At once the lightning flashes, shakes the ground,
The trembling bulwarks echo to the sound,
The pest, that never spends in vain its force,
But shatters all that dares oppose its course,
Whizzing impetuous flies around the wind.

When the invincible Orlando succeeded in overcoming this redoubtable enemy with a gun and could choose from the rich booty:

. . . nothing would the champion bear away
From all the spoils of that victorious day
Save that device, whose unresisted force
Resembled thunder in its rapid course.

Then he sailed out on the ocean, plunging the weapon into the sea and exclaiming:

O! Curs'd device! base implement of death!
Fram'd in the black Tartarean realms beneath!
By Beelzebub's malicious art design'd
To ruin all the face of human kind. . . .
That ne'er again a knight by thee may dare,
Or dastard cowards, by thy help in war,
With vantage base, assault a nobler foe,
Here lie for ever in th' abyss below!

Near the end of the century, the emotion and force in that poem was put into prose form by Cervantes. Consider this selection from Quixote's curious discourse on arms and letters (Cervantes, 1964 ed.:391-392):

> Blessed were those ages that were without the dreadful fury of those diabolical engines of artillery, whose inventory, I truly believe, is now receiving in hell the reward for his devilish invention, by means of which a base and cowardly hand may deprive the most valiant knight of life. While such a knight fights with all the bravery and ardor that enkindle gallant hearts, without his knowing how or whence there comes a random bullet (discharged by one who perhaps ran away in terror at the flash of his own accursed machine) that cuts short and ends in an instant the life of one who deserved to live for centuries to come. When I consider this, I have a mind to say that I am grieved in my soul at having undertaken this profession of knight-errantry in so detestable an age as this we live in. For although no peril can daunt me, still it troubles me to think that powder and lead may deprive me of the chance of making myself famous and renowned for the strength of my arm and the edge of my sword over all the known earth.

SON OF A GUN

During the fifteenth century the gun had acquired a rich store of symbolic and associative overtones and was already rivalling the sword as the embracing symbol of war. After its introduction and widespread use, the antagonism of townsman and knight increased. These devices were the products of urban arts and crafts; they resulted from the economic, social and intellectual changes that disintegrated feudalism and were manufactured by the foes of warrior-knights–city dwellers and artisans. Books and manuals were printed, schools of instruction arose preparing the sons of townsmen in the new warfare; foundries and arsenals proliferated everywhere. These are some of the first factors noticed as a result of the invention of the gun.

The art of gunnery produced a new type of warrior, the cold-blooded, technically inclined man who in the middle of the fight had to carry out a series of measurements and calculation, no matter how rough and imprecise. The growing anonymity of the individual soldier, the indiscriminate death dealt by shot and ball: these factors, it was claimed, had ruined war as a finishing school for the knightly character. The new type of fighter vividly contrasts with the hot-blooded warrior of the old days who daringly threw himself into the mêlée with feathers, flags and sword, screaming and shouting and perspiring as much as humanly possible. "The result of these combats was no longer regarded as a Divine judgement, but as a triumph of personal merit, and to the minds of the spectators seemed to be both the decision of an exciting competition and a satisfaction for the honour of the army or the nation" (Burckhardt, 1950:63).

Seeing the growing disoccupation of the feudal warrior, some members of the new middle class were congratulating themselves over their recently acquired powers and others were gloating over the slipping anachronism. Let us listen to the self-praise of Artillery Captain Michael Mieth in the Emperor's service.

"Where are now those numerous robber castles, built on high mountains, in which not a few shamefully robbing and burning murderers, preserving themselves safely, not only made whole territories unsafe, but even defied the highest and crowned heads? Have they not been intimidated by the guns, like chickens, and are their residences not turned into stone-heaps and dens of owls, snakes and bad spirits" (cited by Vagts, 1937:43).

Not only did gunpowder blast the feudal strongholds, but also the ideals of their owners. As portable firearms were multiplied, the medieval contempt for unmounted troops (cf. Hatto, 1940) was undermined, until in tactical importance, gun-toting foot soldiers were raised to the level of the mounted men-at-arms. Thus it came about that, whereas among the feudal knights ruses of war, surprisals, pursuits and even the exploitation of the enemy's defeat were considered dishonorable and unchivalrous, they now became customary. At the end of the fifteenth century Machiavelli (1940 ed.: chap. xl, bk. iii) says: "Although in all other affairs it is hateful to use fraud, in the operations of war it is praiseworthy and glorious."

According to the mythology of the time, it was not chivalrous to be superior in numbers or differently armed, or to fight at a distance. The knight did not consider the bow and arrow, the cannon and handgun as fair weapons. The sword and lance knew where and when the adversary was struck, the arrow or ball or bullet did not. Consider this vignette of aristocratic disdain toward the gun. In 1582, Alexander Farnese, Duke of Parma, was besieging Dudenarde. One day in early spring Farnese had a table laid for himself and his staff, to dine in the open air near to the entrenchment:

> Hardly had the repast commenced, when a ball came flying over the table, taking off the head of a young Walloon officer who was sitting near Parma. A portion of his skull struck out the eye of another gentleman present. A second ball destroyed two more of the guests as they sat at the banquet. The blood and brains of these unfortunate individuals were strewn over the festive board, and the others all started to their feet, having little appetite left for their dinner. Alexander alone remained in his seat. Quietly ordering the attendants to remove the dead bodies, and to bring a clean tablecloth, he insisted that his guests should resume their places. [Motley, 1856: III, 555-556]

The new mode of warfare seemed treacherous and dishonorable to those looking back wistfully to a nobler age, now closed. In olden times he received great praise and honor who let his enemy have equal arms. Challenges went out in good order to those who were good knightly people. Now no one is a good captain who cannot beat his handicapped enemy. Now he is praised and extolled in war, who is able and knows how to cheat his enemy. Now "the novice was more likely to learn how to stab a comrade in a drunken quarrel or fake a muster roll, than to face a danger nobly" (Hale, 1962:23).

With the rise of strong kings and rich towns, most of the feudal warriors were faced with the necessity of finding some new employment. Some strove to enter religious orders: the effort of knights to recover prestige and posts in the Church formed part of the Jesuit movement, which was a counterrevolution of knights as well as a counterreformation in religion. This did not solve the problem; nor did the field of law offer an answer. That expanding profession, preparing and providing for a slowly growing bureaucracy, was monopolized by the keen-witted sons of townsmen. Only a small, rich section of the high nobility could avoid the consequences of technological unemployment. For the lower nobility and squirearchy of Europe there seemed no future but a steady sinking into boorish sloth on their meager estates. Driven by hunger from their cold castles, they were for hire and could not always make their own conditions. Since the new standing armies were recruiting townsmen, they found themselves competing with erstwhile inferiors. In 1524 a German book *Nobility and War* complained that the wealth and luxuries of merchants and craftsmen were casting feudal warriors into the shade.

FRUEH-KAPITALISMUS

From the mid-fifteenth century the demand for guns entered a secular phase of rapid growth. The establishment of the great national states with big armies and navies and their incessant wars, together with geographical exploration and overseas expansion, all added to the demand for cannon. The sovereigns themselves became personally interested in the matter of ordnance and developed not only enthusiasm but real, technical expertise in the "art of gunnery." They patronized gunners and gun-founders and devoted a good deal of their resources to the building and improvement of arsenals and artillery trains (Cipolla, 1965:26).

The making of guns brought about some concentration of industry in large establishments, which anticipated the factories of the nineteenth century, though machinery, such as it was, depended not on steam or hydroelectric power, but the pull of horses or the rush of water. The increasing scope of warfare promoted large-scale industry, both directly and indirectly: directly because it led to the building of extensive plants for the production of the new armaments; indirectly, because the growing military demands for supplies of ore and metal (especially iron and copper) stimulated the mining and metallurgical industries, which, like the armament industries proper, could often be carried on with more economic efficiency in larger more expensive establishments, employing many workers (Sombart, 1913).

Copper, the basic raw material for the making of bronze ordnance, came mainly from Hungary, Tyrol, Saxony, and Bohemia. Tin, the metal to be mixed with copper, came mainly from England, Spain, and Germany. Although the raw materials were produced in only a few areas, the casting of bronze guns was carried on almost everywhere by artisans who had no difficulty in shifting from producing bells to producing guns and vice versa. The trade in raw copper and in bronze ordnance became one of the flourishing and profitable activities of the day. Much of the first European wealth had its origins firmly rooted in this very fertile trade: the Fugger, to quote the most conspicuous example, were great merchants of copper and had a prosperous gun foundry at Fuggerau, near Willbach (Carinthia).

The growth in the number of men under arms and the increasing cost of supplying them made it necessary to assemble capital in large units and led to the development of large-scale enterprise in industry, commerce, and finance. These increased costs compelled rulers to have recourse to the financiers. As pointed out by Mumford (1934:76):

> As security for the loan, the lender took over the royal mines. The development of the mines themselves then became a respectable avenue of financial enterprise, with returns that compared favorably with the usurious and generally unpayable interest. Spurred by the unpaid notes, the rulers were in turn driven to new conquests or to the exploitation of remote territories: and so the cycle began over again.

The demand for guns gave birth to new types of men. In addition to factory owners, financiers, military entrepreneurs, traders, and miners, others rose up to fill the swelling middle class. Take, for example, the men in the foundries. These artisans no longer worked to specific orders or were hired for definite periods of time; now, more or less permanent governmental arsenals were established in which guns were produced by a permanent staff or by experts temporarily hired. Also the engineer and the mathematician became full-time workers. "War established a new type of industrial director who was not a mason or a smith or a master craftsman—the military engineer. It was to the Italian military engineers from the fifteenth century on that the machine owed a debt quite as high as it did to the ingenious British inventors of James Watt's period" (Mumford, 1934:88). So when Iago sneered at Cassio as "a mere arithmetician," he represented the contempt of a whole school of blunt, impetuous warriors for the new soldier, so called because of money income, with his slide rule and tables of embattling. The art of war broadened the interest in applied mathematics and so helped contribute to the changed atmosphere in which real scientific advance became possible in vital physical or chemical research.

By 1500 European affairs were coming more and more under the control of new social groups that had a taste for organization rather than splendor, for efficiency rather than gallantry. And such groups could count on an increasingly numerous class of craftsmen with a taste for mechanics and metallurgy. The very factors that had originally favored the development of the new technology continued to operate and fostered its further progress powerfully. Thus war, based on gunpowder, played a prominent part in the rise of a state economy. The rise in the cost of armies, due mainly to the increase in artillery, and the ever-increasing demands on industry for standardized arms and equipment, hastened factory organization. Military demands fostered mass production, which, in turn, stimulated the growth of armies and the advance of mercantilism.

THE MODERN STATE

The modern state is European in its origin and definitely stems from the period which was marked by the first widespread use of the gun. Its emergence was largely the product of the related supersession of central government over feudal decentralization, and state autonomy over transcendent religious and secular authority, during the sixteenth and seventeenth centuries.

When the word "feudal" is used it generally refers not to nobles only, but all sorts of component groups having rights within the state, and so includes towns and provinces, and even craft guilds and courts of law, in addition to the church and the noble class. Concerning medieval states, Strayer (1963:17-18) points out:

> It is clear that such a regnum could not be a cultural unit any more than it was an ethnic unit—there were always many dialects, frequently many languages, always different customs, and usually different laws for each of the constituent groups. Even geography does not help much, for a regnum was only roughly a geographical unit. It might have had a core, but would be hard to define its boundaries—there were everywhere, contested districts and loosely attached, more or less autonomous dependencies.

States existed territorially in medieval Europe, but these were seldom political units internally ordered under the authority of central governments or ruling houses. Instead, the predominant units of political organization in medieval Europe were feudal and were smaller than medieval states—baronial fiefs, walled towns, monasteries, tradesmen's guilds, secular and clerical social classes, and the like—and were often completely autonomous in their domains within the states. Central authorities in the medieval states were often deficient in legitimacy, and consequently kings and princes could influence or control the activities of autonomous feudal groups only to the extent that they were willing and able to bring force to bear. Medieval history records numerous instances in which the coercive capabilities of central authorities were markedly inferior to the capabilities of feudal groups within their states. Hence, feudal groups within states could and did war against central authorities and against one another for autonomy and aggrandizement almost continuously, a reflection of the relative anarchy within medieval states. This is a far cry from the internal order and central governmental control generally characteristic of modern sovereign states.

Just as internal order was not characteristic of the medieval state, neither was external autonomy. During the medieval era, all states were formally, and from time to time actually, under the transcendent dominion of both a Holy Roman Emperor, charged with the maintenance of European political unity, and a Pope, responsible for the spiritual orthodoxy and unity of Christendom. Therefore, the external autonomy of medieval states was at least formally controlled and constrained by the efforts of temporal and religious authorities. Even as internal control in the medieval era depended on force and the ability to use it, the influence of transcendent authority over medieval states depended largely upon the military capabilities of these higher authorities. States maneuvered and fought to thwart external control, and Holy Roman Emperors and Popes maneuvered and fought to impose and exercise overarching control. This struggle between local and transcendent authority became another phase of medieval political interaction.

The wars of religion, as they were called, were no more religious than they were political, despite the religious ferocity shown by partisans of both sides. They were essentially a new form of the old phenomenon of feudal rebellion against higher central authority. Palmer (1957:130), a serious student of the era, concludes:

> The Peace of Westphalia marked the advent in international law of the modern European system of sovereign states. No one any longer pretended that Europe had any significant unity, religious, political, or other. Statesmen delighted in the absence of any such unity, in which they sensed the menace of "universal monarchy." Europe was understood to consist in a large number of unconnected sovereignties, free and detached atoms, or states, which moved about according to their own laws, following their own political interests, forming and dissolving alliances, exchanging embassies and legations, alternating between war and peace, shifting position with a shifting balance of power.

Hence, two developments combined during the sixteenth and seventeenth centuries to destroy the medieval state and feudal system, and to initiate the rise of the modern state and the modern state system. First, central authorities within medieval states succeeded, after decades or even centuries of civil strife, in undermining and dashing the political and military autonomy of feudal units within their domains. Next, and relatedly, these same kings and princes managed ultimately to seal their states against the demands and incursions of secular and religious transcendent authorities.

The first notable development is the centralization of power in the hands of the king. In medieval times, power was distributed among the feudal units; now it became concentrated in the monarchy. The cost of artillery and the expenses entailed in equipping large numbers of soldiers with guns were too great to be borne by any individual, and in consequence were met by the state (Barker, 1944). Further, this concentration of power in secular hands raised the monarchy above the church; for war, becoming a political instrument, ceased to be a moral trial. It is during the sixteenth century that we see the rise of standing armies, the development of competitive armaments, and the introduction of the balance of power as a policy. Military service ceased to be the perquisite of a class and became a state profession. The development of mass fighting, if not of mass armies, was a characteristic of this age. If Machiavelli was not the first in modern times to suggest conscription, he nevertheless composed the decisive memoranda on the basis of which was promulgated the Ordinanza (1506), that is, the law which established obligatory military service in Tuscany for all men between 18 and 30.

Numerous factors combined to make it possible for central authorities ultimately to gain superiority and impose order within their territorial domains: accretions in wealth in central treasuries from exploration and exploitation in the New World, improvements in central administrative organization and efficiency, and impacts from religious schism that enhanced the legitimacy of secular authority, among others (Friedrich, 1950). But the central reason for the rise of the modern state remains the same: improvements in military technology—especially in artillery—which rendered baronial castles and walled towns vulnerable.

The impact of internal consolidation in medieval states led directly to the enforcement of external autonomy and the emergence of the modern international system. One of the most important results of the internal consolidation of princely authority in medieval states was the greatly increased power in the hands of central governments. In effect, the victory of "central authority" over "feudal decentralization" transferred absolute control over the human and material (and hence military and economic) resources of territorial units to the authorities governing these units. With the exception of the tiny German states, or the Italian city-states, most of the newly ordered territorial units, like Spain, France, England, and Russia, were sizable and therefore usually well endowed with resources that could be transformed into central governmental power.

New power was wielded by governments first to irreversibly complete their internal ascendancy, and then to exert and enforce their independence from transcendent authorities. New capabilities under the control of central governments served to render their territorial domains defensible against, and largely impermeable to, military thrusts directed by Holy Roman Emperors and Popes seeking to extract tribute or to otherwise realize their nominal hegemonic control. The result was that the imperial claims of these transcendent authorities were undermined; and in consequence, the international order of Europe was changed, in fact, from mythical unity in a Holy or Holy Roman empire, to fragmentation and a system of internally ordered and externally autonomous territorial political units. By the time the medieval jurists met at Westphalia in 1648, state sovereignty had become a fact. The modern state system had emerged.

SUMMARY

By an invention deemed devilish at the time, we see the fall of feudal warriors along with their practices and ideals and the rise of new soldiers whose loyalty is not to a piece of land or to an overlord but to cash and the state; the concentration of industry and capital and new types of men following new types of occupation performed in cities; and the victory of the modern state over feudal decentralization which could only be maintained through land-bounded personal relationships.

There was always an opportunity for the Church to come out against the new modes of warfare. After all, about one-third of the land in Europe during the medieval ages was held by the Church as fiefs. The Church did not fulminate against the gun primarily because it needed a force capability with which to restrain the more aggressive princes and towns. Apart from not speaking out, the best evidence of acceptance of the gun is that the Church provided gunners with a patron saint of their own, St. Barbara.

The gun was first used in the fourteenth century and no serious outcry was raised about it. For example, in the 1350s Petrarch in his *De Remediis Utrinsque Fortunae* (Lib. I, dialog. 99) wrote that "these instruments which discharge balls of metal with most tremendous noise and flashes of fire . . . were a few years ago very rare and were viewed with greatest astonishment and admiration, but now they are becoming as common and familiar as any other kind of arms. So quick and ingenious are the minds of men in learning the most pernicious arts." At that time, the gun was cumbersome and extraordinarily big. It cannot have been an easy weapon to use in the field.

But in the fifteenth century all that changed; the art of warfare developed with great innovations. After the problem of metal and gun-casting was solved with new techniques to make guns lighter and more portable, there was left only the problem of powder (White, 1962:100-101):

> The chief difficulty of the gun-masters of the later Middle Ages was that their gunpowder was a loose mixture of carbon, sulphur, and saltpetre: any shaking during transport sent the heavier saltpetre to the bottom and the light carbon to the top. Likewise, the lack of sufficient air-spaces between the particles retarded the explosion. Slow and relatively inefficient combustion forced gunners to pack the powder into the gun with a wooden block, and then to pack the shot with rags or clay to contain the gas until enough had been generated to reach shooting pressure. This exasperating problem was largely solved in the 1420s by the invention of corned gunpowder. By holding the three components in even relationship throughout the mass of the powder, and by providing an equal distribution of larger air-spaces, corned powder made the explosion uniform and practically instantaneous. The cannon became an efficient engine of war, and the fact that packing could be less elaborate raised the hand-gun from the level of a psychological weapon to that of an instrument of slaughter.

So at the very moment when it became such a formidable instrument in the art of warfare, and its potential fully realized by those in positions of power, did the knights inveigh against the gun in no uncertain terms. But then it was too late and they could not really adapt to it. With guns an infantry of social nobodies could mow down a whole cavalry charge, a portent of the end of the leisurely, honorable, and not very dangerous way of life of the knights.

The emergence of the modern state in Europe and the impact of that state on societies around the world was brought about by the absolute monarch and his royal servants in the sixteenth century. The autonomous jurisdictions and private armies of feudal society were replaced by a centralized administration and a standing army of paid soldiers or mercenaries. "The whole process is a complete parallel to the development of the capitalist enterprise through the gradual expropriation of the independent producers," wrote Weber (1946 ed.:82). "In the end, the modern state controls the total means of political organization, which actually come together under a single head."

The revolutionizing role of the bourgeoisie against feudal society and its worldwide repercussions in the development and spread of modern civilization has been celebrated by Marx and Engels (1948 ed.:11-13) in The Communist Manifesto:

> The bourgeoisie, wherever it has got the upper hand, has put an end to all feudal, patriarchal, idyllic relations. It has pitilessly torn asunder the motley feudal ties that bound man to his "natural superiors," and has left no other bond between man and man than naked self-interest, than callous "cash payment." . . . It has accomplished wonders for surpassing Egyptian pyramids, Roman aqueducts, and Gothic cathedrals. . . . The bourgeoisie, by the rapid improvement of all instruments of production, by the immensely facilitated means of communication, draws all nations, even the most barbarian, into civilization. . . . It compels all nations, on pain of extinction, to adopt the bourgeois mode of production; it compels them to introduce what it calls civilization into their midst, i.e., to become bourgeois themselves. In a word, it creates a world after its own image.

By ousting an old system of warfare, gunpowder created a new system of peace. In the fifteenth century it revolutionized not only the method of fighting, but also the way of living, and in consequence civilization itself. In fact, it established an outlook on things in general as different from the outlook of the Medieval Age as its outlook differed from that of the Classical. Therefore, with the advent of firearms we do not merely turn over another page in human history, instead we open a new volume, one that might be entitled, The European Conquest of the World.

The firearms of the fifteenth century were crude and inaccurate by modern standards, but against natives armed with spears and arrows the men who used them were invincible. By 1500, European ships were capable of crossing any ocean and finding their way back again. The small cannon they carried gave them absolute control of any harbor they entered. Their horses and firearms enabled them to capture any inland city they could find before the horses died or provisions ran out (Parry, 1966).

Since the tools produced by the marriage between science and technology in the West were unprecedentedly potent, the Western weapons forged out of these tools were irresistible when they were pitted against the antediluvian weapons which were all that the rest of the world yet possessed. (During the fifteenth century, the Turks, Indians, Moslems, and Chinese actually possessed cannon and in fact used them. But, and this is most important, in no way were they improved on; their technological capacity simply withered, it seems, at that point in time. The only other people to develop improvements on the gun were the Japanese, the only people to develop a modern state, other than the Europeans, before the turn of the nineteenth century.)

These weapons were felt earliest and most urgently by the professional soldiers in the service of non-Western governments; and this explains why, in a number of non-Western countries, army officers have been the spearhead of the Westernizing revolution which the military impact of the West has eventually set in motion. The application of successive Western technical inventions to the art of war is what has given the West its modern ascendancy over the rest of the world.

The attractiveness of Western weapons for non-Westerns thus presents no puzzle. It is tragic, but it is also rational. It is rational because there is no denying that the strategy of fighting the West with its own weapons has been the only means by which the non-Western majority of mankind has been able to save itself from falling under Western domination, or has been able to extricate itself from Western domination after having fallen under it.

Thus was social change of the most extensive nature, if not actually brought about, then at least expedited and facilitated, its influence amplified, by a revolutionary technological development. Like many innovations and inventions, the gun was denounced and scorned, its users the object of social hostility which is the touchstone, for many, of the identification of people or groups as deviant. While this hostility was manifested by the representatives and symbols of the most powerful groups in the societies, the latter could not stay the hand of the new technology. The deviants became the innovators, the midwives of social change, with rapidity and repercussions seldom equaled in human history.

REFERENCES

ARIOSTO, L. (1516). Orlando Furioso (J. Hoole, trans.). London: G. Nicol, 1785.

ATKINSON, G. (1935). Les nouveaux horizons de la Renaissance française. Paris: E. Droz

BARKER, E. (1944). The development of public services in Western Europe, 1660-1930. London: Oxford University Press.

BURCKHARDT, J. (1950). The civilization of the Renaissance in Italy. London: Phaidon Press.

CERVANTES, M. (1964). Don Quixote of la Mancha (W. Starkie, trans.). New York: New American Library.

CIPOLLA, C.M. (1965). Guns, sails, and empires. New York: Minerva Press.

FRIEDRICH, C.J. (1950). Constitutional government and democracy. Boston: Ginn & Co.

FULLER, J.F.C. (1946). Armament and history. London: Eyre & Spottiswoode.

HALE, J. (1962). "War and public opinion in the fifteenth and sixteenth centuries." Past and Present, 21:18-33.

HATTO, A.T. (1940). "Archery and chivalry: A noble prejudice." Modern Language Review, 35:40-50.

HOWARD, M. (1976). War in European history. London: Oxford University Press.

MACHIAVELLI, N. (1940). The Prince and The Discourses. New York: Modern Library.

MARX, K., and ENGELS, F. (1948). The communist manifesto. New York: International Publishers.

MOTLEY, J.L. (1856). The rise of the Dutch republic. 3 vols. New York: Harper & Bros.

MUMFORD, L. (1934). Technics and civilization. New York: Harcourt, Brace.

NEF, J.U. (1952). War and human progress. Cambridge: Harvard University Press.

PACKARD, F.R. (1921). Life and times of Ambroise Paré. New York: P. B. Hoeber.

PAINTER, S. (1940). French chivalry: Chivalric ideas and practices in Mediaeval France. Baltimore: Johns Hopkins Press.

PALMER, R.R. (1957). A history of the modern world. 2nd ed. New York: Knopf.

PARÉ, A. (1634). Of wounds made by gunshot, in Workes (T. Johnson, trans.) London: T. Cotes and R. Young.

PARRY, J.H. (1966). The establishment of the European hegemony, 1415-1715: Trade and exploration in the age of the Renaissance. 3rd ed., revised. New York: Harper Torchbooks.

PETRARCH (1350). De Remediis utrinsque fortunae. Venice.

SOMBART, W. (1913). Krieg und kapitalismus. Munich: Duncker & Humblot.

STRAKER, E. (1931). Wealden iron. London: G. Bell & Sons.

STRAYER, J.R. (1963). "The historical experience of nation-building in Europe." Pp. 17-26 in K.W. Deutsch and W.J. Foltz (eds.), Nation-building. New York: Atherton Press.

TAYLOR, F.L. (1921). The art of war in Italy, 1494-1529. Cambridge: Cambridge University Press.

VAGTS, A. (1937). A history of militarism. New York: W.W. Norton.

VIRGIL, P. (1868). De Rerum Inventoribus Trans. by T. Langley. New York: Agathnian Club. Original publication in English in 1546.

WEBER, M. (1946). From Max Weber. (H.H. Gerth and C.W. Mills, trans. and eds.). New York: Oxford University Press.

WHITE, L. (1962). Medieval technology and social change. New York: Oxford University Press.

6

SOCIAL CHANGE AND POLITICAL CRIME
The Making of a Political Criminal

RICHARD MORAN

During the late 1960s and early 1970s a small yet significant number of young people came to believe that political crime and violence were both proper and necessary to bring about social change. Most case history analyses of political criminals have focused on the idiosyncrasies of particular individuals. The "true believer" of Hoffer (1951) commits himself to a cause out of his own psychological rather than political needs or authentic desire for social change. By equating the state with the father figure, Freudians like Flugel (1921) contended that the political criminal creates a political theory that enables him to give vent to his father-hatred without feelings of guilt. Similarly, Stekel sketched the political criminal as someone who displaced a small personal problem into the life of a nation. He writes: "Perhaps Booth was beaten by a drunken father, so Lincoln died" (see Mannheim, 1965:327). Although on occasion certain political actions of particular individuals can be explained in psychoanalytic terms, an analysis of political crime in general requires more than reduction to the realm of personal pathology.

Psychoanalytic explanations are not in themselves sufficient to account for political crime; perhaps they are not even necessary. In fact, when psychoanalytic assumptions are made, they tend to obscure collective modalities of explanations, not to uncover them. Although the public may be more comfortable with explanations of political crime (especially assassinations) rooted in personal pathology, as a comprehensive thesis it seems oversimple and unconvincing. [1] The "genuine" political criminal is not a rebel without a cause, nor is he a rebel in search of a cause, he is a rebel with a cause.

The people in the present study were not simply following a fashionable trend to bomb or terrorize, but had developed a high degree of moral awareness and political sophistication. Their behavior was not criminal action in search of a political rationale, but political conviction expressed through criminal action.

DATA COLLECTION

The research data consisted of twenty case histories. A political criminal was defined as an individual who, motivated by his conviction, committed an unlawful act designed to bring about a reorganization of society (Moran, 1974). The term implies no value judgment as to the propriety of their acts or of their goals; it is meant to be purely descriptive. The twenty persons constitute all individuals who fit the definition, and about whom sufficient information on their personal lives and backgrounds, as well as their political activities, was known in order to conduct an analysis.

The individuals used in this study (not all of whom are specifically discussed herein, but information on those not specifically mentioned was used for analysis and conclusions) were the following: Jane Alpert, Dwight Armstrong, Karl Armstrong, Bill Ayers, Daniel Berrigan, Philip Berrigan, Stanley Bond, Kathy Boudin, H. Rap Brown, Stokely Carmichael, Bernardine Dohrn, Daniel Ellsberg, Ted Gold, Samuel Melville, Diana Oughton, Katherine Powers, Terry Robbins, Mark Rudd, Susan Saxe, and Cathlyn Wilkerson. Some were convicted of violent acts, some have not been tried because they continue (at the time of this writing) to be fugitives; others were tried for what might be considered illegal but not violent activity (as the raid on a draft board and the burning of records); in a few cases, the illegal political acts would not fall within the purview of violence.

Nevertheless, they lend themselves to single analytic study. All violated the law for political reasons, fit the above definition of political crime, committed their acts in America between 1965 and 1972. They were distinct from "young radicals" and "student activists" studied by Kenneth Keniston and others in the seriousness of their violations (Keniston, 1968; Harrington, 1968; Lipset and Wolin, 1965; Lipset, 1970). More than merely *drift* in and out of civil disobedience, most made life commitments to social change, as expressed by the seriousness of their acts and the risk of long-term imprisonment. It is this commitment to the implementation of their beliefs—including in most instances resort to violence—that distinguished them from other politically active people who shared their feelings and analysis about society. The remark of a staff member of *Kaleidoscope*, an underground weekly, during an interview concerning the August 24th, 1970 bombing of the Army Mathematics Research Center at the University of Wisconsin, illustrates the wide disparity between those who merely advocate and those who actually commit political crime. "We told them to bomb it, to blow it up. And they blew it up. And we said, My God they blew it up!" (New York Times, 1970a).

A DEVELOPMENTAL SEQUENCE

Although the sociological research conducted to date on political criminals is sparse and undistinguished, it generally suggests that "such characteristics as age, sex, ethnicity, and social class do not differentiate political offenders as a whole from the population in general" (Clinard and Quinney, 1967:180). The present research tends to support this assertion. In the population used in this study, the average age was 27.3 years compared to 28.1 years for the general population; Dwight Armstrong, age 18, was the youngest, and Daniel Berrigan, at 47, the oldest. There were 13 males and 7 females compared to 94.8 males per 100 females in the general population. The study contained two blacks (10%) compared to 11.1% in the general population (U.S. Bureau of the Census, 1972:55-57). Although they ranged from Diane Oughton, the daughter of a millionaire, to Samuel Melville, the son of a laborer, the overwhelming majority of subjects were middle class.

The middle-class backgrounds of the political criminals may be illustrated in the following brief life histories of Bernardine Rae Dohrn and Jane Alpert.

> Bernardine Rae Dohrn was born in Chicago on January 12, 1942, the elder daughter of Bernard Dohrnstein, a Hungarian Jew (he later shortened his name for business purposes), and Dorothy Sodergerb, a Swede. The family lived in a North side tenement until Bernardine was eight and her sister Jennifer was five years old, when they moved to Whitefish Bay, Wisconsin, a middle class, all-white, predominantly German and Jewish suburb just north of Milwaukee. . . . In her senior year, Bernardine was chosen as Whitefish Bay's delegate to Badger Girls State, a Wisconsin-wide convention whose major concerns were promulgating good citizenship and school spirit. She spent her freshman and sophomore years at Miami University of Ohio and later transferred to the University of Chicago where she earned a B.A. in history. In 1964 she entered the University of Chicago Law School, where she became involved in social reform and protest. She progressed through the usual stages of liberal reformism to radical politics. In late February or early March, 1970, Bernardine disappeared. Later that month she failed to show in court in Chicago on charges growing out of the Days of Rage. She was indicted on March 17, 1970, for unlawful interstate flight to avoid prosecution for mob action. On April 2, 1970, she was indicted for conspiracy and violation of federal anti-riot laws, and

on July 23 for conspiring to bomb buildings in Detroit, Chicago, New York, and Berkeley. Currently, she is being sought by the FBI. [Gelder, 1970:164, 170]

Jane Alpert's life history is strikingly similar.

Jane Laren Alpert was about half way between her 22nd and 23rd birthdays when she was arrested on November 13, 1969, on charges of conspiring to bomb federal property. She was born on May 20, 1947, in Lenox Hill Hospital, the daughter of John and Corinne Alpert. Her father is a vice-president of Jelrus Technical Products of New Hyde Park, Long Island, a dental equipment firm. Her mother is a junior high school mathematics teacher in the city public school system. She has a brother, Skippy, who is a 19 year old student at Brandeis University. Her family lived in a seven-story, white trimmed brick apartment building at 67-71 Yellowstone Boulevard. Up until the time of Jane's arrest, they had lived there for 15 years. The Alperts lived in a 4½ room apartment on the fifth floor overlooking a neighborhood of similar pseudo-Colonial buildings. The family holds membership in Temple Isaiah, a liberal reform synagogue in Forest Hills where social consciousness and the ethical values of Judaism rather than ritual are stressed. It was here that Jane attended bas mitzvah classes.

After graduation from High School Jane entered Swarthmore, a relatively small co-education Quaker college, about 30 minutes from Philadelphia. She graduated with honors in June, 1967, and almost immediately secured a job as an editorial secretary with the American Office of Cambridge University Press in New York City. During that summer, Jane decided to work for a Master's degree in Greek at Columbia University. She stayed at her job, carrying almost a full load of academic work as she simultaneously progressed at Cambridge Press. Then, in early November, 1968, she dropped out of Columbia. In mid-April, 1969 she told Mr. Mansbridge at Cambridge University Press that she was quitting. "She was a bit reticent about her reasons" he recalled. "I had to press her about her reasons." In essence, he gathered, she had decided to devote her life to working for the betterment of society. On May 8, 1970, Jane appeared in District Court to plead guilty to conspiracy to commit a series of politically motivated bombings in New York City. A few days later Jane Alpert jumped bail to avoid imprisonment. [New York Times, 1970b:1, 56]

In November, 1974, she surrendered to authorities and was sentenced by a federal judge to 27 months in jail (Time, 1975:63).

In this case, the failure of the data to reveal distinct demographic variables indigenous to political criminals becomes important when viewed in combination with the fact that ordinary criminals (at least those arrested) can be so distinguished. Hence, it follows that political criminals are distinct from ordinary criminals because ordinary criminals can be demographically distinguished from the general population. Nevertheless, the failure of the data to provide adequate points of demarcation forces us to seek the explanation of political crime elsewhere, perhaps in a series of sequential stages which in successive combination might account for the development of a political criminal.

Although the analysis of case histories lacks the quantitativeness necessary to make empirical predictions about who will become a political criminal, it is applicable in affording a basis for understanding the process by which an individual becomes a political criminal (Turner, 1953). The research traces this developmental process through several stages. Mainly, it investigates two types of conditions. First, there are predisposing conditions or background factors, the conjunction of which forms a pool of potential political criminals. These conditions exist prior to an individual's decision to commit a political crime and by themselves do not account for the behavior. Second, there are situational contingencies or conditions which lead to the commission of political crimes by predisposed individuals.[2]

Predisposing Conditions

Strain. Common to all subjects is the strain or tension produced by an early recognition of the wide discrepancy between the American ideal and the American way of life. On the whole, the twenty political criminals were part of a generation that took the "house platitudes" seriously. They apparently believed in what they were told as children about American freedom, equality, world peace, and morality (Harrington, 1968). They were 100% American in their ideals and found what they saw as American hypocrisy disturbing and sometimes even painful. For example, Jennifer Dohrn, Bernardine's sister, recalls a vacation trip to Florida when Bernardine was about thirteen. "I remember driving past those tar-paper shacks and seeing the 'white-only' signs. It was the first time we ran into racism. We were both horrified" (Gelder, 1970:164).

Diana Oughton's childhood illustrates the acute tension or strain she experienced when she began to perceive the discrepancy between her own privileged social position and the lives of other children.

> Diana never accustomed herself to the special position enjoyed by the Oughtons in Dwight. In school the other children sometimes teased her by calling her "Miss Moneybags." When she was six she asked her nanny, Ruth Moreheart, "Ruthie, why do we have to be rich?" On another occasion, when money problems forced a girl friend to move away, Diana went to her father in tears and asked, "Why can't we be ordinary like them?" When she was a little older, Diana quietly wondered if her uniformly good marks in school had anything to do with the fact that several of her teachers rented houses from her father. [Powers, 1971:10]

During her college years Diana began to develop the feeling that privilege somehow made one unworthy. She had begun to question her worldly values and to feel that important things were wrong in America. In short, her tension began to grow:

> Diana was in the process of changing as her senior year at Bryn Mawr came to an end. She was like a person with a nagging religious doubt, a sense that questions of overriding moral importance exist in the world. She had begun to reject worldly values and the proprieties of society; she sensed that most people put too much importance on the trivial things and too little on the important ones; she was sensitive about herself, vaguely aware that privilege made one somehow unworthy. She knew that America was far larger than Dwight, that the world she had known was only the complacent veneer of American life, that important things were wrong in the country, that honesty and sincerity and moral commitment were the qualities which gave size to people and ways of life. [Powers, 1971:21]

After graduation from Bryn Mawr, Diana joined the Voluntary International Service Assignments (VISA) and was assigned to Chichicastenango, Guatemala. Her tension continued. "She hated poverty but she hated affluence, too. Transistor radios struck a jarring note in the market, and yet the Indians wanted radios, cars, sewing machines and all the other doubtful (to Diana) benefits of modern life" (Powers, 1971:27).

For Stokely Carmichael the strain occurred at the age of eleven when his family moved from Port of Spain in his native Trinidad to Harlem. Although from a different sociocultural context, Carmichael's case is similar to Diana Oughton's. His strain or tension, however, generated from a sense of deprivation rather than privilege, with an important racial theme.

> "In Trinidad," Carmichael said in an interview with Robert Penn Warren, "some 96 per cent of the population had been Negroes; all immediate authority—police, teachers, ministers, civil servants—all the storekeepers and entrepreneurs in general were Negroes. The 4 per cent white population lived in 'Mansions,' " he continued, "but then many Negroes lived in mansions too, and the question of exploitation of black by the white had not occurred to . . . [him]. In America all was different. Immediate authority was white, and the storekeeper was white." Carmichael was surprised and shocked. [New York Times, 1966:137]

As in the previous cases, Daniel Berrigan recognized from early childhood the suffering and poverty in the world. Coming from a devout Catholic home, Daniel Berrigan focused his aspirations on becoming a priest:

> Daniel felt the call of the priesthood since childhood; at the age of seventeen he applied for the Society of Jesus and in 1939, aged eighteen, Daniel left his home in Syracuse for the seminary to begin the arduous thirteen-year training that is imposed on the men before ordination. "From the time he was ordained," a Catholic educator who worked closely with him in those years has said, "Daniel was obsessed with two issues: alleviating poverty and breaking down the traditional structures of the priest-layman relationship." [Gray, 1970:56]

Although not as abruptly made aware of the disparities of American life, Ted Gold came from a family structure which made him particularly attuned to what he saw as American hypocrisy:

> Theodore Gold was born in New York City on December 13, 1947, into a milieu that is by now almost predictable for contemporary activists. He was an only child. His parents were liberals of the upper West Side Jewish variety, living in a pleasant apartment on tree-lined 93rd Street, comfortably well-off if not exactly rich. . . . Most sociological studies suggest that activist youth come from just this kind of background, where both parents work and the dinner table ideas are likely to be at least liberal. What they don't go on to say is that when both parents are away all day and the child is raised by a black maid, as in Ted Gold's case, the resulting psychological dislocations may be as great an impetus to radicalism. [Sale, 1970:424]

Although these examples underscore early concerns of the political criminals, they should not be regarded as typical or qualitatively different from the concerns apparently experienced by a significant, albeit unknown, proportion of the general population. Most children have similar experiences and make similar observations. Jennifer, as well as Bernardine, was horrified by the tar-shacks and the "white-only" signs. What is different about the twenty cases is an unwillingness or inability to accept or adjust to these discrepancies. For example, Susan Le Grand, a frequent companion of Mark Rudd, has been quoted as saying: "Mark just sees so much around him that is wrong and he just has to do something about it. He just has to" (New York Times, 1970c:31).

A perception of the discrepancy between "what is" and "what ought to be" can often be the basis for disillusionment and cynicism, but to the twenty political criminals it became an incentive to act. According to Leon Festinger (1957), people experiencing dissonance or strain are ordinarily motivated toward its reduction or elimination. They can do so by (1) adjusting their beliefs, (2) seeking new information to reduce dissonance while avoiding dissonance-increasing information, or (3) acting to change the existing dissonance-producing situation. Peculiarly, the political criminals under examination refused to choose the first two alternatives, as is commonly the case. Rather than attempting to reduce the dissonance by compromising their beliefs, or denying the evidential validity of existing discrepancies by becoming quietly content with the everyday satisfactions of the status quo, including family life and career advancement, these men and women attempted to eliminate the dissonance or strain by changing the situation.

For example, on October 26, 1973, the final day of his mitigation of sentence hearing, Karl Armstrong took the witness stand to tell his story. His remarks speak directly to this point.

> I think I'd like to start talking about my own life, . . . You know, I was born on the day they hung the Nazis at Nuremburg. My father used to talk

> to me about the war. He couldn't understand why the German people didn't resist, because he thought that any act, almost any act of resistance, would be justified against the Nazis. That really left a lasting impression on my mind. I tried to understand the German Nazi experience and how it came about. I resolved then that nothing like that, as long as I was alive, would happen in America. The only real resolution I ever made in my whole life was that I would be prepared to give up my life so that that wouldn't happen here in America . . . there would be no purpose in living. [Schipper, 1973:48]

Similarly, in a June 1968 interview, Cathlyn P. Wilkerson was asked whether she ever gets fed up trying to disrupt what she considers massive corruption at the seat of power:

> Fed up is an establishment term. People who are organizers see themselves as working for human beings, trying to help them find out what it means to be free. At times, I get exhausted, but the concept of getting fed up is not relevant. All organizers are underfed, underpaid, underslept, but to me, it's the only liberating thing to do. I can't, I couldn't withdraw. The struggle to be human is primary. [Washington Star, 1968:10]

On May 17, 1968, Daniel Berrigan and eight other individuals carried 378 draft files classified 1-A out of the local board number 33 in Catonsville, Maryland, and set them afire with napalm in an adjacent parking lot. The Catonsville Nine were tried for conspiracy and destruction of government property in the United States District Court in Baltimore in October 1968. On the witness stand, Daniel Berrigan explained why he participated:

> One simply cannot announce the Gospel from his pedestal . . . when he was not down there sharing the risks and burdens and the anguish of his students. I burned some paper because I was trying to say that the burning of children was inhuman and unbearable, and . . . a cry is the only response. [Berrigan, 1970:92]
>
> In a 1970 interview, Daniel Berrigan was quoted as saying:
>
> The first generation of Jesuits worked in the streets; the second generation bought a house; the third air-conditioned it. I belong to the first generation, and the men inside don't like my *facon d'agir.* [Gray, 1970:66]

The twenty men and women refused "to grow up and learn better." To them, maturity meant exchanging their youthful idealism, moral sensitivity, and hope for a better world for adult responsibility with its accompanying need for conciliation, selective morality, and emphasis on settling down. Jane Alpert stated, in writing about Sam Melville, "He told me how much he envied the kids at Columbia who realized that middle-class life was a pile of shit before they got sucked into it, as he had been, and that he identified more with eighteen and nineteen year olds than he did with friends he's known since his early twenties" (Alpert, 1972:6).

Wilkerson and her friends (1968:8) express their repugnance toward what the middle class had defined as success and happiness. Under the title, "A False Privilege," they write

> What is the reality of the promise of success we've been offered? What jobs should we take? Do we want to join the managerial staff of some corporation and look into the empty faces of fellow businessmen eight hours a day, drink their faces out of our minds at night, and play the game of competing to have the best job in the biggest corporation that exploits the most people?

Because the subjects generally occupied a social position that largely excluded them from conventional participation in major social institutions (such as marriage, occupational careers, or politics), they were in amost favorable position to act on their political beliefs. Their isolation in colleges and universities freed them from traditional family ties and influences that might otherwise restrain idealism and prevent action on political or moral feelings. It may be that the young and somewhat affluent can more readily afford the luxury of embarking on a search for answers or solutions to the contradictions and inconsistencies of the social system (Wolfgang, 1969). This situation, combined with what has been termed the Kennedy "politics of expectation" that flourished in the early 1960s, and the increasing premium placed on the youth culture, produced an intense pressure which in concert created new possibilities to resist choosing the two previously mentioned common dissonance-reducing alternatives. Confounding the pressure were the ever-widening inconsistencies and discrepancies between American ideals and the American experience. With the social system thought to be on the verge of disintegration, it became more difficult to put on the adult lens of responsibility that would blind one to the current state of affairs. Ergo, with the evidence of discrepancy becoming greater and the opportunity for action becoming more and more compelling, some young people were prepared to act.

The making of a political offender does not end here. The attempt to bridge the gap between the actual and the ideal could eventuate in a number of various choices. The strain experienced is only a small part: "such persons may be candidates for membership in religious sects . . . as well as radical political and economic organizations. It is not happenstance that religious leaders have sometimes turned to radicalism, and that a number of radicals have, on disillusionment, turned to the solace of religion" (Lemert, 1951:214). Rennie Davis, for example, a defendant in the 1968 Chicago Seven Trial, five years later led 3,500 youths in worship of a 15-year-old Indian guru, whom he described as the "living perfect master–the answer to all the world's ills" (Boston Globe, 1973:2). Likewise, Eldridge Cleaver, former Black Panther and fugitive from America, upon his return did evangelical television commercials for Baptist General Convention of Texas (Montagno and Huck, 1977).

A Political Problem-Solving Perspective. The commission of a political offense is certainly not the only way to solve the tension or strain problem. There are numerous other possible solutions. In fact, because of the ready availability of both conventional and unconventional ameliorative solutions, very few individuals become political criminals. Most accept the conventional definitions and solutions to their problems and consequently are not candidates for political crime. However, because the political criminal rejects the psychiatric axiom that current problems of living have their origin in his personal or family history, he does not consider adjustment or manipulation of self as a viable solution. Instead he locates the sources of problems in phenomena external to him. His approach is extrapunitive rather than intrapunitive. [3] For example, Samuel Melville felt quite strongly that problems of self-respect and dignity had their origins in the external world. He believed that the only way to personal change was through social change.

John Cohen (1972:77), in his introduction to Samuel Melville's *Letters From Attica,* has written:

> Sam was seeking a sense of personal worth. Shortly after his arrest, in a brief, beautiful note to Jane [Alpert] he said that he was proud of what he had done–I think he wrote, "At least we have not bent our knees to their false gods, or kissed their flag." Sam's goal was a sense of self-respect and dignity. Although in this sense his concern was individual and personal, he argued against any attempt to separate personal salvation from the struggle for social justice: "I don't think you can have inner peace without outer peace, too. . . . There is no individual change without social change."

In a letter written while in Attica serving a 13-to-18-year term for a series of politically motivated bombings in New York City, Sam Melville (1972:139) wrote to his brother John:

> The unavoidable conclusion i arrive at is that i was not born in a vacuum; that i see my reflexion in many, many faces. Now, it follows that if i am a sociological phenomenon and i suffer a sociological disease i must have a sociological prognosis

Under an extrapunitive perspective an individual can define the nature and origins of the discrepancies and inconsistencies he finds in society in four fundamental ways: religious, moral, social, or political. These four perspectives share the common belief that society can be changed for the better. In this sense they do not differ markedly from one another. In fact an individual may hold each perspective in his lifetime, or they may coexist within him and compete for his attention and loyalty. Philip and Daniel Berrigan are good examples. One summer when Daniel Berrigan was working with a team of students in Yonkers on problems of racism in white suburbia, a student asked: "What did you hope to accomplish at Catonsville?" "Well," Daniel answered, "how different was it from Christ's overthrowing the tables of the money-changers?" (Gray, 1970:48). In answer to a further query on the practicality of his actions, Daniel Berrigan replied, "How useful were the acts of martyrs? How many martyrs ever had a practical program for reforming society? Since politics wasn't working anyway, one had to find an act beyond politics, a religious act, a liturgical act, an act of witness. If only enough men could offer this kind of witness, it would purify the world" (Gray, 1970:48).

The development of a radical political problem-solving perspective is exemplified in the case of Diana Oughton (from Powers, 1971:19-74, passim):

> In the fall of 1959, *Diana Oughton* entered Bryn Mawr College. She was a Midwestern Republican, which meant she was close to being a right wing conservative in the eyes of most of her friends at college. She was against social security, federal banking regulations, and she supported Richard Nixon against John Kennedy in the 1960 Presidential elections.
>
> During her last year she joined a special tutoring program for black children with reading problems in Philadelphia's ghetto. The volunteers were only supposed to tutor one child each but Diana, horrified to discover that seventh graders could not read *at all,* soon had three. Diana had never paid much attention to the fact there were no blacks at Madeira, an exclusive boarding school in Greenway, Virginia; by her senior year at Bryn Mawr, she understood it was no accident that there was only one black in her class.
>
> After graduation Diana joined the Voluntary International Service Assignments (VISA) run by the American Friends Service Committee and was assigned to Guatemala where she had her second experience with poverty. By the spring of 1964, Diana's attitude toward Guatemala had begun to take on definition. The poverty had been immediately apparent, of course, but at first it had seemed as if the country itself were poor. Gradually, it became apparent that only the lower classes within the country were poor, while the upper classes were very well off indeed. There was nothing startling about the presence of rich and poor in the world, but in Guatemala Diana began to see for the first time that the rich are afraid of the poor, and that the poor hate and envy the rich.
>
> Diana's recognition of the poverty of Guatemala and of the half-hidden war between rich and poor led to the formation of political opinions after she met Alan Howard, a Fulbright scholar living in Guatemala City. Howard, a graduate of Hamilton College from Newton, Massachusetts, was working on an experimental reading program in the federal prison. Long conversations with political prisoners had given him a decidedly cynical view of Guatemalan politics and a sense that traditional parliamentary methods would never end the inequities which divided the country. Soft-spoken, intelligent, with a vaguely clean-cut look that belied his politics, Howard lived alone in La Roja Zona, the red-light district of Guatemala City. After meeting him through the IGA, Diana would often spend long evenings talking about politics in Howard's austere apartment, plainly furnished but always cluttered with books and papers. Howard argued that the VISA program would never change Guatemala in fundamental ways. At best, he said, reformist programs like Diana's might hold

> isolated individuals; at worst they would dilute the anger and desperation which alone could prompt the people to rise up and destroy the old system.
>
> When Diana had arrived in Guatemala she had been a liberal, believing the only way to make a better world was to identify the problems, and devise their solutions, one by one. Guatemala made her into a radical: she began to feel that things had to be changed all at once, or not at all. Step by step, she acquired a new sense of the world and its troubles, simple in outline but broad in its application: the name of the problem is capitalism, she concluded, and the name of the solution is socialism. She did not acquire her faith in a flash; it was a slow conversion, but nonetheless complete.
>
> Back in the United States Diana moved to Powelton Village in Philadelphia where she took a $100 a week teaching job with an adult reading program funded by the Office of Economic Opportunity (OEO). She became disappointed in the bureaucratic structure and in late 1965 she moved to Ann Arbor, Michigan. In January of 1966, she enrolled in a Master of Arts program at the University of Michigan and nine months later began teaching part-time at Ann Arbor's year-old Children's Community School. There she met Bill Ayers, an Ann Arbor radical. Together, they worked at the experimental school for two years and when the school failed they became active in the Ann Arbor SDS.

Meanwhile, they were becoming convinced that direct action rather than education and peaceful reform was the way to social change. In the fall of 1968 Diana Oughton and Bill Ayers joined the "Jesse James Gang"–the most radical wing of the Ann Arbor SDS. By the summer of 1969 she and Bill had joined the Weathermen–the underground direct-action group in the SDS.

The people here under study did not select illegal activity as their initial political act. Usually they began from a social perspective in which the experience with poverty was of primary importance. They were not compelled by the poverty that they themselves experienced (most were middle class) but by the poverty and suffering of others. However, the potential political criminals' direct experience with trying to ameliorate poverty and suffering in the urban centers and distant corners of the world eventually led them into a confrontation with politics. They began to realize that no matter how hard they worked, raising the educational level of the poor and establishing social welfare agencies, a social change would not be brought about. They felt that the real problem was the uneven distribution of political power and the only way to rectify the situation was through direct action. Initially, this action took the form of electoral politics and mass nonviolent demonstrations. Jane Alpert began as an enthusiastic supporter of Senator Eugene J. McCarthy's bid for the Democratic nomination in 1968 (Charlton, 1970:56), and Stokely Carmichael began by picketing Woolworth's lunch counter in New York City (Life, 1967:80). However, each began to find conventional political channels inadequate as a means of providing a solution. Their confrontation with the existing institutions of social change and their growing disenchantment with their ability to remedy social injustice eventually caused them to turn reluctantly toward more radical solutions—solutions that stressed the need to destroy the old institutions and build new ones. Carmichael, for example, was arrested 27 times during peaceful demonstrations before he uttered the "inflammatory" slogan "Black Power" (New York Times, 1966).

Concomitant with the development of a radical political perspective, all developed friendship ties with one or more persons who shared their political perspectives and desire for social change. As effective bonds with similar persons increased, contact with conventional individuals was neutralized and in time became absent. This situation led to an increasing isolation from conventional society and a heightened tendency to impose political meaning on everyday events. Consequently, rather ordinary events began to be interpreted as part of a larger process destined to bring about a revolution in society. For example, at his trial Karl Armstrong recounted the sequence of events that led to his bombing the Army Mathematics Research Center at the University of Wisconsin:

> Then came Cambodia, people at Kent State got killed, and, to me, that meant that the U.S. Government had declared war on the students. And, after all the protests by all the thousands, with all the trashing, I felt that the University of Wisconsin could no longer ignore the demands to abolish AMRC. I was literally stunned when I returned to the UW and found that the University was, in fact, ignoring the demands. It was then that I made the decision to destroy AMRC. [Schipper, 1973:48]

The failure of conventional channels of political protest and the despair thus engendered encouraged the development of more extreme and radical attitudes. The tendency to gather into affinity groups helped provide the social and group support necessary to the continuing commitment to one's convictions. As a consequence, individuals become more and more isolated from those with different views of reality. In time they begin to lose perspective; they think that a revolution is about to begin, and that they are part of the powerful vanguard.

Powers (1971:101) describes the mood upon return from Cuba of a thirty-six member SDS delegation that included Diana Oughton, Kathy Boudin, and Ted Gold: "They began to feel that history was escalating, that the rise of blacks in the United States and the defeat of Americans abroad might occur even before they had a chance to play their part in the revolution."

Bernardine Dohrn (1971:3) reflected on the tendency of isolated affinity groups to develop more extreme and radical attitudes:

> This tendency to consider only bombings or picking up the gun as revolutionary, with the glorification of the heavier the better, we've called the military error. After the explosion, we called off all armed actions until such time as we felt the causes had been understood and acted upon. We found that the alternative direction already existed among us and had been developed within our collectives. We became aware that a group of outlaws who are isolated from the youth communities do not have a sense

of what is going on, cannot develop strategies that grow to include large numbers of people, have become "us" and "them."

These two stages persist for some time before the potential political offender decides on the seriousness or gravity of his commitment to radical social change. Many persons who otherwise qualified as potential political criminals on the basis of predisposing factors entered into interpersonal relations with similar persons that isolated them from conventional views of reality, but because the proper situational conditions were not met, they never became political criminals.

Situational Contingencies

Turning Point. When an individual arrives at a stage in which old methods of action fail, are exhausted, or are discredited, he must face the necessity of doing something different, i.e., more extreme, or abandon his cause altogether. To the potential political criminal it is a matter of immanent logic. Once the initial inertia had been overcome the pendulum kept swinging along the continuum from political awareness to political commitment to political crime. Mass action, community organization and control, even riots in the street had failed. Only political crime was left. Yet this was a difficult decision to make. It meant severing relationships with friends and family; it was more serious than breaking windows in Chicago or throwing sticks and rocks at policemen in Cambridge or taking over Sproul Plaza at Berkeley. It meant that there would be no chance for a normal life–it meant no turning back.

A statement, dated December 6, 1970, was sent to a number of underground newspapers; it was signed by Bernardine Dohrn (1971:3) and accompanied by her thumbprint in order to establish authenticity:

> Two weeks before the townhouse explosion, four members of this group had firebombed Judge [John M.] Murtagh's house in New York as an action of support for Panther 21, whose trial was just beginning. To many people this was a very good action. Within the group, however, the feeling developed that because this action had not done anything to hurt the pigs materially, it wasn't very important. So within two weeks' time, this group had moved from firebombing to anti-personnel bombs. Many people in the collective did not want to be involved in the large scale, almost random bombing offensive that was planned. But they struggled day and night and eventually, everyone agreed to do their part.

Because the potential political criminal is confronted with the apparent necessity to take more forceful action to bring about social change, before normative and utilitarian justifications for political crime or violence are fully established, he experiences a dramatic intrapsychic dilemma. First, as a socialized member of the larger society, he has internalized the normative prohibitions against crime and violence. It is only as he begins to neutralize these prohibitions and develop normative justifications that he becomes eligible for criminal candidacy. For example, at his mitigation of sentence hearing, Karl Armstrong testified:

> I'm a very nonviolent person, basically . . . I don't feel comfortable with violence and even as I was firebombing ROTC and conducting the aerial attack at Baraboo, I felt very alienated from the violence I was using. But, in the case of the Indochina war, I could justify for myself the use of violence used to deter even greater violence. Even the judicial system acknowledges that belief. . . .
>
> I can say, in good conscience, under exactly the same circumstances, I would do it again to end the war. [Schipper, 1973:48]

Second, he must hold a belief in the utility of criminal action. Those who remain unconvinced that it is useful to oppose government with violence never become political criminals; for, not being able to believe that such action can produce constructive social change, they consider it madness. For example, the "young radicals" studied by Keniston (1968) doubted the effectiveness and historical inevitability of the success of violence and terrorist tactics in bringing about social change; hence, although they shared the necessary normative justification, they never expressed their convictions through criminal action. Instead they confined their activities to political organization and protest, sometimes committing acts of civil disobedience but always avoiding serious political crime.

Concerning Bill Ayers and Diana Oughton's need to believe in the utility of criminal action, Thomas Powers has written:

> At the beginning of 1968 Bill and Diana had assumed, like the vast majority of the radical movement, that American stability precluded any possibility of a genuine revolution. By the end of the year the country seemed bitterly divided and morally bankrupt. With the right kind of push, they felt, anything might happen. They were tired of waiting and they no longer had the slightest allegiance to democracy as they found it in America.
>
> In its early years SDS had been concerned with questions of political morality. By the end of 1968 it was obsessed by the moral crimes of Vietnam; they felt anything was justified if it might end that crime and prevent its repetition. To do this, SDS felt a revolution was needed; the only question which preoccupied them was how to bring it about. [Powers, 1971:61-62]

To be sure, normative and utilitarian justifications are analytically separate and distinguishable. Those who believe crime and violence are proper are not necessarily required to believe that they are also useful. However, the two concepts so directly impinge upon each other that what is proper often becomes interchangeable with what is useful or effective. This phenomenon may be referred to as instrumental morality or what Weber (1964) called the "ethics of responsibility." In either case the morality of a particular behavior hedges on the foreseeable results of one's actions. When utilitarian justifications are sufficiently strong, normative prohibitions against crime and violence ordinarily become modified. Consequently, individuals who believe violence is effective in bringing about a new social order may in time come to believe that it is also proper.

Capital punishment illustrates this point. National opinion polls have repeatedly shown that approximately two-thirds of the public are in favor of the death penalty, presumably believing it to be a deterrent to crime (Gallup, 1976). Let us suppose that social scientists could demonstrate conclusively that capital punishment not only fails to deter crime, but its implementation actually contributes to the death of innocent victims. Society then would have to reexamine its normative imperative concerning capital punishment and adjust it in the light of this new evidence. People who formerly believed it was proper to execute convicted criminals would now believe it to be improper, not because their morality or sense of justice had changed, but because its negative utility had been demonstrated.

With respect to instrumental morality, the development of a radical political perspective is a crucial step. This perspective provides the necessary explanation for the contradiction between democratic ideals and undemocratic reality in American society, giving purpose, rationale, and direction to its adherents. Although this perspective does not amount to a comprehensive belief system involving European history and theory (they descended more from the Abolitionists and Wobblies than from Marx), the slogans, rhetoric, and other simplified fragments of the broader unarticulated ideology form a powerful *tour de force* (Harrington, 1968). To nonadherents, revolutionary ideals must appear impractical and visionary, yet the offering of "illusions as solutions" provided its followers with a sense of the possible, so necessarily, so desperately needed for combining their growing militancy with a marching mysticism (cf. Toch, 1965).

Jane Alpert (1972:19-20) has written about Sam Melville's search for a political framework to justify his commitment to violent social change:

> The more he informed himself about the war, about foreign policy, and about the economic structure, the more he felt it was all doomed and that the only right action was whatever would push its physical destruction a little closer. He began to fantasize about sabotage.
>
> This was not a sudden development in Sam, although it seemed to occur over a short period of time. He was by nature an intensely passionate man. His hostility to stupid and vicious forms of authority had long predated his political activism. The analysis of the New Left had given him a framework which justified his commitment to violent change, but the Left itself could not move fast enough for him.

Once the potential political criminal acquires the belief that social change is possible, perhaps even inevitable (i.e., he moves from social theory to political ideology), he believes himself an historical actor merely playing out his part in the "natural order" of things.

> Throughout the summer and early fall of 1969 everything the Weathermen did was designed to steel themselves for a pure act of the will. In Jim Mellen's phrase, they were to become the "tools of necessity," the agents of history. They sometimes joked about "Mellen's Hegel rap," but they took it seriously. They were going to surrender themselves into history, to make themselves into history's cutting edge, to become the catalyst of historical change. [Powers, 1971:89]

The adoption of this perspective protected them from a paralyzing ambivalence which might otherwise have required the morality of their actions to depend on the foreseeable consequences. Here the foreseeable consequences were established and the morality predetermined.

Commitment. The above three conditions combine to bring a person to the point where he believes that criminal activity is both proper and useful. Yet, if he is to place his life at the disposal of a cause, he must have intensive reinforcement and elaboration of his initial tentative inclination to effect social change through criminal behavior before he does so. Diana Oughton, for example, doubted the feasibility of terrorist activities in the United States. However, the commitment to terrorism had been made by the group and in the end she succumbed.

According to Darley and Latane (1972), there are three basic criteria necessary to make people respond in a crisis. First, they must perceive the crisis. Second, they must know how to respond to it. And third, they must feel a responsibility to act. The persons examined here fulfilled all three criteria. They perceived the crisis, generally early in life. Their development, socialization and education provided the knowledge of how to respond; and the first two factors in combination enabled them to feel the responsibility necessary to act. The entire thrust of their politics was an emphasis on personal responsibility and commitment. The "every man his own leader" ideal was primarily designed to prevent cooptation, neutralization, and imprisonment of leaders as a way of destroying a social movement (Krause, 1971), but it also served to underscore the importance and responsibility of each for meaningful social change.

> Bernardine Dohrn told the Weathermen War Council in Flint, Michigan, "we f—ed up a lot anyway. We didn't fight around Bobby Seale when he was shackled at the Conspiracy Trial. We should have torn the courtroom apart. We didn't smash them when Mobe peace creeps hissed [Black Panther leader] David Hilliard on Moratorium Day in San Francisco. We didn't burn Chicago down when Fred [Hampton] was killed. [Gelder, 1970:164]

Bernardine Dohrn (1970:11) further wrote:

> The parents of 'privileged' kids have been saying for years that the revolution was a game for us. But the War and racism of their society show that it is too fucked up. We will never live peaceable under their system.

Much of the radical press urged people to resist the forces of war and violence in their daily lives. By "living the revolution" one could prove one's commitment, not only to others, but to oneself as well. The typical radical asked himself, "Do I really think armed struggle is years away, or am I just not committed enough to give up my comforts?" (Gelder, 1970:170). In order to silence their own doubts they began to give more and more emphasis to an "ethic of ultimate ends." The purity of one's intentions became more important than the foreseeable results of one's deeds (Weber, 1964).

Not only were many of the subjects willing to act criminally or even violently, but they were willing to die, if necessary, for their ideals. For them the exemplary held utility, at least historically, for it kept the flame of political protest kindled.

> They [Philip and Daniel Berrigan] criticized any anti-war protest that stopped short of Philip's. "One becomes convinced that equivalent risk is going to be the only source of community worth talking about," Daniel wrote to James Forest after preaching a sermon on the "softness and bureaucracy" of the Catholic Peace Fellowship which created a crisis in their friendship. "And that the expressive acts such as Phil's, once they are thoughtful and proceed from a sacrificing heart, must be multiplied. You sound as though we were keeping house in normal times. Ha. Give us a bit of anguish, or why talk about hope?" [Gray, 1970:114]

In time it became honest and moral to be involved in revolutionary activities, whether or not they worked. As a result, those who accepted the responsibility and commitment to revolutionary change took on the characteristics of martyrdom. No longer was it enough to do penance for the sins of society by going into the ghetto and slums and working among the impoverished. Something more was needed to affirm one's commitment. Words were no longer adequate.

In February, 1968, three thousand members of Clergy and Laymen Concerned About Vietnam arrived in Washington, D.C., for an annual rally.

> It seemed that every religious leader in the peace movement was there except Philip and Daniel Berrigan. Clergy and Laymen Concerned About Vietnam had become for the Berrigans, "another liberal bag." As soon as it grew fashionable for progressive clergymen to march, picket, and lecture against the war, the Berrigans bowed out of the movement they had helped to create. "You can't criticize the Berrigans this year," one of their friends said. "They look down on anyone who hasn't risked as much as they have. They'll barely break bread with you if you haven't burned your draft card. Talk about ghettos! That ghetto of martyrs is the most exclusive club of all." [Gray, 1970:115]

Daniel and Philip Berrigan saw their role and the role of Christians to be constant critics of the state and guardians of Christian values.

> As advocated by the Berrigans, it [commitment] also demands a return to early styles of Christian martyrdom. "Originally, as you recall, one was not

> brought to the baptismal font in his mother's arms," Daniel had written in the early essay in which he condemned the Catholic sheepfold. "One came to baptism somewhat as Paul did: by a shattering change of heart, by many deliberate renunciations. . . . And this inner death to all that ordinary men live by was dramatized in the occurrence of martyrdom, which sealed publicly what one had already pledged to become in the sacred waters." [Gray, 1970:115]

In this respect, it is interesting to note in the case histories a frequent reference to Herman Melville's *Moby Dick.* Jane Alpert was obsessed with the book's symbolism during her high school years. She and a classmate went through the entire manuscript trying to ascertain whether it was Ahab's right or left leg that was missing, believing it to be somehow crucial (New York Times, 1969). Similarly, on December 27, 1969, during the Weatherman meeting in Flint, Mark Rudd urged radicals to be like Captain Ahab who lived with one thought, "to bring down the white whale" (Powers, 1971:133). Samuel Grossman desired so strongly to be identified with Ahab, that he changed his name to Melville in order to pretend ancestry. He wanted to devote his life, like Ahab, to the pursuit of the superhuman enemy (Alpert, 1972).

These are not the idiosyncratic beliefs of a few individuals, but represent a dominant cultural theme borrowed from literature and often symbolized in popular folk music of the time. For example, P.F. Soans' "Eve of Destruction" was expressive of the apocalyptic thinking of the time. As Carl Belz has written, "It featured an accelerating bear which slowly developed into the impact of a forceful marching song. . . . This resulted in the paradoxical and disturbing aesthetic impression that the predicted destruction might be a glorious and appealing event" (Belz, 1969:169). Yet it was the belief in the possibility of a real revolution that provided these persons with the courage of their convictions. As J. Kirk Sale has written concerning Ted Gold: "No one wants to die, but when he is finally prepared for it, or thinks he is, the only way to keep going is with the belief that history will keep his ideas . . . alive" (Sale, 1970:514).

The Commission of a Political Crime. For the conventional politician and common criminal there are relatively precise and measurable symbols of commitment and success, unavailable to or unacceptable by the political criminal. With virtue and success attributed to the self, in contrast to external objects and achievements, new symbols need to be uncovered and shaped. Commitment became defined by one's willingness to risk arrest; one's political savvy and experience became measured by the length of one's police record. Hence, the best way to prove commitment and achieve recognition was to commit a crime and go to jail, or to commit the crime and successfully elude and frustrate authorities.

Lacking the necessary political power to change existing social institutions from within, the political criminal attacks established symbols of society as a way of calling attention to his cause.

Philip Berrigan at Baltimore:

> We are entering the Customs House in Baltimore, Maryland, to deface the draft records there with our blood. We shed our blood willingly and gratefully in what we hope is a sacrificial and constructive act. We pour it upon these files to illustrate that with them and with these offices begins the pitiful waste of American and Vietnamese blood ten thousand miles away. We implore our countrymen to judge our action against this nation's Judeo-Christian tradition, against the horror in Vietnam and the impending threat of nuclear destruction. [Gray, 1970:110]

Daniel Berrigan at Catonsville:

> Today, May 17th, [1968] we enter Local Board No. 33 at Catonsville, Maryland, to seize Selective Service records and burn them with napalm. . . . We destroy the draft records not only because they exploit our young men but because they represent misplaced power concentrated in the ruling class of America. . . . Now this injustice must be faced, and this we intend to do, with whatever strength of mind, body, and grace that God will give us. May God have mercy on our nation. [Gray, 1970:116]

This exercising of destructive or disruptive power forced the political offenders into an untenable position. They become confronted with the paradox of denouncing the political system for its creation and perpetuation of human suffering and misery, and then employ the same means to reach their new humanitarian goals. By using the ethic of ultimate ends they began to lose claim to their higher morality and ethical superiority. Although they could argue that what they were doing was no worse than what the social system was doing, they could no longer claim that it was any better.

The axiom that the end justifies the means began to break down when the question was asked, "Which end should justify which means?" As Max Weber (1964:120) has written:

> We encounter the ever renewed experience that the adherent of an ethic of ultimate ends suddenly turns into a chiliastic prophet. Those, for example, who have just preached "love against violence" now call for the use of force for the *last* violent deed. . . . In the same manner, our officers told the soldiers before every offensive: "This will be the last one: this one will bring victory and therewith peace."

This is an awkward position to defend and its uncertain validity becomes increasingly difficult to maintain. With each act of violence the social message becomes more obscure. In time the violent medium begins to overshadow the peaceful message until the medium becomes the message.

This situation often led to a tenuous alliance between those who employed criminal techniques for political purposes and those who utilized political rationales for criminal purposes. In Boston, for example, Susan Saxe and Katherine Powers, two political activists at Brandeis University teamed up with Stanley Bond, a convicted armed robber who had been politicalized while serving his prison term, and Robert Valeri and James Gilday, two straight criminal types without political convictions. Together they robbed the Brighton Branch of the State Street Bank and Trust Company of $26,000 (Sackman, 1970). To Saxe, Powers, and Bond it was "a legitimate declaration of war . . . to steal money to buy guns to steal more money to create havoc" (Morse, 1970:56), but to Valeri and Gilday, it was simply a bank robbery.

The willingness of at least some political criminals to join ranks with ordinary criminals inevitably led to the complete obfuscation of the symbolic nature of their crimes. To a public already confused about the social message of these new politicians, this was the final bit of evidence that such crimes were straight criminal actions disguised as political acts. For a while even the political criminals themselves seemed confused. Bernardine Dohrn's endorsement of Charles Manson–notorious for his statements against blacks and women–let alone the crime he stood accused of–indicated a readiness to defend anyone who had "off[ed] some rich honky pigs" (Gelder, 1970:170).

It is not unusual that men who are inclined toward a dislike of the existing order join together to seize the standard of progress and revolution. As Cesare Lombroso wrote: "The army of progress is recruited from all ranks and conditions–men of genius, intellectual spirits who are the first to realize the defects of the old system . . . lunatics, enthusiastic propagandists of the new ideas . . . [and] criminals, the natural enemies of order" (Lombroso-Ferrero, 1911:297). This alliance is not essentially illogical, although it is sufficiently at variance with the political norms of society to be easily construed as such. When the public came to a realization that the revolution was dead and the movement lost its power, its social message extinguished.

SUMMARY

These five stages have been presented as separate and distinct in order to meet the requirements of the analytical method employed. In reality, they may occur simultaneously or out of sequence, with the partial completion of one stage complementing and helping to complete another.

Although the developmental model attempts to formulate principles applicable to all twenty cases, there are a few interesting exceptions. Daniel Ellsberg's status as a white-collar political offender (his position at the Rand Corporation enabled him to commit a politically motivated violation of the law) may set him somewhat apart. He apparently did not actually progress through stages one and two as described. After many months of agonizing over his decision (stages three and four), Ellsberg attempted to release the Pentagon Papers to the Senate Foreign Relations Committee and to several prominent United States Senators. It was upon the Senate's repeated refusal to utilize his information that he decided to go to the *New York Times* to make them public. Likewise, Samuel Melville did not progress through the usual stages of social reform and liberal protest. His father was a member of the Communist Party who worked at organizing taxi drivers' unions in New York. In the late sixties Samuel Melville began to act on the political beliefs he had learned as a child.

The series of developmental stages which in successive combination might account for the development of a political criminal can be summarized as follows: First, the individual must experience strain or tension produced by a perceived discrepancy between the ideal and the actual state of affairs, and he must resolve to eliminate the strain by closing the gap between "what is" and "what ought to be." Second, the individual must develop a political problem-solving perspective which emphasizes the need to destroy the old institutions and build new ones. Third, the individual must arrive at a turning point where old methods of action have been exhausted, have failed, or have been discredited. He must face the necessity of doing something different or abandoning this cause altogether. It is only as he begins to develop normative and utilitarian justifications for political violence that he becomes eligible for criminal candidacy. Fourth, even if the individual comes to believe that criminal activity is both proper and useful, he must experience a feeling of personal responsibility and commitment before he is willing to place his life or liberty at the disposal of a cause. Fifth, the individual must commit a politically motivated crime.

NOTES

1. For a presentation of the thesis that Presidential assassins have almost always been young men with delusional thought processes who tended toward lives of alienation and socioeconomic deterioration, see Kirkham, Levy, and Crotty, 1969.
2. This breakdown is similar to one found in Lofland and Stark, 1965.
3. For a full discussion of these concepts, see Rosenzweig, 1934.

REFERENCES

ALPERT, J. (1972). "Profile of Sam Melville." Pp. 4-54 in S. Melville, Letters from Attica. New York: Morrow.

BELZ, C. (1969). The story of rock. New York: Oxford.

BERRIGAN, D. (1970). The trial of the Catonsville Nine. Boston: Beacon.

Boston Globe (1973). "Names in the news." August 10, p. 2.

CHARLTON, L. (1970). "Girl next door turns radical: A study in modern alienation." New York Times, December 1, p. 56.

CLINARD, M.B., and QUINNEY, R. (1967). Criminal behavior systems: A typology. New York: Holt, Rinehart & Winston.

COHEN, J. (1972). "Introduction." Pp. 47-80 in S. Melville, Letters from Attica. New York: Morrow.

DARLEY, J.M., and LATANE, B. (1972). "When will people help in a crisis?" Pp. 326-331 in Change: Readings in society and human behavior. Del Mar, Cal.: CRM Books.

DOHRN, B. (1971). "New morning." Rat, Dec. 17, 1970/Jan. 6, 1971, p. 3.

--- (1970). "Declaration of war." Great Speckled Bird, June 8, pp. 1, 11.

FESTINGER, L. (1957). A theory of cognitive dissonance. Stanford, Cal.: Stanford University Press.

FLUGEL, J.S. (1921). The psycho-analytical study of the family. London and New York: International Psycho-Analytical Press.

Gallup Poll (1976). "Two Americans in three say convicted murderers should face death penalty." March, pp. 22-24. Princeton, N.J.

GELDER, L. VAN (1970). "Bernardine Dohrn is weighed in the balance and found heavy." Esquire, April, pp. 164-170.

GRAY, F. DU P. (1970). "Profiles." New Yorker, March 14, pp. 14ff.

HARRINGTON, M. (1968). "The mystical militants." Pp. 684-689 in R. Perrucci and M. Pilisuk (eds.), The triple revolution. Boston: Little, Brown.

HOFFER, E. (1951). The true believer: Thoughts on the nature of human movements. New York: Harper & Row.

KENISTON, K. (1968). Young radicals: Notes on committed youth. New York: Harcourt Brace & World.

KIRKHAM, J.F., LEVY, S.G. and CROTTY, W.J. (1969). "Assassination and political violence." Pp. 49-69 in Staff Report to the National Commission on the Causes and Prevention of Violence, Task Force Report, Vol. 8. Washington, D.C.: U.S. Government Printing Office.

KRAUSE, E.A. (1971). The sociology of occupations. Boston: Little, Brown.

LEMERT, E.M. (1951). Social pathology: A systematic approach to the theory of sociopathic behavior. New York: McGraw-Hill.

Life Magazine (1967). "Whip of black power." May 19, p. 80.

LIPSET, S. (1970). "The activists: A profile." Pp. 244-255 in C.H. Anderson (ed.), Sociological essays and research. Homewood, Ill.: Dorsey Press.

LIPSET, S., and WOLIN, S.S. (eds., 1965). The Berkeley student revolt. Garden City, N.Y.: Doubleday.

LOFLAND, J., and STARK, R. (1965). "Conversion to a deviant perspective." American Sociological Review, 30:862-875.

LOMBROSO-FERRERO, G. (1911). Criminal man: According to the classification of Cesare Lombroso. Reprinted by Patterson Smith, Montclair, N.J., 1972.

MANNHEIM, H. (1965). Comparative criminology. Boston: Houghton-Mifflin.

MELVILLE, S. (1972). Letters from Attica. New York: Morrow.

MONTAGNO, M., and HUCK, J. (1977). "The selling of Jesus." Newsweek, February 28, pp. 48-49.

MORAN, R. (1974). "Political crime." Unpublished doctoral dissertation. Philadelphia: University of Pennsylvania.

MORSE, J. (1970). "The enigma named Susan Saxe." Boston Sunday Advertiser, November 1, p. 56.

New York Times (1966). August 5, p. 137.

--- (1969). December 1, p. 1.

--- (1970a). December 14, p. 1.

--- (1970b). November 30, pp. 1, 56.

--- (1970c). April 7, p. 31.

POWERS, T. (1971). Diana: The making of a terrorist. New York: Bantam Books.

ROSENZWEIG, S. (1934). "Types of reaction to frustration: a heuristic classification." Journal of Abnormal and Social Psychology, 29:298-300.

SACKMAN, M. (1970). "Police charge three with robbery, murder." The Justice, September 20, p. 56.

SALE, J.K. (1970). "Ted Gold: Education for violence." The Nation, April 13, pp. 423-429.

SCHIPPER, H. (1973). "Trapped generation on trial." The Progressive, 38(1):45-59.

Time (1973). "Implications of mercy." March 5, p. 70.

--- (1975). "Underground odyssey." January 27, p. 63.

TOCH, H. (1965). The social psychology of social movements. Indianapolis, Ind.: Bobbs Merrill.

TURNER, R.H. (1953). "The quest for universals in sociological research." American Sociological Review, 18:604-611.

United States Bureau of the Census (1972). Census of Population, General Population Characteristics, Final Report PC(1)-B-1. United States Summary. Washington, D.C.: U.S. Government Printing Office.

Washington Star (1968). "Portrait of an organizer." June 6, page 10.

WEBER, M. (1964). From Max Weber. Trans., and ed. by H. Gerth and C.W. Mills. New York: Oxford.

WILKERSON, C., SEGAL, M. and COLEMAN, L. (1968). "A false privilege." New Left Notes, October 7, p. 8.

WOLFGANG, M.E. (1969). Violent Behaviour. Churchill College Overseas Fellowship Lecture no. 4. Cambridge, Eng.: W. Heffer & Sons.

7

THE PSYCHOLOGY OF POLITICAL DEVIANCE

ALBERT ELLIS
LINDA ECKSTEIN

No one seems to have definitely defined political deviance, and possibly no one ever will, since it ranges all the way from extreme right wing to left wing ideology and activity, and appears to have almost an infinite number of in-between shadings. For the purpose of this article, we shall give it quite a limited or restricted definition; and even at that, we shall probably get into several kinds of difficulty.

We shall start with some distinctions made by Holland (1967), who in turn takes off from criteria for deviant behavior of Clinard (1963) and Siporin (1965). Clinard and Siporin suggest that such behavior follows three major criteria: (1) it includes the social visibility of the "deviant" individuals; (2) it exceeds the tolerance limits of the social environment in which it occurs; and (3) it deviates from the norm in a disapproved direction.

Going further, Holland lists three main kinds of deviant behavior: (1) anticonforming behavior, which has as its primary purposes the public expression of negative attitudes toward values of the dominant culture; (2) subconforming behavior, which fails the standards set by society by virtue of inadequacy or incompleteness on the part of the deviant individuals; and (3) nonconforming behavior, which includes value-oriented or value-directed behavior in which the values involved do not constitute those predominant in the culture.

In regard to political deviance, we shall ignore, in the present article, both subconforming and nonconforming behavior. Thus, many individuals in most societies, including our own, seem apolitical or peculiarly political because of what Holland would call their "inadequacy or incompleteness." Mental defectives, for example, usually would not vote or show any interest in politics. Most alcoholics, drug addicts, and residents of mental and penal institutions would also tend to cop out of politics, and we could view them as subconforming politically. A great many nonconformists would also have little or no interest in politics—for example, hippies, hermits, artists whose only interest lies in esthetics, and romantics and idealists who abjure all forms of political involvement or who may sometimes think of themselves as "armchair liberals," but who still rarely vote, let alone participate in other forms of political activity. We shall ignore both subconformists and nonconformists in the present paper.

This leaves us with what Holland calls the "anticonformists." Here, too, we have a number of problems. For political anticonformists range from the extreme right wing to the extreme left wing; and even if we stick with one of the largest of these groups, the left-wing activists or the political dissenters, we run into quite a bit of difficulty: for this group, too, turns out rather "impure" and includes quite a number of different shadings and colorings. As Keniston (1973) has noted, research on student radicals and militants at first assumed that asking subjects to label themselves on a continuum from left to right or from moderately to very radical has the virtue of great simplicity and seems to hold great promise; but it soon showed the vice "of glossing over the growing likelihood that any two self-labelled 'radicals' would hold very different beliefs and behave in very different ways" (Keniston, 1973:xii).

Various studies have also found that not only do political "militants" differ significantly over the "proper" role of confrontation, resistance, disruption, and violence, but they also include dissenters who favor hippie, counterculture, and new life-style modes, and those who favor sociopolitical activism rather than psychocultural issues. Thus, Block, Haan, and Smith (1969) found differences between campus "activists," "constructivists," and "dissenters."

Deviation, as Clinard and Siporin suggest, includes behavior that deviates from the norm in a disapproved direction. And Holland, as noted, includes under anticonforming behavior that which has as its primary purposes the public expression of negative attitudes toward values of the dominant culture. In a considerable amount of political deviation as defined in this manner, however, research indicates that the militant activity in question has shown a good many "constructive" qualities on the part of the deviants that society by no means always disapproves of and that, in fact, it sometimes considers among its "finest" values.

In this connection, Derber and Flacks (1968) studied 51 student activists and found that a factor analysis of eight of their main values produced two rotated factors: romanticism and humanitarianism. Doress (1968), in an investigation of Boston University student activists, found that left activists (as compared to right-wing and moderate activists) showed lower dogmatism, greater inner-directedness, self-actualizing values, feeling reactivity and intimate contact, and higher achievement via independence and flexibility. Gurin (1971) found student activism associated with social maturity, religious liberalism, and identity-seeking definition of college goals.

Haan, Smith, and Block (1968) showed that male activists described themselves as idealistic, perceptive, empathic, and altruistic. Katz (1968) found activists of both sexes higher than other students on social maturity and estheticism. Kerpelman (1970) discovered both rightist and leftist activists higher on independence than centrist students. Paulus (1967) found student activists high on social conscience and satisfaction with the administration. According to a study by Schneider (1966), left-wing student activists proved other-oriented and focused on moral injustices.

Somers (1965) showed that militant students did significantly better on their college grades than did conservatives. Whitaker and Watts (1971) found student activists higher than nonactivists on achievement and self-confidence.

Fairly consistently, then, researchers have turned up socially acceptable traits in student militants and rebels compared to nonrebellious groups. Keniston, considering these and other data, therefore concludes that student radicals constitute an elite group and not a "rabble of rejects." They show unusually high moral development. They by no means act upon, or violently act upon, their radical beliefs. He concludes (Keniston, 1971:307):

> Furthermore, psychological studies of student radicals indicate that they are no more neurotic, suicidal, enraged, or disturbed than are nonradicals. Indeed, most studies find them to be rather more integrated, self-accepting, and "advanced," in a psychological sense, than their politically inactive contemporaries. In general, research on American student rebels supports a "generational solidarity" (or chip-off-the-old-block) theory, rather than one of Oedipal rebellion.

What can we say to all this? Nothing very sensational. Perhaps, as Brzezinski (1971), Bettelheim (1969), and Feuer (1969) maintain, student rebels either have unresolved Oedipal feelings and still foolishly act out against their parents, or perhaps they unrealistically will not accept the fact that times have changed, technology has largely taken over, and Luddite rebellion will do them no good. Perhaps.

On the other hand, dissent, even when it takes a somewhat violent nature, has its social advantages as well as its psychologically healthy aspects (Deutsch, 1969; Douglas, 1969; Ellis, 1969; Hentoff, 1970; Keniston, 1968, 1971, 1973; Kiev, 1975, Newfield, 1970, Wolff, 1969). Thus, student rebellion in the 1960s, for all its excesses at times, had some distinctly constructive elements: (1) It seriously shook the authoritarian foundations of many colleges and universities. (2) It mobilized many previously apathetic and inert students into fighting seriously for what they believed right and proper. (3) It helped create a wider sense of community among the students and sometimes among other elements in society. (4) It brought to the fore several important issues, such as racial discrimination in the system of higher education, that subsequently got faced, discussed, and sometimes solved. (5) It highlighted, for many thinking individuals, several basic weaknesses of our culture and encouraged discussion and research that may eventually produce profound changes in our social system.

Student dissent, of course, also includes right-wing as well as left-wing activities. Not only are there such radical groups as the Free Speech Movement at Berkeley, the Students for a Democratic Society, and the Weatherpeople, but on the conservative side there are the Young Americans for Freedom, the Young Conservatives, and the Young Republicans. However we may personally disagree with the viewpoints and activities of any of these organizations, it seems a healthy sign of the times that, especially during the course of military effort like the Vietnam affair, this wide spectrum of student opinion and dissent continues. A mass of young people who have homogenized, one-sided views of the way things do and had better exist would hardly bode good for the present and future of the United States or any other country.

THE PSYCHOLOGY OF POLITICAL EXTREMISTS

Because ordinary forms of political dissent do not seem to produce or to make systematic use of highly disturbed individuals, and because studies of some violent-prone groups (such as the Berkeley Free Speech Movement and the Students for a Democratic Society) also do not seem to find unusually aberrant members in the majority of such groups, attention will here be focused on the psychology of extreme right-wing and left-wing groups that consciously and actively pursue violence. These are people who call for revolution at all costs, as a means of backing up their dissenting political views. They include ultraconservative extremists, such as the American Nazi Party and the Ku Klux Klan, on the one hand; and the Weatherpeople and the Symbionese Liberation Army, on the other.

Unusual difficulties are encountered by the researcher seeking to gather facts about the members of such groups and about their psychological makeup. The organizations, by their very nature, tend to act in secretive and underground ways, and therefore virtually no reliable studies of their membership have appeared in the literature. A few members of these extremist groups, such as Stern (1975), have published detailed accounts of the activities and the personalities of themselves and some of their associates, but not enough material of this sort has yet appeared to substantiate any detailed analysis of their psychological makeup.

On theoretical grounds, however, it would definitely appear that members of violent revolutionary groups, such as the Weatherpeople and the SLA, fulfill the criteria of deviance as defined by Clinard (1963), Siporin (1965), and Holland (1967). Their behavior includes: (1) anticonformity which has as its primary purposes the public expression of negative attitudes toward the values of the dominant culture; (2) social visibility; and (3) action that exceeds the tolerance limits of the social environment in which it occurs.

On more psychological grounds, the views and actions of members of these extreme revolutionary groups also appear distinctly "deviant" or "disturbed," because in several important respects they seem exceptionally inconsistent, illogical, and self-contradictory. Thus, members of the American Nazi Party or the Ku Klux Klan supposedly want to preserve the existing social system and increase its degree of organization and law and order. They presumably hate the "disorder" and the "disorganization" wreaked on society by overpermissive liberals. Yet, their practice of vigilantism, torture, blackmail, and sometimes downright murder does not seem to square with many of their vaunted ideals. Unlike left-wing visionaries (e.g., Marx, Engels, Lenin, and Trotsky), who hypothesize that after the revolution the state will somehow wither away and that pure democracy (or a form of civilized anarchy) will prevail, these right-wing visionaries seem to believe that a strong centralized state will continue in power forever—but that somehow "democracy" and "freedom" will also prevail, and that the masses will benefit enormously from endless dictatorial rule.

On the extreme left-wing side, the contradictions seem equally obvious and acute. Ostensibly, the revolutionaries of the left stand for freedom, democracy, humanity, and virtually every other "idealistic" view imaginable. But they believe, peculiarly enough, that they can only obtain these goals through deliberately instigating considerable authoritarianism and violence. They consequently attack, as Rader (1970) shows, not only the property but the person of the ruling class. And they use almost exactly the same tactics against reactionary oppressors as they accuse these oppressors of illegitimately using against them.

Although highly "practical" and "hard-headed," they also seem to follow a highly utopian philosophy. Although the members of the proletariat and the blue-collar class seem to get more reactionary with the passing decades, these extreme left-wing radicals still expect them to support the revolutionary cause and, eventually, take over and run the state in an enlightened manner. Where almost the entire history of political revolution, from at least the French Revolution to the modern Russian and Chinese revolutions, tends to show that a group that takes over the government by somewhat violent means remains in power for quite a period of time, and if anything increases political incarceration, torture, and murder, the modern radical extremists still seem to think that this will not occur if they fight their way into power.

As Rader (1970:211) notes in this respect:

> The great contradiction of the bomber and terrorist is that he goes beyond the logical to assert a very desperate and profoundly human hope; that through the selective use of violence, violence itself can be defeated. Sometimes, they say, men must kill the killers to end the killing. . . .

> Where the terrorist makes his fatal mistake is that he assumes death is foreign to man, that violence repels him because man, like Ionesco's Berenger, longs to be cured of death, and that—and this is the greatest irony for those who struggle against American racism and imperialism—he finally believes, like a child, in the essential goodness and decency of the average man.

Although one cannot easily obtain data on the personality traits of extreme right- and left-wing radicals who resort to violence, and who are political deviants, what data we do have seems to fairly clearly indicate that they lead rather disturbed lives. As a remarkable case in point, we have the autobiography of Susan Stern (1974), *With the Weathermen: The Personal Journal of a Revolutionary Woman.* With candor rarely revealed in other similar documents, Stern bares herself in this journal.

The Stern Story

According to her own story, Stern steadily experienced (1) severe bouts of abysmal depression, (2) frequent suicidal feelings, (3) severe anxiety, (4) continual self-downing, in spite of her unusual activism, outstanding accomplishments, and heroism, (5) overindulgence in all kinds of drugs, including marijuana, LSD, mescaline, speed, barbiturates and other downers, and alcohol, (6) obsessive-compulsive and often destructive sex indulgence, (7) arrant egomania and addiction to attention-getting, (8) dire needs for love and approval, (9) fanatical commitment to revolutionary activity even when it proved clearly against her own interests, and various other kinds of emotional disturbance. Although she and many of her revolutionary companions would naturally tend to blame her emotional turbulence on the conditions of her upbringing and the reactionary state of the nation during her childhood and adolescence, note that the vast majority of other people who had a fairly similar upbringing turned out, even when in a radical frame of mind not too dissimilar from hers (e.g., members of Students for a Democratic Society which spawned the Weathermen), not to resort to the political activist extremes that she did.

The Case of Joe Remiro

Susan Stern came from an intellectual, permissive, upper middle class, New York Jewish home. Joe Remiro, by contrast, became one of the shooting members of the Symbionese Liberation Army, an extremist left-wing group that in 1973 took over the mantle of the Weathermen and in some ways made the latter look almost like pacifists. Not only did the SLA deliberately execute black educator, Marcus Foster on November 6, 1973, with many cyanide-filled bullets, but on February 4, 1974, they successfully executed the first political kidnapping in the United States—that of Patty Hearst. Joe Remiro, quite unlike Susan Stern, had a Chicano father, who Joe himself describes as "still patriotic" and "still telling World War II hero stories," an Italian-Catholic mother, a typical parochial school background (graduated from Sacred Heart High School in San Francisco), and a lower-middle-class upbringing.

Yet, Joe's biographer, a highly competent liberal-hippie journalist, John Bryan (1975), outlines for Joe a set of personality traits amazingly similar to those of Susan Stern including deepseated feelings of anxiety and guilt, dogmatic rebelliousness, enormous insecurity, rabid and exceptionally violent commitment to revolution, inability to relate very long to another person, serious bouts of drug and alcohol addiction, great feelings of alienation, extreme homicidal tendencies, and various other kinds of emotional difficulties. Bryan, a fine observer but a somewhat prejudiced interpreter, lays the responsibility for most of Joe's aberrations squarely on his experiences in the Vietnam War. But just as we can point out that exceptionally few well-to-do Jewish women from New York adopted Susan Stern's revolutionary life style, so we can note that less than a handful of Vietnam veterans, from San Francisco's parochial school lower-middle-class background, threw in their lot with the SLA. Hence, this kind of sociological and psychological analysis seems neither necessary nor sufficient to explain the personalities of these two extreme revolutionists.

Backgrounds of Extremists

The thesis that either sociological backgrounds or family upbringing primarily cause extremist radical behavior seems even less tenable when one looks at the psychological manifestations of left-wing revolutionaries in the United States who served as Susan Stern's and Joe Remiro's main companions in their underground activities. Although a fairly high percentage of these extremists came from middle-class intellectual Jewish homes, the majority did not. Among the leading SLA members, for example, Nancy Ling Perry, a WASP from Santa Rosa, California, had an ultraconservative furniture store owner for a father. Patricia Soltysik came from the small California city of Goleta and conservative midde-class parents. Camilla Hall, daughter of a Minnesota Lutheran minister, had a German-Swedish background. Angela DeAngelis Atwood, daughter of a New Jersey Teamster organizer, had a fairly conservative upbringing. Although Emily Harris was born into a wealthy Jewish family, Bill Harris had army officers as both his father and (after the father died) his stepfather. During his childhood, he served as an acolyte in St. Christopher's Episcopal Church in Fort Sill, Oklahoma.

The Rader Story

Another most revealing story of the "insides" of a radical extremist, as well as the inside of the left-wing activist movement in America, comes from Dotson Rader (1973), whose autobiography, *Blood Dues,* tells the story of an all-American boy's involvement in deviant politics—including innumerable gory details of

Rader's personal life and feelings. This again is a rather gruesome personality picture. According to Rader's own story, he joined and continued in the extremist movement largely as a result of (1) his severe feelings of personal inadequacy and his determination to prove himself as a "man" by taking violent risks, (2) his neurotic obsession with the "beauty" of violence, (3) his nihilistic thinking, (4) his compulsive imbibing of drugs and alcohol (including cocaine, Demerol. Phanaphen, and Quaaludes), (5) his deepseated feelings of guilt, (6) his "paranoia and a sense of defeat before life which was oppressive enough for me to take in the middle of the night shivering in a cold sweat and pray, when I did not believe in prayer, that I would make it through the night," and (7) his tendencies toward severe depression and suicide, which began at the age of nineteen (long before he joined the radical movement) and continued up to the time he wrote his autobiography in his thirties. Although Rader's family, social, and religious backgrounds seem far different from those of Susan Stern and Joe Remiro, his emotional disturbances and the part they apparently played in his revolutionary involvement have many amazing similarities to theirs.

Common Personality Traits

There are insufficient details on the lives of radical extremists other than Susan Stern, Joe Remiro, and Dotson Rader, to conclude that they had similar personality difficulties. However, there is a good deal of general information on such extremists, in the first-hand reports of Stern, Remiro, and Rader, as well as in a number of observations by other writers. Thus, reports by a fairly wide spectrum of observers include the Black Panther leader, Eldridge Cleaver (1970), the Brazilian educator and idealist, Paulo Freire (1970), the young liberal, James Simon Kunen (1970), the conservative leftist, Norman Mailer (1968), and the insurrectionist "crazies," Jerry Rubin (1970) and Abbie Hoffman (1968). Adding these views to those of Stern, Remiro, Keniston, Newfield, Rader, and some of the other authors previously cited, a fairly consistent picture emerges. The most extreme, violence-prone radicals seem to have, in many instances though not in all, personality characteristics along the following lines:

Actions that Contradict Ideologies. Although the extreme left-wing radicals in the United States ostensibly oppose limitations on democracy and free speech, they frequently act (and even talk) in a manner that seems directly opposed to this view. They think nothing of interrupting others' rights to free speech; they silence their own members; they act dictatorially rather than democratically (and frankly advocate "temporary" dictatorship *after* the revolution); and they often behave in a manner that seems just about as Joe Remiro said to Bryan (1975:176):

> A nation doesn't have the right to come off and become capitalist and imperialist. When they do they have no rights. They lose their rights. If we allowed a free election in this country and a Nixon were elected again, I'd say, "Well, bullshit! There ain't gonna be no more motherfuckin' free elections."

Devout Dogmatic Beliefs. Leftist extremists (like rightist extremists) believe what they believe in an exceptionally dogmatic, absolutistic, unarguable way. As Paulo Freire (1970), himself a noted activist, reports:

> While the rightist sectarian, closing himself in "his" truth, does no more than fulfill his "natural" role, the leftist who becomes sectarian and rigid negates his very nature. Each, however, as he revolves about "his" truth, feels threatened if that truth is questioned. Thus, each considers anything that is not "his" truth a lie. As the journalist Marcio Moreira Alves once told me: "They both suffer from an absence of doubt."

Delusions of Strength and Success. Because of their dogmatic adherence to their own views, extreme activists frequently believe that they have enormous numbers with them and will soon succeed in their revolutionary attempts, when actually they have little or no mass following. Eldridge Cleaver (1970) believed, along with Huey Newton, that the Black Panther Party (now defunct) would soon have millions of members and, along with Jerry Rubin (now retired from politics), that even the kindergarten children "are a rising wave of Yippies." Mark Rudd, in 1968, predicted that within eighteen months a leftist revolution would occur in America.

Distortions of Facts. Because of their dogmatic allegiance to a monolithic way of looking at things, extreme revolutionists tend to misperceive reality. Jerry Rubin (1970) stated that "every arrest in Amerika is political." The SLA members felt positive that by killing Marcus Foster they would win enormous approval. But as Bryan (1975:193) states: "The Black Panthers condemned the killing and its perpetrators, as did most other leftist groups. It was, in fact, the Foster assassination which almost certainly doomed SLA to a lonely and little-lamented extinction in the end."

Fanaticism and Extremism. By definition, one would expect deviant radical groups to act fanatically and extremistically; and they certainly do. Of the SLA members, Bryan (1975:116) says:

> Like the Narodniki, who had little understanding of then-developing Russian dialectical materialism, but an enormous mystical confidence in their own half-informed vision and in "the people," the S.L.A. chose terrorism, assassination, bank robbery, and kidnap to gain the respect and following of this "lowest strata" and to undermine what they felt was an absolutist government.

The Weathermen, as Susan Stern tells us, decided that monogamy existed as a deterrent to their collectives and to the revolution, and they waged relentless war against their own monogamous couples, driving some of the most ardent and active members out of their movement.

Mysticism. True to their highly romantic outlook, extreme revolutionists tend to often adopt mystical views—in spite of the fact that many of them, influenced by the Marxists, think of themselves as materialists. Nancy Ling Perry profoundly believed in astrology and let the charts guide her life. Several other members of the SLA had a considerable interest in the occult, and they made use of the ancient mystical symbol of the seven-headed cobra as one of their insignia. As Norman Mailer (1968:279) noted, Jerry Rubin "was a mystic, a revolutionary mystic—his roots were in Bakunin." To give substance to this estimate, Rubin himself, almost a decade later, turned from revolution to the most mystical elements of Esalen and the transpersonal psychology movement.

Drug and Alcohol Abuse. Although revolutionists supposedly stick to quite Spartan rules and abjure the overuse of drugs or alcohol, the facts in the case of American extremists show otherwise. As noted above, Susan Stern, Joe Remiro, and Dotson Rader all abused various kinds of drugs as well as liquor. Jerry Rubin exulted that "a new man was born smoking pot while besieging the Pentagon." But Norman Mailer, in more sober style, insists that in the one main battle where the radical extremist Wedge tried to have it out deliberately with the forces of the Army, "the pot had deprived them of force," and they easily lost the skirmish. Stern, Rader, and Remiro's biographer, Bryan, report that boozing and drugging often ran rampant among the most violence-prone revolutionists. Nancy Perry, at one time, smoked "twelve or thirteen joints a day." Russell Little, arrested with Remiro for Marcus Foster's assassination, confessed that in college he "chased the women around and boozed it up as often as I could afford." General Field Marshall Cinque of the SLA steadily drank wine and beer as he and his comrades shot it out with the Los Angeles police and went to their deaths.

Feelings of Guilt and Inadequacy. Many of the other radical extremists besides Stern, Remiro, and Rader, downed themselves abysmally. An SLA member characterized the whole movement of rabid radicalists as "based on guilt." Donald (Cinque) DeFreeze upset himself so much when his wife, Gloria, contemplated walking out on him as a result of his kidnapping and burglary rampages, that he decided to kill her and his children "to keep them from leaving me." Many of the Weathermen and SLA exploits of bravado and violence stemmed from egotistic attempts, on the part of those who perpetrated or incited them, to cover up their own feelings of inadequacy and ego deficiency.

Nihilism. Well-ordered revolutionism, such as that of Lenin and Mao, solidly aims to overthrow the forces of government and to replace it with a highly systematized form of lasting alternative political rule. Many of the extreme American radicals in recent years, however, took an almost completely nihilistic view and appeared much more interested in destroying, at all cost, existing order than in replacing it with a better system. Eldridge Cleaver, in a pamphlet, *On Weathermen,* wrote that "in times of revolution, just wars and wars of liberation, I love the angels of destruction and disorder as opposed to the devils of conservation and law and order" (cited in Cleaver, 1970). He also spoke about sharing with Jerry Rubin "the total desire to smash what is now the social order in the United States of Amerika." Rubin called upon people not only to burn their draft cards, but also dollar bills, MA and doctoral degrees, and to become a new race of individuals who see property as theft. He proposed that, once the revolution came, "there will be no such crime as 'stealing' because everything will be free" (Rubin, 1970:256). When Kunen asked Mark Rudd if he would do anything, including slashing a priceless Rembrandt, to build the revolution, he replied, "There's nothing I wouldn't do."

Romanticism and Utopianism. Presumably a hard-headed realist and fighter, the typical radical extremist actually often winds up as an arrant romanticist. Susan Stern, Mark Rudd, and Jerry Rubin at first thought they would get 500,000 activists to the Democratic Convention in Chicago in 1968; they then toned down to a "realistic" expectation of 50,000. Actually, as Rubin admits, maybe 2,000 to 3,000 showed up. In the Pentagon affair, too, Mailer points out, Rubin had an "apocalyptic vision." A San Francisco commentator referred to the members of the SLA as "romantics, unbelievable nineteenth-century revolutionary romantics." A British reporter called them "a bunch of muddled romantics who probably owed far more to Hemingway than to Ho Chi Minh."

Addiction to Hatred and Violence. One would naturally expect violent rebels to deify hatred and violence, and they do. Said Jerry Rubin (1970:127): "The more people you alienate, the more people you reach. If you don't alienate people, you're not reaching them." And Kunen (1970:118): "If you want to make it with the activists, hatred is supposed to be all right with you." Rubin again (1970:127): "When in doubt, burn. Fire is the revolutionary's god. Fire is instant theater. No words can match fire." A joint communique put out in 1970 by the Berkeley Commune and Up Against the Wall/Motherfucker said: "There is no separation in the revolutionary movement. Every act is assimilated into the struggle, if it furthers revolt. . . . We must be flexible to rally one day and bomb the next." Susan Stern reports that the Women's Militia of the Weathermen, during the Days of Rage in Chicago in October 1969, literally fought to get into the heaviest street fighting, even after several of them had been injured. She herself felt somewhat frightened at the Weathermen's obsession with violence:

> But most of the others seemed thrilled—even the youngest, newest recruits. To be a criminal at large in the United States, a tapeworm in the belly of the monster, eating it up alive from the inside out. To make bombs. See big buildings topple. IBM got it last week—how about AT&T next?

Of the TDA (The Day After) demonstration that she helped arrange in 1970, Stern writes: "Eighty-nine people were arrested that day; hundreds were injured. Damages were over $75,000. Dozens of pigs were hurt and pig cars had been destroyed. By all criteria, TDA in Seattle had been an outstanding success" (Stern, 1975). Dotson Rader, by no means one of the most violent-prone activists of the late 1960s and early 1970s, also exults about "the bombings and the widespread terrorism" (over four thousand bombings in the United States in the 1969-1970 period), and admits that he favored such violence

> not because I was a radical or because I had spent the time since the early sixties actively on the left. No, it was because I was a romantic, and as

> such I found violence, dissent, defiance, sedition, rebellion by the young against the old, against the past, true and (yes, declare it), beautiful [Rader, 1973:22].

Rader, who like Stern has written an exceptionally honest portrayal of himself and his values during his revolutionary days, notes (1973:107):

> I still believed in the efficacy of violence. I responded to it positively on many levels, esthetically, sexually. I even discovered myself wishing to die violently, shot, say, coming out of my apartment building in the afternoon as I stopped in the doorway to open an umbrella because it was raining; seeing assassination as the ultimate flattery, a deadly kiss.

More self-searching than most other extreme activists, Rader fully admits his own and other revolutionists' profound feelings of inadequacy, and the need to earn their "manhood" or "womanhood" by taking undue physical risks and thereby "prove" their value to themselves, that lay behind their intense urges to destroy property and other humans: "Of course the attractiveness of this image of violence and my insistence on giving it political content were based upon sexual disorder, feelings of sexual inadequacy and dysfunction, insecurity over my manhood" (1973:8).

Intersectarian Aggression. As seems typical of radical movements of the last few centuries, the violence of the American rebels in recent years has notably expressed itself in intersectarian (and, for that matter, intrasectarian) warfare. Both Rader and Stern, and especially the latter, show how members of extremist left-wing groups, such as the Weathermen, viciously and unhesitatingly attacked other factions of the same group who happened to disagree with them. According to these observers (and many other commentators) the Weathermen and the Progressive Labor (Trotskyite) factions of the Students for a Democratic Society fought each other so nastily in June 1969 that they completely disrupted and brought to an end the SDS itself, which at one time had about a half million adherents and represented the largest student activist group in the history of the country.

Hardly content with that "victory," the Weatherman faction (first reduced to about 2,000 and soon to a few hundred members) went on to massacre its own dissidents. On the antimonogamy issue, for example, a mere handful of Weathermen leaders ruthlessly steamrollered or kicked out the monogamous-prone majority. As Stern reports, Mark Rudd sent J.J., one of the central office people, to "reorganize" the Seattle Weathermen group:

> Like a bulldozer, he swept through the leadership collective with his list of lines, leaving no alternatives. Rudd had lined us all up for the kill—J.J. was shooting us down, one by one. Ty and Jean were massacred—end your monogamy, or split the collective. Sara and Bill were told they must live in separate houses or split the collective. Tim and Toddy were told they had to live in separate houses or split the collective.

On other issues of intragroup disagreement the same grim tactics prevailed. Writes Stern (1975:199-200) again:

> The second day of the War Council, Seattle began a criticism session that lasted the next two days. It was generally overseen either by Rudd or J.J. It was the old routine, only more severe than ever. The prime target of the criticism, the real reason it had been called, was Mike Justesen, one of the most active and most loyal of the Weathermen. He was pronounced a pig early in the War Council, and for two days, the Seattle collectives spent their time smashing Mike. . . . Only through total smashing of his defenses could he really see himself and his role in the revolution and begin to change. We were exorcising Devil America out of Mike Justesen. . . . Hour after hour we screamed and shouted at Mike. Not only did we carefully explain to him why he was such a pig, exactly how he manipulated and undermined people, but we made sure that all his rationales for why he acted as he did were smashed. We put Mike on the rack, and pulled, until he was stretched to the breaking point, and then we pulled some more, until we could see him begin to snap.

Hatred of Police and Military Forces. As one of their main complaints, extreme revolutionists often point out that systems such as capitalism, the state, or even technology fail to see humans as humans, but only see them abstractly as cogs in the wheels of the system itself; consequently, they dehumanize people and make them into almost insensate "things." Presumably, violent revolutionism idealistically fights this tendency: insists that the system itself, by fair means or foul, gets destroyed, so that this kind of system-imposed dehumanization stops. Unfortunately, as Dotson Rader incisively points out (1973:110), inciting total war against a presumably totalitarian state or system has its own inner contradictions:

> To be a revolutionary engaged in violence required the abandonment of one human quality to assert another. One had to abstract life from its particular context and assert that abstract Life could be salvaged only by wasting individual lives. A revolutionary had to disengage himself sufficiently from personal feeling to be able to view his enemies as abstractions, not people, as classes rather than as individuals. The enemy had to be drained of individual substance so that violence could be done to him; he had to be seen as part of the gang in the dock at Nuremberg awaiting execution, as outside human limits.

Nowhere more clearly do we see this tendency of violent revolutionists to dehumanize their opponents than in the extreme leftists' attitude toward members of the police or military forces—whom they monolithically label as "pigs." Even the few revolutionists with a sense of humor, such as Jerry Rubin and Abbie Hoffman, go rabid at the mere mention of these "pigs." Other extremists turn positively, and often literally, homicidal. Thus, ignoring completely the fact that policemen and military personnel have their own ideas, loyalties, family ties, friendships, desires to earn a living, and other human qualities, and that they have wide individual differences (as do, of course, revolutionaries), Abbie Hoffman quite unhumorously writes, "Cops are our enemies." And, in regard to himself and Dick Gregory participating in a demonstration: "The other pigs (having a leader-follower head) wouldn't touch us. He said what if they did? I replied I would kill the Top Pig and I meant it" (Hoffman, 1968:119).

Tim Leary, at the height of his acid-tripping stage, noted that "to kill a policeman is a sacred act" (Bryan, 1975:82). Stern (1975:49) hit her first pig with a Coke bottle, across his forehead. "He staggered back looking stunned. I waited to feel nauseated as I saw the red ribbon of blood deepen across his face and begin to drip down his nose. But I felt exhilarated." Again (Stern, 1975:148):

> The reports from Chicago were good. We had done hundreds of thousands of dollars' worth of damage. We had injured hundreds of pigs. Greatest of all, one of Richard Daley's chief counsels, Richard Elrod, was paralyzed from the waist down. I had a right to walk with my head high.

Social and Personal Causation

From the foregoing material it can be seen that although radical extremists may protest loudly and long that they have largely idealistic motives and that they want to help their fellow humans, both their words and actions belie these claims; and it seems clear that a great deal of their motivation springs from personal problems, feelings of alienation, hostility to other people, and low frustration tolerance. One can note almost exactly the same things about right-wing extremists—since they, too, frequently mouth noble ideals and then behave in an exceptionally ignoble manner.

Theorists have made and still often do make the point that the psychological aberrations of radical extremists on both sides of the continuum stem from the very social conditions that they strive to correct. To some extent this is true. But obviously, all members of a social group do not develop into radicals or revolutionists, even though they tend to live under the same "exploitative" or "alienating" system. And the radicals themselves, virtually all of whom oppose the system in some concerted left-wing or right-wing manner, rarely end up in the same extremist camp, using the same violent tactics, as a small percentage of their theoretical cohorts do. So although a given social system may well *contribute* to or *encourage* extreme radicalization of many of its citizens, it hardly exclusively or directly *causes* that kind of deviant behavior.

THE STUDY OF ASSASSINS

Another aspect of extreme political deviance exists in the behavior of many assassins. A survey of the psychology of many of the notorious political assassins in recent years led to the conclusion that "almost all of them are characterized by severe emotional instability or outright psychosis" (Ellis and Gullo, 1971:222). Some of the findings are briefly summarized below.

Lee Harvey Oswald had a long history of disturbance, beginning in early adolescence; and when brought into Youth House in New York City because of chronic truancy from school, obtained the diagnosis of "personality pattern disturbance with schizoid features and passive-aggressive tendency" and "a seriously detached, withdrawn youngster" (Hartogs and Freeman, 1965). He kept getting into serious difficulties throughout his life; unsuccessfully tried to assassinate Major General Edwin A. Walker a year before he succeeded in killing President John F. Kennedy; could not adjust in the Soviet Union any more than he could in the United States; and, according to Manchester (1967), had a complete breakdown when his wife, Marina, left him the day before the assassination:

> That was the breaking point. He had nothing left, not even pride. In Marina's later testimony, "He stopped talking and sat down and watched television." She glanced in once and saw him staring at an old film of a World War II battle. Apparently, he was intent upon the flickering screen. In fact, he was going mad. Madness does not strike all at once. Lee Oswald's disease had been in process all his life.

Jack Ruby, Oswald's own assassin, also seems to have suffered from severe disturbance from his earliest years. Dr. Walter Bromberg reported that he had a "brain disease, a subtle one." Dr. Manfred Guttmacher testified at his trial that Ruby had suffered

> a rupture of his ego. . . . I think he was struggling to keep his sanity during this period. I think that he had an unusual degree of involvement in the whole tragedy. . . . He came upon the perpetrator of the tragedy . . . there was a disruption of his ego, a very short-lived psychotic episode in which the hostile part of his makeup, which is very strong, became focused on this one individual.

Dr. Louis J. West (Wilford, 1970) described Ruby as suffering from a "paranoid state," called him "obviously psychotic," and held that he required hospital treatment.

Sirhan B. Sirhan, who murdered Senator Robert F. Kennedy in the midst of a large public function, had a history of severe emotional disturbance that we would have difficulty duplicating even in the histories of many institutionalized psychotics. According to Dr. Martin Schorr, a clinical psychologist, he exhibited "paranoid and schizophrenic tendencies" and had "not only had impulses for homicide but for suicide" (Robinson, 1969). Dr. Bernard L. Diamond, who hypnotized Sirhan in his jail cell and got him to reenact the killing of Senator Kennedy, testified that his act stemmed from "an outgrowth of chronic psychosis." Diamond reported that "the expert witnesses were not in serious disagreement over the diagnosis, only over the conclusions to be drawn from it. Ten of the eleven psychologists, anthropologists, and psychiatrists who examined the raw data were in substantial agreement: chronic paranoid schizophrenia" (Harris, 1969).

James Earl Ray, the convicted assassin of Martin Luther King, had a school record marked with absence and misbehavior. He got convicted several times, during the eighteen years before his crime, of burglary, armed robbery, car theft, and forgery. He acted notably withdrawn much of the time, especially when the conversation got personal. He "seemed governed by a curious, even touching unreality" and behaved in an exceptionally bigoted, unreliable and disturbed manner (O'Neil, 1968).

Ramon Mercader, Leon Trotsky's assassin, underwent an exhaustive examination by Dr. Jose Gomez Robledor and Dr. Alfonzo Quiroz Cuaron. In their huge report on Mercader, they reported these things about him: "Complete inability to make close human contacts. . . . He spent almost the entire time in bed, often with his face down and the sheet pulled over his head. . . . His answers showed superficiality and emotional dissociation. . . . He is shown to be fearful and self-destructive in his inner self" (Levine, 1959).

Assassins from the past also show signs of severe emotional disturbance (Ellis and Gullo, 1971:231-239). These include Marat's assassin, Charlotte Corday; Felice Orsini, an Italian revolutionist who attempted the assassination of Napoleon III; John Wilkes Booth, Lincoln's assassin; Charles J. Guiteau, who killed President James A. Garfield; Prendergast, who shot and killed Carter H. Harrison, a mayor of Chicago; Richard Lawrence, who attempted to shoot President Andrew Jackson; and Giuseppe Zangara, who tried to assassinate President-elect Franklin D. Roosevelt and killed Mayor Anton Cermak of Chicago instead.

SOURCES OF DISTURBANCE OF POLITICAL DEVIANTS

Thus it would appear that extreme radicals tend to have a considerable degree of emotional disturbance. Many students of dissent have come to somewhat similar conclusions, except that they have made them in regard to dissenters in general, including those who have participated in violent and revolutionary actions to only a moderate degree. However, such a conclusion may rest on shaky grounds.

Assuming that political extremists do act, during their early lives and in their later behavior, in disturbed ways, most theorists have related their disturbance to their relationships with their parents and to the over-permissive ways in which such parents have presumably reared them. Keniston (1973) reviews many studies in this connection and finds no conclusive evidence that student dissenters largely acted out Oedipal rebellions against their parents, nor that they dissented because they were "spoiled brats" whose parents did not exert sufficient control over them. However, practically all the studies that he considers included what we might call "fairly normal" radicals and not the extremists who can properly be called "deviant." Hence, a case has yet to get made which would prove, one way or the other, that these deviants had "abnormal" childhood backgrounds and that these significantly contributed to their disturbances.

Even when such aberrant childhood "influences" turn up—as they largely do in the cases of many of the assassins mentioned above—the question arises: Where does the real "cause" of these "influences" reside? Lee Harvey Oswald's mother, for example, seems to have pampered him, excused him from responsibility for his actions, denied wrongdoing on his part, and placed the blame for his behavior squarely on others rather than on her son (Ansbacher et al., 1966). But, considering how badly her son tended to act during his childhood and adolescence, it seems possible that he distinctly influenced her "pampering" rather than that she "caused" his aberrant behavior. Also, Mrs. Oswald acted so peculiarly in her own right, during Lee's childhood and into her later adulthood, that one can suspect that she may well have passed on to him, through hereditary as well as environmental channels, some of the tendencies that he displayed (Ellis and Gullo, 1971; Stafford, 1966).

Causal influences on human behavior, in other words, include interactional, transactional, and dialectical relations between children and their parents and between "hereditary" and "environmental" factors (Riegel, 1976). Parents certainly influence their children to some important degree; but children also influence their parents—and, at least in part, determine what kind of an upbringing they will receive. Cognitive, emotive, and behavioral styles of people, moreover, have strong biological predispositions behind them, and in some respects the major part of the variance stems from these predispositions rather than from environmental conditioning. In fact, conditioning itself largely depends on inherited tendencies to get conditioned—for if people did not come into the world as individuals strongly predisposed to learning, how could they possibly learn anything (Ellis, 1976a)?

Rather than resort to general "causes," such as heredity or environment, to explain extreme political deviance, we shall try to track down some of its origins in cognitive-emotive terms. The question arises: What goes on in the heads of radical extremists to encourage them to act the way that they do?

The theory of rational-emotive therapy and personality formation explains this kind of behavior largely in terms of philosophic orientation or cognitive style. It assumes that humans tend, from birth onward, to pursue two main goals: first, that of remaining alive; and, second, that of trying to feel reasonably happy or satisfied, and simultaneously free from unnecessary pain or deprivation, while they remain alive. They do this by rationally pursuing these goals and by attempting to remove any major blocks that interfere with these pursuits; but, at the same time, they also irrationally tend to block their own goals and defeat their own purposes.

The theory of rational-emotive therapy (RET) assumes, in other words, that virtually all humans have the basic goals or values of survival and happiness; and that they think, feel, and behave appropriately (or "rationally") when they abet these goals and think, feel, and behave inappropriately (or "irrationally") when they sabotage these goals. Rational behavior, according to this view, does not consist of an end in itself, and one cannot absolutistically justify it. But once humans decide, choose, or set virtually any goals—such as those of survival and satisfaction—they act "rationally" when they work to attain those goals and "irrationally" when they work against them.

In political life, people choose to survive and remain relatively happy, just as they do in other aspects of life—e.g., sex, love, marriage, family, economic, social, recreational, and other affairs. One group, which we usually call conservative, picks the kind of political ideologies and practices that it thinks will best aid human survival and happiness; and another group, which we call radical, selects the kind of ideas and applications that it thinks will favor human existence and satisfaction. Both groups, then, have basically the same *ultimate* values; but both differ sharply on how to arrange politics so as to implement these values.

Using RET methodology, many clinical studies of people have originated during the last two decades (Ellis, 1958, 1962, 1971, 1973, 1975, 1976b, 1977a; Ellis and Harper, 1971, 1975; Hauck, 1973, 1974, 1975; Maultsby, 1975; Goodman and Maultsby, 1974; Knaus, 1974; Lembo, 1974, 1976; Young, 1974). To back up the hypotheses formulated by these case histories, a great many experimental studies have appeared, which fairly conclusively validate most of the major RET theories (diGiuseppe and Trexler, 1977; Ellis, 1977b; Murphy and Ellis, 1977). To solidify the RET approach still further, a good many authors have published related cognitive-behavior therapy writings that also have a great deal of clinical and research evidence to support their main premises (Beck, 1976; Goldfried and Davison, 1976; Kelly, 1955; Lazarus, 1971, 1976; Mahoney, 1974; Meichenbaum, 1974; Rimm and Masters, 1974). Although still new to the field of politics, some applications of the tenets of RET have already gotten under way there (Long, 1976a, 1976b, 1976c).

RET says the same thing in regard to political behavior that it does regarding other types of human behavior: namely, that as long as people stay with their wants, desires, and preferences, and refrain from escalating them into needs, demands, musts, and absolutes, they will not get into serious trouble—at least, into what is called emotional trouble. Take, for example, the radical extremists. They start with a quite legitimate set of premises or assumptions: "Since the present political system includes various deficiencies, and since it hardly leads to our solving some of the serious political, economic, social, and other problems of our society, it would seem highly preferable if distinct changes occurred in it. Moreover, since the system and its ills have prevailed for quite a long period of time; since various attempts to change them slowly, by conventional means, have rather miserably failed; since the ills created or encouraged by the system still indubitably exist and take a huge toll in the form of needless human suffering; it would seem extremely desirable that we change this system radically and rapidly; and no nonsense about it!"

This kind of preference on the part of political radicals clearly has some good sense to it: since one can easily see that the existing political system, in virtually every large community in the world, has its distinct failings and evils, and that quite a number of its citizens suffer in various ways as a result of its limitations. For the left- and right-wing dissenters, therefore, to strongly desire to change the existing setup and for them to want to do so radically and rapidly does not seem unusually crazy. Debatable—yes; for many less radically inclined individuals could well argue for less of a political change—or for a change that people and politicians could effect less radically and, hence, disruptively. But difference and debatability lies at the core of virtually all human views of change. So the preferences of the political radicals—if they really remained on that level—seem arguable but reasonably sane.

Rational-emotive therapy (or RET) has developed a set of techniques for the analysis of irrational behavior (see Ellis, 1973, 1977b). In this model, the thwarted desires of the radicals, when they could not, at least for the present, change the system that they wanted to change, would lead to pronounced feelings of displeasure on their part and to some kind of action that would possibly rid them of their displeasure, and might contribute toward the social goals they try to implement. Their desires, their feelings of frustrations, and the consequent activities would all attempt to get them what they want: (1) general survival and happiness, and (2) political changes that they believe (rightly or wrongly) would help them and other citizens of their land survive and feel happy.

The extremists consume much time and energy with their feelings of anxiety, despair, depression, horror, and intense hatred. Having these feelings, they tend to have disruptive and disordered motivation. They consume much time and energy with these feelings, which detract from goal-oriented rational activities. Further, they tend to seek their political goals in such a fanatical manner that they reduce their chances of obtaining those goals.

A similar situation prevails in the political area. People who obsessively-compulsively strive to make money, to win a particular person's love, or to gain success in athletics, may possibly accomplish these ends: for monolithic determination to succeed against all odds may bolster them to overcome almost insurmountable obstacles. It also may not: for other people, seeing the compulsive striving, may deliberately create roadblocks.

In the field of politics, obsessive-compulsiveness occasionally works out very well—but probably under special conditions which favor the overly determined individual's rise to power. Thus, both Stalin and Hitler would never have made it had they not had the advantage of unusual socioeconomic and political conditions. For political rebels, in the final analysis, have to somehow win the allegiance of the majority of the electorate; and the more fanatical and extremely they behave, the more the likelihood exists that they will turn off large numbers of people and finally sabotage their own efforts.

This seems to have happened with both right- and left-wing extremists in the United States in recent years. Even during the late 1960s, when the war in Vietnam continued and seemed never-ending, and when student revolt reached maximum proportions, the Nazi-minded extremists won practically no popular support (although the Young Americans for Freedom, a much less rabid group, flourished fairly actively); and the Weatherpeople seemed to lose more and more sympathizers as they acted more terroristically and desperately in their attempts to foment left-wing revolution. Also: violent suppression of civil rights in countries where left- and right-wing dictatorships rule does not really stop opposition from a sizable minority of activists and guerrillas—as we have constantly seen in the Soviet Union, China, and a number of Latin American and African nations.

Another human factor also tends to enter the scene here. Where political extremism starts to hold sway and one group righteously and dogmatically declares violent war on another group instead of doing its best to settle their differences more peacefully, hate seems to beget hate, and both groups wind up thinking and behaving more suicidally and homicidally. Part of the "counterrevolutionary" activity that terroristic "revolutionaryism" inspires may arise on a rational basis: since if I go after you with a gun instead of trying to settle our differences through discussion and argument, you may have little practical choice other than to shoot at me in return. But a great deal of the counterviolence that follows one political group's violence seems sparked off by the same kind of irrational thinking and inappropriate emoting that helped the original violence get going.

It seems most unlikely that the members of any extreme radical group, once they have made up their minds that they must have what they want in regard to political change and once they begin to feel angry at their opponents and to act violently against them, will sit down and examine the irrationality leading to their thoughts, feelings, and actions; and that they then will go on logically and empirically to question their thinking and reweigh their decisions. By the time such a group gets into action, the time for rational rethinking has long passed.

What then? Can the problem of radical deviance, and particularly the kind of extremism that leads to rampant violence of a revolutionary nature, ever get resolved? Theoretically, yes. For the RET technique of rational disputing of irrational beliefs has preventive as well as curative aspects. Just as we now teach people the value of democratic discussion and voting, as opposed to the disadvantages of authoritarian and dictatorial methods of "persuasion," so can we teach them the value of RET-oriented disputing.

Thus, long before they incense themselves to the point where they irrationally believe that their political views *must* prevail and that virtually all their opponents amount to utterly *rotten individuals,* people can get taught, in the course of their regular education, to observe their own political (and other) feelings and to distinguish fairly clearly between their appropriate emotions of frustration, disappointment, and sorrow and their inappropriate feelings of depression, hatred, and low frustration tolerance when they do not achieve some of the things they want. They can also learn, after distinguishing between their appropriate and inappropriate feelings when politically (and otherwise) frustrated, to look at the enormous disadvantages of the latter and the advantages of the former. Finally, they can learn to seek out their irrational beliefs that mainly contribute to (or directly "cause") their inappropriate feelings and to rationally dispute these beliefs until they give them up and have them only infrequently reoccur.

This does not mean, of course, that political extremists *have* to see the errors of their ways and to do something about their disadvantageous and self-destructive thoughts, feelings, and actions. No reason exists why they *must* do this. The world won't turn out *awful* if they don't. The rest of us non-extremists can *stand* the unfortunate results of continued political extremism (as well, of course, as some of the good results that accrue from the same kind of thinking and behaving). And rabid extremists and terrorists do not amount to *rotten people* if they don't mend their ways and behave somewhat saner. After all, the human race has withstood the effects of extreme political deviance for thousands of years, and it will probably continue to do so in the future.

It would seem highly *preferable,* however, if we had a better understanding of extreme political dissent and its absolutistic demands and commands and if we could do something to alleviate it. The approach used in rational-emotive therapy to understand and deal with other kinds of human absolutism may well prove useful in the area of radical extremism. Let us, educationally and preventively, try it out and see.

REFERENCES

ANSBACHER, H., ANSBACHER, R., SHIVERICK, D., and SHIVERICK, K. (1966). "Lee Harvey Oswald: An Adlerian interpretation." Psychoanalytic Review, 53:55-68.

BECK, A.T. (1976). Cognitive therapy and the emotional disorders. New York: International Universities Press.

BETTELHEIM, B. (1969). "Children must learn to fear." New York Times Magazine. April 13:125ff.

BLOCK, J.H., HAAN, N., and SMITH, M.B. (1969). "Socialization correlates of student activism." Journal of Social Issues, 25:143-177.

BRYAN, J. (1975). This soldier still at war New York: Harcourt Brace Jovanovich.

BRZEZINSKI, Z. (1971). Quoted in Keniston, q.v.

CLEAVER, E. (1970). "Introduction" to J. Rubin, *Do It!* New York: Ballantine Books.

CLINARD, M.B. (1963). Sociology of deviant behavior. New York: Holt, Rinehart and Winston.

DERBER, C., and FLACKS, R. (1968). "An exploration of the value system of radical student activists and their parents." Paper presented at American Sociological Association, San Francisco.

DEUTSCH, M. (1969). "Conflicts: Productive and destructive." Journal of Social Issues, 25:7-41.

DI GIUSEPPE, R., and TREXLER, L. (1977). "Outcome studies of rational-emotive therapy." Counseling Psychologist, in press.

DORESS, I. (1968). "A study of a sampling of Boston University student activists." Unpublished doctoral dissertation, Boston University.

DOUGLAS, J.H. (1969). "The child, the father of the man." Family Coordinator, 18:3-8.

ELLIS, A. (1958). "Rational psychotherapy." Journal of General Psychology, 59:35-49.

--- (1962). Reason and emotion in psychotherapy. New York: Lyle Stuart.

--- (1969). "Toward the understanding of youthful rebellion." Pp. 85-111 in P.R. Frank (ed.), A search for the meaning of the generation gap. San Diego: Department of Education, San Diego County.

--- (1971). Growth through reason. Palo Alto: Science and Behavior Books.

--- (1973). Humanistic psychotherapy: The rational-emotive approach (Edward Sagarin, ed.). New York: Julian Press and McGraw-Hill.

--- (1975). How to live with a "neurotic." Rev. ed. New York: Crown.

--- (1976a). "The biological basis of human irrationality." Journal of Individual Psychology, 32:145-168.

--- (1976b). Sex and the liberated man. New York: Lyle Stuart.

--- (1977a). How to live with–and without–anger. New York: Reader's Digest Press.

--- (1977b). "Rational-emotive therapy: Research data that supports the clinical and personality hypotheses of RET and other modes of cognitive-behavior therapy." Counseling Psychologist, in press.

ELLIS, A., and GULLO, J.M. (1971). Murder and assassination. New York: Lyle Stuart.

ELLIS, A., and HARPER, R.A. (1971). A guide to successful marriage. Hollywood: Wilshire Books.

--- (1975). A new guide to rational living. Englewood Cliffs, N.J.: Prentice-Hall.

FEUER, L.S. (1969). The conflict of generations. New York: Basic Books.

FREIRE, P. (1970). Pedagogy of the oppressed. New York: Seabury Press.

GOLDFRIED, M., and DAVISON, G. (1976). Clinical behavior therapy. New York: Holt, Rinehart and Winston.

GOODMAN, D., and MAULTSBY, M.C., Jr. (1974). Emotional well-being through rational behavior training. Springfield, Ill.: Charles Thomas.

GURIN, G. (1971). A study of students in a multiversity. Ann Arbor: University of Michigan Press.

HAAN, N., SMITH, M.B. and BLOCK, J.H. (1968). "Moral reasoning of young adults: Political-social behavior, family backgrounds and personality correlates." Journal of Personality and Social Psychology, 10:183-201.

HARRIS, T.G. (1969). "Sirhan B. Sirhan: A conversation with Bernard L. Diamond." Psychology Today, 3(4):48-56.

HARTOGS, R., and FREEMAN, L. (1965). The two assassins. New York: Crowell.

HAUCK, P. (1973). Overcoming depression. Philadelphia: Westminster Press.

--- (1974). Overcoming frustration and anger. Philadelphia: Westminster Press.

--- (1975). Overcoming worry and fear. Philadelphia: Westminster Press.

HENTOFF, N. (1970). "Degrees of exile: America in the 70's and beyond." In D. Rader (ed.), Defiance: A radical review, no. 1. New York: Paperback Library.

HOFFMAN, A. (1968). Revolution for the hell of it. New York: Dial Press.

HOLLAND, G.A. (1967). "Non-conforming thoughts on non-conformity." Rational Living 2(2):7-9.

KATZ, J. (1968). "The activist revolution in 1964." Pp. 386-414 in J. Katz et al. (eds.), No time for youth: Growth and constraint in college students. San Francisco: Jossey Bass.

KELLY, G. (1955). The psychology of personal constructs. New York: Norton.

KENISTON, K. (1968). Young radicals. New York: Harcourt, Brace and World.

--- (1971). Youth and dissent. New York: Harcourt, Brace, Jovanovich.

--- (1973). Radicals and militants. Lexington, Mass.: Lexington Books.

KERPELMAN, L.C. (1970). Student activism and ideology in higher education institutions. Office of Education, Project No. 8-A-028, University of Massachusetts.
KIEV, A. (1975). "The nonconforming adolescent." Reprinted from Exerpta Medica.
KNAUS, W. (1974). "Rational-emotive education." New York: Institute for Rational Living.
KUNEN, J.S. (1970). The strawberry statement: Notes of a college revolutionary. New York: Avon.
LAZARUS, A.A. (1971). Behavior therapy and beyond. New York: McGraw-Hill.
––– (1976). Multimodal therapy. New York: Springer.
LEMBO, J. (1974). Help yourself. Niles, Ill.: Argus Communications.
––– (1976). The counseling press: A cognitive-behavioral approach. Roslyn Heights, N.Y.: Libra Publishers.
LEVINE, I.D. (1959). The mind of an assassin. New York: Farrar, Straus and Cudahy.
LONG, S. (1976a). "Cognitive perceptual factors in the political alienation process: a test of six models." Unpublished paper.
––– (1976b). "Irrational ideation and political reality: A theory of political alienation." Unpublished paper.
––– (1976c). "Irrationality and systematic reflection: Insights from Ellis' rational behavior therapy." Unpublished paper.
MAHONEY, M. (1974). Cognition and behavior modification. Cambridge, Mass.: Ballinger.
MAILER, N. (1968). The armies of the night: History as a novel. New York: New American Library.
MANCHESTER, W. (1967). The death of a president. New York: Harper & Row.
MAULTSBY, Jr., M.C. (1975). Help yourself to happiness New York: Institute for Rational Living.
MEICHENBAUM, D. (1974). Cognitive behavior modification. Morristown, N.J.: General Learning Press.
MURPHY, R., and ELLIS, A. (1977). A comprehensive bibliography of rational-emotive therapy and cognitive-behavior therapy. New York: Institute for Rational Living.
NEWFIELD, J. (1970). "This movement, this new left." Pp. 11-23 in D. Rader (ed.), Defiance: A radical review, no. 1. New York: Paperback Library.
O'NEIL, P. (1968). "Ray, Sirhan–What possessed them?" Life, June 21, page 24
PAULUS, G. (1967). "A multivariate analysis study of student activist leaders, student government leaders, and nonactivists." Unpublished doctoral dissertation, Michigan State University.
RADER, D. (1970). "On revolutionary violence." Pp. 194-212 in D. Rader (ed.), Defiance: A radical review, no. 1. New York: Paperback Library.
––– (1973). Blood dues. New York: Knopf.
RIEGEL, K.F. (1976). "The dialectics of human development." American Psychologist, 31:689-700.
RIMM, D.C., and MASTERS, J.C. (1974). Behavior therapy. New York: Academic Press.
ROBINSON, D. (1969). "Psychologist, testifying for the defense, says tests indicate Sirhan has paranoid tendencies." New York Times, March 11.
RUBIN, J. (1970). Do it! New York: Ballantine Books.
SCHNEIDER, P. (1966). "A study of members of SDS and YD at Harvard." Unpublished bachelor's thesis. Wellesley College.
SIPORIN, M. (1965). "Deviant behavior theory." Social Work, 10:59-67.
SOMERS, R.H. (1965). "The mainsprings of the rebellion: A survey of Berkeley students in November 1964." Pp. 530-557 in S.M. Lipset and S.S. Wolin (eds.), The Berkeley student revolt: Facts and interpretations. New York: Doubleday Anchor.
STAFFORD, J. (1966). A mother in history. New York: Bantam Books.
STERN, S. (1975). With the Weathermen. New York: Doubleday.

WHITAKER, D., and WATTS, W.A. (1971). "Personality characteristics associated with activism and disaffiliation in today's college-age youth." Journal of Counseling Psychology, 18:200-206.

WILFORD, J.N. (1970). "Psychiatrist urges brain tests for suspects in violent crimes." New York Times, November 18, page 35.

WOLFF, R.P. (1969). Review of L.S. Feuer's *The Conflict of Generations.* New York Times Book Review, March 30, pp. 3, 32.

YOUNG, H.S. (1974). A rational counseling primer. New York: Institute for Rational Living.

8

FROM DEVIANT TO NORMATIVE

Changes in the Social Acceptability of Sexually Explicit Material

CHARLES WINICK

In 1963, Ralph Ginzburg was fined $42,000 and sentenced to five years in prison for publishing the magazine *Eros,* which a federal judge had found to be obscene. In 1976, Ginzburg found some copies of the magazine in a warehouse and donated all of them to the American Civil Liberties Union, which announced its intention to sell them at public auction. In 13 years, what was once obscene had become tame; what had been deviant was now accepted. Any such substantial change in public morality is likely to be overdetermined, and the shift from sex prohibition to sexual script in the arts is no exception.

One of the relationships between deviance and social change, which is the subject of this paper, is the normalization of behavior which had previously been frowned upon. Beginning in the 1950s, increasing during the 1960s, and approaching new levels of explicit expression in the 1970s, sex-oriented media and art content that had formerly been regarded as deviant became relatively acceptable, as a result of a variety of kinds of social change.

Over the last 20 to 30 years, there has been a vast expansion of the audiences for sex-oriented materials in all of the arts and media of mass communication. Complementarily and simultaneously, there has been greater explicitness in the manner in which sexual material is presented in many different formats. The changes in content during this period are more dramatic than the analogous changes occurring in the previous two centuries of American history. Sex content that was once proscribed is now almost prescribed for many media and art forms.

The alteration in perception of what constitutes acceptability would appear to represent almost a case history of how material that was once labeled deviant has been relabeled positively. However, social scientists have seldom addressed themselves to identifying either the dimensions of the change in sex-related material or the reasons for its development. Some social philosophers, like Sorokin (1956), have decried what has happened but very few have attempted to understand why it occurred. It is reasonable to speculate that the changes in content reflect pushes from audiences and pulls from the arts and media and are the end products of deep-rooted social and institutional trends.

On the level of mass psychology, the Nuremberg Trials and the coming into our awareness of the Holocaust, by the late 1940s, probably helped to make us more willing to accept other previously hidden aspects of human behavior. A related residue of World War II was the reluctant recognition that some national leaders, like Adolf Hitler, had been quite mad. If our leaders had been so disturbed, perhaps some of the givens of our society might be reevaluated and found to be irrelevant to current society. A loss of confidence in leadership could lead to an erosion of confidence in values which had been taken for granted.

The Nuremberg and other post-World War II disclosures affected many Americans still recovering from the depression, anxiety about communism, concern about the impact of automation and the technocratic state, and receptive to the loneliness and vulnerability of existentialism. Such challenges to the integrity of self provided the background for a considerable range of shifts in social and community life that have facilitated a movement toward hedonism and privatization. The most obvious change has been a decline in the work week and a sharp increase in the time available for leisure. Early retirement is a growing trend that provides more leisure for older persons. Persons with increased leisure often use it in order to give more time to consumption of the media and popular arts.

Private satisfaction rather than public participation has become a growing feature of American life. Sennett (1977) has suggested some reasons for our general loss of interest in public life. Previously, Karl Mannheim (1950) had explained how legitimation had been eroded and meaning lost from many activities. On the basis of his analysis of data from the Detroit Area Study, Lenski (1961) questioned whether Max Weber's concept of the Protestant Ethic could fruitfully be applied to contemporary American society. The Protestant Ethic was probably a group of characteristics which were important at a particular time in history but which no longer are part of one constellation. Most notably, asceticism has surely ceased to be a significant part of American national character. Many television stations, newspapers, magazines and other media now have "life style" editors who regularly report on the new good life, the life of enjoyment.

One analysis posits hedonism as the appropriate ideological companion to the loss of legitimacy and meaning from our declining and alienating institutions (Etzioni, 1972). Hedonism seems to complement critiques of society as oppressive.

Recent decades have seen an intensive scrutiny of our social and moral values. The turbulence of a period of racial conflict, assassinations of national leaders, new communal living arrangements, questioning of the nuclear family and other existing life styles, disclosures of deceit and chicanery by high government officials, Watergate, youth rebellion, widespread drug use, substantial increases in the crime rate, the Vietnam War, decriminalization of abortion, and other extraordinary events led to very searching examination of major institutions.

As work has become less satisfying, it appeared less rewarding in terms of deeper needs, values, and relationships and increasingly functioned as a source of money with which to enjoy the leisure that was a central locus of gratification. Many kinds of work lead to atonie, or a lack of resonance with reality (Winick, 1964). Workingmen's taverns no longer provide discussions of industrial or political issues but rather an opportunity for gaiety and frivolity (Cavan, 1966; Le Masters, 1975).

Marxists have argued that the source of social relations, culture, and ideology has shifted to a mass culture of consumerism (Alt, 1976). This trend has involved a privatization of daily existence mediated by new forms of popular culture, many aspects of which have increasingly expressed sex-oriented themes.

All of the social critiques noted above may have some etiological relevance. In order to explore some other causal contributors to the change and to document its parameters, some reasons for, and explication of, the details of the transformation of previously deviant sexual content in popular arts and media into relative acceptability will be discussed below under five headings: larger social forces, court decisions and other statements, content of the arts, functions served by sex-oriented material, and the future.

LARGER SOCIAL FORCES

A number of larger social forces have contributed to the changing climate for sex-oriented materials during the last few decades. They include a disaffection with government, disasters and recessions, the role of youth, perceptual and emotional isostasy, the importance of looking, and shifting sex roles and morality.

Disaffection With Government

The upsurge of interest in all aspects of sex during the 1960s was one of many responses to the loss of interest in government. As people became less confident in government, they increasingly moved to more private satisfactions.

Many citizens' feelings of cynicism and powerlessness are reflected in a survey conducted with a national sample (New York Times, 1976). Of the respondents, 55% agreed with the statement that "public officials don't care much about what people like me think." Almost three-fifths (59%) felt that government "is pretty much run for a few big interests."

A direct measure of withdrawal of interest from participation in political life was the very low degree of voter interest in the 1976 Presidential election, which provided a clear-cut choice between candidates. Only 53% of the citizens over 18 actually voted, which was the poorest turnout since 1948. The single most frequently cited reason for not voting, in postelection polls, was a lack of confidence in government.

Media reflect and reinforce such underlying feelings. During 1976, a number of successful films *(The Parallax View, Marathon Man, Three Days of the Condor, The Next Man)* dealt with a dread but unnameable government-linked conspiracy of vast magnitude, usually involving torture, poisoning, and murder. The popularity of such films suggests the public's readiness to accept a paranoid view of government, a view that was certainly reinforced by the FBI, CIA, and Watergate scandals.

Congressmen who had been linked to sexual or personal scandals generally won reelection in 1976. Their reelection implies the extent to which the general public had grown to accept irregular behavior in its elected officials and had decreased expectations of its political leadership.

Corruption in the institutions of American life had been foreshadowed in many pre-Watergate media, most remarkably in the character played by Burt Lancaster in the movie *The Sweet Smell of Success* (1957). As many people were turned off government by such films and by real events, they increasingly turned inward. Transcendental meditation, yoga, Zen, interest in Eastern religions, Esalen seminars, EST, Arica, autogenic relaxation, biofeedback, and many other methods for expanding personal satisfactions became very popular (Smith, 1976).

Disasters and Recessions

Americans have, in recent decades, been assured that they faced several kinds of imminent disaster and economic catastrophe. Advised that his insolent chariot (Keats, 1958) was unsafe at any speed (Nader, 1965), a representative organization man (Whyte, 1956) who was a member of a lonely crowd (Reisman, 1969) had to confront the limits to growth (Meadows, 1972). Told to think about the unthinkable (Kahn, 1964), he faced a crisis in black and white (Silberman, 1964) while his children confronted a crisis in the classroom (Silberman, 1971) or even death at an early age (Kozol, 1970). Future shock,(Toffler, 1970) awaited those hardy enough to survive.

Many television shows, articles, and books have relentlessly warned Americans that they were hurrying, or at least slouching, into catastrophe. We can anticipate that persons living under a threat are especially likely to cope with anxiety via sexual outlets, like the men and women in the Decameron who distracted themselves by revelry in a large country house during the plague. We know that in previous times of social upheaval, like Restoration England, Germany in the latter part of the 18th century and the Weimar Republic, and America after World War I, there was an increase in the range of acceptable sexual behavior and the availability of such material in the popular arts.

For three decades, more and more problems have surfaced in this country and a number of them have been related to our several periods of concentrated economic difficulties, which it is customary to describe euphemistically as "recessions" or, more recently, as "stagflation." Beginning in 1973, the United States became aware, however reluctantly, that it was entering an economic depression that was the worst since the 1930s. Sexual gratification is especially important during such a time. When loss of a job, participation in marginal work, or anxiety about losing a job may cause people to become atonic and question their worth, the ability to express oneself sexually becomes particularly important (Winick, 1964). Such gratification may be derived from sexually oriented media, which can present fantasy or other vicarious experiences in a controllable and nonthreatening manner.

Just how gratifying a sexual fantasy may be can be inferred from the case of Sultan Shah-riyar, in the Thousand and One Nights. The sultan killed every woman with whom he made love. Knowing this, Scheherezade told so interesting a story that the sultan wanted her to finish it on the following night. She would always stop the tale at its most provocative moment. For a thousand nights, the stories about love were so gratifying to the sultan that he fell asleep every morning without having had intercourse—but fully satisfied. Fiction and movies similarly may present sexual provocation, pleasure without any potential letdown, for their audiences.

Anxiety has become pervasive because of problems like inflation, decreasing availability of oil and other sources of energy, food shortages, awareness of corruption, environmental pollution, threat of war in the Middle East, and a pervasive helplessness in the face of larger realities that, for the first time, many Americans feel they can no longer control.

Observing sexual activity on the screen and in books and magazines may, in fantasy, give the viewer a sense of fulfillment which could be particularly important for persons with misgivings about the directions that society is taking and when other kinds of achievement are becoming less available.

During the Great Depression of the 1930s, for some of the same reasons that have made them so appealing today, a number of sexually oriented pictorial materials were very popular. At that time, such content could not be sold openly but enjoyed a substantial covert popularity. Sexualized versions of popular comic strips like Mutt and Jeff and Tillie the Toiler had widespread distribution, and stag films were shown very frequently at many kinds of gatherings. With the end of the depression, and the beginning of World War II with its unifying national goals, such sex-oriented materials became less important. They became salient again in the 1950's, with the Korean war, McCarthyism, and other divisive movements. The conflict-riddled decade of the 1960s witnessed their full flourishing.

The Role of Youth

Mass media and the popular arts are perhaps more influential over young people, particularly adolescents and young adults, than over any other age group. The media and arts offer role models, methods for making contact with the world outside, vehicles of socialization, a current vocabulary of emotion, a social context for courtship, pleasant ways of spending leisure time to an age group which has such time, a continuing subject for conversation, subjects for hobbies and fan clubs, symbols of achievement, publicized exemplars of masculinity and femininity, training in consumer behavior, and objects of fantasy. Such attractions of the arts and media have been so important in recent decades because the American population has been relatively young, with a current median age of 28.9.

Among the larger social attitudes feeding the interest in media expressions of sexuality is the dramatic increase in educational levels during the last two decades. Millions of young people, born in the post-World War II baby boom, made education a major growth industry. Even in 1976, with widespread questioning about the utility of college education, over ten million students were enrolled in colleges and universities. The more education people have, the more extensive is their moviegoing and other media consumption and the more varied are their sex interests likely to be. A major finding of the first Kinsey (1948) report was that there was a positive and high correlation between education and range of sexual expression.

Increases in education have also often been linked with questioning the traditional values of a society. For many youths, the first opportunity for radicalization comes from colliding with society's restrictions on sexual expression. When they begin to question the rationale for various sexual restraints, they may also scrutinize the reasons for other kinds of limitations. Many young people identified with poet William Blake, who had, some 200 years earlier, argued that repression was the major political problem of the day and that society's goal should be freedom, the chief symbol of which was sexual freedom.

The more education a person has, the greater the likelihood of seeing a sexually oriented film. In the General Social Survey, college graduates were twice as likely to have seen an X-rated film during the year as those with less than a high school education (National Opinion Research Center, 1976). When a new opportunity for experience presents itself, college graduates are more likely than persons with less schooling to respond positively to the opportunity for innovation.

The increase in education among young people is additionally relevant because the movie audience is very young, with 73% of all movie admissions provided by persons between 12 and 29, who constitute only 39% of the United States population. Seven out of ten of frequent moviegoers, defined as those who attend movies at least twice a month, are under 30 (Newspaper Advertising Bureau, 1974). The youthful population is, especially in the last several years, the most sexually emancipated part of the population.

Yankelovich (1974), in the most ambitious recent study of the attitudes of young people, concluded that the more liberal casual sexual attitudes which had been confined to a minority of college students in the late 1960s had spread to mainstream college youth as well as mainstream working-class youth by the early 1970s, in a remarkably abrupt transition. The new code of sexual morality centered on the acceptability of nonmarital sex.

One reason for youths' interest in sex in films is that they are responding to the decline of rites of passage (Winick, 1968). Consider how little ceremonial observance there is of a teenager's getting a driver's license, one of the most significant changes in status. The decline of age-graded experiences, and in ceremonies and benchmarks of social life, has led many people to seek ritualistic satisfaction elsewhere. The ritualistic aspects of sex in movies may appeal to this need.

Young people have also been the primary audience for rock and roll music, a significant part of which is concerned with love and sex. Thus, Ray Charles' famous record of "I Got A Woman" is an account of coitus. In fact, "rock" etymologically connotes entrance of the penis into the vagina and "roll" refers to the organs' interaction (Winick, 1970a). Some famous performers, like Jim Morrison and Chuck Berry, would masturbate their guitars. The popularity of rock and roll among youth since 1953 coincides with the period within which movies and other media have become heavily sexualized.

Sex in rock music reached new candor in the 1970s. Andrea True, previously known as an actress in sex-oriented movies, recorded a major hit record of the decade called "More, more, more" ("how do ya like it . . . more, more, more"). "Love to Love You Baby" is 17 minutes of the title phrase, along with sexually explicit gasps and moans, repeated by Donna Summers, the "queen of sex rock." Another recent successful record, "Lady Marmalade," by the Labelle group, repeated the refrain, "Voulez-vous coucher avec moi?"

Identification of youths with such rock music is unusually intense because the composers, performers, and often record company executives involved in the music are likely to be young. In contrast, the composers, performers, and producers of the pre-rock, pre-1950s popular music of the "June-moon" type were likely to be older than its youthful consumers. Older composers like Cole

Porter, George Gershwin, Jerome Kern, and Irving Berlin wrote from a European tradition; rock composers are super-contemporary and "now."

The success of sex-related rock records among young people is important for many reasons. One reason is the relationship between competition and sex. Wherever young people turn, they see many others competing for the same goals, such as school grades or jobs. Some have dealt with this competition by drug use or "dropping out" and others retreat into hedonism. Interest in sexually oriented media may represent another escape from competition and demands for accomplishment.

Also, particularly among young adults, notions of fun, communication, and pleasure have entered importantly into thinking about the recreational aspects of sex. At the same time, the procreational possibilities of sex are lesser sources of anxiety because of the development of laparoscopy as a simple technique for sterilization and significant advances in contraceptive technology represented by the pill and IUD. The pleasurable spectator pastime of watching sex in films and print materials fits in with young people's recreational outlook and the desire to improve their sexual-communicative skills.

Jet planes and charter flights have dramatically expanded opportunities for travel and helped to expose many young people to different approaches to sexuality in other countries. Moviegoers are twice as likely as nonmoviegoers to have made an airplane trip in the last three years (Newspaper Advertising Bureau, 1974). Many travelers to Europe have doubtless observed the more casual attitudes toward prostitution and sex in the arts in many countries and transferred such attitudes to their expectations in America.

Perceptual and Emotional Isostasy

The notion of perceptual and emotional isostasy may help to explain the popularity of media sex-related content. In geology, the principle of isostasy expresses the way in which the earth's high reliefs are compensated by variations in the density of materials extending below the surface. Highs and lows, in effect, balance each other. In economics, the analogous concept of countervalence has been used in order to express the manner in which a strong force, such as an aggressive corporation, is met by a competitive element, such as the consumer movement (Galbraith, 1956).

We suggest that there is an isostasy of the audience's responses to mass media, a reciprocal relationship between the number and severity of the country's problems and the amount of time which it devotes to media, and particularly to movies. Another way of expressing this notion is that the worse times become, the better will movie attendance be. The peak of moviegoing was reached during the Great Depression of the 1930s. 1974–the year of the energy crisis, a recession, Watergate, President Nixon's resignation, and a threat of war in the Middle East–was also the year in which American moviegoers spent more money at the box office ($1.9 billion) than ever before. Two escapist films—*The Sting* and *The Exorcist*—far outpaced the other films.

The notion of isostasy not only applies to the frequency of moviegoing; it also helps to explain why sexually oriented content is so popular in movies and other popular arts. All the media are likely to emphasize war, crime, and other violence-oriented materials. As a result, many consumers of the arts are seeking a balancing experience that is pleasurable. During the last decade, sexually oriented materials have increasingly provided such a pleasurable experience.

Another factor is the audience's response to television fare. There can be no doubt about the growing sophistication of television content, or about the heavy involvement of Americans with television. Viewing has continued to increase fairly steadily, reaching a current average of 45 hours weekly per household. Now that 98% of American homes possess television and 70% own color television, there has been a tremendous increase in exposure to sound pictures. As a result, there has been a revolution of rising expectations in terms of visual stimuli, and sexuality in the movies represents an effort to compete with the bombardment of free stimuli from television.

The increase in visual sophistication has been coterminous with a sharp decline in illusions about other aspects of American life. Race, international relations, and personal morality are some of the areas of social living in which traditional beliefs are becoming less binding. Attitudes toward sex are always closely intertwined with other attitudes. Greater acceptance of new options in various aspects of social life has been both cause and effect of the greater acceptance of sex reality in visual media.

The Importance of Looking

Looking may provide sexual satisfaction even if the object of the looking does not seem to be sexual. Interview studies with persons who witnessed but did not report crimes of violence involving women victims, as in the 1964 murder of Kitty Genovese in New York City, indicated that many derived a parasexual response from witnessing the event (Winick, 1968). Thirty-eight persons heard Miss Genovese being murdered but none of them called the police. In studies of similar witnesses to a crime who did not report it, a recurrent finding is that seeing such events is so provocative that the excitation takes precedence over summoning law enforcement authorities. In a less extreme term, this kind of sexual gratification from looking, or optical lubricity, can be found in the general population.

One expression of Americans' continuing interest in sexual gratification by looking is provided by our continuing enthusiasm for burlesque, which became more popular in the United States before World War II than ever before in any other country. Every town of more than 100,000 was likely to have its own burlesque theater (Gorer, 1937). Burlesque was and is unique in providing a visual satisfaction complete in itself, in contrast to other cultures which provided erotic spectacles as a prelude to direct sexual activity. In Mediterranean seaport cabarets, for example, there is a long tradition of erotic dancing, but the performers are available for subsequent sexual relations.

After a brief hiatus in the 1940s, burlesque made a comeback in the 1950s, with over 200 theaters now presenting it. Burlesque is expanding because it offers sex without the risk of obscenity prosecutions. Our desire to look without touching also expresses itself in the popularity of topless waitresses. There is probably no other country in the world where such waitresses could go about their business, confident that men would not try to touch them. There are topless bars all over America; New York City, for example, has 225 such bars.

Some patrons find sexual looking more satisfying than alcoholic beverages and it may be more profitable for cabarets to have the former than the latter. When the Supreme Court ruled, in 1972, that First Amendment rights may be curtailed in California clubs that served liquor and also presented what the Court called "bacchanalian revelries," a number of the clubs chose to give up their liquor license rather than abandon their topless or bottomless shows.

Shifting Sex Roles and Morality

In the 1960s, the women's liberation movement became a significant force in terms of women's rights to self-expression of all kinds, including sexual satisfaction. Although some feminists have complained that sexually explicit magazines, books, and movies derogate women, respondents to the General Social Survey who had a high score on a scale of female equality were twice as likely as those with a low equality score to have seen an X-rated film (National Opinion Research Center, 1976). We may speculate that sexually explicit films and the women's movement both represent a form of social change and that there is a generalized responsiveness to the new, as in the marketing concept of the "tryer" or "upscale" purchaser.

In some ways, the most important change in attitudes toward sexual behavior occurred in women. As women increasingly entered the labor force and became economically self-sufficient, they were less likely to accept older ideologies like the double standard for sex, whereby what was prohibited for women was approved for men. Concern about overpopulation and families' need for wives' incomes to cope with inflation led to less children and contributed to women's assumption of roles outside the home, a trend which was enormously enhanced by the availability of the birth control pill after 1961.

Magazines that addressed themselves to sexually liberated women became very popular. *Cosmopolitan,* which had been facing bankruptcy when it carried conventional features on homemaking, recipes, and other service content, became enormously successful after it began, in the 1960s, concerning itself with women's sexual satisfaction and pleasures. Its editor had previously been known as the author of a "how-to" book on *Sex and the Single Girl* (Brown, 1962).

The women's movement spawned a new dimension in sexually oriented materials. Magazines *Playgirl* and *Viva,* which began publication in 1973, are directed to women and show extensive photographs of nude men. A typical issue of *Viva* ("the international magazine for women") contains a pictorial feature on "crotch watching, the only female spectator sport," and ten different photographs of nude men (Anonymous, 1975). A new literature of sexual awareness for women became very popular, with books which provided details on masturbatory techniques (Dodson, 1975) and self-pleasure (Barbach, 1975) emerging as best sellers.

One effect of women's liberation has been to increase the proportion of women attending sexually oriented movies. Jokes about "the raincoat crowd" attending such movies are largely historical, now that couples represent so large a proportion—almost half, in many theatres—of their audiences. The increased attendance of women at erotic theatrical events can also be inferred from the near-disappearance of the word "striptease," which was common in the 1930s when women stripped for audiences of men, but which is less used today when so many couples attend the performances of what is now called "exotic dancing."

The women's movement could only become institutionalized, via *MS* magazine and the National Organization of Women, after the country began to face the consequences of the unisex trend. During the 1960s, when unisex moved from being a pejorative adjective to a positive description, many Americans experienced uneasiness about what constituted masculinity and femininity, and questioned if such concepts still had any utility. There is little doubt that some persons were eager audiences for sexually oriented films and fiction because the latter's sex roles were unequivocal and clear-cut and thus reassuring. In fiction and movies, men were men, women were women, and they knew how to express their gender via sexual behavior.

At the same time, discussions of sexual ethics tended to stress the interpersonal nature of the sexual situation rather than absolutes or doctrinal considerations. During the last two decades, situation ethics became a significant component of discussions about morality. Situation ethics were generally set forth as the right and good thing being whatever is the most living thing in a situation (Fletcher, 1966). In terms of sex, the notion that a wide range of behavior was normal was accepted by a large proportion of the population, which demanded freedom for the individual to satisfy his needs, desires, and tastes as he sees fit. The notion of "sexual minorities" as persons with unusual interests who are entitled to the same kind of protection as other minority groups was accepted fairly widely (Ullerstam, 1966). The propositions that sex is a significant part of happiness, and that sex should be approached with openness, encouraged the treatment of varieties of sexual expression in films, books, and magazines.

The idea that a person has value in and of himself, apart from possessions or accomplishments, has been assuming salience since the 1960s. This concept relates to sex in that sexual interaction increasingly is seen as one kind of self-expression. Movies and other popular arts provide an opportunity to see sexual interactions, not unlike one's own, elevated to the status of art. Furthermore, our increasing technocracy and bureaucracy tend to downgrade individuality, the loss of which may be seen as a kind of spiritual death. Equating sex with aliveness tends to make sex in the arts a testament to the individual's struggle to affirm his or her importance.

Such affirmation became more important as conventional marriage appeared to pose increasing problems and the divorce rate began climbing in the 1950s. Sexual expression in the popular arts represented an outlet for "getting off" impulses or feelings which could not be expressed in marriage. Tacit recognition of such a safety valve function could have been one reason that so many social institutions, by the 1950s, seemed to be reinforcing the growing acceptance of sex in the arts.

Freedom in the arts was reinforced by the new freedom of clothing, beginning in the late 1950s. Clothes as a way of concealing the body gave rise to clothes as a way of revealing it. Greater candor about the body via clothes facilitated and reflected sexual candor in the arts and media. As guilt and shame were less likely to be related to revealing the body, they were also less likely to be associated with sexual expression in behavior and the public arts.

COURT DECISIONS AND OTHER STATEMENTS

In addition to social trends, there were pronouncements, from some important agencies of social control, on the subject of the kind of sex-related content that is and is not acceptable in the popular arts. They included court decisions, the report of the Commission on Obscenity and Pornography, and other writings.

Court Decisions

Between 1957 and 1969, under Chief Justice Earl Warren, the U.S. Supreme Court issued a number of decisions which liberalized the nation's attitudes toward sexually oriented materials and thereby effected significant social change (Fahringer and Brown, 1973-1974). The Warren court probably achieved more social change than did legislatures, in obscenity as well as other areas. In U.S. v. Roth (1957), the Court created the formula of "whether to the average person applying contemporary community standards, the dominant theme of the material, taken as a whole, appeals to the prurient interest" as the test of obscenity. Scienter, or the seller's knowledge of material's content, was said by the Court to be a required constitutional predicate to an obscenity conviction (Smith v. California, 1959).

In Jacobellis v. Ohio (1964), the Court set forth the concept of a national community standard and two years later added the requirement that material must be "utterly without redeeming value" to be obscene (Memoirs v. Attorney General, 1966). In Redrup v. New York (1967), the Court said that materials that were not pandered, sold to minors, or foisted on unwilling audiences, were constitutionally protected. The Warren Court's last important opinion on obscenity was Stanley v. Georgia (1969), which found that mere possession of obscenity in a person's home was not criminal.

On June 21 and 24, 1973, the Court, now dominated by appointees of President Nixon and headed by Warren Burger, announced major decisions on obscenity (Miller v. California, 1973; Paris Adult Theatre, 1973), which discarded the Roth test. The Court now held that, to be obscene, the work must depict, in a patently offensive way, sexual conduct specifically defined by the applicable state law; lack serious literary, artistic, political, or scientific value; and appeal to the prurient interest of the average person, applying contemporary community standards. The Court also held that the prosecution did not have to produce proof on the issue of obscenity and that there was no national community standard.

Each community was free to clarify what its standards were. In New York State courts, "community" has been defined as the whole state, while in adjacent New Jersey, it means the individual county, and in federal prosecutions, it is generally construed as the geographic area serviced by each of the 90 courts. What is obscene in one "community" may not be obscene in the very next "community."

Because the 1973 decisions clearly favored the prosecution and because of uncertainty over what "community" standards would be observed, it was originally thought that the 1973 decisions would brake the expansion of the production of sex-oriented materials. However, exactly the opposite seems to have taken place, in the case of both hard- and soft-core materials. Hard-core involves erection, coital penetration, oragenitalism, and closeups of genitalia. Soft-core may involve the presentation of "ultimate sexual acts" but the organs are not shown, there is no erection, no closeups of penetration, and the activity may be simulated.

Expansion of the number of areas willing to permit hard- and soft-core material has occurred, even though the 1973 decisions are more stringent than previous Supreme Court rulings and leading erotica publishers Mike Thevis and William Hamling were convicted of selling obscene materials and given substantial prison sentences. There is considerable public and prosecutional apathy toward obscenity, which may be seen as a "victimless crime," requiring large sums of taxpayers' money to be spent pursuing convictions that are increasingly difficult to obtain. Burt Pines, city attorney of Los Angeles, noted in 1974 that the city, after spending $500,000 in unsuccessful efforts to convict the movie *Deep Throat,* had abandoned the case.

Other prosecutors have been more successful. For example, a number of persons were convicted in Memphis in 1976 of conspiracy to violate the federal obscenity laws by distributing *Deep Throat* in Memphis, and in 1977 Larry Flynt was convicted of engaging in organized crime for publishing *Hustler.* These convictions appear, however, to have been the result of atypical local political conditions. Overall, the number of prosecutions since the 1973 decisions has declined. Although the decisions facilitate a prosecutor's task, there has been no increase in convictions. Defense attorneys now try harder to win an acquittal during a trial because they expect to be less successful in winning an appeal from a conviction.

Recent cases in many different states have involved the introduction into evidence of polls which tend to show that the majority of an area's citizens feel that it is acceptable for media to show actual or pretended sex acts and that adults should have the right to see such materials, if they want to do so. In a 1976 survey conducted in the heartland community of Hamilton County, Ohio, for example, 74% of the respondents felt that adults had the right to see publications depicting nudity and sex.

A number of states, such as Oregon, Vermont, New Jersey, New York, and Indiana, had their obscenity statutes declared unconstitutional during the 1970s. For varying periods of time, therefore, such states had no obscenity prosecutions. Many persons noted that the total absence of obscenity prosecutions seemed to have no measurable effect on the quality of life in the affected states and this awareness further downgraded the salience of obscenity as a social problem. In a 1970 survey, the Commission on Obscenity and Pornography (1970) had found that only 2% of the nation's population felt that obscenity was a "serious problem." It ranked 14th out of 14 problems cited.

By the late 1950s, many state legislatures were liberalizing laws on homosexuality, sodomy, fornication, and other kinds of sexual activity. The National Gay Activists Task Force, sparked by prominent educators, scientists, and artists, urged legislatures to implement more open attitudes toward gays. "Homosexual" increasingly was used as an adjective connoting a tendency rather than as a noun denoting an unalterable condition, especially after the American Psychiatric Association had officially changed its classification of homosexuality, in 1974, from a disease to a sexual option which did not imply pathology. Such highly publicized official actions helped to create a more accepting attitude toward sex in the media and arts.

Report of Commission on Obscenity and Pornography

Another contributor to the dramatic change in the climate of acceptance for sexually oriented materials was the final report of the Commission on Obscenity and Pornography (1970), which concluded that sexually explicit materials had no harmful effect. The Commission's report recommended that federal and state obscenity laws, in terms of adults, be repealed. Although the subsequent dismissal of the report by President Nixon and the U.S. Senate was briefly publicized, the dismissal had less impact than the fact that a federal commission considering the effects of sex-oriented print and visual materials had found them harmless. The report served to alert many Americans to the issue of obscenity. The Commission was unable to find any valid and acceptable definition of obscenity and recommended that the term be abandoned; its report used the terms "sexually explicit" and "sexually oriented" materials.

Publishers, moviemakers, writers, and artists generally interpreted the report as a green light to expand content. Some publishers and producers took advantage of the ambiguous or seemingly favorable legal situation after 1970 in order to introduce previously prohibited sexual content. The new freedom was expressed both in soft- and hard-core films for general release, magazines, books, and "comix."

During the 1960s, there were several prominent literary critics, like Paul Goodman (1961), Stanley Edgar Hyman (1966), Peter Michelson (1966), Susan Sontag (1966), and Kenneth Tynan (1968), who wrote widely discussed essays in favor of sex-oriented materials, calling attention to their positive aspects. These essays contributed to a climate of acceptance for such materials in a number of different art forms, which began to reflect increasing candor and openness. Sontag's (1966) widely discussed "The Pornographic Imagination" was particularly influential in arguing that some sexually explicit works, like Pauline Réage's famous 1954 novel *The Story of O,* reach the level of literature, and she defended the artist's right to arouse the audience sexually. A number of these critics argued that we expect to respond to a work of art, but society does not want the audience to respond sexually to a work of sex-oriented art, and that such a double standard is unrealistic.

Beginning in the 1960s and into the 1970s, a number of nonliterary but very popular writers helped to provide an ideology of rejection of technocratic society and enthusiasm for self-expression and hedonism. Theodore Roszak (1969) urged his readers to resist "technocratic totalitarianism." Charles Reich (1970) viewed consciousness expansion as a harbinger of revolution. William I. Thompson (1972) saw increased hedonism and depoliticalization on the horizon. Although such writers did not address themselves specifically to sex-oriented materials, their best-selling books were often perceived to be expressing a message of free sexual expression. Reich (1976), however, actually later made the specific connection between rejection of modern technology and sexual freedom.

CONTENT OF THE ARTS

All of the arts, high as well as popular or mass communications, have participated in extraordinary liberalization of sex-related content which would have been considered deviant or even illegal only a few decades ago. The changes, which can be seen most clearly in films, books, magazines, and theatre, represent the expression and outcome of the complex political, sociological, economic and psychological forces noted above.

Films

One of the most remarkable changes in sexually oriented content is its penetration of conventional Hollywood films which are directed to the general public. Since the early 1960s, sexual activity increasingly tends to be shown on the screen rather than implied. During the 1950s, sexual intercourse had been suggested in films by various metaphors. The director would move the camera away from the couple to some symbolic parallel activity: crashing waves hitting a shore (*From Here to Eternity,* 1954), fireworks (*To Catch a Thief,* 1955), rearing stallions (*Not as a Stranger,* 1955), a train entering a tunnel (*North by Northwest,* 1959).

Such indirect expressions of sexual activity were necessary for films made under the Motion Picture Association Production Code, observance of which was necessary for a film to get a seal of approval. Getting a seal was an either-or matter, and a film without a seal was likely to be denounced by religious groups and spurned by the majority of theaters. There were rigid prohibitions against sexually explicit content when the industry Code was in effect.

Through the decade of the 1950s, "love goddesses" like Jane Russell, Jayne Mansfield, and Marilyn Monroe were making increasingly blatant appeals, as movies tried to offer what was not available on television. By the end of the decade, in *Room at the Top* (1959), when Susan asked Joe, "Wasn't it super?" she was probably the first movie heroine who admitted that she enjoyed making love. *The Pawnbroker* (1965) was the first Hollywood Code-approved film to show bare breasts.

In 1964, *The Carpetbaggers* added a new dimension of dialogue that clearly communicated sexual content without showing it on the screen ("What do you want to see on your honeymoon, darling?" "Lots and lots of lovely ceilings"). Similarly provocative dialogue, sexy titles, magazine spreads of near-nude scenes from films, and daring advertising copy combined to make many community elements feel that the Production Code had lost its ability to regulate movie content.

The major Hollywood studios, which had long opposed any introduction of a system of classifying films like England's–U (unrestricted), A (adult must accompany child under 16), and X (no one under 16 allowed)–finally realized that such a system was the only alternative to censorship. Adoption of the rating system in 1968 provided movie makers with new freedom because material not suitable for children could be identified as such.

Attitudes changed so rapidly that two years after the rating system began in 1970, the X-rated *Midnight Cowboy,* which featured a homosexual assault and heterosexual seduction, received the Academy Award as the year's best film.

And hard-core movies became so popular that two of them–*Devil in Miss Jones* and *Deep Throat*–were, respectively, the sixth and eleventh most successful films of 1973, in terms of box office receipts. *Last Tango in Paris,* a soft-core film starring Marlon Brando and with anal intercourse as part of its extensive sexual content, was the year's third most successful film.

Deep Throat soon became a landmark because it was the first hard-core movie to get national distribution, as a result of publicity originating in a widely discussed obscenity trial in New York City. The $25,000,000 profit which the film earned–on an investment of $25,000–encouraged other producers to make hard-core films, which were readily distributed. Because it dealt with a woman's quest for sexual satisfaction, it was hailed as an expression of women's liberation, just as Erica Gavin had previously been applauded in the soft-core film *Vixen* (1968) because of her "take charge" qualities.

Deep Throat was particularly important in obtaining acceptance for other sex-oriented films. It created "porno chic," was the first such film to attract many couples, and a major media event, seen by many famous "square" celebrities. Linda Lovelace, the star, was interviewed widely and achieved a fame unapproached by any previous performers in sexually explicit films. The film's humor provided an escape value by permitting audiences to feel at ease while watching the sexual material. *Deep Throat* was discussed positively in major media like *The New York Times.* Its title became a verb, and a phrase from the movie–"different strokes for different folks"–entered the general language. And when *Deep Throat* became a camp success, seeing it became almost obligatory for many people who would not ordinarily have seen such a movie.

Another 1973 hard-core film which profited from publicity was *Behind the Green Door,* which starred Marilyn Chambers, who had previously been featured as the model on the package of Ivory Snow. The incongruity between the purity connotations of Ivory Snow and the ravishment of the actress in the film helped to attract huge audiences. Audience fantasies about the movie's content were probably enhanced by Miss Chambers' remaining mute throughout a considerable range of sexual activity.

He and She (1971), *Censorship in Denmark* (1970), and *History of the Blue Movie* (1971) were widely shown sexually explicit documentaries. *Mona* (1969), which dealt with a woman who engaged in oral sex in order to preserve her virginity till marriage, was typical of many fellatio-oriented films. *The Lovers,* which clearly suggested oral sex, had been upheld as not obscene by the Supreme Court as long ago as 1959.

Because the Swedish film *I Am Curious, Yellow* (1968) linked extensive sexual activity with the young heroine's quest for a better life, it received extensive discussion as a realistic and honest representation of contemporary youth. By 1968, a number of major Hollywood theatrical films were dealing frankly with homosexuality *(The Fox, The Sergeant, The Detective).*

Contributing to the trend toward expansion of the limits of candor were some famous directors who made very successful and widely discussed films which contained sexual innovations. Michelangelo Antonioni, then generally regarded as the world's premier director, showed two nude women seducing a man in the very influential *Blow-Up* (1967). In *The Damned* (1970), Luchino Visconti presented incest. The film's sadomasochism was anticipated in Luis Bunuel's *Belle de Jour* (1967) and its tranvestism had been a significant element of Federico Fellini's *I Vitelloni,* as long ago as 1953. These directors were so famous that their presenting such sex content encouraged other film makers to follow suit.

The first closeups of the sexual organs during coitus in a nationally distributed film could be seen in *Pornography in Denmark* (1970), a widely shown documentary. Around 1971, film makers began routinely showing coitus on the screen, fellatio could often be seen in 1972, bestiality figured in some 1973 movies (e.g., *Animal Lover*), and dominance-submission was prominent in 1974 titles (e.g., *Defiance*).

There may be a lag of just several months between a previously táboo sexual activity being shown in "adult" movies and its appearance in conventional Hollywood movies that go into general release. Thus, the first conventional film concerned with dominance-submission was *The Night Porter* (1974), a major studio production directed by Liliana Cavani and with two prominent stars (Dirk Bogarde and Charlotte Rampling), rated R. The heroine wears chains, steps on broken glass, enjoys being punched and nicked with glass by her lover, and smears his body with jam before she crawls on him for coitus. She is married to another man and had previously met her sadistic lover when he was an officer of a Nazi prison camp in which she was a prisoner. The film's huge commercial and critical success led to many more dominance-submission movies in the following year, both hard-core *(The Story of Joanna)* and soft-core *(The Story of O).*

The year 1975 also saw the enormous success of *Shampoo,* in which Julie Christie uses the most popular slang words for fellatio as she dives under a table in order to perform fellatio on Warren Beatty. In the same film, Beatty also has sexual intercourse with a mother and her daughter, within ten minutes of each other. The mother is married to one of Beatty's business associates.

No star of sexually explicit films enjoys as established a reputation as Warren Beatty. Up to the early 1970s, the performers in such films were essentially anonymous, using fanciful names, e.g., Bob Superstud. Today, acceptance of hard-core films is so widespread that they have developed their own stars, women like Linda Lovelace, Darby Lloyd Rains, Tina Russell, Marilyn Chambers, Georgina Spelvin, and men like Jamie Gillis, Harry Reems, Johnny Holmes, and Marc Stevens. Each of these performers is sufficiently well-known to have published an autobiography and attracted substantial followings. They are regularly interviewed in leading publications and their films are given comparative ratings equivalent to the four-star system used by some newspapers, as in *Screw's* percentile Peter-Meter and *Hustler's* erection ratings.

Another dimension of acceptance has been provided by Hollywood unions. In 1975, for the first time, Screen Actors Guild members appeared in a hard-core film *(Sometimes Sweet Susan)*, insuring reasonable rehearsal time and equitable salaries. Since then, more performers from television and "straight" movies have been appearing in hard-core films.

New audiences may be attracted as some hard-core films devote proportionately less footage to showing actual sex. In *Memories within Miss Aggie* (1974), a highly praised film made by Gerard Damiano, the director of *Deep Throat*, only about one-fifth of the film shows sexual activity, whereas most hard-core films devote much more of their footage to sex. Some members of the audience may find the sex more acceptable if there is less of it, just as many fans now enjoy the considerable amount of hard-core humorous content. The humor, as in *Deep Throat* and the French import *Pussy Talk* (1975), serves to ease the adaptation of some audience members to actual sex scenes.

Through the 1960s, sex-oriented films had generally been made in 16 millimeter prints. By the end of the decade, it was not uncommon for such films to be made in the more expensive 35 millimeter, with its superior clarity and detail. At the same time, budgets for such films began to escalate. By the 1970s, budgets of several hundred thousand dollars per film were reported. Such budgets permitted more time, a range of settings, name performers, and other contributors to the quality of the product.

As one result of such changes, there has been an increase in the number of theaters showing sex-oriented films. Since 1973, more theaters than ever before—over 1,100—now show hard-core movies and about 4,500 run soft-core, out of approximately 14,650 theaters in the United States. The only states not showing hard-core films are Arkansas, Kansas, Missouri, Oklahoma, and Tennessee, in addition to the District of Columbia. Within a state, not all cities will show hard-core materials. In Texas, for example, Houston will and Dallas will not show such films, while in Massachusetts, Boston refuses but Gloucester is willing to do so. To accommodate such differences, a hard-core movie is often also made in a soft-core version.

Most of the theaters which began showing sexually oriented films were not newly built but were already in existence in suburban shopping centers or metropolitan areas and found such films to be more profitable than traditional features. Admission prices were substantially higher than for traditional films so that the theater could show a profit more easily. There was a steady supply of sex-oriented films and more (212) were actually made in a representative year (1975) than conventional theatrical films (208).

The near-exponential growth of sex-oriented movies in the last decade could reflect one additional factor: the unique ability of movies to appeal to the primary process—the unconscious—in a multidimensional manner. A movie can communicate directly with the unconscious of members of the audience sitting in a darkened theater by presenting a visual and auditory image, as it might be experienced in a dream or fantasy. For example, in *Naked Came the Stranger* (1975), the heroine follows her husband to the apartment where he is engaging in sexual activity with another woman. The heroine listens, outside the door, to the sounds of lovemaking inside the apartment. She raises her dress–she is wearing no underwear–and masturbates herself in rhythm to the sounds coming from the other side of the door. She continues to do so while several strangers walk down the stairs and go past her. The audience knows that such a scene would not take place in "real" life, although on an unconscious level its members enjoy and identify with the "action."

The unique power of movies to present similar intersensory material facilitates the ability of an audience to enter fully into sexual activity on the screen, on the unconscious level, and merge with it. Seeing a film in a darkened theater, with other people, maximizes involvement. To the extent that movies have been able to reflect the primary process rather than the secondary process of reality testing, they have offered a gratification that is very appealing to many people.

Books and Theater

There has been a major change in the quality and certainly the quantity of consumer-oriented books on sex. How-to books like *Sex Without Guilt* (Ellis, 1957), *The Sensuous Woman* (J., 1969), and *The Joy of Sex* (Comfort, 1972) sold millions of copies and helped to make the notion of sexual interest more acceptable. Such books are direct and factual and far removed from the euphemisms and poetic language of Van de Velde (1930), whose book had, for several decades, been the country's leading sex manual.

During the late 1950s and 1960s, fiction classics which had been unavailable in the United States *(Lady Chatterley's Lover, Memoirs of a Woman of Pleasure, Tropic of Cancer)* were published here after the Supreme Court declared them to be not obscene. New writers like Frank Newman, Marcus Van Heller, Marco Vassi, Terry Southern, Larry Townsend, and Alex Trocchi were, at the same time, writing books that were much franker, wittier, and presented a broader range of sexual content than the euphemisms of previous years (e.g., "his manhood throbbed").

In the late 1960s, there was an expansion of paperback fiction for "adults only," which is available not only in specialized book stores but at newsstands and regular book stores. Over 30 publishers specialize in such books, each of which is constructed around a number of sex episodes with transition pages of nonsexual activity. The sex ratio, which is the number of pages devoted to sex in relation to the number of pages in the whole book, went from .29 in 1967 to .47 in 1969. In 1972, it jumped to .61 and was .63 in 1974, based on a representative sample of 428 titles (Smith, 1974). In books appearing after 1970, there are increases in the incidence of fellatio, cunnilingus, and anal intercourse.

The enormous publicity accorded the books by Masters and Johnson (1966, 1970) and other scientists continued the process of general acceptance of research on sex, a process which had begun with the first Kinsey (1948) book. The respectability given to sex research by such scientists had a ripple effect which extended to sex in mass media. Such changes in book content are important because regular moviegoers are much more likely to be book buyers than nonmoviegoers (Newspaper Advertising Bureau, 1974). And, of course, movies often derive from books.

The content of books is related to what is shown in theaters, and live theater has become much more sexually expansive since the Folies Bergère first used nudity in Paris in 1918 and London's Windmill Theatre featured static nude scenes in the 1950s. The American stage has not been the same since *Hair* (1967) presented nude men and women together in a famous scene.

Although ballet dancers like Mikhail Baryshnikov and Rudolf Nureyev are huge popular successes, there are complex relationships between a high art like classical ballet and more mass-oriented arts. But it is probably no coincidence that a nude ballet was performed at New York's Metropolitan Opera House, the showcase of Lincoln Center, for the first time in 1976. The ballet, Flemming Flindt's "The Triumph of Death," was danced by the Royal Danish Ballet, one of the world's leading classical troupes.

Various nonballet stage successes also helped to broaden the scope of what was acceptable. New approaches and content tend to get to movies from two to three years after they first appear on the stage and reach television in around five years, in a kind of trickle-down effect.

Famous writers like Jules Feiffer, Joe Orton, and Kenneth Tynan contributed skits to *Oh, Calcutta* (1969), a nude stage review that was deliberately designed to stimulate the audience sexually. It ran four years in New York and was successful in many other cities. In 1974, the nude sexual musical *Let My People Come* opened in New York and ran for three years. "Come in My Mouth" was a representative song from the show. In the play *Futz* (1967), a young man is in love with a sow. Billy the Kid, a character in *The Beard* (1967), buries his head beneath the skirts of Jean Harlow and licks her to orgasm. In *Fortune and Men's Eyes* (1967), there is a nude homosexual rape scene.

The existential playwrights in France had provided a new legitimacy for dominance-submission on the stage. In plays that were very influential in the United States, famous writers like Jean-Paul Sartre (*Les Séquestres d'Altona,* 1959), Albert Camus (*Caligula,* 1944), and especially Jean Genet (*Les Noirs,* 1958) presented sadism as a complex and important dimension of behavior.

It was hardly surprising that by 1970 the most popular play in New York was called *The Dirtiest Show in Town.*

Magazines

The modern era of sex in American magazines began in 1934 with the publication of *Esquire.* Its Petty and Vargas drawings of girls conveyed the notion of sex as fun. During the 1940s, Robert Harrison issued a number of picture magazines *(Flirt, Whisper, Eyeful)* primarily directed to lonely servicemen and featuring photographs and drawings of women in semi-undress.

None of Harrison's magazines showed photographs of women's breasts. One reason for the ability of *Playboy* to provide an attractive alternative to the realities of the 1950s, and the blandness of the first Eisenhower administration, was its daring in running such photographs. From the first issue in 1953, circulation rose slowly but steadily to 2,000,000 ten years later. Its real growth came in the 1960s, when it reached 5,500,000 circulation. The great increase during the decade in the number of college students, many of whom embraced Hugh Hefner's "Playboy Philosophy" of sexual gratification for its own sake, helped expand the magazine's readership. To many "young urban males," the magazine seemed to implement countercultural attitudes like a liberal view of psychotropic drug use. When so much of America was coming apart because of the Vietnam War and other problems of the 1960s, *Playboy* offered sexual freedom as the centerpiece of a life style which would be further implemented via a huge corporate network of resorts, night clubs, television programs, book clubs, and a book publishing firm.

A key feature of *Playboy* was, and is, the nude centerfold. Typically, the model would be shown fully dressed and going about her regular business (e.g., sitting in the stacks of Harvard's Widener Library, carrying out her assignments as a graduate student of Sanskrit), then she would be presented nude and in bed, and finally shown fully dressed once more, shopping for groceries. The reader could thus, in fantasy, undress her and then dress her again. This opportunity to strip a woman in the pages of the magazine was an innovation which surely contributed to its enormous success. A related interest in peeping was probably responsible for the magazine's peak, the 6,500,000 copies of the November 1976 issue, feature Jimmy Carter's candid views on lust and sex.

In 1969, *Penthouse* began publication, showing the female pubic hair which had previously been airbrushed in *Playboy.* By 1976, *Penthouse* was selling 4,400,000 copies per month. Former madam Xaviera Hollander regularly replies to correspondence from readers.

Oui was started by *Playboy* to attract young people who wanted "harder" material. *Gallery,* which features amateur erotic photographs of "the girl next door," and *Club,* concentrating on the female posterior, each have a circulation of 1,000,000. *Players* is written for the black male. *Chic* stresses quality paper and photography. *Cheri* is the news magazine of sex. *Swank, Genesis, Cavalier, Club* and *High Society* are other successful magazines for men that are heavily sex-oriented.

Perhaps the most spectacular success of any recent sex-oriented magazine was that of *Hustler,* which began in 1974 and featured color photographs of the female genitals, original humor, an antiwar policy frequently enunciated by provocative editor Larry C. Flynt "the newsstand is the poor man's art gallery" and 16-page, life-size foldouts of nude models.

Some 35 other sex-oriented magazines for men seem to be flourishing at the present time. What is most extraordinary about their number is that each one appears to expand the market without taking away readers from its predecessors.

Never before in any country have there been so many magazines for men featuring photographs of nude women.

In 1968, *Screw* commenced publication as a weekly celebration of sex and wittily irreverent guide to consumers of sex-oriented materials, and many other sex tabloids have since appeared and flourished. The editor of *Screw,* Al Goldstein, became a courageous national spokesman for sexual freedom in the arts, whose ideas were adopted by many others.

During the 1960s, as one outgrowth of the Free Speech Movement at the University of California, underground weekly newspapers like the *Los Angeles Free Press* and *East Village Other* began carrying "comix," or outspoken sex-oriented comic strips. Robert Crumb, a cartoonist, put out the first issue of *Zap,* a magazine that dealt humorously but explicitly and often kinkily with sex. Other "comix" magazines, like *Snatch, Suck, Jiz, Ball,* and *Fetish Times,* appeared and flourished. A representative feature, in the first issue of *Snatch,* was Crumb's "Adventures of Andy Hard-on." The "comix" had become so institutionalized that in May 1976 a special "dirty comics" convention was held at the Berkeley campus of the University of California.

FUNCTIONS SERVED BY SEX-ORIENTED MATERIAL

One reason for the enormous increase in sex-oriented media materials is a sense that they may not only be a source of entertainment and pleasure but might serve a variety of other positive personal and social functions. Discussion of such functions was facilitated by the considerable publicity given the many studies sponsored by the Commission on Obscenity and Pornography (1970). In addition to the more generalized social gratifications discussed previously, sex-oriented content may meet informational, personality, and other needs.

There has been growing awareness that films and other media provide an opportunity to explore and indirectly experience sex situations which, in real life, might be less accessible. A man may see a bondage relationship, for example, which he has never actually had and thereby facilitate an expression of his fantasy while not risking it in his everyday life.

Sex-oriented content may offer an important avenue of expression for persons who, for whatever reasons, have no partner for sex activity. Such content not only gives a fantasy release, it also may provide considerable detailed information that is not otherwise available. Interviews conducted for the Commission on Obscenity and Pornography indicated that a considerable proportion of consumers of sexually explicit movies and publications derived information about sex organs and positions from seeing sexual activity on the screen and were seeking satisfaction of a healthy curiosity about various aspects of sex (Winick, 1970b). Couples may find that their ability to communicate with one another about sexual matters may be enhanced by looking at such materials together. Various sexual positions are shown so clearly that some psychotherapists recommend specific films or publications to patients, with considerable success. Pictures or movies can present details of appearance and interaction that are simply not as communicable in any other way.

Magazines like *Forum* and *Sexology* have flourished because they answered readers' detailed questions on various aspects of sexual behavior. However, it is much easier for a person seeking information to buy a movie ticket or a book and not face the possible embarrassment of submitting his or her name in a letter to a magazine, which will answer the letter in words rather than pictures.

Seeing a sexually explicit film or other picture may cut through defenses which a patient has erected to verbal communication in an individual psychotherapy or group therapy situation. People who may have harbored feelings of guilt or anxiety about some sexual practices often feel less guilty or anxious after seeing such practices in a book or magazine or on a movie screen. Similarly, cartoons have been used by psychotherapists with patients whose verbosity is self-defeating and who need a pictorial vocabulary of emotion that is more accessible than words (Kadis and Winick, 1973).

For some persons, there is an element of connoisseurship in attending sexually oriented movies. Like other movie buffs, they compare actors with their performance in previous films, seek evidence of a director's style, look for production values and unusual settings, relate the sexual behavior to the personality style, respond to the manner in which transitions are handled, evaluate the music, and otherwise critically view the film. Such dimensions have assumed increasing importance as sexually oriented films are being shown in more theaters, have larger budgets, and enjoy increasing acceptance by the public.

A number of students of sex offenders believe, on the basis of anamnestic data from the offenders on their earlier experiences, that exposure to sex-oriented materials could be a useful preparation for adult sexual functioning. Sex offenders often report relative inexperience with erotic materials, perhaps reflecting a deprived sexual environment which is an indicator of atypical and inadequate sexual socialization. The decline in such crimes as sexual molestation in Denmark, after the 1967 legalization of sexually explicit materials, suggests that such materials may drain off, in a socially harmless way, impulses which could otherwise involve antisocial expression (Committee on Obscenity and Pornography, 1970).

The continuing debate over sex-oriented materials has identified a number of other functions they serve and needs they meet. Increasingly, sex therapy centers and other "square" institutions are exploring newer methods of using such content in educational and therapeutic settings.

THE FUTURE

How are the trends of the last few decades likely to fare in the future? Most of the large-scale social factors that have led to the current popularity of sex-oriented popular arts are unlikely to reverse themselves. Furthermore, artistic freedoms that have been gained are seldom ever given back. In the past, however, there has often been a cyclical pattern of sexual freedom in the arts, so that the excesses of the Reformation theater in England were subsequently balanced by the repression of the Victorian era.

Some organizations, like Morality in Media, are resisting the expansion of sex-oriented materials. Questions have been raised about the long-term effects on the quality of life in American communities of so much sex-related content (Cline, 1974). Although a number of earlier commentators had been concerned about sex-oriented materials leading to sex crimes, the largest study of sex offenders found no such connection (Gebhard, 1965).

Even though active opposition to the spread of sex-oriented materials is sporadic, it would be wrong to assume that acceptance of such content is complete. Many Americans undoubtedly feel ambivalent or uncomfortable about the proliferation of sex in the arts. In some quarters, there is uneasiness about the ultimate effects of making public that which had previously been so private.

The consequences for sex roles, morality, and the family of so much sex in the public arts are not clear. It is also uncertain how exposure to such content affects actual sexual behavior—whether consumption of these materials is a stimulant or serves to drain off libidinal energy which might otherwise go into sexual interaction, or whether one or another outcome is particularly likely with specific kinds of audiences. Another possibility is that continued contact with sex-related content may lead to satiation and boredom, once the mystery and tension are removed from the presentation of sex. The boredom may extend to sexual activity as well as its presentation in the arts.

A number of communities have sought to control the spread of sex-oriented popular arts. One way in which communities are dealing with the sexual explosion in the arts is to have a European kind of "zoned-in" segregated district where such materials are freely available. In Boston, the area popularly known as the Combat Zone is reserved for adult entertainment, including bookstores and movies. Detroit has used the "zoned-out" dispersal approach to zoning in order to scatter the distribution of such places. American communities will doubtless continue to attempt to cope with sex-oriented content in the arts, in ways that reflect local problems and conditions.

The producers of such materials will probably try to continue to expand their market and use new technology, like cable television, pay TV, and videodiscs, to disseminate new formats which are not subject to any voluntary self-regulation. There is enough ambiguity in the ability of the Federal Communications Commission to regulate cable television so that *Deep Throat* has been presented on cable. We may expect that in any such unclear situation, some entrepreneurs will be willing to take risks in order to attract audiences and make money.

Rivalry between movies and television is likely to continue and to spur each medium to try to be more daring than the other. Theatrical movies attempted to attract consumers in the 1950s by presenting much more sex-oriented material than television was then able to show. In retaliation, television soap operas in the 1960s became much more liberal in terms of sex content, and other kinds of programs followed suit. The opening week of the most successful new series of the 1975-1976 television season, *Mary Hartman, Mary Hartman,* involved the arrest of an exhibitionist who was the heroine's grandfather. The heroine complained bitterly, in the same week, that her husband no longer had sexual intercourse with her. In order to counter such material, contemporary movies present more sex, to which television will again reply, and the cycle shows no sign of abating.

Another reason for expecting at least the temporary continuation of current trends is the commercial and marketing libidinization of youth. The most popular doll in American history was the Barbie, a sexy preadolescent whose play consisted of dates with her boy friend Ken. During the 1960s, twenty million such mannequin dolls were sold annually (Winick, 1968). Nine out of ten American girls in the 5-to-10 age bracket own at least one Barbie. The girls who play with Barbie, Dawn, and their successors can rehearse sexual fantasies during very impressionable years. Such girls, when they become adults, may be ready to accept and perhaps even extend the trends noted above. Small wonder that women have so clearly been the leaders in the "sexual revolution."

Continuation of current directions is also likely to be reinforced by the growing erotization of advertising (Key, 1976). Television advertising is subject to the constraints of the Television Code, but print media are not so regulated. Some $35 billion a year is spent on advertising in America in a typical year, and its use of sex appeals has been increasing steadily. Sex in advertising helps to maintain an awareness of sex and to legitimate related content in entertainment media. A comparison of the sexual content of advertising in the 1970s (Winick, 1973) as compared with the 1940s (McLuhan, 1948) is almost startling in terms of how much more daring its content has become. The pervasiveness of advertising, with the representative American exposed to over 500 messages daily, gives such changes in its themes a unique power.

Advertising is a key contributor to the furniture of the American mind. Its importance, in the context of sex-oriented art and media materials, is that so many of our attitudes derive from and are influenced by advertising. The "sexual revolution" of our time is essentially attitudinal, and the public's willingness to explore more open attitudes is one reason for the expansion of the market for sex-oriented content.

One irony of the attitudinal revolution is that it is occurring in America, the exemplar of capitalism, while revolutionary countries like China are puritanical and repressive. Not too long ago, sexual freedom in the arts used to be associated with revolution and anarchism. Today, with American movies showing sexual intercourse with a fish *(Fireworks Woman)* and a man sucking his own penis *(Every Inch A Lady),* and similar content in other media, the leading capitalist country now permits what would be anathema in the Communist countries.

In this country, demographic considerations could be especially important in the future. The fertility rate of American women has been declining dramatically, from 122.7 per 1,000 women aged 15 to 44 in 1957 to 65.7 per 100,000 in 1976. At the same time, there has been a steady decline in the death rate, so that the population is getting older. Since many of the trends which fed the interest in sex-oriented materials were related to the needs of young people, it is possible that the increase in age of the American population will modify the attitudes toward such materials in the popular arts. If other social changes of the last several decades are equally inconsistent with the trends of the next few decades, the future role of sex in the arts could be different.

REFERENCES

ALT, J. (1976). "Beyond class: The decline of industrial labor and leisure." Telos, 28(summer):55-80.
Anonymous (1975). "Crotch watching." Viva, 2(4):12-20.
BARBACH, L.G. (1975). For yourself. New York: Doubleday.
BROWN, H.G. (1962). Sex and the single girl. New York: Bernard Geis.
CAVAN, S. (1966). Liquor license: An ethnography of bar behavior. Chicago: Aldine.
CLINE, V.B. (1974). Where do you draw the line? Provo: Brigham Young University Press.
COMFORT, A. (1972). The joy of sex. New York: Crown.
Commission on Obscenity and Pornography (1970). Final report. Washington, D.C.: U.S. Government Printing Office.
DODSON, B. (1975). Liberating masturbation. New York: Bodysex Designs.
ELLIS, A. (1957). Sex without guilt. New York: Lyle Stuart.
ETZIONI, A. (1972). "The search for political meaning." The Center Magazine, 5(2):2-8.
FAHRINGER, H.P., and BROWN, M.J. (1973-1974). "The rise and fall of *Roth*–A critique of the recent Supreme Court obscenity decisions." Kentucky Law Journal, 62(3):731-768.
FLETCHER, J. (1966). Situation ethics: The new morality. Philadelphia: Westminster Press.
GALBRAITH, J.K. (1956). American capitalism: The concept of countervailing power. Boston: Houghton Mifflin.
GEBHARD, P.H., et al. (1965). Sex offenders. New York: Harper & Row.
GOODMAN, P. (1961). "Pornography, art and censorship." Commentary, 32(November): 203-212.
GORER, G. (1937). Hot strip tease. London: Cresset Press.
HYMAN, S.E. (1966). "In defense of pornography," in Standards. New York: Horizon.
J. (1969). The sensuous woman. New York: Lyle Stuart.
Jacobellis v. Ohio (1964). 378 U.S. 184.
KADIS, A.L., and WINICK, C. (1973). "The cartoon as therapeutic catalyst." Pp. 106-123 in H.H. Mosak (ed.), Alfred Adler: His influence on psychology today. Park Ridge, N.J.: Noyes Press.
KAHN, H. (1964). Thinking about the unthinkable. New York: Avon.
KEATS, J. (1958). The insolent chariot. Philadelphia: Lippincott.
KEY, W.B. (1976). Media sexploitation. Englewood Cliffs, N.J.: Prentice-Hall.
KINSEY, A.C., et al. (1948). Sexual behavior in the human male. Philadelphia: Saunders.
KOZOL, J. (1970). Death at an early age. New York: Bantam.
LE MASTERS, E.E. (1975). Blue collar aristocrats. Madison: University of Wisconsin.
LENSKI, G. (1961). The religious factor. Garden City, N.Y.: Doubleday.

MANNHEIM, K. (1950). Freedom, power, and democratic planning. London: Routledge and Kegan Paul.
MASTERS, W.H., and JOHNSON, V.E. (1966). Human sexual response. Boston: Little Brown.
——— (1970). Human sexual inadequacy. Boston: Little Brown.
McLUHAN, H.M. (1948). The mechanical bride. New York: Vanguard.
MEADOWS, D.R. (1972). The limits to growth. Washington: Universe Books.
Memoirs v. Attorney General of Massachusetts (1966). 383 U.S. 413.
MICHELSON, P. (1966). "An apology for pornography," The New Republic, 155(December 10):21-24.
Miller v. California (1973). 413 U.S. 15.
NADER, R. (1965). Unsafe at any speed. New York: Grossman.
National Opinion Research Center, University of Chicago (1976). General social survey. Chicago: Author.
New York Times (1976). November 16.
Newspaper Advertising Bureau (1974). Moving going and leisure time. New York: Author.
Paris Adult Theatre (1973). 413 U.S. 49.
Redrup v. New York (1967). 386 U.S. 767.
REICH, C.A. (1970). The greening of America. New York: Random House.
——— (1976). The sorcerer of Bolinas Reef. New York: Random House.
REISMAN, D. (1969). The lonely crowd. New Haven: Yale University Press.
ROSZAK, T. (1969). The making of a counter-culture. New York: Doubleday.
SENNETT, R. (1977). The fall of public man. New York: Knopf.
SILBERMAN, C.E. (1964). Crisis in black and white. New York: Random House.
——— (1971). Crisis in the classroom. New York: Random House.
SMITH, A. (1976). Powers of mind. New York: Random House.
SMITH, D.D. (1974). "Sex and sex roles in 'adult only' paperback fiction." Paper presented at the annual meeting of the American Association for Public Opinion Research, May 1974.
Smith v. California (1959). 361 U.S. 147.
SONTAG, S. (1966). Styles of radical will. New York: Farrar, Straus, and Giroux.
SOROKIN, P.A. (1956). American sex revolution. Boston: Sargent.
Stanley v. Georgia (1969). 394 U.S. 557.
THOMPSON, W.I. (1972). At the edge of history. New York: Harper & Row.
TOFFLER, A. (1970). Future shock. New York: Random House.
TYNAN, K. (1968). "Dirty books can stay." Esquire 70(October):168-170.
ULLERSTAM, L. (1966). The erotic minorities. New York: Grove.
United States v. Roth (1957). 354 U.S. 476.
Van De VELDE, T.H. (1930). Ideal marriage. New York: Covici, Friede.
WHYTE, W.H., Jr. (1956). The organization man. New York: Simon and Schuster.
WINICK, C. (1964). "Atonie: The psychology of the unemployed and the marginal worker." Pp. 269-286 in G. Fisk, (ed.), The frontiers of management psychology. New York: Harper & Row.
——— (1968). The new people. New York: Bobbs Merrill.
——— (1970a). A study of consumers of explicitly sexual materials, Commission on Obscenity and Pornography. Technical papers, vol. iv:245-262.
——— (1970b). "Sex and dancing." Medical Aspects of Human Sexuality, 4(9):122-132.
——— (1973). "Sex and advertising." Pp. 162-167 in R.J. Glessing and W.P. White (eds.), Mass media: The invisible environment. Chicago: Science Research Associates.
YANKELOVICH, D. (1974). The new morality. New York: McGraw-Hill.

9

FEMINISM, DEVIANCE, AND SOCIAL CHANGE

NANETTE J. DAVIS

The fate of our times is characterized by rationalization and intellectualization and, above all, by the "disenchantment of the world." Precisely the ultimate and most sublime values have retreated from public life.

Max Weber, 1946

That the scientific revolution has had virtually no effect on feminism only illustrates the political nature of the problem: the goals of feminism can never be achieved through evolution, but only through revolution. Power, however it has evolved, whatever its origins, will not be given up without a struggle.

S. Firestone, 1970

The problem of modern social order has been a critical one for sociologists. Whereas a few thinkers believe social change to be benign or positive, a "transitional" process toward a new and enhanced social life (Park and Burgess, 1969), other theorists hold social change to be essentially destructive of moral and social order, as it disrupts traditional maps of the world that detailed the individual's place and identity in social relations. The absence of a comprehensive and authoritative ideological system, critics note, is an inevitable corollary of industrial transformation (Wilensky and Lebeaux, 1965).

According to Weber, rationalization replaces sacred values and demystifies traditional rules and relations (Gerth and Mills, 1946). Individualism flourishes as persons calculate ends in practical (not ethical) terms; operate by abstract rules, not personal ties; and play "performer" roles as "merchants of morality" (Goffman, 1963), rather than acting within moral imperatives. Science, technology, modern accounting systems, all strip away the protective cover of social life, rendering it comprehensive, simplified, objectified, often trivialized. In the process, meanings become central problems to modern men and women.

The rationalized market, as a central institution, dominates all relations, and transforms persons into commodities in that individuals become more interchangeable, replaceable and removable at lower costs (Marx, 1956; Gouldner, 1970). At the same time, labor market participation, and the education and training that accompanies it, is a critical indicator of modernism. Participating in this market exposes persons to the stratified nature of social order and their often disadvantaged position within that order. It hastens an awareness of social order as "flat, uninspiring, and unhappy" (Mannheim in Wolff, 1971:xcv). In a world dominated by the market, though, the nonparticipant may experience a two-fold exclusion: resource deprivation and institutional outsider.

Whether viewed as benign or destructive, social change has had a profound impact on women's social participation, producing an accumulated institutional effect, as Mannheim (in Wolff, 1971:xcix) proposed for drastic change, generally, that "threatens to smash the whole subtle machinery of social life." Dramatic transformation of family and work life as fertility declines, economic and political access remains problematic, and the empty nest looms earlier have generated new frustrations, anxieties, and insecurities, exposing women to new work and social roles (Sullerot, 1971). The loss of traditional ideologies and social relations, then, characterizes modern life. How it affects women's propensity for conformity and deviance, initiates a collective response to change, and generates institution building are central concerns of this paper.

SOCIAL CHANGE, GENDER ROLES, AND DEVIANT INVOLVEMENT

The anomaly of increased extra-familial social participation among women simultaneous with their status decline is related to role dislocation and devaluation. Lower fertility, privatization of the nuclear family, segregated labor market, consumerism, and social distributions based on equality of competition, not equality of results (George and Wilding, 1976), have profoundly altered family and gender structures, and probably worsened women's condition, especially among already disadvantaged groups (Smart, 1976). At the same time, modernization intensifies individualism and aspiration for independence and self-fulfillment.

For women as a social category, the demystification process accompanying structural change and the demise of paternal authority tentatively frees them from traditional barriers and rewards. In the absence of genuine social power, however, spurious claims to equality and emancipation, promoted by dominant classes, undermine social ties and weaken conformity to externally imposed order.

A major structural change has been the drastic decline in the birthrate in the United States since 1900, but especially since the late 1950s, having profound demographic and life-style implications (Westoff et al., 1973). Demographers report that fertility is falling to the replacement level, the average age of reproduction is rising, the annual number of births is stabilizing, and the population is aging appreciably. The shift from a four-child family in the 1950s, to a two- or one-child family in the 1970s, made possible by improved contraceptive techniques and legalized abortion, frees women from early pregnancy and childbearing. Once considered women's fate, childbearing and childrearing have become a personal choice, ostensibly freeing women to pursue formerly restricted personal and social goals.

Focusing on the widespread benefits of controlled births to women and society, demographers often ignore the "dark side" of the fertility change. For example, reduced childbearing has not lessened, but rather has expanded, women's time and energy commitment to children and household maintenance (Oakley, 1974). Chase Manhattan Bank estimates that the average housewife works a 99.6 hour work-week (Morgan, 1970). Firestone (1970) asserts that fewer children, coupled with commercialization of childhood, contributes to an "ideology of childhood," sentimentalizing and romanticizing this age period, with questionable social effects for parent and child. The social construction of childhood by commercial and professional interests extolls the virtues of expensive toys, games and records; children's industries grow as comic books and television programs replace the classics; and children's specialists–pediatricians, psychologists, orthodontists, music teachers–increasingly define the reality of the childbearing and childrearing experiences. The production of consumerism begins young and translates into heavy personal and financial burdens for parents as they attempt to cope with their offspring's ever-rising economic expectations. Because the psychological burden of raising children falls heaviest on the mother, her inability to negotiate unrealistic demands is often interpreted as *her* failure, leading to spouse and parental conflict and mutual resentment.

The privatized nuclear family may yield contradictory and socially negative results for many women and children, as some examples indicate:

1. The increased incidence of child abuse across social classes, as familial isolation and failure to realize personal goals alienate parents and children, encouraging parental mistreatment and physical violence (Fontana, 1976).

2. The rising incidence of illegitimacy, especially among teenage girls, as they attempt to reproduce the image, not the reality, of the American dream family. Although pregnancies among young, single women could be interpreted as choice behavior in that pregnancy validates the female identity, the host of attendant personal and social problems (e.g., high infant mortality, pregnancy-related illnesses, lowered education and job mobility, dependence on welfare) suggest that the gap between the cultural ideal and the everyday reality falls most heavily on those least prepared or resourceful to bear the strain (see Menken, 1972).

3. The mandated intensity of the mother-child relationship in the early years of childrearing is offset by adolescent rebellion and alienation at a later period.

The absence of extended kin and failure of any viable institutional child support system privatizes the woman's troubles. Maternal depression and psychosomatic illnesses are directly related to female powerlessness and the necessity to cope individually with the cultural discontinuity in child socialization (Bart, 1971).

4. Fewer children for full-time housewives implies an earlier and protracted empty nest. The result may be involutional melancholia, which may contribute to the husband's withdrawal and eventual divorce, further complicating the woman's distress.

5. Freedom from unwanted pregnancy and decision to reduce family size may be more directly related to bureaucratic career mobility for husbands, than to enhanced personal goals for wives. Job and geographic mobility for men require frequent movement and readjustment of families in new settings. "Women provide the stable pole in the flux of events," says Coser (1975), as relocation falls heaviest on the wife, severing her from familiar persons and places, while opening up new opportunities for husband and children (Weissman and Paykel, 1972). The two-person career, whereby husband and wife strive to further *his* mobility, creates additional dependencies: economic and social subordination to the husband, and unpaid submissive organizational wife (Mainardi, 1970).

The privatization of the nuclear family, cherished as a cultural ideal, actually isolates women from self-actualizing or independent activities (Glazer, 1976). Exclusive or near-exclusive feminine and wife-mother roles often have counterproductive outcomes. Gove and Tudor (1973) have examined differential mental hospitalization rates, and indicate that more severe mental breakdowns tend to be concentrated among married women, rather than single females or males. Studying "invisible deviance" among women, Pollak (1950) concludes that domestic seclusion masks women's private crimes: child abuse, illegal abortion, infanticide, and husband or lover murder by poisoning or other unobtrusive techniques. Less seriously deviant, but no less alienating for self and family, is compulsive housewifery. This involves obsessive concern over cleanliness and house care unrelated to self or family needs; or means supplanting goal-oriented behavior, a deviant adaptation that in the paradigm of Merton (1957) would be "ritualism." Separated from the larger society, lacking extrafamilial goals, badgered by media commercials that romanticize housework, and preoccupied by deadening routine, the housewife may substitute ritualized housecleaning for unsatisfying family interaction.

The demise of the patriarchal order and lack of alternative life-support systems brings women into contact with unfamiliar situations and structures. Women are proving to be willing risk-takers, moving into deviance at rates that equal or exceed those of men. Their increased participation in serious crimes (Adler, 1975; Loving and Olson, 1976), drug addiction (Greenberg and Adler, 1974), suicide (Schrut and Michaels, 1969), and stress-induced illnesses demonstrates a characteristic pattern in modernization: enhanced conventional social participation, or expectation thereof, exposes the individual to new choices, anxieties, and life-styles. On the one hand, failure to achieve, having tried a new course of action, may be as significant for inducing a deviant response as fear of experimentation. On the other hand, resentment over the apparent successes of others, and low self-esteem can also engender deviance. Whether for status enhancement, class resentment, experimentation, simple opportunity, peer pressure, rebellion, economic need, or other motivated sources, female deviance is a direct outcome of being in the world, rather than being secluded or protected from competitive relations and the struggle for economic and social survival.

Criminal activity is a case in point. Women have probably always engaged in "hidden" or invisible crimes (Pollak, 1950), and so long as violence or theft was perpetrated on kin or local community, the family could deal with socially disruptive or antisocial behavior. As women moved out of the home and into the workshop, welfare lines, supermarkets, and schools, their experiential repertory grew. As consumers, they may calculate the odds of getting caught shoplifting, and decide in favor of a chancy outcome. As taxpayers, they may willfully withhold money owed the government, if they can find a safe means to dodge payment. As unemployed mothers or self-supporting women, they may choose prostitution or check forgery, depending on their class and social skills. As gang members in a "tough" neighborhood, they may learn to battle with fists, knives, or guns, or whatever other weapons are available, to protect their turf.

Few of these criminal acts are predicated on explicit grounds of rebellion or antiestablishment sentiments. Most female crime, like male criminal behavior, appears to arise out of calculated risk or a "drift into deviance" (for a review of deviant motivations, see Davis, 1975). Women are not toppling institutions, although some are carrying guns. A few very notorious cases have involved senselessly violent acts (i.e., Charles Manson's "girls") or assassinations, indicating women's capacity for ruthlessness. Female violence continues to be overwhelmingly a family affair (Rosenblatt and Greenland, 1974). The conventional criminal, including the woman, is apolitical, a situation that may change as minorities and women politicize their criminal acts (for example, see Minton, 1971).

Adler (1975) has been criticized for overemphasizing increased rates of female delinquency and crime without adequately taking into account the relatively low number of females arrested, compared to males. It is significant that female arrests are no longer restricted to sex-related or status offenses. Instead, females are approximating males in their involvement in serious crimes, a trend primarily manifested among the 17-and-under group.

While female arrests account for 15.3% of the total arrests in 1973, involvement in violent crime is low (10.2% of total arrests) and represents only a fraction of total female arrests (3%). The relatively higher arrest rates for property crime is mainly for larceny (where women account for 31% of total arrests), and reflect the consumer-oriented role women play in industrial societies. Victimless crimes, long attacked by critics because enforcement procedures violate due process, provide ready-made categories for controlling female morality, accounting for nearly 60% of all female arrests. For example, vagrancy and suspicion are catch-all categories for picking up suspects when no more specific charge can be made (Quinney, 1975). Laws against prostitution apply for both men and women in all but five states, but men are rarely arrested for this "female crime" (see Schur, 1965; Kadish, 1967; Packer, 1968, for a critique of criminalizing private morality).

Experimenting with drug and alcohol, attempting new life-styles, deserting home and school at earlier ages, enhances exposure to deviant groups. Criminalizing female deviance, though, encourages dependence on outsider groups, and curtails access to conventional jobs and persons.

While gender changes induce psychosocial dislocations among all classes of women, their impact is particularly profound for maritally unattached and poor women. A report from Lexington, Kentucky, federal hospital for drug addicts shows two significant shifts in the socioeconomic status of female addicts between 1961 and 1967: (1) women admitted in 1967 were much more likely to be divorced than in 1961; and (2) the number supporting themselves through illegal activity as their primary source of income increased from 10% to 30% among whites and from 36% to 67% among blacks (Cuskey et al., 1971). And while female users of illicit drugs constitute only 20% of the 1970 addict population, they have a relatively heavier dependence than males on sedatives and tranquilizers, often freely prescribed by physicians for functional and psychosomatic disorders. Prescription drugs may serve as a parallel escape hatch from a social context that denies autonomy within the family sphere and lacks compensatory rewards and mobility in the economic world.

Changing roles of women, as traditional values of "Kinder, Kuche, and Kirche" conflict with social and economic demands, create highly contradictory expectations, and for some women, severe psychological stress. Mental illness is now more common among women than men (Gove and Tudor, 1973), and when present among mothers is a primary contributor to adolescent depression and deviance (Weissman, 1972a).

Once fairly rare among women, suicide is a frequent response to isolation and anxiety, with women now attempting suicide two to three times more often than men. Weissman's (1974) clinical findings show suicide to be concentrated among women who are relatively younger (30-35), single or divorced, or who are unwed teen mothers, excessive users of medication, or who express a wide variety of psychosomatic complaints. While males complete the suicide act more often than females (because of more effective methods of self-destruction), women are successfully taking their own lives more frequently than ever before. A Los Angeles study shows that women accounted for 35% of the successful suicide attempts in 1960; ten years later, the figure has risen to 45% and it continues to rise (Adler, 1975).

Another consequence of changing roles for women is evident in the rise of stress-related diseases. Coronary disease, ulcers and hypertension, previously restricted to males, are now major health problems among women (Stoll, 1974).

ECONOMIC ORGANIZATION AND SOCIAL MARGINALITY

Tracing the recruitment of women into deviance to the declining status and power of traditional family roles presents only a partial interpretation of deviant phenomena. Women actually experience dual institutional failure as they shift from the customary domestic sphere, formerly offering a modicum of social and economic support, to the labor market, wherein blocked access and mobility, a double standard for job participation, and low pay both reflect and reinforce structured sex inequality and social marginality. As developed by Park and Burgess (1969) and Stonequist (1937), marginality is a result of social change, whereby discredited persons, who fall in between well-defined and well-separated groups and are never accepted fully by any group, experience serious problems of identification and role ambivalence. Immigrants, minorities, "night people," and denizens of the "cool world" all occupy an alien position in social relations (see Sagarin, 1975).

Working women also confront similar problems of role marginality and malintegration. Glazer and associates (1976) have summarized the peculiar circumstances surrounding women's job participation by noting that they are multiple job holders, combining full-time homemaking with paid employment depriving them of full participation in either family or work spheres.

No longer is work an option for women, but an economic necessity for both single and married women, as delayed marriage and high divorce rates mandate self-support and cycles of inflation and recession severely restrict the husband's capacity to support the family without his wife's supplementary earnings. Labor market participation has cumulative social effects on women and children, as these figures, summarized in Glazer et al. (1976), indicate:

- Over 65% of women work because of financial need.
- Almost half of employed men have wives who are employed, and who contribute about 25% of the family income.
- There are 13.6 million women with children under 18 years old who work outside the home, representing 38% of all employed women.
- Among 7.2 million families headed by women, accounting for over nine million children, 54% were in the labor force.
- Twenty-five million children under 18 years have employed mothers.
- The work-life expectancy of American women has increased from 6.3 years in 1900 to 22.9 years in 1970.

Whether full-time or supplementary breadwinners, women's work life is marked by the same discriminatory effects as characterizes racial minorities: sex and race-typed jobs, pay and benefit differentials, and blocked mobility. Women's occupations continue to command lower salaries, as Table 1 summarizes, that severely restrict their capacity to remain single or to leave an undesirable marriage.

The income gap is not explained by educational differences, as Glazer (1976) emphasizes, for women earn substantially less than men with comparable education. Not only are women concentrated in sex-segregated, low-pay, low-status, last-hired and first-fired jobs, but also career discontinuities because of parenthood pull them out of the labor market and confirm their marginal position in the work force.

Nor does advanced education assure occupational status advantages as it does for men (Reskin, 1976). Whether in academia, business, or the professions, women's entrance to higher status and decision-making positions remains blocked. Male-sponsored mobility and informal networks typically exclude women as protegés, colleagues, and friends, and anti-nepotism regulations act as de facto barriers that discourage entry into preferred jobs, especially for married women. The achievement-based model of status attainment fails to materialize for women. The institutional location of women, as described by Weiss, Ramirez, and Tracy (1976) is "incorporation at the rear of the bus."

Media reports proclaiming the "breakdown of sex barriers" across formerly restricted occupations may reinforce the equality myth (see "Women's News," 1976). Publicity attending such rare events as a woman personality earning a million dollars per annum (e.g., Barbara Walters), or gains by a handful of women admitted to political or corporate life, really masks the larger social reality. For every highly successful woman careerist, there are tens of thousands of underemployed and minimum wage-earning women whose occupational power and prestige resembles little more than nineteenth-century industrial conditions: an unprotected market for surplus workers (International Labour Conference, 1975).

Table 1. MEDIAN ANNUAL EARNINGS OF WOMEN AND MEN IN THE TOP FIVE OCCUPATIONS OF WOMEN WORKERS[a]

Occupation[b]	Women	Men	Percentage of Women in Occupation	Earnings of Women as Percentage of Men's Earnings
Public elementary school teachers	$6,883	$8,366	84	82
Secretaries	4,803	7,536	98	64
Bookkeepers	4,477	7,401	82	60
Retail salesclerks	2,208	5,482	65	40
Waitresses/waiters	1,662	3,894	89	57

a. Table drawn from Glazer (1976). Originally published in *Monthly Labor Review*, U.S. Department of Labor, August, 1974.

b. These are the five largest women's occupations, including 25.4% of the female labor force.

If the career woman persists as an anomaly, a freak event, or as Fred Davis (1961) points out, a classic deviant type, female industrial workers are simply invisible. Lacking the minimum job prerequisites of tenure and a living wage, clerical workers, machine operators, waitresses, domestics, and other low-skilled female workers serve as subterranean social types. Largely disconnected from union, community, and political organizations, the larger mass of women workers remain politically and economically disadvantaged, despite their formal legal equality (see Glenn and Feldberg, 1976; Glazer and Waehrer, 1972).

The central thesis in the conflict analysis of social relations revolves around the themes of class exploitation, underclass oppression, and dominant groups' mystifications about the productive and political systems of control. These power strategies divide society and promote conflict. In this view widespread deviance is an expression of conflict between mutually hostile groups and as such is a form of social protest (Davis, 1975). Until recently, rebellion among women has been inchoate, unorganized, and mainly psychological. Operating at a low level of class consciousness, rebellion was typically turned inward or against members of their own class. The current feminist revitalization movement, explicitly addressing these class-caste issues, takes up what the early feminist movement evaded or failed to accomplish: a critical examination of the institutional roots of sexism. Organizational attempts to balance power inequities aim to destigmatize female behavior, either by demanding equal or preferential access to coveted professional and management positions, or by offering new institutional solutions to problems of social change.

FEMINISM AS COLLECTIVE MOVEMENT AND COUNTER IDEOLOGY

The rise of the current feminist movement is a response to liberation efforts that began in the 1950s to rectify glaring legal and educational discrimination for blacks. By the mid 1960s, the benign civil rights movement had assumed a more radical form, involving a larger corps of dissidents—younger, more educated blacks, Indians, intellectuals, welfare recipients and workers, students, women, and others who were reacting to unpopular government policies and persistent social problems. This prefeminist movement represented a diffuse collective outrage against the Vietnam War, minority ghettoization, structural poverty, political assassinations, and urban disorganization in the context of national affluence and military expansionism (see G. Marx, 1971, for an overview of this period).

Sex inequalities among movement groups ("the position of women in our movement should be prone," black leader Stokely Carmichael said) certainly provided a necessary spur for many women's collective disenchantment. Undoubtedly, the abortion movement sweeping Europe and North America also served to rally many educated women, as well as to link feminist activity to other reforms: pollution, population pressure, health and welfare issues, and corporate waste (see Chafe, 1972). Movement symbols captured media attention, as bra burning replaced draft-card burning. Widespread sex inequality in public and private sectors was publicized as a result of federal antidiscrimination policies. Initially developed to integrate minorities into schools and jobs, middle-class, educated women soon became the chief beneficiaries, as they sought federal relief for long-standing deprivations (Bird, 1974). Token relief, often years after the complaint had been filed, stimulated rather than quelled demand. Recession, the "backlash" effect, minority/women competition for scarce positions, and government reluctance to enforce compliance among resisting institutions slowed down what many proponents presumed to be inevitable progress. Economic pressure and continuing sex discrimination and sex segregation in employment practices (Levinson, 1975) mobilized formerly quiescent groups: developed working-class women's movements, unionized clerical workers, and stimulated the growth of women's caucuses, centers and other unions (Liss, 1975). The demystification process, initiated by technological change and bureaucratic revolution, filtered down the class structure. No longer restricted to educational elites, the feminist ideology appeals to both economically deprived and advantaged classes of women, although its greatest impact continues to be on college-educated and working women (Ferree, 1976).

While feminism lacks the cohesion and unity of movements of self-segregated groups, it is possible to identify three major ideological themes articulated by both liberal and radical feminists: destigmatizing female social roles and life styles; opening up closed or unequal access to institutional benefits; and developing nonhierarchical, participatory institutions to mitigate widespread distress and isolation among women. These efforts have had a profound impact on the social reconstruction of women's deviance.

Redefining gender roles, that traditionally restricted women to sex object or mother, involves altering the stigma associated with alternative moral careers and social types. Recognizing that the double bind constrains women and imposes a limited role repertory, feminists eschew the "feminine" style, wherein a passive and submissive demeanor is the counterpart to male aggression and control (de Beauvoir, 1953). Promoting a new assertiveness and independence, consciousness-raising, self-defense, and political groups emphasize the need for collective action against sex inequality and exploitation both at home and work. Culturally stigmatized groups–career women, black welfare mothers, lesbians, abused wives, rape victims, and older women–become redefined as politically oppressed, serving as models of women's capacity to endure despite the harsh physical, psychological and economic treatment (Morgan, 1970).

Attacking institutional discrimination, feminists reject as sexist any status quo arrangements that exclude women or involve unequal treatment based on sex differences. Whereas radical feminists often reject standard job or political careers for women on grounds that token participation fails to transform fundamentally sex, class, and race divisions, other feminists are more moderate.

Most accept dominant institutions, but demand that outmoded master institutions drastically retool to accommodate formerly excluded groups. Middle class movement leaders, such as Freidan (1963), DeCrow (1975), and Bird (1974), articulate a revivalist, not a revolutionary, doctrine. Expressing a preference for legal and economic emancipation, "middle-roaders" pressure existing institutions to match practice with rhetoric. Demanding full social equality, cultural feminists are more likely to struggle for equal wage and welfare benefits, for litigating job discrimination, for eliminating sexism in textbooks, and for improving economic opportunities for women who seek prestige positions.

Although less representative among movement influentials, radical feminists, as Millett (1970), Mitchell (1971), and Firestone (1970) articulate a strong counterestablishment position, serving as ideological benchmarkers for revolutionary goals. Asserting that the reproduction of institutional sexism and caste in all social relations begins with biological reproduction, these writers attack outmoded nuclear family arrangements that reinforce women's economic and social dependence on men. Equally militant feminists focus on economic institutions, especially capitalism, as the source of sexist, classist, and racist relations. The anticapitalist position may be less tenable, however, in view of recent data that show women in socialist societies to be almost equally burdened with multiple roles as family services conflict with work commitments. Radical feminists reluctantly face the problem that changing the political structure does not necessarily alter the productive process of family life in which women continue to carry the largest burden. Child and working-mother support systems, nearly nonexistent in capitalist societies, have made some significant differences for women in socialist countries, freeing women for self-advancement and limited leisure time (Rowbotham, 1974; Nuss, 1976). If structured sex inequality persists even in socialist societies, as many feminists believe, it is apparent that social change models must offer more than reshuffling of power distributions.

Perhaps the most significant thrust of contemporary feminism is not, after all, encouraging token or marginal participation in existing institutions. For this really reaffirms dominance relations. Instead, developing counterideologies and alternative organizational models helps to erode traditional hierarchies by exposing the normal order as problematic, by normaling women's defiance, and by reversing deviant labels, expose the "dark underside" (Sagarin, 1975) of dominance relations. In this way, the movement dramatizes and personalizes the causes, costs, and consequences of female dependence.

SOCIAL POWER, DEVIANT LABELING, AND THE POLITICAL RECONSTRUCTION OF REALITY

The strength of a social rule is measured by the amount of stigma attached to its violation. Because social rules define moral boundaries and assign penalties for their rupture, they are justified by their makers as natural, inevitable, or inherent to the order of things. Even questioning cultural stereotypes that underlie rules may result in relatively severe condemnation, as when children confront adult lapses between saying and doing, bringing forth angry outbursts. The power to make and enforce rules initially requires controlling social definitions. This is a hierarchical matter, Becker (1973:204) claims:

> Elites, ruling classes, bosses, adults, men, Caucasians–superordinate groups generally–maintain their power as much by controlling how people define the world, its components, and its possibilities, as by the use of more primitive forms of control.

Violation of taken-for-granted gender roles, whether by choice or coercion, calls into question the most mundane assumptions of everyday life, and contains the possibility of fractionating social routines and accustomed relations. Goffman (1963) observes that a "pathology of interaction" characterizes relations of normals with stigmatized persons: homosexuals, transvestites, lesbians, prostitutes, career women, and unwed mothers, to cite examples, elicit reactions of hostility or humor, self-consciousness or contempt, embarrassment or indifference. These responses signal a regression of mutual consideration, inviting intervention and control over defective or morally maimed persons.

Control involves both symbolic and structural features. A stigma theory is constructed; an ideology to explain the inferiority and account for the threat. Specific terms are developed that provide a source of imagery, imputing a wide range of imperfections. Defensive responses among the discredited are interpreted by normals as a direct expression of the defect. Face-saving devices are discounted or disallowed, and publicly prescribed and publicly validated measures are employed that reaffirm core values and institutions. Thus, deviance is group-constructed and group-governed, not an intrinsic attribute of persons, classes, or social types (see, for example, Goffman, 1963; Garfinkel, 1956; Davis, 1975).

Sociologists' preoccupation with flagrant gender-role transgressions may miss a more crucial point. This is the process by which gender mythology and gender stratification, that accompany rather simple biological differences, largely determine the social enterprise, affecting roles, rewards, costs, and identities. Because men have been the principal definers of basic human categories in all societies, they have held a virtual monopoly over myth-making and organizational resources. The male ideology has imposed severe constraints on gender roles, prescribing, proscribing, suppressing, and stigmatizing social variants. Through its influence in knowledge systems, it has also distorted our understanding of how social structures and human personality become intertwined (see Smith, 1974, 1975). Consequently, the attacks on sexism and gender categories have come from the women (Stoll, 1974).

The "woman's problem" (I am unaware of any analogous phrase for men) is a male construct that suggests the difficulties men have with socially defining and placing adult women. "Woman's place," in man's world, to paraphrase Janeway (1971), sums up a whole set of traits, attitudes, and ways of relating that have been considered proper to women along with the obligations and restrictions that it implies. Assumptions once thought to be ordained by nature—physical differences (caste) and social and behavioral differences (class and status)—are employed to grant privileges and penalties to some persons on the basis of such distinctions. The moral legitimacy of these differences, however, has been seriously eroded by social and technological change. As central actors in the changing scenario, the contemporary feminists' movement is very much involved with reconstructing the social realities about what constitutes the "woman's problem," and hopefully, by redefining woman's place, to move women into an equal position in the human universe.

Social problems theorists note that value-relevant problem definers are most effective in articulating and disseminating their ideological and social bases by attacking traditional social problems, rather than inventing new ones. Bensman (1976) says: "What appear to be different are not the problems, but the evaluation of the seriousness of the problems, the conception as to who are the victims and what are their causes, costs, and consequences."

RECONSTRUCTING THE DEVIANT EVENT: SOURCES, COSTS, AND CONSEQUENCES

Scapegoating, exclusion, and the conferring of invidious attributes is the stuff out of which society maintains order. When controlling discredited classes and groups, authority systems may ignore or deny social injustices among the morally maimed by blaming the victim. This entails negating or trivializing the costs and consequences of socially inflicted injuries or destructive acts, reaffirming powerlessness and inferior status. As moral entrepreneurs, feminists have dramatized the evil of women's victimization, as documented in three examples of feminists' research on social problems: rape, wife abuse, and mental disorder.

Rape and the Victim Status. Legal ambiguities surround the rape act and confound the victim status. Drawing on common law, a *Yale Law Journal* study (1952) points to the historical involvements of males as victims in the rape act. On the one hand, forcible rape violates the male's possession of a woman and threatens the status of father or husband by decreasing the value of his possession. On the other hand, women cry rape as vengeance against males who involve them sexually, and then desert the relationship.

Until recently, a wife had no legal recourse against rape by her husband, on the grounds that rape is the forcible penetration of a woman not his own wife: "Since his wife is a man's sexual possession already, he cannot be convicted of rape. He would have robbed himself" (Medea and Thompson, 1974:13). In many societies, the ravished woman is further punished by being ignored, ridiculed, branded, forced to marry her assaulter, or stoned to death. Rape is shrouded in misconceptions, prejudice, indifference, and the silence of victims, and if this is less the case today than in the past, feminism can be credited with having instituted the change.

Nor is rape typically considered a serious crime for men, especially if the victim is deemed "undeserving" or morally suspect. If the assaulted woman is black or poor, if she previously knew her assailant or had sexual relations with him, if she is single and sexually active, if she lacks evidence of resisting her attacker, if the assault is part of a "date-rape," or if she is violated as a hitchhiker, all of these conditions subject the woman to blame or censure (Griffin, 1971; Burgess and Holmstrom, 1974; Brownmiller, 1975).

In the past, legal requirement for conviction necessitated corroboration to prove that a rape had actually occurred: proof of physical evidence of penetration and struggle, proof of outcry, proof of immediate complaint, or outside testimony to prove the woman's nonconsent to the crime. Other barriers to prompt legal justice include problems of obtaining legally admissible evidence, judge and jury stereotypes about female sexuality, criminologists' conception of rape as victim-precipitated (Amir, 1971), the unknown incidence of false rape claims, and harsh sentences for convicted rapists.

Two conflicting interpretations exist regarding the validity of rape reporting data. On the one hand, several writers state that many false accusations of rape are made, motivated by the woman's anger or rejection (Kling, 1965; Gunn, 1973). Other incentives viewed as promoting false rape charges are: shame, protection of an innocent party, blackmail, revenge, hatred, and notoriety (LeGrand, 1973). Suspicion of the victim has contributed to law enforcement agencies' insensitivity in dealing with rape victims.

The other argument is that increased reporting of rape (62% increase between 1968 and 1973) represents an actual increase in the incidence of the crime. Official statistics often cloud, rather than illuminate, the rate problem. What data show is a heavy case mortality, or attrition of rape cases as they are processed through the criminal justice system. Goldner (1972) rejects the notion that rape is increasing "disproportionately to population increases." Rather, a more responsive system appears to encourage increased reporting, although various obstacles to reporting, investigating, apprehension, and conviction persist. Attrition-of-justice effects probably contribute to underreporting (estimated at 50% of all cases). And while the conviction rate for rape is rising, it remains the lowest for any violent crime (Horos, 1974:24).

Goldstein (1976) has summarized the problems that rape victims have when they report the crime to police, hospitals, and other institutional authorities. Victims face stereotyped police notions about how victims should look and act, remain ignorant of and lack confidence in the legal system, and are further jeopardized by police failure to collect pertinent evidence. Hospital treatment by staff often involves further humiliation and delays, absence of psychological services, hospital rejection of the victim, and lack of privacy. Court failure to prosecute offenders is often linked to allegations of the woman's promiscuity that justifies admitting prior sexual history, but invalidates the victim's case. The practice of trivializing sexual assault as "friendly rape," "felonious gallantry," or "assault with failure to please" (Brown, 1974) severely demeans the significance of the violent crime and contributes to the woman's trauma.

One consequence of feminist intervention is improved treatment for rape victims. Rape crisis centers are nonhierarchical, volunteer-staffed groups that provide immediate physical and emotional aid and assist the woman through her encounters with the legal-medical system.

Wife Abuse and Structured Violence. Evidence on the source and consequences of wife abuse, although more sketchy than for rape, presents a similar picture of the victimization of females. Both crimes entail legally proscribed violent acts, but unlike other violent crimes, are more commonly treated as unenforceable (involving the willing-victim notion). Both acts entail a discredited victim whose evidence is questioned or negated by officials. Both offenses serve as extralegal control measures, often severely restricting freedom of movement and choice. And both crimes are underreported and underprosecuted.

The battered wife syndrome is an increasingly common problem in American society, actually exceeding rape in number of victims affected. For example, FBI statistics show that there were 18,387 arrests for forcible rape in 1973; during a comparable period, 14,000 wife-abuse complaints reached the New York City family courts (Gingold, 1976). A tentative profile of this crime reveals the following: While unrelated to class—neither urban or suburban families have a monopoly on family violence—the middle-class wife is less likely to report the crime and more likely to endure abuse until children are in school or otherwise independent enough for mothers to reenter the job or marriage market. According to the Harris Poll, the middle class is more prone toward physical assault than the poor (quoted in Loving and Olson, 1976). Among reporting wives, many are pregnant and almost always are economically dependent on husbands. Excessive drinking by the man is involved in most outbursts. Resistance on the woman's part frequently engenders a more violent reaction, thus contributing to the stereotype of the submissive, abused wife (Fojtik, 1976). Secrecy, shame, and self-blame combine with social rejection and refusal of families to intervene on the woman's behalf. Wives who leave physically abusive spouses often face a loss of their husband's economic support and trouble with legal agencies which tend to blame women for domestic difficulties.

The crime of wife abuse is rarely taken seriously, even when life-threatening injuries result. Police claim that women rarely follow through an arrest warrant, which reduces police incentive to intervene. Moreover, domestic violence is potentially highly threatening to police, as when an enraged husband shifts his attack from his wife to police officers responding to a call for help. Men involved in both rape and wife assault are reported to deny their culpability, denying the victim ("she asked for it") and the seriousness of the crime ("everyone does it").

Most battered wives drop charges against their offending spouses, reportedly out of love for husband and children, or because of fear, remorse, or economic need. Few women really have a choice. Lack of personal or institutional resources, coupled with the secrecy and scorn that surrounds family violence, effectively closes off other options (Martin, 1976; Rockwood, 1976).

Among women who seek legal redress and support, the social and psychological costs are great. Public and professional indifference prevails. Red tape, agency hostility, attorney's fees, and unsympathetic judges, if the case reaches the court, make prosecution time-consuming, expensive, and humiliating. Convictions are rare, not only because courts are reluctant to place employed men in jail, leaving wives and children to welfare, but also because many professionals (and feminists) believe the criminal justice system is not a proper remedy for society's problems (see Green, 1975).

The success of the programs to publicize, combat, and give aid to victims of wife abuse may be a chief factor accounting for increased reporting. Alternatively, there may be an absolute increase in number of wives beaten by husbands, either because women are increasingly rejecting the vestiges of male dominance in the home or because violence itself has accelerated as a response to private frustrations and unresolved public problems.

Following Durkheim, many sociologists have documented the regularities and persistence of crime in urban-conflict societies, considering it to be a normal part of the social order and that its complete eradication is impossible (Inciardi and Siegal, 1977). The rediscovery of violence, including rape and domestic assault, is evident in public opinion polls and victimization studies that report increased concern over personal safety.

It is necessary to explain why males are disproportionately more involved in violent crime than females (Simon, 1975). Geis (1967:358) holds that traditional sex roles may actually encourage masculine-style truculence, whereas alternative status symbols and roles discourage the ideal of aggressive masculinity:

> Violence that warps and destroys will be controlled . . . only when societies no longer insist that virility and similar masculine status symbols be tied to demonstrations of aggression and violence. Sex roles seem blurred among "hippies" and it is sometimes difficult to distinguish the girls from the boys. The use of drugs by juveniles also represents withdrawal from combat, a disinvolvement from matters physical and forceful.

Shelters, counseling, and improved law enforcement will not eliminate wife beating, just as rape clinics and legal revisions of outmoded rape laws will not eradicate rape. The battered-wife syndrome is rooted in traditions of sex inequality and culturally approved counter roles of male machismo and female passivity. For the assaulted wife, it is a Catch-22 situation; a vacuum of dependency, despair, and nonresponse.

Women and Madness. The social construction of madness, publicized by psychiatric critics Szasz (1960), Scheff (1966), and others, addresses the problem of how institutions, organized to prevent and cure mental disorder, actually create moral careers organized around illness. Feminists have launched their own assault on Freudian thought and the clinical industry, claiming that psychoanalysis is merely an old form of social control in modern dress in that it perpetuates myths about female abnormality, sex role stereotypes and inherent female inferiority. Feminists maintain that the ideology is conservative and supports a two-value standard. Women are healthy if adjusted to feminine and wife-mother roles; unhealthy if they exhibit "male" behaviors, such as this description of the "angry-woman syndrome":

> an inability to brook criticism or competition, bursts of uncontrollable temper; the use of foul language; possessiveness and jealousy; the use of alcohol or drugs; and consorting with spouses who accept such behavior. [Rickel, 1971]

Ironically, women are psychologically healthy if they adopt the behavioral norms for their sex, despite high agreement among clinicians that the concept of "healthy, mature adult" does not differ significantly from their notion of healthy, mature men—independent, aggressive, adventuresome, competitive, and objective, traits viewed as inappropriate for adult women (Broverman et al., 1970).

What Chesler (1972) calls the "Freudian vision" of woman, as breeders and bearers, implies a biological, not social, interpretation of female symptoms. Depression, frigidity, psychoneurosis, self-deprecatory attitudes, suicide attempts, and anxiety are "female" psychiatric symptoms; conditions supposedly linked to functional irregularities (i.e., menses, menopause), or inability to bear children. The structures and situations of women's everyday lives are subsequently ignored or interpreted as residual. While males are also disturbed (e.g., destructive aggressiveness, hostility, pathological self-indulgence, alcoholism), women usually have far fewer socially acceptable channels for self-expression, reflected in the range and extent of symptoms centering around socially conditioned and socially approved self-destructive behavior (e.g., excessive self-criticism and overidentification with husband and children). Nor is mental illness among women taken seriously despite their higher incidence of psychiatric contact. Illness behavior may be punished, suppressed or "managed," not fundamentally changed or redirected.

Hospital data suggest how differential diagnosis by sex may be directly related to differences in sex role expectations. Females are two to three times more likely to be hospitalized for depression as males and comprise the largest proportion of diagnosed schizophrenics admitted to outpatient clinics, and private and public hospitals. British hospital data show 35 women patients to every man, a ratio that is reversed in prisons (Chesler, p. 92). Depression is a common response to disappointment or loss, and tends to be associated with a denial of the "bad" in significant others, an inability to express hostility, and a negative self-image (Friedman, 1970). Bart (1971) has studied depression in middle-aged women, and found that such women had completely accepted their role, and were depressed because that role was no longer possible or needed. Alternative careers may be perceived as unavailable or no longer possible.

Laing and Esterson (1970) identify schizophrenia as a self-estrangement process in which the person's wants, values, and realities are negated by "violence masquerading as love." Choosing women as subjects, and the family as experiential framework, they describe how human experience becomes invalidated:

> Jack may act upon Jill in many ways. He may make her feel guilty "for bringing it up." He may invalidate her experience. This can be done more or less radically. He can indicate merely that it is unimportant or trivial, whereas it is important and significant to her. Going further, he can shift the modality of her experience from memory to imagination: "It's all in your imagination." Further still, he can invalidate the content: "It never happened that way." Finally, he can invalidate not only the significance, modality and content, but her very capacity to remember it at all, and make her feel guilty for doing so into the bargain.

Although sociologists are disinclined to make blanket condemnations of the nuclear family, research underscores the dysfunctionality of traditional roles for adapting to new environments and social conditions. Especially among full-time housewives, home- and kin-based networks tend to close off meaningful extra-familial exchanges, and isolate the woman into sex-segregated relationship (Bott, 1957). And low social power in family decision-making (Blood and Wolfe, 1960) combines with limited personal development to induce "identity crisis" and a disesteemed self-image (Bernard, 1975). Women's madness, interpreted as deviant by clinical and popular opinion, is actually generated by conventional roles and serves as a normal response to structured inferiority and powerlessness.

DEVIANCE DISAVOWAL: DELABELING AND RELABELING GENDER IDENTITIES

Ascribed gender categories are so pervasive that even women who otherwise benefit from class, caste, and status arrangements have shared self-deprecatory and self-hatred identities. More females express a preference to be males than the reverse—few men wish they were women. Many women expressly reject having a woman supervisor or physician. Controlling for occupation, education, and age, public opinion polls show that women have been slower than men to accept contraception, abortion and other emancipating measures (see, for example, Jones and Westoff, 1972).

If self-blame, voluntary withdrawal, and conservatism are by-products of stigma and control, increased social participation is more likely to result in "deviance disavowal" strategies. These are techniques used by socially visible deviants to neutralize their physical or moral handicaps. Instead of denying or concealing their physical differences, a stigmatized group may seek to normalize relationships and to affirm their right of social acceptance by insisting on the use of positive labels and rejecting negative attributions. According to Davis (1961) and Goffman (1963), repudiating putative differences enables deviants to manage strained relations with normals, mitigating the awkward, embarrassing or negative aspects of social interaction. In this way, devalued groups make claims on persons and institutions for reclassifying and reevaluating their social status and for improving their situations in various ways. Collective action hastens the acceptance of new classifications and social opportunities (Ball-Rokeach, 1976).

Replacing stigmatizing labels with others that are socially acceptable involves two processes: delabeling and relabeling. Delabeling entails changing community norms such that offending behavior becomes acceptable or is interpreted as a normal response to social conditions. Relabeling occurs as mutual aid organizations press for positive labels that normalize the deviant groups' involvement in educational, occupation, and community roles as well as creating images that are socially acceptable (Trice and Roman, 1970). Berger (1963) refers to this two-fold process as "alternation" or meaning changes resulting from shifts in a group's structural position, changing role requirements, or lifeworld of the labeled. Thus, individual mobility and relative structural openness favor the temporality of deviant careers.

The chronic problem affecting the acceptance of women into standard occupational and community roles is the attribution of the taint of permanent defectiveness and incompetence, alleged to have physiological origins—menstruation, pregnancy, menopause—or to derive from psychological differences—inherent emotionality, passivity, and dependence. To neutralize the sex stigma women must either change these negative characteristics or alter their response to such disabilities. Similarly, they must offer contravening ideas or evidence that the undesirable behavior is beyond their control and responsibility. Permanent stigma is avoided if stereotypes of offensive behavior as natural, normal, or preferred can be successfully diffused in the community.

FEMALE SEXUALITY AND THE NEW WOMAN

Originally defined as offensive and immoral, female sexuality, especially within a monogamous relationship, is accepted as normal and appropriate. The cult of the female orgasm has replaced Victorian silence and embarrassment about women's capacities for profound and protracted sexual feeling. The decline of a socially acceptable age appropriate for sexual activity among females coincides with increased tolerance of elective abortion and unwed parenthood. Whereas illegitimacy continues to be defined as a social problem, the ideology of lower fertility promotes abortion as a pragmatic response to unwanted pregnancy. The women's movement, public perceptions of overpopulation, and recent judicial decisions are interrelated influences prompting medical acceptance of abortion on personal grounds, rather than for life-threatening circumstances only. Agitating for abortion on demand as a woman's right, movement ideology helped to shape the 1973 Supreme Court decision that struck down the various state criminal abortion codes as violating "guarantees of personal privacy" (*Supreme Court Reporter,* 1972:706). Formerly tainted with criminality, abortion has changed from a costly, dangerous, and stigmatizing act to a fairly inexpensive, low-risk medical procedure, especially for early terminations. Teenagers, single women, minorities, and the poor, at one time excluded from "therapeutic" abortions, are now primary users, with teens receiving nearly 40% of all medical abortions in some states (Davis and Farr, 1977).

As sexual permissiveness becomes commonplace, the conception of female deviance as sexual misconduct has come under attack. For example, girls are more likely to be involved in "status offenses"–violating curfew, runaway, truancy, ungovernability, and "promiscuity"–that account for 70% of all female referrals to the juvenile court in 1972 (compared to 31% of all boys referred for similar offenses). What Chesney-Lind (1974) calls the "sexualization of female juvenile crime" entails a discriminatory structure in which females charged with status crimes are:

(1) More likely to be incarcerated than those convicted of criminal offenses.
(2) Twice as likely to be detained over 30 days than other delinquents.
(3) More likely to be detained prior to trial.
(4) More likely to have a longer sentence than boys.

Imputations of sexual misconduct are apparent in institutional practices that routinely provide vaginal smears for incoming female residents. Regardless of the charge, incarcerated girls are treated as sex-norm violators, a definition that reinforces correctional biases regarding female misconduct as moral "deficiencies" (Chesney-Lind, 1974; Klein, 1973).

Prostitution laws have come under special attack by feminists and other critics who urge the decriminalization of morality offenses, as these promote, not reduce, female felonies (Packer, 1968; Schur, 1965; DeCrow, 1975; Davis, 1976a). Prostitution myths that justify existing policies abound. One is that prostitution causes widespread venereal disease; therefore, to ease laws would cause a VD epidemic. Another is that prostitution is directly involved with organized crime activities. A third myth is that prostitutes are responsible for serious crime, especially robbery, assault, and drug offenses.

Claiming that such myths sustain unconstitutional prostitution laws, feminists argue that such legislation discriminates against women in that it violates the equal protection clause, invades individual privacy, undermines due process, and implicates police in illegal methods for arrest purposes. The law differentially punishes women for street soliciting while ignoring men who catcall and openly solicit women. Law enforcement reflects the growing social ambivalence about criminalizing sex offenses. Prostitution laws are underenforced but remain on the books, either for plea bargaining purposes or for exploiting hustlers as informants.

Mutual aid groups (COYOTE–an acronym for Cast Off Your Old Tired Ethics) and feminists have labored to delabel prostitution as a sexual offense and relabel it as an economic activity, dramatizing the economic and social conditions that move women "into the life." One streetwalker reports: "It looked good to me; I didn't have any money, I was on welfare, trying to raise a baby, getting high, running the streets." In other words, prostitution is a normal response to economic and social deprivation. Moral gatekeepers may resist social acceptance of such deviance; alternatively they may tolerate the behavior in disguised forms–"party girls," call girls, massage parlors, sauna baths (Rasmussen and Kuhn, 1976)–or in ecologically restricted settings (Skolnick, 1966; Castle, 1974).

Secrecy, shame, and stigma–these attributes were once considered as invariably shaping the lesbian's life style, severely constricting social interaction and inducing numerous psychological problems. Although the "double life" continues to be a major adaptation to stigma, "counterfeit secrecy" (or playacting straight to socially aware heterosexual audiences to reduce dissonance) and verbal disclosures of gayness express the newer ethos. Over the past several years with the advent of both gay liberation and the rise of the feminist movement, there has been increasing resentment against secrecy. Legitimation of homosexuality becomes a possibility once gays are willing to risk the hazards of "coming out" for the rewards of being accepted as normal human beings.

Younger lesbians are also less intrigued with seeking ultimate "causes" of their sexual preference. Because most theories embrace a pathological explanation–psychoanalysts citing regression, castration complex, or unresolved sexual attraction with the father (Electra complex) and sociologists focusing upon social rejection or social ineptitude–little attention is directed to normal features of same-sex relationships. Simon and Gagnon's (1967) review of female homosexuality reveals that, rather than perverse or destructive, lesbian relations tend to be stable and monogamous, a model learned from parents (see also, Winslow and Winslow, 1974). Erotic attachments for another woman usually occur in late adolescence or early adulthood, following an extensive or intense emotional relationship with another female. Even the "butch role," adopted by a few lesbians, tends to emulate conventional ideas of male-female relationships and the culturally male functions of work and responsibilities. In lesbianism, homosexual behavior thus constitutes only a small portion of life organization and activity.

As this adaptation is usually viewed as nonthreatening, we may anticipate that the open ethos, increasingly espoused by the gay community, will accelerate social acceptance of this alternative sexuality. The media report of an openly committed lesbian priest suggests how far beyond Victorian morality the current generation really is.

Countering stereotypes of woman as incompetent, passive, and sexually miscreant, feminists propose their model of the "ideal woman." In one version, the new woman is morally and physically strong, independent and self-reliant; she selectively chooses "male" attributes (e.g., dominance, intelligence, wittiness), rather than adopting wholesale the masculine role. Among active feminists such traits are compatible with a strong self-image (for a review of these issues, see Mednick et al., 1975).

Another model goes beyond this tempered approach. Stereotypes of the violent woman compete with media portrayals of "libbers," both of whom are depicted as aggressive bullies who "beat the system" to further their selfish ends. Despite differences both stereotypes–independent woman and hardened deviant–reveal a common theme, stressing assertiveness and self-confidence, attributes heretofore restricted to men.

SOCIAL CONTROL AND FEMALE DEVIANCE

Alternatively, the emergence of a radically different model of female behavior may actually reduce social acceptance, as the "new" woman confronts a resistant system. Arrest and sentencing practices show that chivalry is dead, if it ever existed for most working class and minority women. Although women continue to be overwhelmingly underrepresented in arrest and prison figures, among those women entering the system, a double standard of justice prevails (Nagel, 1972). Women are not only more likely than men to be arrested for trivial crimes (e.g., shoplifting and victimless offenses), but, inevitably, they also bear the additional burden of being unskilled, undereducated, poor, young, and minority, and of having child-rearing responsibilities. Lenient treatment may be a myth in view of the evidence showing women as more likely than men to receive indeterminate sentencing, to spend more time in jail (where few or no social services are available), to be denied bail, to lack jury trials, and to receive longer sentences for similar offenses. Jailing exacerbates personal and social deficiencies. Women report that chronic problems are boredom, lack of privacy, inadequate work and medical treatment, persistent worry over children and anxiety about their ability to assume conventional roles after release (preliminary interviews with Oregon State women inmates). Women's detention centers, jails, and prisons are notoriously understaffed and underfinanced (Chandler, 1973; Burkhart, 1973). Administrators justify low expenditures on the basis of limited enrollment.

Rigid behavioral expectations for women in prison preclude self-direction, but probably contribute to "familying" or fictional kin groupings usually found only in female institutions with and without sexual expression (Heffernan, 1972; Giallombardo, 1966). High recidivism rates among women parolees, however, are directly related to differential conduct standards. California data show that agency decisions to return women to prison are typically based on factors unrelated to the criminal activity of the parolee—"bad" companions, immoral conduct, and the like (Berecochea, 1972).

On the whole, sociologists have remained mute about women's experiences in the criminal justice system, having assumed womanhood and motherhood operate as extralegal pressures discouraging police and judicial processing (Simon, 1975). Lower incidence of sentencing among women is presumed to be linked to their "very conventional" behavior (Millman, 1975), incapacity for criminal activity (Cohen and Short, 1976), and to dependency on older, influential male companions who initiate and direct the deviance (Wheeler, 1975; Simon, 1975). Women who commit crimes are perceived as less culpable, because they "have a good many more escape hatches and receive a good deal more forgiving than do male offenders" (Wheeler, 1975). In some earlier accounts, some criminologists wrote off the woman offender altogether. Elliott (1952:227) stated, "The average woman offender is actually a rather pathetic creature, a victim of circumstances, exploitation and her own poor judgment." Such views represent unexamined assumptions that reinforce negative stereotypes, repudiate the seriousness of female deviance, ignore the punitive and arbitrary criminal process, and block acceptance of women as responsible actors.

Public evaluation of women lawbreakers suggests an interesting dichotomy. A Washington State study found, on the one hand, that citizens consider crime among women to be more serious than for men and recommend harsher treatment for female offenders; on the other hand, women offenders rate high on a social acceptability scale.

Incongruities abound. As the evidence makes clear, once actually processed by the criminal justice system, women offenders experience harsher punishment than men, but evidently not as harsh as the public prefers. Judicial treatment may discriminate in favor of middle-class women, who are viewed as nonculpable, while rigorously prosecuting lower-class females who are perceived as threatening. If courts respond to public pressure, it is likely that proportionately more women will be sentenced. The more resourceful may avoid conventional corrections and, instead, wind up in various community-based diversion programs.

Public sentiment and court judgments are not completely at odds, as both accept the dominant culture pattern. Female deviance violates basic gender role prescriptions dictating passivity, compliance and noninitiative behavior. Although perceived as nondangerous, community and enforcement persons continue to define such women as "social offensive" (Rasche, 1974), controlling the behavior, while tolerating the deviant actor.

Under such conditions, neutralizing the sex stigma may require an alternative strategy. Repression and discriminatory treatment can trigger what Wilkins

(1965) defines as a "deviance-amplification" process, whereby stringent control measures for reducing criminality actually foster isolation, alienation, and a higher crime rate among outsiders. Militancy may be one response to social contradictions and discriminatory treatment. Little publicized strikes and riots by protesting women prisoners is one variant of the new rebellion (Baunach and Murton, 1973). Another is "prisonization" involving identification with deviant and inmate subcultures, especially among lower class, blacks, and those experiencing protracted confinement (Zingraff, 1976). Sex as a basis for sentencing has been justified on grounds that women's greater dependency and passivity facilitated rehabilitation if confinement were longer. Under the impact of changing roles, rather than achieving pro-social goals, official policies may generate intransigence and truculence as normal responses by once-compliant women to irrational and arbitrary control.

CONCLUSIONS AND COMMENTS

In overviewing changing roles among women and their propensity to deviate, three major conclusions can be drawn. First, social change is the major source for role dislocation among women, having initiated both deviance and collective reaction to structured strain. Second, the feminist ideology offers a fundamental reconstruction of gender roles, that involves rejecting the notion of deviance as individual phenomena. Third, feminists' attempts to normalize female sexuality have been successful, as permissive sexual trends precede the women's movement.

Efforts to reconstruct updated versions of the "ideal woman" suggest that upper-middle class versions, incorporating some "male" attributes (e.g., dominance, wittiness) may be most acceptable. Alternatively, visible deviant outbursts and inadequate impression management among lower-class minority women may create strong official reaction. Blamed as "libbers" because of their putative aggression, anger, and "masculine" demeanor, such women are usually cut off from feminist networks in community and work groups. Their truculence and resentment is primarily class- and caste-inspired, not gender-centered. If official repression and deviance amplification persist, we may anticipate increased alienation among lower-class women as class and race divisions harden, and the women's movement becomes perceived as merely a racist, classist tool for integrating educated or affluent women.

How can social science help to resolve the splintering of meanings into myriad conflicting and unresolved ideologies? Constructing new social maps will obviously not be achieved by spurious assumptions of social unity and consensus. Denying the reality of race, class, gender, status, and other social differences neither eradicates them nor obliterates the negative consequences following such divisions. In sociological discourse, unexamined assumptions about race, class, gender, age, and other fundamental statuses restrict knowledge, reflecting only particular views of the world and shutting out others. As Wilden (1972) notes, "the social sciences, in general, have repeatedly falsified their observations by unrecognized epistemological and ideological closures imposed on the system under study."

The social scientist appears caught in a dilemma. Distance and objectivity, tools of the trade, bound observer's sensitivities to abstract categories far removed from the suffering and turmoil of oppressed groups. Conversely, the advocate's perspective may be equally distorting if it closes off access to information or confines observations to underdogs. A way out of the dilemma has been proposed by Manis (1976) and others, who argue for a value-oriented social problems perspective. This presumes that sociologists seek to uncover hidden agendas that reinforce elites' definitions of crime, deviance, and social problems. The near-monolithic interpretation of social change and social problems, as a view from the top, neglects the range of meanings and experiences of less-advantaged actors. In most criminological studies female offenders are not mentioned at all. Smart (1976) contends that the deviant, the criminal or central actor is always male: "it is always *his* rationality, *his* motivation, *his* alienation, or *his* victim." This approach excludes women and makes them invisible. It also supports what critics have observed as the dominant criminology that serves as a management tool, confirming enforcement ideologies and practices (Jeffery, 1960; Davis, 1976b).

A conception of deviance is not simply an analytic description, but entails a variety of moral, political and practical implications. Lay and official stereotypes create the "facts" of deviance, implying persons so labeled to be immature, inadequate, irresponsible, unsocialized, destructive, degenerate, and so on. Categorical treatment of deviants as a special social type justifies authoritarian techniques of social control, sometimes under the guise of a benevolent science. Popular renderings of women as deviant or violent types, sometimes pictured as mirror images of male psychopaths, may titillate the uninformed, but reinforce destructive stereotypes. As an analytic category "deviance" may have outlived its usefulness.

Examining social change requires that sociologists remain open to newly emerging groups and their alternative perspectives. Radical feminism offers a disquieting political critique of our most unconscious taken-for-granted social relations. We may choose to call the rejection of traditional gender roles as "deviant," and treat anger and boisterousness as violating "ladylike" tactics and rules of the game. Alternatively we may consider the world from the perspective of feminists, noting that structures and ideologies of social inequality are perverse, inhumane, and undermine the entire social enterprise.

REFERENCES

ADLER, F. (1975). Sisters in crime: The rise of the new female criminal. New York: McGraw-Hill.

AMIR, M. (1971). Patterns in forcible rape. Chicago: University of Chicago Press.

BALL-ROKEACH, S. (1976). "Receptivity to sexual equality." Pacific Sociological Review, 19:519-540.

BART, P. (1971) in Gornick and Moran (eds.). Women in sexist society. New York: Basic Books.

BAUNACH, P.J. and MURTON, T. (1973). Women in prison: An awakening minority. Crime and Corrections 1:4-12.

BECKER, H. (1973). Outsiders: Studies in the sociology of deviance. New York: Free Press.

BENSMAN, J. (1976). "Social theory and social problems." Social Problems Theory Division Newsletter. The Society for the Study of Social Problems (summer).

BERECOCHEA, J. (1972). "Recidivism among women parolees: A long term survey." Sacramento: California Department of Corrections.

BERGER, P. (1963). Invitation to sociology. New York: Doubleday.

BERNARD, J. (1975). The future of motherhood. New York: Penguin.

BIRD, C. (1974). Born female. New York: David McKay.

BLOOD, R., and WOLFE, D. (1960). Husbands and wives. Glencoe, Ill.: Free Press.

BOTT, E. (1957). Family and social networks. London: Tavistock.

BROVERMAN, I., BROVERMAN, D., CLARKSON, F., ROSENKRANTZ, P., and VOGEL, S. (1970). "Sex role stereotypes and clinical judgements of mental health." Journal of Consulting and Clinical Psychology, 34.

BROWN, K. (1974). "The crime of rape." Reprint of a series appearing in the Fort Worth Star-Telegram.

BROWNMILLER, S. (1975). Against our will: Men, women and rape. New York: Simon & Schuster.

BURGESS, A., and HOLMSTROM, L. (1973). Rape: Victims of crisis. Bowie, Md.: Robert Jay Brady Publishing.

BURKHART, K. (1973). Women in prison. New York: Doubleday.

CASTLE, R. (1974). "Ash meadows: A fly-in brothel." Pp. 41-52 in J. Jacobs (ed.), Deviance: Field studies and self-disclosures. Palo Alto, Calif.: National Press.

CHAFE, W. (1972). The American woman: Her changing social, economic and political roles: 1920-1970. New York: Oxford University Press.

CHANDLER, E.W. (1973). Women in prison. Indianapolis: Bobbs-Merrill.

CHESLER, P. (1972). Women and madness. New York: Avon.

CHESNEY-LIND, M. (1974). "Juvenile delinquency: The sexualization of female crime." Psychology Today, 7(July):43-46.

COHEN, A., and SHORT, J. (1976). "Crime and juvenile delinquency." Pp. 49-100 in R.K. Merton and R. Nisbet (eds.), Contemporary social problems (4th ed.). New York: Harcourt, Brace, Jovanovich.

COSER, R. (1975). "Stay home, little Sheba: On placement, displacement, and social change." Social Problems, 22(April):470-480.

CUSKEY, W., MOFFET, A., and CLIFFORD, H. (1971). "Comparison of female opiate addicts admitted to Lexington Hospital in 1961 and 1967." H.S.M.H.A. Health Reports, 86(April):332-340.

DAVIS, F. (1961). "Deviance disavowal: The management of strained interaction by the visibly handicapped." Social Problems, 9:120-132.

DAVIS, N.J. (1975). Sociological constructions of deviance: Perspectives and issues in the field. Dubuque, Iowa: Wm. L. Brown.

--- (1976a). "Prostitution and social control: Use and abuse of the criminal sanction." Unpublished paper.

--- (1976b). "Social problems theory: Explanation or ideology." Paper presented to the Society for the Study of Social Problems, New York City, August.

DAVIS, N.J., and FARR, G. (1977). "Social effects of alternative abortion policies: Toward

a theory of law and social change." Paper presented to the Pacific Sociological Society, Sacramento, April.
DeBEAUVOIR, S. (1953). The second sex. New York: Knopf.
DeCROW, K. (1975). Sexist justice. New York: Vintage Books.
ELLIOTT, M. (1952). Crime in modern society. New York: Harper.
FERREE, M. (1976). "Social networks and the diffusion of feminism." Paper presented to the annual meeting of the American Sociological Association, New York.
FIRESTONE, S. (1970). The dialectic of sex. New York: Bantam.
FOJTIK, K. (1976). "Household violence." NOW Newsletter (June).
FONTANA, V. (1976). Somewhere a child is crying: Maltreatment–Causes and prevention. New York: New American Library.
FRIEDAN, B. (1963). The feminine mystique. New York: Norton.
FRIEDMAN, A. (1970). "Hostility factors and clinical improvement in depressed patients." Archives of General Psychiatry, 23.
GARFINKEL, H. (1956). "Conditions of successful degradation ceremonies." American Journal of Sociology 61:420-424.
GEIS, G. (1967). "Violence in American society." Current History, pp. 354-358.
GEORGE, V., and WILDING, P. (1976). Ideology and social welfare. London: Routledge & Kegan Paul.
GERTH, H.H., and MILLS, C.W. (eds., 1946). From Max Weber: Essays in sociology. New York: Oxford University Press.
GIALLOMBARDO, R. (1966). Society of women: A study of women's prison. New York: John Wiley.
GINGOLD, J. (1976). "One of these days–pow–right in the kisser." Ms (August):54-55, 94.
GLAZER, N. (1976). "The captive couple." Pp. 263-291 in D.H. Zimmerman, D.L. Wieder, and S. Zimmerman, Understanding social problems. New York: Praeger.
---- MAJKA, L., ACKER, J., and BOSE, C. (1976). "The homemaker, the family and employment: Some interrelationships." Paper prepared for American Women in a Full Employment Economy: A Compendium. The Joint Economic Committee of Congress.
---- and WAEHRER, H.Y. (eds., 1972). Woman in a man-made world. Chicago: Rand McNally.
GLENN, E., and FELDBERG, R. (1976). "Structural change and proletarianization: The case of clerical work." Paper presented to American Sociological Association, New York City.
GOFFMAN, E. (1963). Stigma: Notes on the management of spoiled identity. Englewood Cliffs, N.J.: Prentice-Hall.
GOLDNER, N. (1972). "Rape as a heinous but understudied offense." Journal of Criminal Law, Criminology and Police Science, 63:402-407.
GOLDSTEIN, C. (1976). "The dilemma of the rape victim: A descriptive analysis." Criminal Justice Monograph 7, Institute of Contemporary Corrections and the Behavioral Sciences. Sam Houston State University, Houston, Texas.
GOULDNER, A. (1970). The coming crisis of western sociology. New York: Basic Books.
GOVE, W.R., and TUDOR, J. (1973). "Adolescent sex roles and mental illness." American Journal of Sociology, 78:812-835.
GREEN, A. (1975). Social problems: Arena of conflicts. New York: McGraw-Hill.
GREENBERG, S., and ADLER, F. (1974). "Crime and addiction: An empirical analysis of the literature, 1920-1973." Contemporary Drug Problems, (summer):221-270.
GRIFFIN, S. (1971). "Rape: The all-American crime." Ramparts, (September):26-35.
GUNN, J. (1973). Violence. New York: Praeger.
HEFFERNAN, E. (1972). Making it in prison. New York: John Wiley.
HOROS, C. (1974). Rape. New Canaan, Conn.: Tobey Publishing.

INCIARDI, J., and SIEGAL, H. (1977). Crime: Emerging issues. New York: Praeger.
International Labour Conference (1975). Equality of opportunity and treatment for women workers. Geneva, Switzerland: International Labor Office.
JANEWAY, E. (1971). Man's world, woman's place. New York: Dell.
JEFFERY, C.R. (1960). "The historical development of criminology." Pp. 364-394 in H. Mannheim (ed.), Pioneers in criminology. Chicago: Quadrangle.
JONES, E., and WESTOFF, C.F. (1972). "Attitudes toward abortion in the United States in 1970 and the trend since 1965." Pp. 569-578 in Demographic and social aspects of population growth. Commission on Population Growth and American Future Research Reports. Washington, D.C.: U.S. Government Printing Office.
KADISH, S. (1967). "The crisis of overcriminalization." The Annals of the American Academy of Political and Social Science, 374(November): 157-170.
KLEIN, D. (1973). "The etiology of female crime." Issues in Criminology, 8(fall): 3-30.
KLING, S. (1965). Sexual behavior and the law. New York: Bernard Geis Associates.
LAING, R., and ESTERSON, A. (1970). Sanity, madness and the family. New York: Pelican.
LeGRAND, C. (1973). "Rape and rape laws: Sexism in society and law." California Law Review, 61:919-941.
LEVINSON, R. (1975). "Sex discrimination and employment practices: An experiment with unconventional job inquiries." Social Problems, 22:533-547.
LISS, L. (1975). "Affirmative action implications for worldwide family systems." Paper presented to Society for Study of Social Problems.
LOVING, N., and OLSON, L. (eds., 1976). National conference on women and crime. Washington, D.C.: National League of Cities.
MAINARDI, P. (1970). "The politics of housework." In Discrimination against women. Hearing before the Special Subcommittee on Education and Labor. Part 1. Washington, D.C.: U.S. Government Printing Office.
MANIS, J.G. (1976). Analyzing social problems. New York: Praeger.
MARTIN, D. (1976). Battered Wives. San Francisco: Glide Publishing.
MARX, G. (ed., 1971). Racial conflict: Tension and change in American society. Boston: Little, Brown.
MARX, K. (1956). Karl Marx: Selected writings in sociology and social philosophy. Ed. by T.B. Bottomore and M. Rubel. London: Atts.
MEDEA, A., and THOMPSON, K. (1974). Against rape. New York: Farrar, Straus and Giroux.
MEDNICK, M., TANGRI, S., and HOFFMAN, L. (1975). Women and achievement. New York: John Wiley.
MENKEN, J.A. (1972). "Teenage childbearing: Its medical aspects and implications for the United States population." Pp. 331-354 in C.F. Westoff and R. Parke, Jr., Demographic and social aspects of population growth. Commission on Population Growth and American Future Research Reports. Washington, D.C.: U.S. Government Printing Office.
MERTON, R.K. (1957). Social theory and social structure. New York: Free Press.
MILLETT, K. (1970). Sexual politics. New York: Doubleday.
MILLMAN, M. (1975). "She did it all for love: A feminist view of the sociology of deviance." Pp. 251-279 in M. Millman and R.M. Kanter (eds.), Another voice. New York: Anchor.
MINTON, R.J. (ed., 1971). Inside prison American style. New York: Vintage.
MITCHELL, J. (1971). Women's estate. New York: Pantheon.
MORGAN, R. (ed., 1970). Sisterhood is powerful. New York: Vintage.
NAGEL, S. (1972). "Double standard of American justice." Society, 9(March): 18-25, 62-63.
NUSS, S. (1976). "The position of women in industrialized socialist and capitalist countries." Paper presented to the American Sociological Association, New York, August.

OAKLEY, A. (1974). The sociology of housework. New York: Pantheon.

PACKER, H. (1968). The limits of the criminal sanction. Stanford: Stanford University Press.

PARK, R., and BURGESS, E. (1969). Introduction to the science of sociology (3rd ed.). Chicago: University of Chicago Press.

POLLAK, O. (1950). The criminality of women. Philadelphia: University of Pennsylvania Press.

QUINNEY, R. (1975). Criminology: Analysis and critique of crime in America. Boston: Little, Brown.

RASCHE, C. (1974). "The female offender as an object of criminological research." Criminal Justice and Behavior, 1(December):301-320.

RASMUSSEN, P., and KUHN, L. (1976). "The new masseuse." Urban Life, 5(October): 271-292.

RESKIN, B. (1976). "Sex differences in status attainment in science: The case of the postdoctoral fellowship." American Sociological Review, 41(August):597-612.

RICKEL, N. (1971). "The angry woman syndrome." Archives of General Psychiatry, 24.

ROCKWOOD, M. (1976). "Battered wives: Help for the victim next door." Ms, (August): 95.

ROSENBLATT, E., and GREENLAND, C. (1974). "Female crimes of violence." Canadian Journal of Criminology and Corrections, (April):173-180.

ROWBOTHAM, S. (1974). Women, resistance and revolution. New York: Random House.

SAGARIN, E. (1975). Deviants and deviance: An introduction to the study of disvalued people and behavior. New York: Praeger.

SCHEFF, T. (1966). Being mentally ill: A sociological theory. Chicago: Aldine.

SCHRUT, A., and MICHAELS, T. (1969). "Adolescent girls who attempt suicide–Comments on treatment." American Journal of Psychotherapy, 23:243-251.

SCHUR, E. (1965). Crimes without victims. Englewood Cliffs, N.J.: Prentice-Hall.

SIMON, R.J. (1975). The contemporary woman and crime. Rockville, Md.: National Institute of Mental Health, Center for Studies of Crime and Delinquency.

SIMON, W., and GAGNON, J. (1967). "The lesbians: A preliminary overview." In Gagnon and Simon (eds.), Sexual deviance. New York: Harper & Row.

SKOLNICK, J. (1966). Justice without trial. New York: John Wiley.

SMART, C. (1976). Women, crime and criminology: A feminist critique. Boston: Routledge & Kegan Paul.

SMITH, D.E. (1974). "Women's perspective as a radical critique of sociology." Sociological Inquiry, 44:7-13.

--- (1975). "An analysis of ideological structures and how women are excluded: Considerations for academic women." Canadian Review of Sociology and Anthropology, 12(November, part 1):353-369.

STOLL, C.S. (1974). Female and male. Dubuque, Iowa: Wm. C. Brown.

STONEQUIST, E. (1937). The marginal man. Chicago: University of Chicago Press.

SULLEROT, E. (1971). Woman, society and change. New York: McGraw-Hill.

Supreme Court Reporter (1972). Roe v. Wade. V. 93 410 (October):705-763.

SZASZ, T. (1960). "The myth of mental illness." American Psychologist, 15:113-118.

TRICE, H., and ROMAN, P. (1970). "Delabeling, relabeling and Alcoholics Anonymous." Social Problems, 17(spring):538-546.

WEISS, J., RAMIREZ, F., and TRACY, T. (1976). "Female participation in the occupational system: A comparative institutional analysis." Social Problems, 23(June):581-592.

WEISSMAN, M. (1972a). "The depressed woman and her rebellious adolescent." Social Casework, (November):563-570.

--- (1972b). "The depressed woman: Recent research." Social Work, 17(September): 19-25.

--- (1974). "The epidemiology of suicide attempts, 1960-1971." Archives of General

Psychiatry, 30(June):737-746.

WEISSMAN, M., and PAYKEL, E. (1972). Moving. Yale Alumni Magazine.

WESTOFF, C.F., et al. (1973). Toward the end of growth. Englewood Cliffs, N.J.: Prentice-Hall.

WHELLER, M. (1975). "The current status of women in prisons." Pp. 82-88 in A. Brodsky (ed.), The female offender. Beverly Hills, Calif.: Sage.

WILDEN, A. (1972). System and structure: Essays in communication and exchange. London: Tavistock.

WILENSKY, H., and LEBEAUX, C. (1965). Industrial society and social welfare. New York: Free Press.

WILKINS, L. (1965). Social deviance: Social policy, action, and research. Englewood Cliffs, N.J.: Prentice-Hall.

WINSLOW, R.W., and WINSLOW, V. (1974). Deviant reality. Boston: Allyn & Bacon.

WOLFF, K.H. (ed., 1971). From Karl Mannheim. New York: Oxford University Press.

Women's News (1976). The Oregonian. Portland, Oregon (December 31).

Yale Law Journal (1952). "Forcible and statutory rape: An exploration of the operation and objectives of the consent standard." V. 62(December).

ZINGRAFF, M. (1976). "The inmate subculture and adaptation patterns of incarcerated female delinquents." Paper presented to the Society for the Study of Social Problems, New York City, August.

10

DIRECTIONS IN THE STUDY OF DEVIANCE
A Bibliographic Essay, 1960-1977

FRED MONTANINO

The recent history of theoretical approaches to the study of deviant behavior is similar to that of other eras in at least one crucial respect, namely, the approaches reflect the shifting interests, polemical disputes, and continual search by scholars for a conceptual perspective that can account for forms and frequencies of social deviance. It is not surprising that among the major orientations (anomie, conflict, and labeling) there are proponents as well as opponents. The exchange of ideas and the constant flow of criticism has led to the refinement of existing perspectives, in such manner as to generate, if not new theories, then at least succeeding waves of interest and research in old ones.[1]

Whether it be new theory, regenerated interest in old, or some combination of both, in a very real sense this oscillation represents the valiant and often unsuccessful efforts of scholars intent on staving off the tyranny of ignorance, of misconception due to lack of accumulated knowledge, and of inappropriate and wasteful response due to misunderstanding the causes, processes and consequences of what has been variously described as aberrant, unconventional, nonnormative, socially rejected, hostility provoking, in short, deviant behavior.

The period from the early 1960s to

AUTHOR'S NOTE: *I wish to thank Professor Kai T. Erikson of Yale University and Professor Edward Sagarin of City College of New York for their many helpful suggestions in the preparation of this paper.*

the late 1970s has been enriched by sociologists united in their search for theoretical precepts for an understanding of social deviance. The differences among them are found in the particular approach that is deemed most fruitful; as Merton describes this:

> After all, what cognitive basis—not, mind you, social or psychological or political basis—what cognitive basis should there be for subscribing to a theoretical perspective, other than believing it to be at once more fruitful, more comprehensive, and more cogent than its rivals? [1976:110]

BACKGROUND OF THE SIXTIES

Both conflict and anomie precede labeling conceptions of misconduct. Conflict theory of crime and deviance can be traced to Louis Wirth (1931), among others. Wirth, a leading thinker in American sociology, pointed to the effect of migration on misconduct and contended that much of his findings need not be restricted to the immigrants and their families but extended to other families and communities as well. Communities, for example, of heterogeneous groupings, weak family ties, and vanishing neighborhood patterns where people live under "loose, transient and impersonal relations," had high rates of misconduct. A few years later, Thorsten Sellin (1938), developed conflict quite differently from the classic Marxist approach, picked up on the work of Wirth and concentrated on how people with different backgrounds (in a society of immigrants, particularly) came together with different norms and committed crimes or deviant acts because what they were doing was normative for them, although not for the social group into which they were catapulted. Wars, slavery, migration (voluntary and involuntary), escape from undesirable political conditions and the like have caused people of different lineages, physical characteristics, and even languages, as well as with dissimilar religious beliefs and practices, to become residents of a single country sharing life as neighbors. Ease of travel, urbanization and industrialization, in addition, have resulted in greater intermingling of such people with one another, whereas previously, in a more agrarian setting, there was little such contact. For Sellin, the myriad of groups brought to a new land varied conceptions of what was right, decent, normative. What was accepted in one group was criminal or deviant in the eyes of another, or in America in the dominant (at the time) Anglo-American culture.

Added to Wirth's and Sellin's work on conflict, Merton's (1938) on anomie exerted early and potent influence upon the academic community, changing the focus from psychological pathology and biological determinism concerning the etiology of deviance, to one in which social structural and sociocultural considerations are stressed. Gibbs (1966) described this (especially with the work of Sellin, and his remarks can be extended for Wirth and Merton) as a shift in interest from the deviant actor and a generation of interest in the acts that are committed, their effects within the wider social milieu, and vice versa (the effect of the milieu on the act). Yet more generally this can be viewed as a shift in interest from the deviant actors not to the acts so much as to the social structure in which the acts are nurtured.

This similarity should not serve to distort the fact that there are major differences in the anomie and conflict perspectives, not the least of which is the respective posture taken toward norms. Anomie involves a distinctly more universalistic view of norms than does conflict; conflict theorists are oriented around the position that the norms are rather relativistic and at times arbitrary. Nonetheless, in the development of these two lines of thought, anomie and conflict, there are those who have come to see overlap, Merton (1976) among them. Sagarin (1975) claims that there is conflict in anomie theory, at least with regard to opportunity, a view in many ways supported by the work of Cloward and Ohlin (1960).

Anomie and culture conflict were major thrusts in deviance theory previous to the 1960s, but were not alone. A more generalized conflict theory than that advanced by Wirth and Sellin was put forth by Vold (1958), and criminology was debating differential association (Sutherland and Cressey, 1966). In sum, deviance theory was having its fashions and fads, a multitude of approaches, many perspectives.

LABELING

As a result of scholarly activity flourishing in the early 1960s, there was developed a major new perspective, labeling. Otherwise known as the societal reaction or interactionist approach, labeling highlights the thought that deviance develops out of an interactive process between the actor and the audience (those who react to him). Related to anomie and conflict in its stand in opposition to individual pathology and biological determinism, labeling rejects the major emphasis on the act and the actor in favor of a study of the reaction thereto.

This major thrust, which brought great stimulation and excitement in the early 60s in the area of deviance, has roots which can be traced back further in time. Although some argue that his full work *Crime and the Community* is rather conflict oriented, seeds of labeling can be found in Tannenbaum (1938) who at the time enunciated the concept which he called "tagging." Even earlier W.I. Thomas (1923) hinted at the labeling approach with his statement, "If men define situations as real, they are real in their consequences." In Merton's famous essay on the self-fulfilling prophecy (1948), there are common threads of both conflict and labeling. Merton pointed out that people who are defined as uneducable then fulfill this definition; although he was using as examples race and ethnicity, he was by implication also pinpointing that these definitions were made by the power groups against the powerless ones in a conflict situation. Edwin Lemert's (1951) work *Social Pathology,* which appeared a full decade before the flowering of interest in labeling, is revered by many as marking the birth of the labeling perspective. Lemert tells us that there is nothing that is evil in and of itself; that there are people that deviate from the "rules" of a society. However, this is not deviance but deviation. Deviance is an interactive process which is twofold: first, deviators are labeled and once they are labeled they develop fears, paranoia, poor self-image, and mental anguish all of which lead to a secondary form of deviation.

What Kitsuse (1972) calls the "germ" or general idea of labeling had thus emerged early but remained, awaiting cultivation. The major cultivators of labeling in the early 1960s (Becker, 1963; Kitsuse, 1962; Kitsuse and Cicourel, 1963; Erikson, 1962, 1966; Schur, 1965; Scheff, 1966) nurtured this perspective, often working almost in seclusion, with little contact among each other. Some of the major tenets of their work revolved around the propositions that actions derive their connotations of "badness" through a process of definition by law-abiders and rule-makers; that emphasis should be placed upon the processes in society whereby some people gain the power to define others as deviant; that placing a deviant label and reacting negatively to those so labeled often involves the matter of who is the transgressor rather than the nature of the particular transgression itself; that labeling a person deviant results in secondary deviation, which can be more damaging to the individual and society than the original transgression; that the labeling process "fixes" an individual in that status; and the exclusion of the labeled from the activity and life of normals or locking those that are stigmatized into categories facilitates the development of deviant careers.

Starting with Gibbs (1966), continuing with Bordua (1967) and Gouldner (1968), the labeling perspective began to become the object of opposition. Attacks resulted in three major events: (1) a general reply by Becker (1971) to his critics, presented to the British Sociological Society; (2) a short book by Edwin Schur (1971) defending labeling against every charge; and (3) a conference called by Gove, which was ostensibly for the purpose of examining labeling, culminating in a volume containing a myriad of criticisms, together with replies by Kitsuse and Schur (see Gove, 1975a).

Problems of Assessment

As one becomes immersed in the critical literature (pro and con) that has been generated over this new perspective in the last few years, it is discovered that the ranks of those that accept as well as query have progressively swelled. It is in itself not unusual that any major perspective experiences this sort of contradictory growth pursuant to the initial statement of its propositions; but, in the case of the interactionist perspective, one must approach an assessment of this period with extra caution. Unlike the role that Merton played in anomie, in the case of labeling there were a number of spokesmen that were involved in the initial formulations. Among them, one is hardpressed to find general agreement.[2] This dissension among the labeling people created corresponding dissension among the critics as to what were the universal propositions espoused by labelists which could be considered inaccurate and vulnerable. If one were to identify the bottom line around which critics of the perspective evolve, it is found that most are expressing the difficulty they have in "fitting" the perspective into their approach to the field.

There are several factors that one should keep in mind in assessing the proliferation of objections to labeling.

First, there is the question of "timing." Both initial and important statements concerning labeling evolved over a relatively broad period, and the critics reflect the labeling literature at the time that they were writing. For example, Gibbs (1966) involves himself with the work of Becker (1963), Kitsuse (1962), Kitsuse and Cicourel (1963), and Erikson (1962), while critical analysis of the work of Scheff (1966) is necessarily absent. Writing one year later, Bordua (1967), in addition to reviewing several of the works cited by Gibbs, also includes the later studies of Erikson (1966) and Scheff (1966) in his general critical analysis. For unavoidable reasons, the nature of the criticisms changed as new type of expressions favorable to labeling appeared.[3]

Second, it can be demonstrated that opponents of the perspective tend to be selective as to just who they will or will not include in their critical assessments. Bordua sees fit to include the work of Lemert (1951) in his analysis because he perceives Lemert's work to be especially embraced by labelists, evidenced by what he describes as the expression of "gratitude" by labelists to Lemert (Bordua, 1967:150):

> Nevertheless, it seems appropriate to cite the work of Edwin Lemert as especially relevant in inspiring more recent developments. This is especially the case as the more recent writers constitute themselves as something of a "school" and acknowledge greater or lesser debt to Lemert.[4]

Reference to Lemert, as well as this particular interpretation of labelists, is absent in the work of Gibbs (1966). Gouldner (1968), on the other hand, in a critique that can be more properly viewed as an attack on Becker, leans heavily in his criticism of the perspective on a still later work by Becker (1967).

Third, various critics of the labeling perspective tend to exhibit great discretion in identifying and analyzing the pitfalls of labeling; that is, each will zero in on those propositions and implications considered especially crucial or vulnerable. Bordua (1967) tells us that the perspective is oriented to the left, tilted too much in favor of the "underdog"; that it places in a dim light, all too consistently, agencies and agents of social control and does not entertain their inherent virtues, such as the deterrence effect. Conversely, Gouldner (1968) contends that labeling is not left enough or, what is worse, only "pseudo-left," not concerned with those fighting back in an oppressive system but with those "on their backs." He argues that labeling adherents fail to identify those in relatively high positions responsible for the miseries of the underdog, but seek to cast light away from them by examining "pawns," those that are merely in intermediate positions in the hierarchy of power.

Consensus and Other Critics

Similarly, steady and growing concern over what is perceived to be labeling's lack of consideration to the etiology of deviant behavior has enjoyed consistent, critical popularity. Gibbs (1966:12) states:

> . . . the three men [Becker, Erikson, Kitsuse] have not specified their goal adequately, i.e., whether they are seeking an explanation of deviant behavior or of reaction to it.

Bordua (1967:153) expresses this same concern in yet another manner:

> . . . it [labeling theory] assumes an essentially empty organism or at least one with little or no autonomous capacity to determine conduct. The process of developing deviance seems to be all societal response and no deviant stimulus.

To these early critics, one can add Akers (1968), who remarks that the label does not create deviance in the first place.[5]

There are those (Cameron, 1964; Mankoff, 1971) that carry this query further and contend that the label does not necessarily lead to career deviance (secondary deviation in the extreme). The questions of ideology (Liazos, 1972; Thio, 1973), etiology (Hagan, 1973a, 1973b;[6] Hirschi, 1973), individual responsibility, and the entrenchment of individuals in deviant careers (Gove, 1970) crop up over and over again (more recently in Gove, 1975; Sagarin, 1975; and Montanino and Sagarin, 1977). Many writers have sought to demonstrate that labeling tenets are not as potent explanations for some as against other substantive forms of deviance.

In reading the literature that has been generated by proponents of the labeling perspective, a wide, but unfortunately far from exhaustive, array of deviant activities and statuses are encountered. Lemert (1951, 1967) deals, for example, with communism, prostitution, paranoia, and stuttering. Becker (1963) concerns himself mainly with marijuana users and jazz musicians. Matza (1964, 1969) was enmeshed in studies of juvenile delinquency as well as marijuana users, while Kitsuse's (1962) early major work dealt with homosexuality. Schur (1965) considered what he called "victimless crimes," such as abortion, homosexuality, and drug use. Scheff (1966) dealt specifically with those that come to be labeled mentally ill, and Scott (1969) with those who are declared "legally blind" although not totally sightless. Erikson (1966) identified what he designated "crime waves" which involved mainly heretics and suspected witches. Combined with what can be perceived as the high priority that labelists place on generating conceptual insight into the processes and consequences of the act of labeling, these types of study of deviance resulted (at least in the eyes of the critics) in the relegation of the substantive form of deviance that is investigated to practical obscurity. Mankoff (1971) points this out in asserting that labelists have paid little attention to developing categorizations of substantive areas of deviance for which their work may apply (and to what degree). Ergo, substantive forms of deviance which labelists have not addressed or directly accounted for (i.e., serious crime, white-collar crime, rape, robbery, etc.) become important and seemingly useful avenues of study for those seeking to advance criticism. This is not to say that the areas that have been studied remain sacrosanct or unassailable. Hindelang (1970, 1974) and Giordano (1976) have challenged Matza's notions of delinquency and drift. Foster, Dinitz and Reckless (1972), more generally concerned with delinquency and the effect of the label or stigma of identification, have expressed similar criticism.

In the application of labeling to mental illness, controversy has raged. While Bord (1971) has had rather ambivalent feelings, Wenger and Fletcher (1969) have demonstrated a positive effect on noncommitment via the participation of defense lawyers in civil commitment hearings, thus buttressing the moral entrepreneur stance of the labeling perspective. On the other hand, Gove and his colleagues have consistently taken a critical stand on the application of the labeling perspective to mental illness that has been put forward by Scheff (1964, 1966, 1967, 1974). Along this line, Gove and Lubach (1969) describe the successful treatment of those involved in psychiatric institutionalization (see also Gove, 1970a, 1970b, 1975a; Gove and Howell, 1974). A summary of this running controversy is provided in an exchange of comments between Gove (1975b) and Scheff (1975).

Response: Defense, Clarification and Expansion

Induced by criticisms and controversies and the sheer excitement with which its initial statements injected the field of deviance, labeling has undergone defense, modification, clarification and in many respects expansion (Becker, 1971; Schur, 1969, 1971, 1974; Scheff, 1974, 1975; Kitsuse, 1972, 1975; Freidson, 1965; Lorber, 1967; Bustamante, 1972; Rotenberg, 1974; Trice and Roman, 1970; Marshall and Purdy, 1972; Lemert, 1967, 1974; Gusfield, 1967; Connor, 1972a, 1972b; Currie, 1968; Cohen, 1965, 1966, 1968, 1974; Lauderdale, 1976; McIntosh, 1968; Weinberg, 1965; Williams and Weinberg, 1970; Harris, 1975; Turner, 1972; Katz, 1972; Blakenship and Singh, 1976; and so the list could continue). [7]

In some instances such works are an attempt to empirically operationalize certain central tenets of the perspective and thereby test them, others are an extension of labeling thought to the study of various forms of substantive deviance that had been perceived as neglected or especially fertile for application, still others are an attempt to modify, interpret, clarify or otherwise add to various existing (and those perceived as neglected or unnoticed) conceptual implications that have been generated within the framework of the perspective. Finally, in such modifications and reinterpretations, there are those who, like Lemert (1974), appear to be expressing serious thoughts and misgivings over a perspective that they had once wholeheartedly embraced.

Criticism has provoked defense and reply. In examining the defense of labeling by Becker (1971), Kitsuse (1972), and Schur (1971, 1974), one discovers a uniform and not unanticipated quality. The noted defenders tend to proceed along the lines of interpreting, modifying, and clarifying positions that have been taken by proponents, thus speaking not only for themselves in a particular instance but for their colleagues as well; in essence, they seek to present a "united front." There is much overlap in the separate defenses (dealing with the questions of etiology, empirical operationalization and the like), with marked tendency to restate and stress what is perceived to be the major emphases of the perspective, especially those which the defenders perceive to have been grossly misunderstood.

Becker (1971) responds to, among others, the criticisms of Akers (1968), Bordua (1967), Gibbs (1966), Gouldner (1968), Gove (1970a), and Mankoff (1968, 1970). He expresses dissatisfaction with the term "labeling theory" and contends that this put the perspective in the position of being criticized for what it is not. Thus, on the question of etiology, critics drew the implication that the perspective was seeking to explain deviance by responses others made to it. Contending that this is not the case, and seeking to speak for those proponents involved in the presentation, Becker (1971:179) states:

> The original proponents of the position, however, did not propose solutions to the aetiological question. They had more modest aims. They wanted to enlarge the area taken into consideration in the study of deviant phenomena by including in it activities of others than the allegedly deviant actor.

To those queries that centered around the concept of secondary deviation and the career entrenchment of individuals in deviant modes of behavior, Becker (1971:180) responds:

> To suggest that defining someone as deviant may under certain circumstances dispose him to a particular line of action is not the same as saying that mental hospitals always drive people crazy or that jails always turn people into habitual criminals.

It is emphasized by Becker (1971:183) that the labeling perspective involves the study of "collective action," and that to "look at all the people involved in any episode of alleged deviance . . . we discover that these activities require the overt and tacit cooperation of many people and groups to occur as they do." It is in this vein that Becker employs the phrase "the interactionist perspective," one he contends more succinctly conveys the labelist stance. Turning his sights on the various levels of ideological attacks (from the left and right) that labeling has come under, he asserts that the interactionist perspective is indeed radical, proof of which is the fact that it has come under attack by "conventional authorities," and that although the perspective does not directly attack the elites of society per se, an attack on the labels that they propagate and on their labeling process is in essence an attack on them.[8]

Becker's defense is lucid, eloquent, logical, and extremely persuasive. It has at once clarified the roots of the perspective and served to narrow the focus of its attention. At the same time, Becker expands the scope of the perspective, with which he is so intimately associated, to include studies of small group and face-to-face interaction (Goffman, 1963), ethnomethodology (Garfinkel, 1956, 1967) or "the drama of moral rhetoric," and symbolic interactionism (Blumer, 1966, 1969). Yet it might occur to the reader that Becker is in many ways exhibiting that which he seeks to study. His identification and avid insistence on the study of moral entrepreneurs can itself be interpreted as a form of labeling; all of which leads one to wonder whether labeling is especially useful and unique to the study of deviance or is more broadly a chronic problem that is invoked with all endeavors wherein man seeks to define, categorize, explain, or communicate.

In an important statement, Kitsuse (1972) traces the roots of labeling to G.H. Mead, and expresses the sentiment that labeling tenets have been misused and misunderstood. He identifies the problem of misuse via the misinterpretation of Becker (1963) and Lemert (1951); then proceeds to review the major tenets of the work of Becker and Lemert, providing for the reader the pitfalls that lead to misunderstanding that are inherent in some of their seminal propositions. Taking to task Bordua (1967) and Gibbs (1966), Kitsuse approaches the question of etiology, this time from the standpoint of norms, by asserting (1972:236) that Lemert (1951) "does not consider the question of etiology a productive line of investigation." Becker, too, it is claimed, is misinterpreted on the question of etiology; Kitsuse (1972:237) states, "Deviance is not a quality of an act, but is the rule that assigns the quality of deviance to the act." What then is the common element among labelists? According to Kitsuse (1972:238), it "is that social norms are problematic as they are invoked by members of the community to identify, define, judge, and treat the persons as deviant."

Why the emphasis on norms? The original criticism, as stated by Gibbs (1966), was that labeling advocates "recognize the norm conception of deviation," which he claims "they do not consistently reject." The point is then made that advocates (Becker, Kitsuse, and Erikson) do not come "to grips" with the problem and do not take a consistent stand. Kitsuse (1975) faces this issue once again, the major thrust of his argument addressing the Mertonian "norm" conception of deviation. In anomie and conflict approaches, Kitsuse contends, the sociologist is put in the position of determining with certainty just what the norm is; such a position fails to treat the norm as problematic, and it leaves the sociologist open to the pitfall of misconstruing what really is or is not a norm.

Kitsuse (1972:241) offers the following conceptions as the major lines of inquiry of the interactionist perspective: (1) the concept of "secondary deviation" and (2) the process of "social differentiation of deviants per se . . .," whereby "persons, groups, and institutions are made different through social interaction." The latter, it is contended, is the more neglected aspect of Lemert's (1951) conception of deviance. Turning his attention to the empirical operationalization of labeling tenets, Kitsuse (1972:242) asserts that the investigation of the interaction process provides not only a theoretical but empirical link for the study of secondary deviation and social control from which can be studied "various categories of deviance as it is reflected in data generated by census and other social agencies," a sentiment which is dealt with in more detail in an earlier work (Kitsuse and Cicourel, 1963).[9]

Of the defenders of labeling, Schur (1969, 1971, 1974, 1975) has been among the most active. Although at times he is seemingly engaged in a great peace mission among scholars in conflict with one another and with himself, his work nevertheless bristles with examples of the fine art of qualitative discourse.[10] In his synthesis of labeling with other major perspectives, Schur (1971) parades before the reader many of the leading thinkers and exponents in the field of deviance, not only the labeling persons but others as well: Becker (1963), Lemert (1951, 1967), Blumer (1969), Cohen (1965), Tannenbaum (1938), Erikson (1962), Matza (1964), Garfinkel (1956, 1967), Kitsuse (1962), Kitsuse and Cicourel (1963), Scheff (1966), Goffman (1961, 1963), Scott (1969), Simmons (1969), Denzin (1969), Schwartz and Skolnick (1962), Skolnick (1965) and one can guess the rest. Thus he expands labeling to embrace many closely and some tenuously related perspectives. Labeling deviance is a process, it is part of a fluid interaction, the perspective itself is totally complementary and is useful to all and any approaching the study of deviant behavior. The roots of the theoretical development of labeling can be traced back to a myriad of social scientific and sociological perspectives. What holds these various outlooks together is the centrality of the concept of interaction.

Among the many assets of Schur's work are the discussions of role engulfment and retrospective interpretation. But perhaps of overriding interest is Schur's (1971:24) rather expanded definition of deviant behavior, something rarely advanced by many of labeling's proponents:

> Human behavior is deviant to the extent that it comes to be viewed as involving a personally discreditable departure from a group's normative expectations, and it elicits interpersonal or collective reactions that serve to "isolate," "treat," "correct," or "punish" individuals engaged in such behavior.

Participant Observation and Ethnographies

Perhaps the locus of consensus that may be found among the defenders is the usefulness of participant observation as a methodological tool which facilitates the study of deviant behavior. Becker (1971:193) states, "The connection between an interactionist theory of deviance and a reliance on intensive field observation as a major method of data gathering can hardly be accidental." Kitsuse (1972:238) tells us that participant observation is essential to a "problematic" approach to norms in the study of deviant behavior:

> The focus and emphasis on the practiced and enforced rules of conduct as they are revealed in interaction rather than on abstract sociological formulations of "normative behavior" is characteristically reflected in the participant observational method of interactionist approach to deviance.

Speaking of the methodological approach of the labeling perspective, Schur (1971:31) writes:

> . . . there is renewed interest among American sociologists in the use of participant observation and related techniques. Such techniques are particularly appropriate to efforts at capturing and depicting the nature and impact of the social processes on which the labeling approach to deviance focuses.

In Schur's view, participant observation within the labeling perspective represents "renewed appreciation and use of some basic sociological methods."

Participant observation has been widely associated with ethnographies, which have a long tradition in anthropology. Anthropologists discussing their studies of primitive peoples described their findings as "ethnographic detail." In retrospect, it is clear that what American sociologists were doing, particularly in Chicago, was somewhat akin to what anthropologists were doing in foreign lands.

The labeling perspective gave a great spurt to participant observation, because there was a conscious effort to take the side of the underdog, and to present the world as the underdog lives and sees it. However, the major emphasis of labeling was not on ethnographic detail (although certainly one can detect much of this), or on writing ethnographies; it was on showing the effect of hostile social reaction on the deviant (secondary deviation). Nevertheless, the descriptions of dance musicians and marijuana users by Becker (1963), and of others in the collection presented by Becker (1964), can for the most part be accurately described as ethnographies.

However, participant observation is not a sine qua non for researchers utilizing an interactionist stance. Erikson (1966), for example, relies heavily on historical sociological reconstruction. Further, he points out (Erikson, 1967) that if participant observation is used in conjunction with disguise, it has many methodological and ethical pitfalls.

There are those of the labeling perspective that have produced ethnographies, and there are ethnographies that are divested of such a perspective. Looking back, one can see some excellent ethnographies from this period: works that were not analytic descriptions of deviants, that did not concentrate on the effects of labeling, but that described the world, how it looked to its inhabitants, and how they survived. Donald Ball's (1967) description of an illegal abortion clinic is such a study, and the fact that he entitled it an ethnography only highlighted this fact. Some of the community studies were ethnographies, and in a sense of deviants: in fact *Tally's Corner* (Liebow, 1967), interestingly enough, was the work of a man more trained in anthropology than sociology. Ethnomethodology, ill-defined as it is, cultist as many claim, nonetheless was incorporated and embraced by many labelists.

Of ethnographies in general (and this holds for those produced within a labeling perspective), they sometimes seem merely descriptive, not profoundly intuitive; sometimes the outsider gets a snow job from those within. But other ethnographies are undoubtedly profound, offering insights that cannot be obtained by interviews. There are works which are totally ethnographic, such as a study of a chiropractic clinic by Cowie and Roebuck (1975). Douglas (1976) has written a guide for the researcher who is doing ethnographic study. Several anthologies contain ethnographic pieces or ones which are at least laden with ethnographic detail: Douglas (1970, 1972), Jacobs (1972, 1974).

THE RESURGENCE OF CONFLICT THEORY

One of the most significant recent trends in deviance theory is the tremendous amount of interest and work on conflict. The new interest in conflict is a resurgence of an old interest. It seems that after the decade of the sixties had come and gone, sociologists no longer harbored illusions as to whether there were major conflicting forces, locked in struggle, in American society. On the one hand, conflict is an outgrowth of labeling, and on the other it gives home to those who feel that labeling has lost its enchantment. It appears to offer an answer to at least one important criticism directed at labeling, that the latter can account only for victimless deviance, not for serious crimes against persons and property.

The interest in conflict should come as little surprise, for if one were to trace the development of conflict and labeling back in time, it is found that they have not been entirely separate. Aside from Marx on the macrosocial level, conflict theory derives in sociology from Simmel, and into American sociology through those greatly influenced by Simmel, namely, Wirth (1931), Coser (1956), and more recently Goffman (1961, 1963). It is not by accident that these thinkers figure prominently in Schur's (1971) defense of labeling.

Conflict theory had been a major thrust in criminology and to a lesser extent in deviance a number of decades ago. Outstanding examples are Wirth and Sellin (mentioned earlier), and in Europe the Dutch socialist criminologist, Bonger (1936). Probably the major theoretical work in criminology (Vold, 1958), while summarizing many thrusts, was particularly conflict oriented. Yet conflict started to recede under the impact of the interest first in anomie, then in labeling, although each of these orientations, in different ways, were continuations of conflict.

Going back to Tannenbaum's (1938) work, while there is much in it that has been misrepresented and misunderstood (Hirschi points this out in his essay in the Gove anthology, 1975b), Tannenbaum did present both labeling and conflict orientations. It seems, however, that he did not intermingle them, did not really combine them, but used them as separate strands in his discussion of crime and delinquency.

Lemert has undoubtedly had a strong input into conflict theory. His early labeling work *Social Pathology* (1951), was not highly conflict-oriented, but his critique of anomie theory was very much so (Lemert, 1964). From the time that Becker's influence started to be felt in labeling, there was an underlying conflict theme. After all, Becker suggested that deviance was the label put upon people by those who had the power to do so; hence there was a struggle between the powerful and the powerless. Lofland (1969) works this out still more, although somewhat obscurely, in his book, *Deviance and Identity.*

For more recent evidence of the upsurge of conflict theory, one need only refer to an entire book devoted to the subject by Denisoff and McCaghy (1973); and an important essay by Lemert (1974) delivered as a presidential address to the Society for the Study of Social Problems, wherein he actually expressed tremendous leanings towards conflict and came close to repudiating at least some of the thrusts of labeling. Lemert (1964) had earlier expressed a desire to go beyond Mead, with his piece in the collection on anomie. Works by Spitzer, appearing in *Social Problems* (1975) and *Criminology* (1976), placed emphasis on conflict. Spitzer particularly, more than others, specifically applied a Marxist perspective for the understanding not of crime, as had been done before, but deviance. Quinney (1974) and Turk (1969) placed crime in a conflict perspective, as did Danzger (1975) and Chiricos and Waldo (1975). In a sociological text, Collins (1975) deals not only with deviance and crime but a myriad of social constellations from a conflict perspective. Sagarin and McCord (1976) stress conflict theory and its relationship to social problems (including crime and deviance). Earlier, there was emphasis on and modification of conflict in Sagarin's (1975) deviance text. An anthology by Reasons (1974), dealing with crime and the criminal, contains many authors who embrace the conflict perspective. And so one could continue, for these are but a few of the many examples one may find among the recent literature.

SOCIAL CONTROL

Additionally, one may identify a steady and growing interest in social control and formal legal processing in recent years, itself, not unexpectedly, an intertwined and concomitant theme of labeling. In his influential work, *Outsiders*, Becker (1963) identified moral entrepreneurs as those persons in a society who take it upon themselves to develop a campaign to arouse public indignation against others on whom they seek to place the label of deviant. Although the thrust of Becker and others was against the moral entrepreneurs, such as crusaders against marijuana, earlier the Prohibitionists, and one can include the Legion of Decency and other anti-pornography groups, it had the effect of generating great interest in the study of the activities of law enforcement officials, and their alleged role in the amplification of deviance. Rafsky (1973), Hartjen (1972), Trojanowicz (1971), Sykes and Clark (1975), Block (1974), and Balch (1972) are all examples of the study of police from an interactional perspective. Rafsky (1973) deals specifically with labeling, while others focus on the behavior of police and citizens in the course of everyday interaction, or in dealing with social-psychological, personality and occupational contingencies of police in their work. Black (1971, 1972) investigated the process of arrest, and has also explored the limitations, possibilities, and promise of sociological investigation of legal processes. Cartwright and Schwartz (1973) explored the implementation of legal norms, while Hawkes (1975) produced an empirical and highly mathematical investigation of the relationship between norms, deviance, and social control, wherein the amount of deviance is correlated with the degree of regulation. Janowitz (1975) looked into the origins of social control, its classical definition as the ability of a social group to regulate itself, and has noted some redefinition of the term over time to encompass "socialization or social repression."

An in-depth study of daily police occupational routine, how the police approach their work, handle themselves in their relations with the community, align themselves within the occupation, assume the role of "professional," and dispatch the discretionary powers they find themselves vested with, has been produced by Reiss (1971). The juvenile/police relationship from the broad perspective of social control has been specifically examined by Black and Reiss (1970). Conger (1976) has explored social control and learning models of delinquency and delinquent behavior, concluding that "a combination of social bonding notion from control theory along with specific principles of social learning lay the groundwork for a more comprehensive theory than either perspective alone." Viewing the repercussions on those that come into contact with legal processes, Galanter (1974) examines the possibility of meaningful change from the viewpoint of the "haves and have nots." Hagan (1974) has been among those who have viewed the process of criminal sentencing, always a popular area of research in social control, assessing it for the reader from a sociological viewpoint. In a more recent work, *The Behavior of Law,* Black (1976) provides what is probably the most ambitious and perhaps encompassing theoretical application of social control to the understanding of crime, deviance and the operation of law in modern society. Law itself is social control and varies inversely with other forms of social control. It is predictive and explanatory and is divorced of considerations of the individual actor. Continuing, Black writes (1976:10):

> Like the theory of law, moreover, the theory of every kind of social control predicts deviant behavior. Deviant behavior is, by definition, an aspect of the behavior of social control.

Although rather an aside in the book, Black argues that the theory of law (which is of more central concern) predicts, explains, and accounts for deviant behavior which had previously been approached and accounted for via theories of *deprivation,* advanced by Merton, Cloward and Ohlin, Short, and Cohen (Black, 1976:30-31); theories of *marginality,* advanced by Durkheim, Hirschi, and others (1976:54-55); *subcultural conformity,* advanced by Sutherland and Cressey, Miller and Feldman (1976:79-80); and, of course, *labeling,* advanced by Tannenbaum, Lemert, Schur, Matza, and Lofland (1976:117-118).

PROLIFERATION: ANTHOLOGIES, READERS AND TEXTS[11]

To the extent that the orientations found in readers and anthologies reflect the continuing interests of scholars in the field of deviance, the labeling perspective has fared well in America and both in Canada and England.

I would say that the interest in anthologies produced its first important book with Becker (1964), and of course the labeling orientation was paramount in most but not all of the pieces. Later, Rubington and Weinberg (1968) produced a reader entitled *Deviance: The Interactionist Perspective.* Interactionism is here a fancy name for labeling, it is in essence Becker's anthology expanded and organized, with an occasional relapse into another orientation. Rushing (1975) gave us a rather large anthology; encountered in it are well-known names, frequently reprinted articles, as well as less known material. With an exception here and there (i.e., an article by Bordua), this collection is similarly infused with a labeling perspective. A collection containing the works of Erikson, Schur, Gusfield, Sudnow, and others whose names are not too hard to guess, has been produced by Rainwater (1974). Another reader with an overwhelming labeling orientation, except for the critique by Gibbs, is that of Filstead (1972). Appearing in the Filstead reader is the major defense of labeling by Kitsuse that has been dealt with earlier in this work. Similarly occupied with labeling, critiques of it, or attempts to go beyond or examine more broadly the collective and interactional elements inherent in it, are works by Davis and Stivers (1975),

Scarpitti and McFarlane (1975), Scott and Douglas (1972), and Dinitz, Dynes, and Clarke (1975). Nevertheless, Scarpitti and McFarlane conceive of positive and negative deviance, which would never be acceptable to Becker or Kitsuse, and Dinitz and his colleagues go into the management and containment of deviance, likewise a departure from a traditional labeling perspective.

Judging from the Canadian readers (Boydell, Grindstaff, and Whitehead, 1972; Haas and Shaffir, 1974; Mann, 1968), the neighbors to the north have embraced the societal reaction stance—Boydell, Grindstaff, and Whitehead—in a massive anthology, with 42 articles. The editors draw heavily on Lemert, Becker, and Schur, seeking to utilize their insights for application to the Canadian experience. Haas and Shaffir offer a smaller anthology, not restricted to the Canadian experience, likewise with a labeling orientation, with the introductory readings coming from Lemert, Becker, Kitsuse, Matza, and Schur. Deviance is here ubiquitous, and the researcher should focus on those who are in a position in society to define it and bring it to the attention of the public. Although these Canadian readers veer toward labeling, they do so in degrees; Haas and Shaffir appear more orthodox, rigid and even intolerant of opposing views.

The British, too, have embraced the labeling perspective; their collections are filled with work written under the influence of Becker, Lemert, Sykes, and Matza, they are somewhat more radical, with a good deal of rhetoric, and all largely influenced by Gouldner. The bulk of the works appearing in British anthologies (Taylor and Taylor, 1973; S. Cohen, 1971; Cohen and Young, 1973; Rock and McIntosh, 1974) are drawn from various symposia held under the auspices of the National Deviancy Conference, that for several years served as the focal point of activity for the unrest of young British sociologists, particularly those interested in crime, delinquency, and related areas. In these works there is healthy skepticism of the power centers both in society and in sociology, a desire to go beyond Becker, a concern with the realities of social class and class conflict, and a recurrent theme analogous to what Schur (1973) has been saying in America: that there are some types of deviance which might best be handled by less social control, or by purposive and radical nonintervention.

One cannot close this section without a discussion of Gove's (1975a) anthology, *The Labelling of Deviant Behavior,* to which reference has been made before. The emphasis Gove sought was on empirical work that would validate or disconfirm (preferably the latter) labeling perspectives, but some of the labeling adherents claim that precisely because it is not a theory but an orientation or an emphasis, it need not be subject to empirical testing.

A problem with labeling, alluded to earlier, is that it consists of the writings of a group of people who have some points of agreement and many of disagreement with one another. Thus it is unlike anomie, where Merton's work is the standard, to be tested, praised, or damned; or unlike differential association where the statements of Sutherland (and later modifications by Cressey) are there for critical examination. It is a strength of labeling that it involves a large number of independent scholars, each speaking only for one person; but it is difficult to refute an argument, only to be told by the most avid of labelists that he agrees with the refutation. To handle this, several of the writers in the Gove work (1975a) first express what it is in that perspective that they understand to be central to it, and then they proceed to criticize it. With Tittle on crime, one can say that labeling was just never meant to apply to ordinary crime, but to victimless crimes and noncriminal deviance; with Sagarin and Kelly on sex, one can note that the conclusions are equivocal, even if more antilabeling than pro. The reader may find it difficult to see how labeling theory can avoid severe and convincing criticisms leveled at it by those who have examined substantive areas of deviance that it had previously ignored. Robins's work on alcoholism is such an example. Powerful arguments against labeling are presented by Gove on mental illness, Hirschi on delinquency, and Gordon on retardation, among others, followed by rejoinders by Kitsuse and Schur.

As the list of readers here encountered may indicate, there has been a spread of international interest in the field of deviance. In England, the National Deviancy Conference for a number of years served as a forum for sociologists to present their views and the results of their studies. Later, an international section of deviance was established by the International Sociological Association, with representatives from about a dozen countries on an international executive board (with James Hackler of Canada as the leading activist). Florence, Italy, appears to have taken the lead in becoming a center of deviance studies in Europe, with the emphasis on left-wing orientations. Most recently, an international conference, under the International Sociological Association, was held in Japan, but the papers from the meeting were not available as of the time that this is being written. However, an examination of the program disclosed that presentations had been made by scholars from Australia, Canada, Germany, Hong Kong, India, Japan, Kuwait, Nigeria, and the United States. Discussions centered around such themes as the politics of social control, reactions to deviance, psycholinguistics, as well as substantive areas, as homicide, alcoholism, and prostitution. The theme of the conference was expressed in the title, "Cross-cultural Aspects of Deviance and Social Control."[12]

The texts on deviance (rather than collections and readers) until recently were few in number. Clinard (1974) dominated the field, from the time that the first edition of the book appeared in 1957. Lemert (1951) could not be considered a text in the traditional sense of the word, and Lemert (1967) was a collection of his significant essays. Becker (1963) was undoubtedly used as a text, although it is not a systematic presentation of the accumulated knowledge in the field, but rather an argument for a particular point of view. All this has rapidly changed. Brief texts have been written by Glaser (1971), Simmons (1969), and Edgerton (1976), the last in a somewhat anthropological perspective. Akers (1973) produced a text which was infused with a single perspective, namely learning theory. There is a brief overall study by A.K. Cohen (1966), and slightly more elaborate books by Davis (1975), Rock (1973), Gibbons and Jones (1975), and Hawkins and Tiedeman (1975); a "once over lightly" review of the field by Bell (1971); a rather lengthy and comprehensive text by Sagarin (1975); a combination of text and readings by Buckner (1971); monographs by S.K. Weinberg (1974) and Schwartz and Stryker (1970). Nor does this exhaust the list. A book by Newman (1976) deals with cross-cultural perspectives on deviance. This interest in the cross-cultural is further reflected by the previously cited work of Connor (1972b) on deviance in the Soviet Union, and by a collection edited by Wilson, Greenblatt, and Wilson (1977) on deviance and social control in Communist China. Stebbins (1971), in a work more in the field of criminology than deviance, nevertheless highlights the latter in the title, an indication of shifting sociological interests, and perhaps a contribution toward coalescence of the two areas. L. Taylor (1971) has likewise combined crime and deviance, in a skillfully interwoven text. A recent work by McCaghy (1976) is a conflict-oriented text; the author had previously co-edited a reader with similar emphasis (Denisoff and McCaghy, 1973).

There were 27 readers reviewed by Sagarin and Montanino (1976), and nine others known to them and listed but not reviewed. Since then, readers continue to appear, including one co-edited by myself (Sagarin and Montanino, 1977). The prolific writer and editor, Jack Douglas, has announced two further collections of previously unpublished articles, on the themes of subcultures of deviance (Douglas, 1977) and official deviance (Douglas and Johnson, 1977).

FIGHT BACK: ANOTHER RECENT THRUST

Other major thrusts of considerable popularity have emerged in the field of deviance in recent times. Theories and descriptions of deviance and of social protest movements (feminist, racial and civil rights) have been brought together by several authors (Sagarin, 1969, 1971; Howard, 1974). The dissatisfaction with one's lot in society has culminated in a general "fight back" movement, a struggle that reached new heights in the 1960s, and is reflected in the literature.

Sagarin (1971:10) has put together a collection of articles all written in an attempt to conceptualize and redefine minority group "to include the collectivities, other than ethnics, that are stigmatized, stereotyped and subject to irrelevant discrimination." In this collection, the various authors attempt to place in the framework of minority/majority relations such statuses as women, homosexuals, adolescents, hippies, the aged, dwarfs, the crippled and physically disabled, ex-convicts, radical right activists, and others. Provocative and stimulating ideas are presented in these works. They were long overdue and far from out of place in the field of deviance. Organizational activities have been aimed at raising the consciousness concerning the oppressive position that some people occupy in society, and at attempts to establish recognition of their plight. But what is apparent in this collection, and what is expressed most profoundly in Goffman's (1963) *Stigma,* is that those traditionally considered deviant by sociologists and those in other denigrated or unequal statuses have elements in common in their relationship to society, a central focus both of labeling and conflict orientation.

A study of voluntary associations of deviants in America by Sagarin (1969) provided a view of such organizations as Alcoholics Anonymous (and such offshoots as Gamblers Anonymous), the Mattachine Society and other organizations of homosexuals, Synanon, ex-convict groups, Little People of America (dwarfs), and the mentally ill (Recovery, Inc. and Schizophrenics Anonymous). Some of these organizations were involved in policies aimed at their own perpetuation. Others were structured in such a manner as to be of service in helping members cope with their particular status in the world of "normals." Still others embodied processes aimed at aiding members in casting off the stigma of their status either by divesting themselves of their deviant attributes and espousing more "normative" life styles, or by lobbying for societal "destigmatization" of the status in question. Since the appearance of the book, other organizations of marginal peoples and deviant groups have sprung up, such as organizations of prostitutes (PONY or Prostitutes Organization of New York) and the "grey panthers," organizations of elderly peoples: these designed to lobby in the interests of those that perceive themselves as persecuted, ostracized, or ignored and separated from the majority in society which acts against their interests.

Katz and Bender (1976) continue and extend the ideas developed by Sagarin in *Odd Man In.* Their work covers some of the same organizations (as Recovery, Inc.), but also others, as groups of stutterers, welfare rights activists, and feminists. It differs from Sagarin's book, first because it is an edited volume, but more significant, Katz and Bender and their authors are on the whole uncritical of self-help groups; they openly take their side, so that it is weak on sociological analysis of organizations, but strong on the stated values of the editors, authors, and the people (deviants and others) whom they are describing.

SUMMING UP

The era of modern research in deviance started with an upsurge in interest in the causes of deviance brought about by the demonstration of sociocultural and social structural forces as etiologic agents. It then became possible in the course of study of various sectors of the social milieu to examine instances of deviance and changes in its form, frequency, and intensity (this by class, ethnic, and geographical considerations). Various mechanisms (the poverty cycle, marginality, alienation and the like) responsible for the action of these agents were hypothesized. This occurred despite the fact that understanding went beyond the concepts of deprivation, marginality, and malintegration as causes of deviance, to the very ways and means of their effect in producing deviance and its manifestation; went beyond an understanding of the ways in which they affect and lead to disturbance of the "social order" to hypotheses for means of prevention, amelioration, and even "cure." Yet such pathways, provided by sound sociological, psychological and other social scientific insights, went largely untrodden.

The evolution of the labeling or interactionist perspective can be viewed in part as drawing major impetus from these very circumstances, frustrations, pressures, and disillusionment in the academic community. A sense of powerlessness to effect lasting solutions to the enigma of deviant behavior in all its varied forms could only add to the popularity of a perspective that proclaimed that nothing is evil in and of itself, that deviance is really differentness that is disapproved by others, that it exists in degrees, and is in large part inevitable. In essence, that deviance is created not by the alleged culprits, but by social control agents, official agencies, moral entrepreneurs, and the hostile audience. One should, in this perspective, look at all the parties involved, and especially place emphasis on those who take part in the negative definition and handling of the alleged outsiders and transgressors. Little wonder that treatments were viewed as processes that brought about more acute symptoms rather than relief. Also of little surprise is the inversion and abandonment of the search for primary etiological factors; hence, one could have anticipated the consternation of critics when confronted with the societal reaction orientation.

All of this has led many to believe that the field of deviance, at least as we know it in sociology, is in a state of poverty, both conceptual and theoretical poverty, the poverty of ideas, yet none of this has dissuaded the academic community from seeking out directions, searching for solutions and attempting to generate understanding which would prove useful in the alleviation of societal distress that emanates from deviance (whether from stigmatization or victimization).

A study of the literature shows that the causative factors of deviance are still unknown, this despite the fact that a host of precipitating and perpetuating elements have been identified. The literature appears to indicate that the etiology of deviance is multiple, and the search for it is not being abandoned because it is difficult to get a "handle" on the problem; the interests of researchers may rightly rest in examining the mechanisms of all these multiple agents, keeping in mind that causation is a composite of many factors or at least many of those factors with which the sociologist is capable of dealing. With this in mind, the essay may be drawn to a close (for now) on an encouraging note; if anything, the last decade has witnessed the resurgence of a focus on often competing and sometimes complementary social scientific approaches to the understanding of deviance; the collapse of paradigms into one another and the resurgence of interest in etiology; the rise in emphasis on the nature and effects of societal reaction, which will have a lasting influence in studies of deviance regardless of the route of orientations in the future; all of which is aided by and coupled with many positive aspects of the general "fight back" movement, the coming to consciousness of those that are afflicted (or at least perceived to be and treated as such), a bringing to the forefront of their voices, and an expansion of the often restricted choices that they are confronted with.

As this essay was being written, two items came to my attention, almost at exactly the same moment, that dramatically illustrated some of the issues raised herein. The American Society of Criminology announced its program for its 1977 annual meeting, and one session was entitled, "The Demise of Labeling." Spector (1976) wrote a review of the role of the journal *Social Problems* in the launching and development of labeling theory, and concluded by stating that "labeling theory is well established, if not the current orthodoxy."

No one can accuse the scholars of having reached consensus.

NOTES

1. This is a constructive view of a process that many envision as a crisis, perhaps with justification in view of the polemical nature of much of the criticism that is exchanged. Merton (1976), from a somewhat broader posture, characterizes this process as a "chronic crisis" both central and beneficial to the field of sociology and crucial in precluding "stasis" (stagnation) via the premature agreement on a sole paradigm that would envelop all relevant inquiries.

2. Although there is enough overlap that the initial spokesmen have been lumped together, there exists enough divergence among them on particular aspects of the perspective so as to preclude total agreement. Indeed, many of the critics preface their remarks with their own understanding (or lack of it) of the common strands that unite the progenitors.

3. Articles by Goode (1975) and Rains (1975), later assessments of labeling, can be considered criticisms of the critics.

4. This observation by Bordua (1967), construing labeling as a school, is one which Becker (1971) addresses, considering it unfortunate and ill-perceived.

5. For Akers' later views on etiology, see *Deviant Behavior: A Social Learning Approach* (1973).

6. For a more expanded discussion of Hagan's work, see the exchange between him and other criminologists (Hagan, 1975).

7. There are no doubt many more examples of work which could fall under the general heading of "dealing with labeling." For example, the many anthologies that have focused around labeling, some generated by authors already mentioned, are not here listed and will be dealt with later in the article. The bulk of citations is to research journal articles and individually authored pieces, which itself is a strong indication of interest in labeling.

8. There is nothing logically contradictory about a criticism of labeling from both the left and the right. The main point of the critics is the contention that labeling is inimical to the search for truth and validity.

9. In addition to responding in defense of labeling, Kitsuse has sought to strengthen the perspective by arguing for expanding its application, for its inclusion as a valid approach to social problems. A more general article seeks to accomplish this (Spector and Kitsuse

1973), and in a later one an analogy has been drawn between labeling in the field of deviance and the value conflict approach in social problems (Kitsuse and Spector, 1975).

10. Schur's most concerted effort (1971), although criticized as "glossy" and deficient in originality by Manning (1973), is perhaps best considered as an effort of synthesis, modification, interpretation, and expansion, all in an effort to disabuse labeling of widespread criticism. An earlier work (1969), which stresses the processual nature of the labeling perspective, is widely inculcated in the later work, *Labeling Deviant Behavior* (1971). The concept of secondary deviation is dealt with in detail in an unpublished manuscript (1974), which grew out of a presentation at the University of Massachusetts at Amherst. Schur (1970) also defined labeling in a short rebuttal to its critics in the previously mentioned conference (in Gove, 1975a).

11. The remarks here on anthologies and readers is in large part a recapitulation of an earlier survey (Sagarin and Montanino, 1976). The reader should refer to the 1976 work for a more expanded discussion of the readers here discussed, as well as of several others.

12. The proceedings and papers of the conference have not been published, but the program and some of the papers were made available to me.

REFERENCES

AKERS, R.L. (1968). "Problems in the sociology of deviance." Social Forces, 46:455-465.

--- (1973). Deviant behavior: A social learning approach. Belmont, Cal.: Wadsworth.

BALCH, R.W. (1972). "Police personality: Fact or fiction." Journal of Criminal Law, Criminology and Police Science, 63:106-119.

BALL, D.W. (1967). "An abortion clinic ethnography." Social Problems, 14:293-301.

BECKER, H.S. (1963). Outsiders: Studies in the sociology of deviance. New York: Free Press.

--- (ed., 1964). The other side. New York: Free Press.

--- (1967). "Whose side are we on?" Social Problems, 14:239-247.

--- (1971). "Labelling theory reconsidered." Pp. 177-212 in Outsiders, 1973 ed.

BELL, R.R. (1971). Social deviance: A substantive analysis. Homewood, Ill.: Dorsey.

BLACK, D. (1971). "The social organization of arrest." Stanford Law Review, 23:1087-1111.

--- (1972). "The boundaries of legal sociology." Yale Law Journal, 81:1086 1100.

--- (1976). The behavior of law. New York: Academic Press.

BLACK, D., and REISS, A.J., Jr. (1970). "Police control of juveniles." American Sociological Review, 35:63-67.

BLAKENSHIP, R.L., and SINGH, B.K. (1976). "Differential labeling of juveniles." Criminology, 13:471-489.

BLOCK, R. (1974). "Why notify the police: The victim's decision to notify the police of an assault." Criminology, 11:555-569.

BLUMER, H. (1966). "Sociological implications of the thought of George Herbert Mead." American Journal of Sociology, 71:535-544.

--- (ed., 1969). Symbolic interactionism: Perspective and method. Englewood Cliffs, N.J.: Prentice-Hall.

BONGER, W.A. (1936). An introduction to criminology. London: Methuen.

BORD, R.J. (1971). "Rejection of the mentally ill: Continuities and further developments." Social Problems, 18:496:510.

BORDUA, D. (1967). "Recent trends: Deviant behavior and social control." The Annals of the American Academy of Political and Social Science, 369:149-163.

BOYDELL, C.L., GRINDSTAFF, C.F., and WHITEHEAD, P.C. (eds., 1972). Deviant behavior and societal reaction. Toronto: Holt, Rinehart and Winston.

BUCKNER, H.T. (1971). Deviance, society, and change. New York: Random House.
BUSTAMANTE, J.A. (1972). "The wetback as deviant: An application of labeling theory." American Journal of Sociology, 77:706-719.
CAMERON, M.O. (1964). The booster and the snitch. New York: Free Press.
CARTWRIGHT, B.C., and SCHWARTZ, R.D. (1973). "The invocation of legal norms: An empirical investigation of Durkheim and Weber." American Sociological Review, 38:340-354.
CHIRICOS, T.G., and WALDO, G.P. (1975). "Socioeconomic status and criminal sentencing: An empirical assessment of a conflict proposition." American Sociological Review, 40:753-773.
CLINARD, M.B. (1974). Sociology of deviant behavior. New York: Holt, Rinehart and Winston, 4th ed.
CLOWARD, R.A., and OHLIN, L.E. (1960). Delinquency and opportunity. New York: Free Press.
COHEN, A.K. (1965). "The sociology of the deviant act: Anomie theory and beyond." American Sociological Review, 30:5-14.
--- (1966). Deviance and control. Englewood Cliffs, N.J.: Prentice-Hall.
--- (1968). "Deviant behavior." International Encyclopedia of the Social Sciences, Vol. 4:148-155. New York: Macmillan and Free Press.
--- (1974). The elasticity of evil. Oxford: Basil Blackwell.
COHEN, S. (ed., 1971). Images of deviance. Baltimore: Penguin.
COHEN, S., and YOUNG, J. (eds., 1973). The manufacture of news: Deviance, social problems and the mass media. Beverly Hills, Calif.: Sage.
COLLINS, R. (1975). Conflict sociology: Towards an explanatory science. New York: Academic Press.
CONGER, R.D. (1976). "Social control and social learning models of delinquent behavior: A synthesis." Criminology, 14:17-41.
CONNOR, W.D. (1972a). Deviance in Soviet society: Crime, delinquency and alcoholism. New York: Columbia University Press.
--- (1972b). "The manufacture of deviance: The case of the Soviet purge, 1936-1938." American Sociological Review 37:403-414.
COSER, L. (1956). The functions of social conflict. New York: Free Press.
COWIE, J.B., and ROEBUCK, J.B. (1975). An ethnography of a chiropractic clinic: Definitions of a deviant situation. New York: Free Press.
CURRIE, E.P. (1968). "Crimes without criminals: Witchcraft and its control in Renaissance Europe." Law and Society Review, 3:7-32.
DANZGER, H.M. (1975). "Validating conflict data." American Sociological Review, 40:570-585.
DAVIS, J., and STIVERS, R. (eds., 1975). The collective definition of deviance. New York: Free Press.
DAVIS, N.J. (1975). Sociological constructions of deviance: Perspectives and issues in the field: Dubuque, Ia.: Wm. C. Brown.
DENISOFF, R.S., and McCAGHY, C.H. (eds., 1973). Deviance, conflict and criminality. Chicago: Rand McNally.
DENZIN, N.K. (1969). "Symbolic interactionism and ethnomethodology: A proposed synthesis." American Sociological Review 34:924-934.
DINITZ, S., DYNES, R.R., and CLARKE, A.C. (eds., 1975). Deviance: Studies in definition, management and treatment. New York: Oxford University Press.
DOUGLAS, J.D. (ed., 1970). Observations of deviance. New York: Random House.
--- (ed., 1972). Research on deviance. New York: Random House.
--- (1976). Investigative social research: Individual and team field research. Beverly Hills, Calif.: Sage.

--- (ed., 1977). Subcultures of deviance. Boston: Little, Brown.

DOUGLAS, J.D., and JOHNSON, J.M. (eds., 1977). Official deviance: Readings in malfeasance, misfeasance, and other forms of corruption. Philadelphia: Lippincott.

EDGERTON, R.B. (1976). Deviance: A cross-cultural perspective. Menlo Park, Calif.: Cummings.

ERIKSON, K.T. (1962). "Notes on the sociology of deviance." Social Problems, 9:307-314.

--- (1966). Wayward Puritans: A study in the sociology of deviance. New York: John Wiley.

--- (1967). "A comment on disguised observation in sociology." Social Problems, 15:502-506.

FILSTEAD, W.J. (ed., 1972). An introduction to deviance: Readings in the process of making deviants. Chicago: Markham.

FOSTER, J.D., DINITZ, S., and RECKLESS, W.C. (1972). "Perceptions of stigma following public intervention for delinquent behavior." Social Problems, 20:202-209.

FREIDSON, E. (1965). "Disability as social deviance." Pp. 71-99 in M.B. Sussman (ed.), Sociology and rehabilitation. Washington, D.C.: American Sociological Association.

GALANTER, M. (1974). "Why the haves come out ahead: Speculations on the limits of legal change." Law and Society Review, 9:95-160.

GARFINKEL, H. (1956). "Conditions of successful degradation ceremonies." American Journal of Sociology 61:420-424.

--- (1967). Studies in ethnomethodology. Englewood Cliffs, N.J.: Prentice-Hall.

GIBBONS, D.C., and JONES, J.F. (1975). The study of deviance: Perspectives and problems. Englewood Cliffs, N.J.: Prentice-Hall.

GIBBS, J. (1966). "Conceptions of deviant behavior: The old and the new." Pacific Sociological Review, 9:9-14.

GIORDANO, P.C. (1976). "The sense of injustice? An analysis of juveniles' reactions to the justice system." Criminology, 14:93-112.

GLASER, D. (1971). Social deviance. Chicago: Markham.

GOFFMAN, E. (1963). Stigma: Notes on the management of spoiled identity. Englewood Cliffs, N.J.: Prentice-Hall.

--- (1961). Asylums: Essays on the social situation of mental patients and other inmates. New York: Doubleday Anchor.

GOODE, E. (1975). "On behalf of labeling theory." Social Problems, 22:570-584.

GOULDNER, A.W. (1968). "The sociologist as partisan: Sociology and the welfare state." American Sociologist, 3:103-116.

GOVE, W.R. (1970a). "Societal reaction as an explanation of mental illness and evaluation." American Sociological Review, 35:873-884.

--- (1970b). "Who is hospitalized: A critical review of some sociological studies of mental illness." Journal of Health and Human Behavior, 11:294-304.

--- (ed., 1975a). The labelling of deviance: Evaluating a perspective. New York: Halsted Press (a Sage publication).

--- (1975b). "The labelling theory of mental illness: A reply to Scheff." American Sociological Review, 40:242-248.

GOVE, W.R., and HOWELL, P. (1974). "Individual resources and mental hospitalization: A comparison and evaluation of the societal reaction and psychiatric perspectives." American Sociological Review, 39:86-100.

GOVE, W.R., and LUBACH, J. (1969). "An intensive treatment program for psychiatric inpatients: A description and evaluation." Journal of Health and Social Behavior, 10:225-236.

GUSFIELD, J. (1967). "Moral passage: The symbolic progress in public designations of deviance." Social Problems, 15:175-188.

HAAS, J., and SHAFFIR, B. (eds., 1974). Decency and deviance: Studies in deviant behavior. Toronto: McClelland Steward.

HAGAN, J. (1973a). "Conceptual deficiencies of an interactionist perspective in deviance." Criminology, 11:383-404.
——— (1973b). "Labelling and deviance: A case study in the 'sociology of the interesting'." Social Problems, 20:447-458.
——— (1974). "Extra-legal attributes of criminal sentencing: An assessment of a sociological viewpoint." Law and Society Review, 8:357-383.
——— (1975). "Setting the record straight: Toward the reformulation of an interactionist perspective in deviance." Criminology 13:421-424.
HARRIS, A.R. (1975). "Imprisonment and the expected value of criminal choice: A specification and test of aspects of the labeling perspective." American Sociological Review, 40:71-88.
HARTJEN, C.A. (1972). "Police-citizen encounters: Social order in interpersonal interaction." Criminology, 10:61-84.
HAWKES, R.K. (1975). "Norms, deviance and social control: A mathematical elaboration of concepts." American Journal of Sociology, 80:886-909.
HAWKINS, R., and TIEDEMAN, G. (1975). The creation of deviance: Interpersonal and organizational determinants. Columbus, Ohio: Charles E. Merrill.
HINDELANG, M.J. (1970). "The commitment of delinquents to their misdeeds: Do delinquents drift?" Social Problems, 17:502-510.
——— (1974). "Moral evaluation of illegal behavior." Social Problems, 21:370-384.
HIRSCHI, T. (1973). "Procedural rules and the study of deviant behavior." Social Problems, 21:159-173.
HOWARD, J.R. (1974). The cutting edge: Social movements and social change. Philadelphia: Lippincott.
JACOBS, J. (1972). Getting by: Illustrations of marginal living. Boston: Little, Brown.
——— (ed., 1974). Deviance: Field studies and self-disclosures. Palo Alto, Calif.: National Press Books.
JANOWITZ, M. (1975). "Sociological theory and social action." American Journal of Sociology, 81:82-109.
KATZ, A.H., and BENDER, E.I. (eds., 1976). The strength in us: Self-help groups in the modern world. New York: Franklin Watts.
KATZ, J. (1972). "Deviance, charisma, and rule-defined behavior." Social Problems, 20:186-202.
KITSUSE, J.I. (1962). "Societal reaction to deviant behavior: Problems of theory and method." Social Problems, 9:247-256.
——— (1972). "Deviance, deviant behavior, and deviants: Some conceptual problems. In W.J. Filstead (ed.), An introduction to deviance. Chicago: Markham.
——— (1975). "The 'new conception of deviance' and its critics." Pp. 273-284 in Gove (1975a), q.v.
KITSUSE, J.I., and CICOUREL, A.V. (1963). "Notes on the uses of official statistics." Social Problems, 12:131-139.
———, and SPECTOR, M. (1975). "Social problems and deviance: Some parallel issues." Social Problems, 22:584-595.
LAUDERDALE, P. (1976). "Deviance and moral boundaries." American Sociological Review, 41:660-676.
LEMERT, E.M. (1951). Social pathology: A systematic approach to the theory of sociopathic behavior. New York: McGraw-Hill.
——— (1967). Human deviance, social problems and social control. Englewood Cliffs, N.J.: Prentice-Hall.
——— (1964). "Social structure, social control and deviation." In M. Clinard (ed.), Anomie and deviant behavior. New York: Free Press.
——— (1974). "Beyond Mead: The societal reaction to deviance." Social Problems, 21:457-468.

LIAZOS, A. (1972). "The poverty of the sociology of deviance: Nuts, sluts and preverts." Social Problems, 20:103-121.

LIEBOW, E. (1967). Tally's Corner: A study of Negro streetcorner men. Boston: Little, Brown.

LOFLAND, J. (1969). Deviance and identity. Englewood Cliffs, N.J.: Prentice-Hall.

LORBER, J. (1967). "Deviance as performance: The case of illness." Social Problems, 14:302-310.

MANKOFF, M. (1971). "Societal reaction and career deviance: A critical analysis." Sociological Quarterly, 12:204-218.

--- (1968). "On alienation, structural strain, and deviancy." Social Problems, 16:114-116.

--- (1970). "Power in advanced capitalist society." Social Problems, 17:418-430.

MANN, W.E. (ed., 1968). Deviant behavior in Canada. Toronto: Social Sciences Publishers.

MANNING, P.K. (1973). "Survey essay on deviance." Contemporary Sociology, 2:123-128.

MARSHALL, H., and PURDY, R. (1972). "Hidden deviance and the labelling approach: The case for drinking and driving." Social Problems, 19:541-553.

MATZA, D. (1964). Delinquency and drift. New York: John Wiley.

--- (1969). Becoming deviant. Englewood Cliffs, N.J.: Prentice-Hall.

McCAGHY, C. (1976). Deviant behavior: Crime, conflict and interest groups. New York: Macmillan.

McINTOSH, M. (1968). "The homosexual role." Social Problems, 16:183-193.

MERTON, R.K. (1938). "Social structure and anomie." American Sociological Review, 3:672-682. (Reprinted in Social theory and social structure. New York: Free Press, 1957.)

--- (1948). "The self-fulfilling prophesy." Antioch Review, 8(summer):193-210. (Reprinted in Social theory and social structure. New York: Free Press, 1957.)

--- (1976). Sociological ambivalence and other essays. New York: Free Press.

MONTANINO, F., and SAGARIN, E. (1977). "Voluntarism and responsibility." In Sagarin and Montanino (1977), q.v.

NEWMAN, G. (1976). Comparative deviance: Perception and law in six cultures. New York: Elsevier.

QUINNEY, R. (1974). Critique of legal order: Crime control in a capitalist society. Boston: Little, Brown.

RAINS, P. (1975). "Imputations of deviance: A retrospective essay on the labeling perspective." Social Problems, 23:1-12.

RAFSKY, D.M. (1973). "Police race attitudes and labelling." Journal of Police Science and Administration, 1:65-68.

RAINWATER, L. (ed., 1974). Social problems and public policy: Deviance and liberty. Chicago: Aldine.

REASONS, C.E. (ed., 1974). The criminologist: Crime and the criminal. Pacific Palisades, Calif.: Goodyear.

REISS, A.J., Jr. (1971). The police and the public. New Haven, Conn.: Yale University Press.

ROCK, P. (1973). Deviant behaviour. London: Hutchinson University Library.

ROCK, P., and McINTOSH, M. (eds., 1974). Deviance and social control. London: Tavistock.

ROTENBERG, M. (1974). "Self-labeling: A missing link in the societal reaction theory of deviance." Sociological Review, 22:335-354.

RUBINGTON, E., and WEINBERG, M.S. (eds., 1968). Deviance: The interactionist perspective: Text and readings in the sociology of deviance. New York: Macmillan.

RUSHING, W.A. (ed., 1975). Deviant behavior and social process. Chicago: Rand McNally.

SAGARIN, E. (1969). Odd man in: Societies of deviants in America. Chicago: Quadrangle Books.

--- (ed., 1971). The other minorities: Nonethnic collectivities conceptualized as minority groups. Waltham, Mass.:Xerox College Publishing.

--- (1975). Deviants and deviance: An introduction to the study of disvalued people and behavior. New York: Praeger.
SAGARIN, E., and McCORD, W. (1976). "Trends in theoretical approaches to social problems." Paper presented to annual meeting, Society for the Study of Social Problems, New York.
SAGARIN, E., and MONTANINO, F. (1976). "Anthologies and readers on deviance." Contemporary Sociology, 5:260-267.
--- (eds., 1977). Deviants: Voluntary actors in a hostile world. Morristown, N.J.: General Learning Press.
SCARPITTI, F.R., and McFARLANE, P.T. (eds., 1975). Deviance: Action, reaction, interaction. Reading, Mass.: Addison Wesley.
SCHEFF, T.J. (1964). "The societal reaction to deviance: Ascriptive elements in the psychiatric screening of mental patients in a midwestern state." Social Problems, 11:401-413.
--- (1966). Being mentally ill: A sociological theory. Chicago: Aldine.
--- (1967). Mental illness and social process. New York: Harper & Row.
--- (1974). "The labelling theory of mental illness." American Sociological Review, 39:444-452.
--- (1975). "Reply to Chauncey and Gove." American Sociological Review, 40:252-257.
SCHUR, E. (1965). Crimes without victims: Deviant behavior and public policy–Abortion, homosexuality and drug addiction. Englewood Cliffs, N.J.: Prentice-Hall.
--- (1969). "Reactions to deviance: A critical reassessment." American Journal of Sociology, 75:309-322.
--- (1971). Labeling deviant behavior: Its sociological implications. New York: Harper & Row.
--- (1974). "The concept of secondary deviation: Its theoretical significance and empirical elusiveness." Paper presented at the University of Massachusetts, Amherst, Dept. of Sociology Colloquium, April.
--- (1973). Radical nonintervention. Rethinking the delinquency problem. Englewood Cliffs, N.J.: Prentice-Hall.
SCHWARTZ, M., and STRYKER, S. (1970). Deviance, selves and others. Washington, D.C.: Arnold M. and Caroline Rose Monograph Series, American Sociological Association.
SCHWARTZ, R.D., and SKOLNICK, J. (1962). "Two studies of legal stigma." Social Problems, 10:133-142.
SCOTT, R.A. (1969). The making of blind men. New York: Russell Sage.
SCOTT, R.A., and DOUGLAS, J.D. (eds., 1971). Theoretical perspectives on deviance. New York: Basic Books.
SELLIN, T. (1938). Culture conflict and crime. New York: Social Science Research Council.
SIMMONS, J.L. (1965). "Public stereotypes of deviants." Social Problems, 13:223-232.
--- (1969). Deviants. Berkeley, Calif.: Glendessary Press.
SKOLNICK, J. (1966). Justice without trial. New York: John Wiley.
SPECTOR, M. (1976). "Labeling theory in Social Problems: A young journal launches a new theory." Social Problems, 24:69-75.
SPECTOR, M., and KITSUSE, J.I. (1973). "Social problems: A reformulation." Social Problems, 21:145-159.
SPITZER, S. (1975). "Toward a Marxian theory of deviance." Social Problems, 22:638-652.
--- (1976). "Conflict and consensus in the law enforcement process: Urban minorities and the police." Criminology 14:189-213.
STEBBINS, R.A. (1971). Commitment to deviance: The nonprofessional criminal in the community. Westport, Conn.: Greenwood.
SUTHERLAND, E.H., and CRESSEY, D.R. (1966). Principles of criminology (7th ed.). Philadelphia: Lippincott.

SYKES, R.E., and CLARK, J.P. (1975). "A theory of deference exchange in police-civilian encounters." American Journal of Sociology, 81:584-601.

TANNENBAUM, F. (1938). Crime and the community. New York: Columbia University Press.

TAYLOR, I., and TAYLOR, L. (eds., 1973). Politics and deviance. Baltimore: Penguin.

TAYLOR, L. (1971). Deviance and society. London: Michael Joseph.

THIO, A. (1973). "Class bias in the sociology of deviance." American Sociologist, 8:1-12.

THOMAS, W.I. (1923). The unadjusted girl. Boston: Little, Brown.

TRICE, H.M., and ROMAN, P.M. (1970). "Delabeling, relabeling and Alcoholics Anonymous." Social Problems, 17:538-547.

TROJANOWICZ, R. (1971). "The policeman's occupational personality." Journal of Criminal Law, Criminology and Police Science, 62:551-559.

TURK, A.T. (1969). Criminality and the legal order. Chicago: Rand McNally.

TURNER, R.H. (1972). "Deviance avowal as neutralization of commitment." Social Problems, 19:308-322.

VOLD, G. (1958). Theoretical criminology. New York: Oxford University Press.

WEINBERG, M.S. (1965). "Sexual modesty and the nudist camp." Social Problems, 12:311-318.

WEINBERG, S.K. (1974). Deviant behavior and social control. Dubuque, Ia.: Wm. C. Brown.

WENGER, D.L., and FLETCHER, C.R. (1969). "The effect of legal counsel on admissions to a state mental hospital: A confrontation of professions." Journal of Health and Social Behavior, 10:66-72.

WILLIAMS, C.J., and WEINBERG, M.S. (1970). "Being discovered: A study of homosexuals in the military." Social Problems, 18:217-228.

WILSON, A.A., GREENBLATT, S.L., and WILSON, R.W. (eds., 1977). Deviance and social control in Chinese society. New York: Praeger.

WIRTH, L. (1931). "Culture conflict and misconduct." Social Forces, 9:484-492.

ABOUT THE CONTRIBUTORS

HENRY BARBERA received a doctorate in sociology from Columbia University, and has taught at the City College of New York and elsewhere. He serves as a council member of the Sociology of World Conflicts (a section of the American Sociological Association) and is a fellow of the Inter-University Seminar on Armed Forces and Society. He is author of *Rich Nations and Poor in Peace and War,* and of several articles on the social structure of world society. His present work, on the linkage between social change and international passions, is called *The Rise of Hope, The Rise of Discontent.*

ARNOLD BIRENBAUM received a doctorate in sociology from Columbia University, and is associate professor of sociology at St. John's University in New York. He has done extensive research and writing in the fields of medical sociology, health care, and mental retardation. He is coauthor of *Norms and Human Behavior, Resettling Retarded Adults in a Managed Community,* and coeditor of *People in Places: The Sociology of the Familiar.*

NANETTE J. DAVIS received a doctorate in sociology from Michigan State University, and is associate professor of sociology at Portland State University. She has written widely on deviance, including her book, *Sociological Constructions of Deviance: Perspectives and Issues in the Field.*

JACK D. DOUGLAS received a doctorate in sociology from Princeton University, and is professor of sociology at University of California at San Diego. He is author, editor, or coeditor of a prolific body of literature on deviance, social problems, and American society, including *The Social Meanings of Suicide, American Social Order, Official Deviance,* and *Investigative Social Research.*

LINDA ECKSTEIN is a graduate student in psychology at City College of New York and is engaged in research for the Institute for Advanced Study in Rational Psychotherapy.

ALBERT ELLIS, Ph.D. in psychology, is executive director of the Institute for Rational Living and the Institute for Advanced Study in Rational Psychotherapy. He is author, editor, or coeditor of more than 450 articles and 39 books, including *Reason and Emotion in Psychotherapy, The Encyclopedia of Sexual Behavior, Growth Through Reason, Sex Without Guilt, A New Guide to*

Rational Living, and *Humanistic Psychotherapy: The Rational Emotive Approach.*

DEAN R. GERSTEIN received a doctorate in sociology from Harvard University, and is assistant research sociologist in the Department of Psychiatry, School of Medicine, University of California at San Diego.

FRED MONTANINO received a master's degree in sociology from City College of New York, and is a doctoral student and teaching fellow at Yale University. He is coeditor of *Deviants: Voluntary Actors in a Hostile World,* is assistant to the editors of *Criminology: An Interdisciplinary Journal,* and has published articles and reviews on deviance and responsibility, victimology, alcoholism, and related subjects.

RICHARD MORAN received a doctorate in sociology from the University of Pennsylvania, and is assistant professor of sociology at Mount Holyoke College. He is a member of the Board of Editors of *Criminology: An Interdisciplinary Journal,* and is currently doing research on political crime and criminal insanity in Victorian England.

TALCOTT PARSONS received his doctorate at Heidelberg in 1927, and is professor emeritus at Harvard University. He is a former president of the American Sociological Association, and is probably the best known and most influential American sociologist of the past four or five decades. His books include *The Social System* and *The Structure of Social Action,* among many others.

EDWARD SAGARIN received a doctorate in sociology from New York University, and is professor of sociology at City College of New York. He has written widely on crime, deviance, and sexual behavior. He is former president of the American Society of Criminology, coeditor of *Criminology: An Interdisciplinary Journal,* and author of *Deviants and Deviance: An Introduction to the Study of Disvalued People and Behavior.*

CHARLES WINICK, Ph.D., is professor of sociology at City College and the Graduate Center, City University of New York. He has published widely in many social science journals; is author of *The New People, The Lively Commerce,* and other books dealing with media and social problems. He has been a consultant for numerous government commissions, including the Commission on Obscenity and Pornography.

HARRIET ZUCKERMAN received a doctorate in sociology from Columbia University, where she is an associate professor. She is author of *Scientific Elite* (1977), many papers in the sociology of science, and is coeditor of *Toward a Metric of Science* (1977).

INDEX